D0140373

THE WILEY BICENTENNIAL–KNOWLEDGE FOR GENERATIONS

*E*ach generation has its unique needs and aspirations. When Charles Wiley first opened his small printing shop in lower Manhattan in 1807, it was a generation of boundless potential searching for an identity. And we were there, helping to define a new American literary tradition. Over half a century later, in the midst of the Second Industrial Revolution, it was a generation focused on building the future. Once again, we were there, supplying the critical scientific, technical, and engineering knowledge that helped frame the world. Throughout the 20th Century, and into the new millennium, nations began to reach out beyond their own borders and a new international community was born. Wiley was there, expanding its operations around the world to enable a global exchange of ideas, opinions, and know-how.

For 200 years, Wiley has been an integral part of each generation's journey, enabling the flow of information and understanding necessary to meet their needs and fulfill their aspirations. Today, bold new technologies are changing the way we live and learn. Wiley will be there, providing you the must-have knowledge you need to imagine new worlds, new possibilities, and new opportunities.

Generations come and go, but you can always count on Wiley to provide you the knowledge you need, when and where you need it!

WILLIAM J. PESCE
PRESIDENT AND CHIEF EXECUTIVE OFFICER

PETER BOOTH WILEY
CHAIRMAN OF THE BOARD

Network Security Fundamentals

Eric Cole, Ronald L. Krutz, James W. Conley,
Brian Reisman, Mitch Ruebush,
and Dieter Gollmann

with Rachelle Reese

BICENTENNIAL
1807
WILEY
2007
BICENTENNIAL

Credits

PUBLISHER
Anne Smith

PROJECT EDITOR
Brian B. Baker

MARKETING MANAGER
Jennifer Slomack

SENIOR EDITORIAL ASSISTANT
Tiara Kelly

PRODUCTION MANAGER
Kelly Tavares

PROJECT MANAGER
Tenea Johnson

PRODUCTION EDITOR
Kerry Weinstein

CREATIVE DIRECTOR
Harry Nolan

COVER DESIGNER
Hope Miller

COVER PHOTO
Tetra Images/Getty Images

Wiley 200th Anniversary Logo designed by: Richard J. Pacifico

This book was set in Times New Roman by Aptara, Inc. and printed and bound by R. R. Donnelley. The cover was printed by R. R. Donnelley.

Microsoft product screen shot(s) reprinted with permission from Microsoft Corporation.

To order books or for customer service please call 1-800-CALL WILEY (225-5945).

ISBN 978-0-470-10192-6

Printed in the United States of America

10 9 8 7 6 5 4 3 2 1

ABOUT THE AUTHORS

Eric Cole is the author of *Hackers Beware, Hiding in Plain Sight: Steganography and the Art of Covert Communication*, and co-author of *Network Security Bible* and *SANS GIAC Certification: Security Essentials Toolkit (GSEC)*. He has appeared as a security expert on CBS News, 60 Minutes, and CNN Headline News.

Ronald L. Krutz is the author of *Securing SCADA Systems* and co-author of *Network Security Bible, The CISM Prep Guide: Mastering the Five Domains of Information Security Management, The CISSP prep guide: Mastering CISSP and CAP, Security+ Prep Guide,* and is the founder of the Carnegie Mellon Research Institute Cybersecurity Center.

James W. Conley is co-author of *Network Security Bible* and has been a security officer in the United States Navy and a senior security specialist on CIA development efforts.

Brian Reisman is co-author of *MCAD/MCSD: Visual Basic .NET Windows and Web Applications Study Guide, MCAD/MCSD: Visual Basic .Net XML Web Services and Server Components Study Guide, MCSE: Windows Server 2003 Network Security Design Study Guide*. He is a technical trainer for Online Consulting, a Microsoft Certified Technical Education Center, and is a contributor to MCP Magazine, CertCities.com, and ASPToday.com.

Mitch Ruebush is co-author of *MCAD/MCSD: Visual Basic .NET Windows and Web Applications Study Guide, MCAD/MCSD: Visual Basic .Net XML Web Services and Server Components Study Guide, MCSE: Windows Server 2003 Network Security Design Study Guide*. He is a Senior Consultant and Trainer for Online Consulting, Inc. He has been deploying, securing and developing for Windows and UNIX platforms for 14 years.

Dieter Gollmann is Professor for Security in Distributed Applications at Hamburg University of Technology. He is also a visiting Professor at Royal Holloway, University of London and Adjunct Professor at the Technical University of Denmark. Previously he was a researcher in Information Security at Microsoft Research in Cambridge.

Rachelle Reese has been designing and developing technical training courses for over ten years and has written a number of books on programming. She has an MA from San Jose State University and is also a Microsoft Certified Application Developer (MCAD).

PREFACE

College classrooms bring together learners from many backgrounds, with a variety of aspirations. Although the students are in the same course, they are not necessarily on the same path. This diversity, coupled with the reality that these learners often have jobs, families, and other commitments, requires a flexibility that our nation's higher education system is addressing. Distance learning, shorter course terms, new disciplines, evening courses, and certification programs are some of the approaches that colleges employ to reach as many students as possible and help them clarify and achieve their goals.

Wiley Pathways books, a new line of texts from John Wiley & Sons, Inc., are designed to help you address this diversity and the need for flexibility. These books focus on the fundamentals, identify core competencies and skills, and promote independent learning. Their focus on the fundamentals helps students grasp the subject, bringing them all to the same basic understanding. These books use clear, everyday language and are presented in an uncluttered format, making the reading experience more pleasurable. The core competencies and skills help students succeed in the classroom and beyond, whether in another course or in a professional setting. A variety of built-in learning resources promote independent learning and help instructors and students gauge students' understanding of the content. These resources enable students to think critically about their new knowledge and to apply their skills in any situation.

Our goal with *Wiley Pathways* books—with their brief, inviting format, clear language, and core competencies and skills focus—is to celebrate the many students in your courses, respect their needs, and help you guide them on their way.

CASE Learning System

To meet the needs of working college students, *Network Security Fundamentals* uses a four-part process called the CASE Learning System:

- ▲ C: Content
- ▲ A: Analysis
- ▲ S: Synthesis
- ▲ E: Evaluation

Based on Bloom's taxonomy of learning, CASE presents key topics in network security fundamentals in easy-to-follow chapters. The text then prompts analysis, synthesis, and evaluation with a variety of learning aids and assessment tools. Students move efficiently from reviewing what they have learned, to acquiring new information and skills, to applying their new knowledge and skills to real-life scenarios.

Using the CASE Learning System, students not only achieve academic mastery of network security *topics*, but they master real-world *skills* related to that content. The CASE Learning System also helps students become independent learners, giving them a distinct advantage in the field, whether they are just starting out or seeking to advance in their careers.

Organization, Depth, and Breadth of the Text

▲ **Modular Format.** Research on college students shows that they access information from textbooks in a non-linear way. Instructors also often wish to reorder textbook content to suit the needs of a particular class. Therefore, although *Network Security Fundamentals* proceeds logically from the basics to increasingly more challenging material, chapters are further organized into sections that are self-contained for maximum teaching and learning flexibility.

▲ **Numeric System of Headings.** *Network Security Fundamentals* uses a numeric system for headings (e.g., 2.3.4 identifies the fourth subsection of Section 3 of Chapter 2). With this system, students and teachers can quickly and easily pinpoint topics in the table of contents and the text, keeping class time and study sessions focused.

▲ **Core Content.** The topics in *Network Security Fundamentals* are organized into 12 chapters.

Chapter 1, Computer and Network Security Principles, introduces basic terminology and concepts related to security and gets the student thinking about why it is important to take security measures to protect a network and its resources. The chapter begins with an overview of different types of attacks. Next it discusses the three key aspects of security: confidentiality, integrity, and authentication. From there it moves on to discuss risk analysis, including identifying and ranking assets, threats, and vulnerabilities. The chapter concludes with an overview of security policies and standards.

Chapter 2, Network and Server Security, discusses some best practices and techniques for mitigating the risk to servers on your network. It begins with a review of the Open Systems Interconnection (OSI) model to ensure that students are familiar with various protocols and the layers at which they operate. From there it moves on to discuss some best practices when securing a network: security by design and defense in depth. Next it presents some techniques for reducing the attack surface of a server. The chapter concludes with a look at perimeter security, including firewalls and Network Address Translation (NAT).

Chapter 3, Cryptography, introduces the fundamental principles of cryptography and discusses various ways it is used to provide network and computer security. The chapter begins with a brief history of cryptography and introduces the cast of characters commonly used to describe cryptographic scenarios. Next it discusses symmetric encryption and introduces the problem of how to share symmetric keys. From there it moves on to discuss asymmetric encryption and one of its common uses, digital signatures. Next it looks at the role of hashes. The chapter then brings the cryptographic techniques together to examine how they can be used to provide confidentiality, integrity, and authentication. The chapter concludes with an overview of public key infrastructure (PKI), using Microsoft®'s Certificate Services as an example of how you can implement a PKI.

Chapter 4, Authentication, discusses the importance of authentication and how credentials can be used to prove the identity of a user or computer. The student is first introduced to some key authentication and concepts, including the entities that must be authenticated, single sign-on, and mutual authentication. Next the chapter examines the types of credentials that can be used to prove the identity of a user or computer. The chapter then looks at some protocols used for network authentication. The chapter concludes with a look at best practices, including using strong passwords and limiting the times during which or locations from which a user can log on.

Chapter 5, Authorization and Access Control, introduces students to concepts and procedures related to limiting who can access resources on a network. The chapter begins by discussing types of access control that have been used historically and that are used today, including mandatory access control (MAC), discretionary access control (DAC), and role-based access control (RBAC). Next it examines how access control is managed on a Windows® network. The chapter concludes with a look at access control in a Unix® or Linux environment.

Chapter 6, Securing Network Transmission, focuses on securing network perimeters and data in transit on the network. The chapter begins with a look at some attacks that target network services and packets on the network. Next it examines some strategies for segmenting a network and securing network perimeters. It concludes with a look at some protocols that can be used to encrypt data on the network, including Secure Sockets Layer (SSL), Transport Layer Security (TLS), and IP security (IPsec).

Chapter 7, Remote Access and Wireless Security, deals with security considerations for a network that extends past the traditional WAN. It begins with a discussion of the dangers of modems and how to secure a network that allows dial-in access. Next it looks at virtual private networks (VPNs). From there it moves on to discuss how Remote Authentication Dial-in User Service (RADIUS) or Terminal Access Controller Access Control System (TACACS) can be used to centralize authentication for remote access clients. The chapter concludes by examining the threats introduced through wireless networking and steps you can take to mitigate those threats.

Chapter 8, Server Roles and Security, examines the different roles servers play on a network and discusses ways to mitigate the threats associated with specific server roles. The chapter begins by discussing establishing a security baseline for the servers on a network. Next it examines risks specific to infrastructure servers, including domain name system (DNS), Dynamic Host Configuration Protocol (DHCP), and Windows Internet Name Service (WINS) servers, and how to mitigate them. It then discusses steps to take to secure domain controllers. Next it looks at considerations for securing file and print servers. The chapter concludes with a look at security issues specific to application servers, such as web and database servers.

Chapter 9, Protecting Against Malware, looks at various types of malware and steps to take to protect computers against viruses, worms, spyware, and other types of malicious code. The chapter begins by defining the types of malware that typically pose a threat to computers. Next it discusses anti-malware programs and the importance of user education in preventing attacks. The chapter then discusses issues related to securely browsing web sites. The chapter concludes with a look at risks specific to email and how to mitigate them.

Chapter 10, Ongoing Security Management, examines some key considerations for keeping a network secure. It begins with a discussion of strategies for ensuring that operating systems and applications are kept up-to-date with the latest security patches. Next, it discusses the importance of auditing and ongoing monitoring. Finally, the chapter examines strategies for both in-band and out-of-band remote management.

Chapter 11, Disaster Recovery and Fault Tolerance, examines the importance of planning for the worst. It begins by discussing three types of plans a company should have in place to define recovery procedures when a disaster or attack occurs. Next, it covers the importance of backups. The chapter concludes with a look at fault tolerance technologies, include Redundant Array of Independent Disks (RAID) and failover configurations.

Chapter 12, Intrusion Detection and Forensics, introduces students to techniques used to detect a potential attack and analyze the nature of an attack. The chapter begins with a look at intrusion detection systems (IDS) and how they can be used to provide advance warning of an impending attack. Next, it looks at how honeypots can be used to analyze an attacker's methods. The chapter concludes with a look at forensics, including procedures for preserving evidence and investigating the extent and methods used in an attack.

Pre-reading Learning Aids

Each chapter of *Network Security Fundamentals* features the following learning and study aids to activate students' prior knowledge of the topics and to orient them to the material.

▲ **Pre-test.** This pre-reading assessment tool in multiple-choice format not only introduces chapter material, but it also helps students anticipate the chapter's learning outcomes. By focusing students' attention on what they do not know, the self-test provides students with a benchmark against which they can measure their own progress. The pre-test is available online at www.wiley.com/college/cole.

▲ **What You'll Learn in This Chapter.** This bulleted list focuses on subject matter that will be taught. It tells students what they will be learning in this chapter and why it is significant for their careers. It will also help students understand why the chapter is important and how it relates to other chapters in the text.

▲ **After Studying This Chapter, You'll Be Able To.** This list emphasizes capabilities and skills students will learn as a result of reading the chapter. It sets students up to synthesize and evaluate the chapter material, and to relate it to the real world.

Within-text Learning Aids

The following learning aids are designed to encourage analysis and synthesis of the material, support the learning process, and ensure success during the evaluation phase:

▲ **Introduction.** This section orients the student by introducing the chapter and explaining its practical value and relevance to the book as a whole. Short summaries of chapter sections preview the topics to follow.

▲ **"For Example" Boxes.** Found within each section, these boxes tie section content to real-world examples, scenarios, and applications.

▲ **Figures and tables.** Line art and photos have been carefully chosen to be truly instructional rather than filler. Tables distill and present information in a way that is easy to identify, access, and understand, enhancing the focus of the text on essential ideas.

▲ *Self-Check.* Related to the "What You'll Learn" bullets and found at the end of each section, this battery of short answer questions emphasizes student understanding of concepts and mastery of section content. Though the questions may either be discussed in class or studied by students outside of class, students should not go on before they can answer all questions correctly.

▲ **Key Terms and Glossary.** To help students develop a professional vocabulary, key terms are bolded when they first appear in the chapter. A complete list of key terms appears at the end of each chapter, and all the key terms, along with brief definitions, appears in a glossary at the end of the book. Knowledge of key terms is assessed by all assessment tools (see below).

▲ **Summary.** Each chapter concludes with a summary paragraph that reviews the major concepts in the chapter and links back to the "What You'll Learn" list.

Evaluation and Assessment Tools

The evaluation phase of the CASE Learning System consists of a variety of within-chapter and end-of-chapter assessment tools that test how well students have learned the material. These tools also encourage students to extend their learning into different scenarios and higher levels of understanding and thinking. The following assessment tools appear in every chapter of *Network Security Fundamentals:*

▲ **Summary Questions** help students summarize the chapter's main points by asking a series of multiple choice and true/false questions that emphasize student understanding of concepts and mastery of chapter content. Students should be able to answer all of the Summary Questions correctly before moving on.

▲ **Applying This Chapter Questions** drive home key ideas by asking students to synthesize and apply chapter concepts to new, real-life situations and scenarios.

▲ **You Try It Questions** are designed to extend students' thinking, and so are ideal for discussion or writing assignments. Using an open-ended format and sometimes based on web sources, they encourage students to draw conclusions using chapter material applied to real-world situations, which fosters both mastery and independent learning.

▲ **Post-test** should be taken after students have completed the chapter. It includes all of the questions in the pre-test, so that students can see how their learning has progressed and improved.

Instructor Package

Network Security Fundamentals is available with the following teaching and learning supplements. All supplements are available online at the text's Book Companion website, located at www.wiley.com/college/cole.

▲ **Instructor's Resource Guide.** Provides the following aids and supplements for teaching a network security fundamentals course:
   ● *Teaching suggestions.* For each chapter, these include a chapter summary, learning objectives, definitions of key terms, lecture notes, answers to select text question sets, and at least 3 suggestions for classroom activities, such as ideas for speakers to invite, videos to show, and other projects.

▲ **PowerPoint Slides.** Key information is summarized in 10 to 15 PowerPoint® slides per chapter. Instructors may use these in class or choose to share them with students for class presentations or to provide additional study support.

▲ **Test Bank.** One test per chapter, as well as a mid-term, and two finals: one cumulative, one non-cumulative. Each includes true/false, multiple choice, and open-ended questions. Answers and page references are provided for the true/false and multiple choice questions, and page references for the open-ended questions. Questions are available in Microsoft Word and computerized test bank formats.

Student Project Manual

The inexpensive *Network Security Fundamentals Project Manual* contains activities (an average of five projects per textbook chapter) designed to help students apply textbook concepts in a practical way. Easier exercises at the beginning graduate to more challenging projects that build critical-thinking skills.

ACKNOWLEDGMENTS

Taken together, the content, pedagogy, and assessment elements of *Network Security Fundamentals* offer the career-oriented student the most important aspects of the network security field as well as ways to develop the skills and capabilities that current and future employers seek in the individuals they hire and promote. Instructors will appreciate its practical focus, conciseness, and real-world emphasis.

We would like to thank the reviewers for their feedback and suggestions during the text's development. Their advice on how to shape *Network Security Fundamentals* into a solid learning tool that meets both their needs and those of their busy students is deeply appreciated.

We would especially like to thank the following reviewers for their significant contributions:

Delfina Najera, El Paso Community College
Jan McDanolds, Kaplan University
Laurence Dumais, American River College

We would also like to thank Carol Traver for all her hard work in formatting and preparing the manuscript for production.

BRIEF CONTENTS

1   Computer and Network Security Principles 1
2   Network and Server Security 30
3   Cryptography 74
4   Authentication 118
5   Authorization and Access Control 149
6   Securing Network Transmission 188
7   Remote Access and Wireless Security 221
8   Server Roles and Security 262
9   Protecting Against Malware 310
10 Ongoing Security Management 356
11 Fault Tolerance and Disaster Recovery 395
12 Intrusion Detection and Response 433

Glossary 462
Index 507

CONTENTS

1   **Network Security Principles** 1

Introduction. 2

1.1   Importance of Computer and Network Security 2
     1.1.1   Exposing Secrets 2
     1.1.2   Causing System Failures. 3
     1.1.3   Profile of an Attacker 4
     1.1.4   Social Engineering 4
     1.1.5   Security Defined. 5
     Self-Check 6

1.2   Underlying Computer and Network Security Concepts 6
     1.2.1   Confidentiality 7
     1.2.2   Integrity 7
     1.2.3   Availability 8
     1.2.4   Accountability 9
     1.2.5   Nonrepudiation 10
     Self-Check 11

1.3   Threats and Countermeasures 11
     1.3.1   Assessing Assets, Vulnerabilities and
            Threats to Calculate Risk 12
     1.3.2   Calculating Risk 15
     1.3.3   Countermeasures—Risk Mitigation 16
     Self-Check 19

1.4   Policies and Standards 20
     1.4.1   Security Policy 20
     1.4.2   Standards 21
     1.4.3   Informing Users of the Importance of Security 23
     Self-Check 24
     Summary 24
     Key Terms 24
     Assess Your Understanding. 26
     Summary Questions. 26
     Applying This Chapter 27
     You Try It 29

2   **Network and Server Security**. 30

Introduction. 31

2.1   Network Protocols Review 31
     2.1.1   Understanding Protocols 31
     2.1.2   The Open Systems Interconnect Model 32

	2.1.3	The TCP/IP Model	39
	2.1.4	TCP/IP Ports	43
	Self-Check		45
2.2	Best Practices for Network Security		45
	2.2.1	Security by Design	46
	2.2.2	Maintaining a Security Mindset	47
	2.2.3	Defense-in-Depth	47
	Self-Check		49
2.3	Securing Servers		49
	2.3.1	Controlling the Server Configuration	49
	Self-Check		56
2.4	Border Security		57
	2.4.1	Segmenting a Network	57
	2.4.2	Perimeter Defense	58
	2.4.3	Firewalls	58
	2.4.4	Network Address Translation	65
	Self-Check		67
	Summary		67
	Key Terms		67
	Assess Your Understanding		70
	Summary Questions		70
	Applying This Chapter		71
	You Try It		73
3	**Cryptography**		**74**
	Introduction		75
3.1	Cryptography Overview		75
	3.1.1.	A Brief History of Cryptography	75
	3.1.2	Cryptographic Primitives	79
	3.1.3	XOR	81
	3.1.4	Cast of Characters	82
	Self-Check		83
3.2	Symmetric Encryption		83
	3.2.1	Understanding Symmetric Encryption	83
	3.2.2	Encryption Strength	84
	3.2.3	Stream Ciphers	84
	3.2.4	Block Ciphers	85
	3.2.5	Sharing Keys	88
	Self-Check		90
3.3	Asymmetric Encryption		90
	3.3.1	Ensuring Confidentiality with Asymmetric Encryption	91

3.3.2   Digital Signatures 92

Self-Check 93

3.4   Hashes 93

3.4.1   Hash Functions 93

3.4.2   Using Hash Functions to Ensure Integrity 94

3.4.3   A Vulnerability When Protecting Passwords 94

3.4.4   Creating Pseudorandom Data with
Hash Functions 95

3.4.5   Keyed Hash Functions 96

Self-Check 96

3.5   Achieving CIA 97

3.5.1   Confidentiality 97

3.5.2   Integrity 97

3.5.3   Authentication 98

3.5.4   CIA 98

Self-Check 99

3.6   Public Key Infrastructure (PKI) 99

3.6.1   Digital Certificates 99

3.6.2   Public Key Infrastructure 100

3.6.3   Designing a CA Hierarchy 103

3.6.4   Security Policy and PKI Implementation 107

3.6.5   Trusting Certificates from Other Organizations 108

3.6.6   Creating an Enrollment and
Distribution Strategy 110

3.6.7   Renewing Certificates 110

3.6.8   Revoking a Certificate 111

Self-Check 112

Summary 113

Key Terms 113

Assess Your Understanding. 115

Summary Questions 115

Applying This Chapter 116

You Try It 117

4   **Authentication** 118

Introduction. 119

4.1   Authentication Overview 119

4.1.1   Interactive Logon 119

4.1.2   Peer-to-Peer Network Logon 120

4.1.3   Computer Authentication. 120

4.1.4   Mutual Authentication 121

4.1.5   Application Authentication 123

Self-Check 125

4.2   Authentication Credentials 125
       4.2.1   Password Authentication 125
       4.2.2   One-Time Passwords 128
       4.2.3   Smart Cards 128
       4.2.4   Biometrics 129
       Self-Check *131*
4.3   Authentication Protocols 131
       4.3.1   LAN Manager-Based Protocols 131
       4.3.2   Kerberos 134
       Self-Check *136*
4.4   Best Practices for Secure Authentication 136
       4.4.1   Password Policies 137
       4.4.2   Account Lockout Policy 139
       4.4.3   Account Logon Hours 140
       4.4.4   Account Logon Workstation 140
       4.4.5   Auditing Logons 141
       Self-Check *141*
       Summary 143
       Key Terms 143
       Assess Your Understanding 145
       Summary Questions 145
       Applying This Chapter 146
       You Try It 148

5   **Authorization and Access Control** **149**
       Introduction 150
5.1   Access Control Models 150
       5.1.1   Discretionary Access Control (DAC) 150
       5.1.2   Mandatory Access Control (MAC) 151
       5.1.3   Role-Based Access Control (RBAC) 152
       5.1.4   Principle of Least Permission 154
       Self-Check *154*
5.2   Implementing Access Control on Windows
       Computers 154
       5.2.1   Principals 154
       5.2.2   Windows Access Control Model 161
       5.2.3   Understanding Active Directory
                Object Permissions 163
       5.2.4   Designing Access Control for
                Files and Folders 165
       5.2.5   User Rights Assignment 172
       Self-Check *173*

5.3   Implementing Access Control on Unix Computers 174
    5.3.1   Principals 174
    5.3.2   Objects 176
    Self-Check *181*
    Summary 182
    Key Terms 182
    Assess Your Understanding 184
    Summary Questions 184
    Applying This Chapter 185
    You Try It 187

6   Securing Network Transmission **188**
Introduction 189
6.1   Analyzing Security Requirements for Network Traffic 189
    6.1.1   Types of Attacks 189
    6.1.2   Considerations for Designing a Secure
          Infrastructure 192
    6.1.3   Securely Transmitting Data 193
    Self-Check *194*
6.2   Defining Network Perimeters 195
    6.2.1   Isolating Insecure Networks Using Subnets 195
    6.2.2   Switches and VLANs 196
    6.2.3   Using IP Address and IP Packet Filtering 199
    Self-Check *201*
6.3   Data Transmission Protection Protocols 201
    6.3.1   SSL and TLS 201
    6.3.2   IP Security (IPsec) 205
    6.3.3   Server Message Block Signing 211
    6.3.4   Secure Shell 212
    Self-Check *214*
    Summary 214
    Key Terms 215
    Assess Your Understanding 217
    Summary Questions 217
    Applying This Chapter 218
    You Try It 220

7   Remote Access and Wireless Security **221**
Introduction 222
7.1   Dial-Up Networking 222
    7.1.1   Dial-Up Networking Protocols 222
    7.1.2   Dial-Up Networking Authentication Protocols 223

		7.1.3	Limiting Dial-Up Access	228
		7.1.4	Preventing Access to the Network	229
		Self-Check		230
	7.2	Virtual Private Networks		230
		7.2.1	Point-to-Point Tunneling Protocol (PPTP)	231
		7.2.2	L2TP and IPsec	233
		7.2.3	Hardware VPN Solutions	234
		Self-Check		235
	7.3	RADIUS and TACACS		235
		7.3.1	Using RADIUS Authentication	236
		7.3.2	Using TACACS and TACACS+	237
		Self-Check		239
	7.4	Wireless Networks		239
		7.4.1	Wireless Networking Standards	239
		7.4.2	Wireless Modes	240
		7.4.3	Preventing Intruders from Connecting to a Wireless Network	240
		7.4.4	Wired Equivalent Privacy (WEP)	241
		7.4.5	WiFi Protected Access (WPA)	244
		7.4.6	802.1x	246
		7.4.7	802.11i	252
		7.4.8	Designing for an Open Access Point	253
		7.4.9	Identifying Wireless Network Vulnerabilities	253
		Self-Check		255
		Summary		255
		Key Terms		255
		Assess Your Understanding		258
		Summary Questions		258
		Applying This Chapter		259
		You Try It		261
8		**Server Roles and Security**		**262**
		Introduction		263
	8.1	Server Roles and Baselines		263
		8.1.1	Trusted Computing Base	263
		8.1.2	Secure Baseline	264
		8.1.3	Preparing to Implement the Baseline	265
		8.1.4	Security Templates	265
		8.1.5	Security Configuration Wizard	270
		8.1.6	Secure Baseline Configuration for Linux Servers	272
		8.1.7	Virtualization	273
		Self-Check		274

8.2   Securing Network Infrastructure Servers 274
        8.2.1   Securing DNS Servers. 275
        8.2.2   Securing DHCP Servers 284
        8.2.3   Securing WINS Servers 287
        8.2.4   Securing Remote Access Servers. 288
        8.2.5   Securing NAT Servers. 289
        Self-Check 289
8.3   Securing Domain Controllers 289
        Self-Check 292
8.4   Securing File and Print Servers. 292
        8.4.1   Securing File Servers 292
        8.4.2   Securing Print Servers 293
        8.4.3   Securing FTP Server. 295
        Self-Check 297
8.5   Securing Application Servers 298
        8.5.1   Securing Web Servers. 298
        8.5.2   Securing Database Servers 301
        Self-Check 304
        Summary 304
        Key Terms 304
        Assess Your Understanding. 306
        Summary Questions. 306
        Applying This Chapter 307
        You Try It 309

9   Protecting Against Malware. 310
    Introduction. 311
    9.1   Viruses and Other Malware 311
            9.1.1   Viruses. 311
            9.1.2   Worms 312
            9.1.3   Trojan Horses. 312
            9.1.4   Browser Parasites 314
            9.1.5   Spyware 313
            9.1.6   Backdoors 313
            Self-Check 315
    9.2   Protecting the Workstation. 315
            9.2.1   Antivirus Software 317
            9.2.2   Anti-Spyware 317
            9.2.3   Computer Configuration Guidelines 318
            9.2.4   User Training 320
            Self-Check 323

9.3   Web Browser Security. 323
      9.3.1   Web Browser Risks. 323
      9.3.2   Web Browser Technologies. 324
      9.3.3   Specific Threats to a Browser Session 327
      9.3.4   Browser Configuration 329
      9.3.5   Internet Explorer Security Zones 334
      9.3.6   Configuring Web Features in Firefox 336

      Self-Check 336

9.4   Email Security 336
      9.4.1   Attacks that Disclose Data 337
      9.4.2   Spam 342
      9.4.3   Protecting Against Malcode Propagated by
               Email 345
      9.4.4   Mail Client Configurations 346
      9.4.5   Architectural Considerations 347

      Self-Check 349

      Summary 350

      Key Terms 350

      Assess Your Understanding. 352

      Summary Questions 352

      Applying This Chapter 353

      You Try It 355

10   Ongoing Security Management 356

      Introduction. 357

10.1 Managing Updates 357
      10.1.1   Configuration Management 357
      10.1.2   Understanding the Components of
               Configuration Management 358
      10.1.3   Importance of Automating Updates 360
      10.1.4   Creating a Security Update Infrastructure. 360
      10.1.5   A WSUS Solution. 362
      10.1.6   Configuring SUS Clients. 362

      Self-Check 365

10.2 Auditing and Logging. 366
      10.2.1   Security Audits. 366
      10.2.2   Monitoring. 368
      10.2.3   Auditing on Unix 368
      10.2.4   Auditing in Windows 369

      Self-Check 371

10.3 Secure Remote Administration 371
      10.3.1   Creating a Remote Management Plan 372
      10.3.2   Remote Management Security Considerations 374

10.3.3   Planning Remote Management Deployment 375
10.3.4   Securing Windows Inbound Management Tools. . . . 376
10.3.5   Securing TCP/IP Remote Management Tools 382
10.3.6   Designing for Emergency
         Management Services 383

         Self-Check 389

11   **Disaster Recovery and Fault Tolerance** **395**

     Introduction. 396

     11.1   Planning for the Worst 396
            11.1.1   Business Continuity Planning. 396
            11.1.2   Disaster Recovery Planning 399
            11.1.3   Designing an Incident Response Procedure 403

            Self-Check 407

     11.2   Creating a Backup Strategy. 407
            11.2.1   Analyzing Backup Requirements 407
            11.2.2   Backing Up System Configurations 408
            11.2.3   Choosing a Backup Tool. 408
            11.2.4   Choosing the Backup Media. 409
            11.2.5   Determining the Types of Backup. 410
            11.2.6   Determining Backup Frequency. 411
            11.2.7   Assigning Responsibility for Backups 413
            11.2.8   Testing Recovery 414

            Self-Check 414

     11.3   Designing for Fault Tolerance. 415
            11.3.1   Eliminating Single Points of Failure 415
            11.3.2   Selecting Fault Tolerant Storage 416
            11.3.3   RAID Levels 416
            11.3.4   Choosing Between Hardware and
                     Software RAID 421
            11.3.5   Storage Area Networks (SANs). 423
            11.3.6   Designing a Failover Solution. 425

            Self-Check 427

            Summary 427

            Key Terms 427

            Assess Your Understanding. 429

            Summary Questions. 429

            Applying This Chapter 430

            You Try It 432

12   **Intrusion Detection and Forensics** **433**

     Introduction. 434

     12.1   Intrusion Detection 434

12.1.1   Intrusion Detection and Response 434
12.1.2   Intrusion Detection Systems (IDS) 434
12.1.3   IDS Issues 438
12.1.4   Intrusion Prevention Systems (IPS) 439
Self-Check 439
12.2   Honeypots 439
12.2.1   Preventing, Detecting, and Responding
to Attacks. 440
12.2.2   Honeypot Categories 441
12.2.3   When to Use a Honeypot 442
12.2.4   Legal Considerations 443
Self-Check 444
12.3   Forensics 444
12.3.1   Understanding Evidence 444
12.3.2   Gathering Evidence on a Live System 445
12.3.3   Preparing a Hard Drive Image 448
12.3.4   Searching for Data on a Hard Drive 450
Self-Check 457
Summary 457
Key Terms 458
Assess Your Understanding. 459
Summary Questions 459
Applying This Chapter 460
You Try It 461

Glossary. 462

Index 507

1

COMPUTER AND NETWORK SECURITY PRINCIPLES

Starting Point

Go to www.wiley.com/college/cole to assess your knowledge of computer and network security fundamentals.
Determine where you need to concentrate your effort.

What You'll Learn in This Chapter

▲ Why networks need security
▲ Types of attacks
▲ Key aspects of security
▲ Threat analysis
▲ Social engineering
▲ Security policies, procedures, and standards

After Studying This Chapter, You'll Be Able To

▲ Identify the key aspects of security and explain why they are important to a business
▲ Describe how social engineering presents a security risk
▲ Compare quantitative risk analysis and qualitative risk analysis
▲ Identify assets and assess their value
▲ Identify vulnerabilities and assess their criticality
▲ Identify threats and assess their likelihood
▲ List the elements of the ISO 17799 standard and describe how they relate to network security

INTRODUCTION

When you begin to learn about computer and network security, you need to understand why you're doing so. The main purpose of this chapter is to get you thinking about the things that can happen when security is not implemented on a computer or network—to increase your paranoia a little—and to give you a foundation in some key security concepts. Therefore, the first section of this chapter describes some potential threats to computer security at a general level. Next the chapter looks at the key aspects you need to consider when implementing security on a computer or network. Then the chapter introduces threat modeling and risk mitigation. The chapter concludes with an introduction to security policies and procedures.

1.1 Importance of Computer and Network Security

Computer security involves implementing measures to secure a single computer. When securing a single computer, you are concerned with protecting the resources stored on that computer and protecting that computer from threats. **Network security** involves protecting all the resources on a network from threats. You must consider not only the computers on the network, but other network devices, network transmission media, and the data being transmitted across the network. In this section, you will learn to appreciate the importance of computer and network security by looking at a few examples of attacks that could occur. These examples should get you thinking about what could happen if computer and network security is not implemented. We'll also define *security* as it will be used in the context of this book.

1.1.1 Exposing Secrets

The more wired our society becomes, the more our confidential data is subject to being discovered by those who will use it maliciously or for their own benefit. For example, in the spring of 2005, hackers discovered the password to Paris Hilton's T-Mobile© Sidekick© and published her address book and other personal information on the Internet. Think about the vulnerability of the data you store on your cell phone or on your personal digital assistant (PDA). Do you use passwords that are hard to guess to protect it?

Similar confidentiality concerns are raised by the use of credit cards to make purchases over the Internet. Figure 1-1 illustrates two potential attacks on your private financial data.

The basic Internet protocols provide no confidentiality protection, so parties located between customer and merchant could capture credit card numbers and use them later for fraudulent purchases. Secure Sockets Layer (SSL) was developed

Figure 1-1

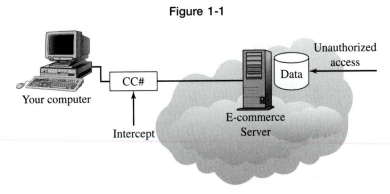

Risks of using an e-commerce website.

by Netscape® to deal with this very problem. SSL defines the **Hypertext Transfer Protocol over SSL (HTTPS)**, which provides encryption of data sent using **Hypertext Transfer Protocol (HTTP)**, the protocol used on the World Wide Web. **Transport Layer Security (TLS)** offers stronger protection than SSL and is gradually replacing it.

Although SSL and TLS can protect data while it is being sent across the Internet (or another unsecured network), its use does not mean your credit card number is safe. Scanning Internet traffic for packets containing credit card numbers is an attack strategy with a low yield. Badly protected servers at a merchant site that hold a database of customer credit card numbers are a much more rewarding target. There is documented evidence that such attacks have occurred, either to obtain credit card numbers or to blackmail the merchant.

Another potential risk is identity theft. **Identity theft,** that is, using somebody else's "identity" (name, social security number, bank account number, etc.) to gain access to a resource or service, exploits an inherent weakness in services that use nonsecret identifying information to authenticate requests.

1.1.2 Causing System Failures

Some attackers are not after confidential data. Instead, they want to disrupt business. These attackers use a variety of techniques to cause damage.

Vulnerabilities in software that accepts user input, such as Internet browsers or email software, can allow external parties to take control of a device. Attackers might corrupt data on the device itself or use the device as a stepping stone for attacks against third parties.

Worms and viruses make use of overgenerous features or vulnerabilities to spread widely and overload networks and end systems with the traffic they generate. The Internet worm of November 1988 is an early well-documented example of this species. Denial-of-service attacks against specific targets have started to occur in the last decade. A **denial-of-service attack** is one that prevents a server from performing its normal job. Resilience against denial-of-service attacks has become a new criterion in the design of security protocols.

1.1.3 Profile of an Attacker

In the scenarios described above, the attacks come from the outside. Keeping the enemy outside the castle walls is a traditional paradigm in computer security. However, typical statistics for the sources of attacks show that attacks from insiders account for a majority of incidents and the largest proportion of damages. Although there have been some very high profile attacks via the Internet, insider fraud remains a considerable concern in organizations and in electronic commerce transactions.

Understanding your enemy is a good first step in learning how to defeat him or her. When designing security, it helps to understand something about why hackers attack and their different levels of expertise.

Attacker Motivation

It has been said that the goal of security engineering is to raise the effort involved in an attack to a level where the costs exceed the attacker's gains. Such advice might be short-sighted. Not every attacker is motivated by a wish for money. Employees who have been fired might want revenge on their former employers. Hackers might want to demonstrate their technical expertise and might draw particular satisfaction from defeating security mechanisms that have been put in their way. Cyber vandals might launch attacks without much interest in their consequences. Political activists might deface the websites of organizations they dislike or launch attacks on a politician's site so that visitors are redirected to a different site.

Attacker Expertise

There is similar variance in the expertise required to break into a system. In some cases insider knowledge will be required to put together a successful attack plan. In this respect, social engineering could be more important than technical wizardry. Hassling computer operators on the phone to give the caller the password to a user account is a favorite ploy. Some attacks require deep technical understanding. Other attacks have been automated and can be downloaded from websites so that they can be executed by **script kiddies**, attackers who have little insight into the vulnerabilities or features of a system, but use scripts to launch attacks.

1.1.4 Social Engineering

One of the common ways attackers gain information is through social engineering. A **social engineering** attack is one that involves people, not computers. This makes it especially difficult for the network administrator to thwart. The following are some examples of social engineering attacks:

▲ An attacker calls an employee on the phone claiming to be an administrator. The person asks for the user's name and password so they can verify the user's network settings.

▲ An attacker who does not work for the company claims to be a temporary employee or contractor. The attacker is allowed access to a computer— or worse, to the server room.

▲ An attacker sifts through documents in the trash bin to discover employee names, organizational hierarchy, or even network configuration data.

These are just a few examples of social engineering attacks. The best way to prevent a social engineering attack is by educating employees about unsafe practices.

1.1.5 Security Defined

Software might crash, communication networks might go down, hardware components might fail, and human operators might make mistakes. As long

---

FOR EXAMPLE

A Network Without Security

You have been hired at a small company as a network administrator. The company has been using peer-to-peer networking to allow users to share files. The company does not have a security policy and users frequently share their passwords with other users so that they can share files.

When you raise concerns to the owner of the company, he shrugs his shoulders. "Nothing has happened so far. Besides, we're not even connected to the Internet," he says.

You explain that a password should be a secret that only a single person knows because that password gives them access to confidential files. You ask the owner to think about the kinds of data that are stored on each person's computer and what would happen if the data fell into the wrong hands. You give the example of a disgruntled employee who leaves with the customer list.

The owner thinks for a moment and turns pale. "You know, I hadn't thought about that before. Your first job is to figure out how I can protect my company from an attack that compromises its confidential data."

as these failures cannot be directly attributed to some deliberate human action, they are not classified as security issues. Accidental failures are reliability issues. Operating mistakes are usability issues. Security is concerned, in contrast, with intentional failures. There might not always be a clear intent to achieve a particular goal, but there is at some stage a decision by a person to do something he or she is not supposed to do. As outlined previously, there can be different reasons for such actions. The root cause of security problems is human nature.

Security practitioners know that security is a "people problem" that cannot be solved by technology alone. The legal system has to define the boundaries of acceptable behavior through data protection and computer misuse laws. However, responsibility for security within organizations resides ultimately with management and with the users on the network. Managers must enforce the company's security policies. Users have to cooperate and comply with the security rules laid down in their organization. Of course, correct deployment and operation of technical measures is also part of the overall solution.

SELF-CHECK

1. List three attacker motivations.
2. How does SSL protect data?
3. What makes a social engineering attack difficult to mitigate?

1.2 Underlying Computer and Network Security Concepts

In this section, we examine some key concepts underlying computer and network security. These concepts include the following:

▲ **Confidentiality:** prevention of unauthorized disclosure of information.

▲ **Integrity:** prevention of unauthorized modification of information.

▲ **Availability:** prevention of unauthorized withholding of information or resources.

▲ **Accountability:** holding users accountable for their actions.

▲ **Nonrepudiation:** the ability to ensure that someone cannot deny (i.e., repudiate) his or her actions.

1.2.1 Confidentiality

Historically, security and secrecy were closely related. Even today, many people still feel that the main objective of computer security is to stop unauthorized users from learning sensitive information. Confidentiality (privacy, secrecy) captures this aspect of computer security.

The terms *privacy* and *secrecy* are sometimes used to distinguish between the protection of personal data (**privacy**) and the protection of data belonging to an organization (**secrecy**). As you examine confidentiality issues, you will also face the question of whether you only want to hide the content of a document from unauthorized view, or also its existence. To see why one might take this extra step, consider traffic analysis in a communications system. If the contents of messages are hidden, an unauthorized observer might simply look at who is talking to whom how often, but not at the content of the messages passed. Even so, an observer could derive useful information about the relationship between the corresponding parties. This very issue has been debated recently in the United States Senate with regard to whether phone companies should be required to provide records of telephone calls to the government and what restrictions apply.

You need to consider the confidentiality of data both when it is stored on a computer and when it is being transmitted across the network. Another consideration is ensuring the confidentiality of data stored on laptop computers or removable devices, such as a USB drive. There have been several recent incidents involving missing laptops that store confidential data. Whenever data leaves a company's site, it becomes vulnerable.

1.2.2 Integrity

It is quite difficult to give a concise definition of *integrity*. In general, integrity is about making sure that everything is as it is supposed to be, and in the context of computer security, the prevention of unauthorized modification of information. However, additional qualifications like "being authorized to do what one does" or "following the correct procedures" have also been included under the term *integrity*, so that users of a system, even if authorized, are not permitted to modify data items in such a way that assets or accounting records of the company are lost or corrupted.

So far we have defined security by specifying the user actions that have to be controlled. From a systematic point of view, integrity is better defined in terms of the state of the system. The Orange Book (or Trusted Computer System Evaluation Criteria, developed by the United States Department of Defense) defines *integrity* in just this way: as the state that exists when computerized data is the same as that in the source documents and that has not been exposed to accidental or malicious alteration or destruction.

Figure 1-2

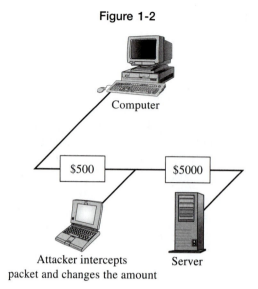

Man-in-the-middle attack.

In this definition, data integrity is a synonym for **external consistency.** The data stored in a computer system should correctly reflect some reality outside the computer system. However, while this state is highly desirable, it is impossible to guarantee this property merely by mechanisms internal to the computer system.

Integrity is often a prerequisite for other security properties. For example, an attacker could try to circumvent confidentiality controls by modifying the operating system or an access control table referenced by the operating system. Hence, we have to protect the integrity of the operating system and the integrity of access control data structures to achieve confidentiality.

Integrity is also an issue when data is transmitted across a network. An attacker could intercept and modify packets of data on the network if that data's integrity is not protected (see Figure 1-2). This type of attack is known as a **man-in-the-middle attack.**

1.2.3 Availability

Availability is very much a concern beyond the traditional boundaries of computer security. Engineering techniques used to improve availability often come from other areas like **fault-tolerant computing** (a computer system or systems that can tolerate the failure of a component). In the context of security, we want to ensure that a malicious attacker cannot prevent legitimate users from having reasonable access to their systems. That is, we want to prevent denial of service.

Figure 1-3

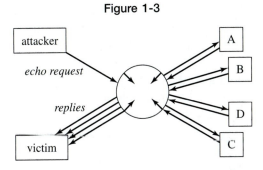

A denial-of-service attack (smurf attack).

There have now been a number of incidents of flooding attacks on the Internet where an attacker effectively disabled a server by overwhelming it with connection requests.

Figure 1-3 shows one of the first denial-of-service attacks, a smurf attack. A smurf attack requires the attacker to **spoof** (pretend to be someone you are not) the identity of the victim. In a **smurf attack,** the attacker sends an Internet Control Messaging Protocol (ICMP) echo request to the broadcast address of some network with a spoofed sender address (the victim's address). The echo request will be distributed to all nodes in that network. Each node will reply back to the spoofed sender address, flooding the victim with reply packets. The amplification provided by the broadcast address works to the attacker's advantage.

In many situations, availability might be the most important aspect of computer and network security, but there is a distinct lack of security mechanisms for handling this problem. As a matter of fact, security mechanisms that are too restrictive or too expensive can themselves lead to denial of service. Designers of security protocols now often try to avoid imbalances in workload that would allow a malicious party to overload its victim at little cost to itself.

A denial-of-service attack can also be launched against network resources. For example, in February 2007, a denial-of-service attack was launched against the domain name system root servers on the Internet. Fortunately, the attack did not disrupt Internet traffic.

1.2.4 Accountability

Confidentiality, integrity, and availability all deal with different aspects of access control and put their emphasis on the prevention of unwelcome events. You have to accept the fact that you will never be able to prevent all improper actions. First, you might find that even authorized actions can lead to a security violation.

Second, you might find a flaw in your security system that allows an attacker to find a way past your controls. Therefore, you might add a new security requirement to your list: users should be held responsible for their actions (accountability).

To provide accountability, the system has to identify and authenticate users. It has to keep an audit trail of security-relevant events. If a security violation has occurred, information from the audit trail could help to identify the perpetrator and the steps that were taken to compromise the system.

1.2.5 Nonrepudiation

Nonrepudiation provides undeniable evidence that a specific action occurred. This definition is meaningful when analyzing the security services that cryptographic mechanisms can provide. Typical nonrepudiation services in communications security are **nonrepudiation of origin,** providing evidence about the sender of a document, and **nonrepudiation of delivery,** providing evidence about the fact that a message was delivered to a specific recipient.

A physical example of nonrepudiation is sending a letter with a return receipt requested. When you do so, a person must sign for the letter. This is an example of nonrepudiation of delivery because you can prove that the letter was delivered. Of course, the person who signs for the letter might not be the person to whom the letter was addressed. This raises a potential weakness in nonrepudiation. Suppose the person who signs for the letter forges the name of the addressee. This means that the delivery can be **repudiated** (denied) by the actual addressee.

An example of nonrepudiation on a network is digital signature. A digital signature allows a recipient to verify that the letter was actually sent by a sender. This is an example of nonrepudiation of origin.

FOR EXAMPLE

Identifying Security Concerns

In speaking with your manager and several other employees at your new company, you identify some documents with confidentiality requirements, some with integrity requirements, and some with both. These documents are listed in Table 1-1.

You also identify a few resources with availability requirements during business hours. For example, one computer in the Sales department stores the "InventoryAndOrders" database. If it cannot be accessed during business hours, salespeople will not be able to check inventory or place customer orders.

Table 1-1: Confidentiality and Integrity Requirements

Data	Confidentiality	Integrity
Payroll records	X	X
Product design specifications	X	X
Health insurance claims	X	
Customer lists	X	
Accounts receivable records		X
Sales records		X
Employee Reviews	X	X

SELF-CHECK

1. Compare confidentiality and integrity. Include areas where they overlap.
2. Explain how availability is a security concern.

1.3 Threats and Countermeasures

Risk is the possibility that some incident or attack will cause damage to an organization's network. An attack consists of a sequence of actions that attempts to exploit weak points in an organization's practices or its network configuration. To assess the risk posed by the attack you have to evaluate the amount of potential damage and the likelihood that the attack will occur. This likelihood will depend on the attacker's motivation and on how easy it is to mount the attack. In turn, this will further depend on the security configuration of the system under attack. The process of identifying a risk and assessing its likelihood and impact is known as **risk analysis.**

Many areas of engineering and business have developed their own disciplines and terminology for risk analysis. This section gives a brief overview of risk analysis for Information Technology (IT) security. Within IT security, risk analysis is applied

▲ Comprehensively for all information assets of an enterprise.

▲ Specifically for the IT infrastructure of an enterprise.

▲ During the development of new products or systems—for example, in the area of software security.

1.3.1 Assessing Assets, Vulnerabilities, and Threats to Calculate Risk

The first step in risk analysis is to identify assets, vulnerabilities, and threats, and to rank them according to their value (assets), impact on the business if they are exploited (vulnerabilities), and likelihood of occurrence (threats). Let's take a look at each of these elements.

Assets

First, assets have to be identified and valued. In an IT system, assets include the following:

▲ **Hardware:** laptops, desktops, servers, routers, PDAs, mobile phones, smart cards, and so on.

▲ **Software:** applications, operating systems, database management systems, source code, object code, and so on.

▲ **Data and information:** essential data for running and planning your business, design documents, digital content, data about your customers, data belonging to your customers (like credit card numbers), and so forth.

▲ **Reputation:** the opinion held by your customers and the general public about your organization. Reputation can affect how likely a person is to place an order with you or provide you with information.

Identification of assets should be a relatively straightforward, systematic exercise. Valuation of assets is more of a challenge. Some assets, such as hardware, can be valued according to their monetary replacement costs. For other assets, such as data and information, valuation is more difficult. If your business plans are leaked to the competition or private information about your customers is leaked to the public you have to account for indirect losses due to lost business opportunities and damage to reputation. The competition might underbid you and your customers might desert you. Even when equipment is lost or stolen you have to consider the value of the data stored on it, and the value of the services that were running on it. In such situations, assets can be valued according to their importance. As a good metric for value, ask yourself how long your business could survive when a given asset has been damaged: a day, a week, a month?

Vulnerabilities

Vulnerabilities are weaknesses of a system that could be accidentally or intentionally exploited to damage assets. In an IT system, the following are typical vulnerabilities:

▲ Accounts with system privileges where the default password, such as 'MANAGER', has not been changed.

▲ Programs with unnecessary privileges.

▲ Programs with known flaws.

▲ Weak access control settings on resources, for example, granting everyone full control to a shared folder.

▲ Weak firewall configurations that allow access to vulnerable services.

Vulnerability scanners (also called **risk analysis tools**) provide a systematic and automated way of identifying vulnerabilities. However, their knowledge base of known vulnerabilities has to be kept up to date. Organizations like the SANS Institute or the Computer Emergency Response Team (CERT) provide this information, as do security advisories of software companies. One vulnerability scanner provided by Microsoft® is the Microsoft Baseline Security Analyzer (MBSA).

Vulnerabilities can be rated according to their impact (level of criticality). A vulnerability that allows an attacker to take over an administrator account is more critical than a vulnerability that gives access to an unprivileged user account. A vulnerability that allows an attacker to completely impersonate a user is more critical than a vulnerability that allows a user to be impersonated only in the context of a single specific service. Some vulnerability scanners give a rating for the vulnerabilities they detect.

Threats

Threats are actions by adversaries who try to exploit vulnerabilities in order to damage assets. There are various ways to identify threats. You can categorize threats by the damage done to assets. For example, Microsoft's **STRIDE threat model** for software security lists the following categories.

▲ Spoofing identities: The attacker pretends to be somebody else.

▲ Tampering with data: Security settings are changed to give the attacker more privileges.

▲ Repudiation: A user denies having performed an action like mounting an attack or making a purchase.

▲ Information disclosure: Information might lose its value if it is disclosed to the wrong parties (e.g., trade secrets); your organization might face penalties if it does not properly protect information (e.g., personal information about individuals).

▲ Denial of service (DoS): DoS attacks can make websites temporarily unavailable; there have been stories in the press that businesses use such attacks to harm competitors.

▲ Elevation of privilege: The term **elevation of privilege** refers to a user who gains more privileges on a computer system than he or she is entitled to.

Figure 1-4

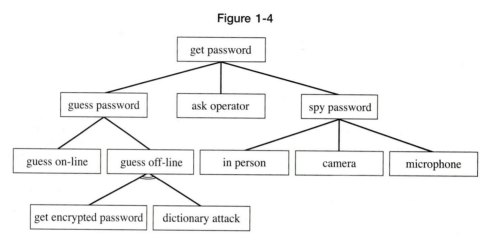

Attack tree for obtaining another user's password.

You can also categorize threats by the source of the attacks. Is the adversary a member of your organization or an outsider, a contractor or a former member? Does the adversary have direct access to your systems or is the attack launched remotely?

You can also analyze in detail how an attack is executed. One way to do this is to draw an **attack tree** (a hierarchical diagram that illustrates how an attack might occur), like the sample in Figure 1-4.

An attack might start with innocuous steps, such as gathering information needed to move on to gain privileges on one computer, and then might progress with more alarming steps such as jumping to another computer, and so on until the final target is reached. To get a more complete picture of potential threats, a forest of attack trees can be constructed. The root of an attack tree is a generic attack. The nodes in the tree are subgoals that must be achieved for the attack to succeed. Subgoals can be broken into further subgoals.

There are AND nodes and OR nodes. To reach an AND node, all subgoals have to be achieved. To reach an OR-node, it is enough if one subgoal is achieved. Figure 1-4 gives a basic attack tree for the attack "get password."

A password can be obtained by guessing, by tricking an operator to reveal it, or by spying on the user. Guessing can occur online or offline. For offline guessing, the attacker needs the encrypted password and has to perform a dictionary attack or a brute force attack. A **dictionary attack** is one in which all the words in the dictionary are tried until a match is found. A **brute force attack** is one in which software tries different combinations of letters, numbers, and symbols until a match is found. The attacker can also spy on the victim in person (so-called **shoulder surfing**), direct a camera at the keyboard to see the keys typed, or direct a microphone at the keyboard to distinguish the keys pressed by sound.

It is possible to assign values to the various strategies represented in an attack tree (e.g., dictionary attack, ask operator). These values can indicate the estimated cost of an attack, the likelihood that it will occur, the likelihood that it will succeed or some other aspect of interest. From these values, the cheapest attack, the most likely attack, or the attack most likely to succeed can be computed. Attack trees are thus a formalized and structured method for analyzing threats.

Threat assessments become reproducible as the overall assessment of a threat can be traced to the individual assessments of subgoals. If the final result appears implausible, the tree can be consulted to see which subgoals were most critical for the final result, and those individual valuations can be adjusted to more plausible values. Note that the construction of attack trees is more an art than a science. You need experience to know when to readjust your ratings for subgoals, and when to adjust your preconceived opinion of the severity of a threat. You also need experience to know when to stop breaking up subgoals into ever more subgoals, a phenomenon known in the trade as **analysis paralysis.**

Threats can be rated according to their likelihood. The likelihood depends on the difficulty of the attack, on the motivation of the attacker, and on the number of potential attackers. **Attack scripts** automate attacks, making it easy to launch the attack. They are also likely to be available to a larger set of attackers. As a result, such attacks would be rated more likely than an individual hand-crafted attack.

1.3.2 Calculating Risk

Having rated the value of assets, the critical nature of possible vulnerabilities, and the likelihood of threats, you now face the task of actually calculating risk. You can calculate risk as follows:

$$Risk = Assets \times Vulnerabilities \times Threats$$

In the process of risk analysis, values are assigned to assets, vulnerabilities, and threats. In **quantitative risk analysis,** mathematical values are used—for example, by assigning monetary values to assets and probabilities to threats, the expected loss can be calculated. In **qualitative risk analysis,** risk is calculated based on rules that capture the consolidated advice of security experts and that do not necessarily have a mathematical underpinning.

In quantitative risk analysis, expected losses are computed based on monetary values for the assets and probabilities for the likelihood of threats. This method has the benefit of being based on a well-established mathematical theory, but also has the considerable drawback that the ratings obtained are often based on educated guesses. The quality of the results obtained cannot be better than the quality of the inputs provided. There are areas of risk analysis where quantitative methods work, but more often the lack of precision in the inputs does not justify a mathematical treatment.

In qualitative risk analysis, the following principles are used:

▲ Assets can be rated on a scale of critical–very important–important–not important.

▲ Criticality of vulnerabilities can be rated on a scale of has to be fixed immediately–has to be fixed soon–should be fixed–fix if convenient.

▲ Threats can be rated on a scale of very likely–likely–unlikely–very unlikely.

A finer method of scaling could be provided for each variable, that is, numerical values from 1 to 10.

Whatever scheme is used, guidance has to be given on how to assign ratings. The mapping of the ratings for assets, vulnerabilities, and threats to risks is often given by a table drawn up to reflect the judgment of security experts. The **DREAD methodology** that complements STRIDE serves as an example of a scheme for qualitative risk analysis, as discussed below:

▲ **D**amage potential: relates to the values of the assets being affected.

▲ **R**eproducibility: one aspect of how difficult it is to launch an attack; attacks that are easy to reproduce are a greater risk than attacks that only work in specific circumstances.

▲ **E**xploitability: relates to the effort, expertise, and resources required to launch an attack.

▲ **A**ffected users: for software vendors, another important contributing factor to damage potential.

▲ **D**iscoverability: When will the attack be detected? In the most damaging case, you will never know that your system has been compromised. If you don't know you've been attacked, then you don't know to take steps to recover.

1.3.3 Countermeasures—Risk Mitigation

The result of a risk analysis is a prioritized list of threats, together with recommended countermeasures to **mitigate** (reduce the likelihood or impact of) risk. Risk analysis tools usually come with a knowledge base of countermeasures for the threats they can identify.

It might seem as if one should first go through a risk analysis before deciding on which security measures to implement. However, there are two reasons why this ideal approach might not work. Conducting a risk analysis for a larger organization will take time, but the IT system in the organization and the world around it will keep changing. So, by the time the results of the analysis are presented, they are already somewhat out-of-date. Moreover, the costs of a full risk analysis might be difficult to justify to management.

For these reasons, organizations might opt for baseline protection as an alternative. This approach analyzes the security requirements for typical cases and recommends security measures deemed adequate. One of the best-known IT security baseline documents is maintained by the German Information Security Agency.

Another trend embraced by operating system manufacturers, including Microsoft is to make their software **secure by default.** This doesn't mean that the operating system does not have vulnerabilities. Instead, it means that known vulnerabilities are closed when the software is installed with default settings. An example of this is the requirement to provide a password for the Administrator account when you install Windows® Server 2003. Another example is the browser security settings configured by default in Windows Server 2003. Although you will most likely need to relax those settings at some point, a default installation will ensure that cookies, ActiveX controls, or other dynamic content cannot be downloaded through a web browser. Another example is that Windows Vista™ includes Windows Defender, an application that protects against spyware, adware, and pop-ups. It also installs with Windows Firewall and is enabled by default.

FOR EXAMPLE

Performing a Risk Analysis

After identifying some of your organizations documents at risk (see previous For Example Box), you take a more formal approach to your investigation. You decide to use qualitative risk analysis to determine where the highest risks to the company lie. You identify your company's assets and assign them values, as shown in Table 1-2.

You identify the vulnerabilities and rate them on how critical they are, shown in Table 1-3.

You identify the threats and rate them according to their likelihood. A partial list is shown in Table 1-4.

For an example, let's take the threat of the denial-of-service attack against the server with the "InventoryAndOrders" database and walk through calculating its risk.

The asset involved is the "InventoryAndOrders" database, which has a value of Medium. A vulnerability affecting the server that could cause a denial-of-service attack is unpatched software, which is assigned a criticality of Medium. Finally, the threat of a denial-of-service attack against this server is also assigned the likelihood of Medium. We'll assign a value of 1 for Low, 5 for Medium, and 10 for High. Therefore, the risk of a denial of service attack against the "InventoryAndOrders" database due to unpatched software is

$$5 \times 5 \times 5 = 125$$

(Continued)

Another vulnerability that can be exploited to launch a denial-of-service attack against the "InventoryAndOrders" database is the lack of a firewall. You assessed the impact of this vulnerability as High, so we'll assign it a value of 10. Therefore, the risk of the attack occurring due to the lack of a firewall is calculated as

$$5 \times 10 \times 5 = 250$$

Let's look at another example. You ranked the likelihood of an employee reading or modifying payroll information as high, giving it a threat value of High, or 10. If the vulnerability that is exploited to launch this attack is weak passwords, the criticality value was rated at Medium, or 5. The asset of payroll records is assigned the value of Medium, or 5. Therefore, the risk of this attack occurring is calculated as

$$5 \times 5 \times 10 = 250$$

However, if the vulnerability exploited is password sharing, which you have assigned an impact of High (10), the risk is

$$5 \times 10 \times 10 = 500$$

You determine that converting the network to use centralized security and establishing password policies can mitigate the worst security threats. Your baseline strategy will also include a firewall on the computer that shares the Internet connection and virus protection on all computers. These are common best practices and are a suitable start for a baseline security plan.

Table 1-2: Assets and Values

Asset	Value
Payroll records	Medium
Product design specifications	High
Health insurance claims	High
Customer lists	High
Accounts receivable records	Medium
Sales records	Low
Employee reviews	Low
"InventoryAndOrder" database	Medium

Table 1-3: Vulnerabilities

Vulnerabilities	Criticality
Unpatched software	Medium
Internet connection with no firewall	High
Antivirus protection missing or not updated	High
Weak passwords	Medium
Common password sharing	High
Employees make decisions about who has access	High

Table 1-4: Threats

Threats	Likelihood
A denial-of-service attack against the server with the "InventoryAndOrders" database	Medium
A denial-of-service attack against the payroll server	Low
Internal employee reading or modifying payroll data without authorization	High
Internal employee accessing employee review records	Medium
Internal employee selling customer lists	Medium
External person obtaining customer lists or product designs	Medium

SELF-CHECK

1. Explain why qualitative risk analysis is often more appropriate than quantitative risk analysis.
2. Describe the three domains that should be considered when calculating risk.

1.4 Policies and Standards

Protecting the assets of an organization is the responsibility of management. Assets include sensitive information like product plans, customer records or financial data, and the IT infrastructure of the organization. At the same time, security measures often restrict people in their working habits and make some activities less convenient. This results in a temptation to flaunt security rules. It is up to a network administrator to enforce the company's security policy without impacting, any more than necessary, usability or the ability of the users to perform their jobs.

The first step in enforcing policies is to define the policies that will be enforced. In this section, we'll discuss security policies, both organizational and those that can be enforced through a computer configuration. Next we'll take a brief look at the recommendations suggested by the ISO 17799 security standard.

1.4.1 Security Policy

A **security policy** is a document that defines the security goals of the business. It should identify assets that need to be secured, how they will be secured, and

---

FOR EXAMPLE

Pencils and Server Room Doors

A security policy often states that all servers must be in a physically secure server room. But being overly strict about this can cause employees to circumvent the policy to do their jobs. Consider a situation in which a credit card bank has contracted with a consulting company to develop an application. The project is being developed on a test server that, due to various test cases, locks up and needs to be physically rebooted. Access to the server room is granted by swiping an employee's identification badge on the access pad by the server room door. The problem is that nobody on the development team is allowed into the server room, nor are they allowed to keep the server (even though it only contained test data) outside the server room. This means that somebody else has to reboot the computer, and since the server operators are busy with projects of their own, they open the door and put a pencil in it so the developers can go back and forth at will without bugging them. This clearly opens the security room to a physical breech of security, but an inflexible and strict security policy that stated only server operators had access to the server room and that all servers must be in the server room opened the door (no pun intended) to this kind of security circumvention in the name of productivity.

a plan that should be followed if an asset is compromised. The policy should also include documentation of server configuration and a process for managing changes to that configuration.

Depending on the industry and where the business is located, you may need to comply with legal regulations. These factors should also be included in your security policy. Some legal regulations your security policy may need to comply with include the following:

▲ Health Insurance Portability and Accountability Act of 1996 (HIPAA)
▲ Federal Information Security Management Act of 2002 (FISMA)
▲ National Industrial Security Program Operating Manual (NISPOM)
▲ Gramm-Leach-Bliley Act (GLBA)

A security policy should also outline an **appropriate use policy,** which is a set of rules employees will be expected to follow. For example, you might restrict users from sharing documents on the network, from visiting websites that host games, or from installing software on their computers.

Keep in mind that the more stringent a security policy, the more likely it is that users will attempt to circumvent it. You need to balance ease of use and user productivity requirements with the need for security.

1.4.2 Standards

Security management standards that specify certain security measures required to be taken by an organization exist for a number of different types of industries. Typical examples are regulations for the financial sector or rules for dealing with classified material in government departments.

Other management standards are best described as codes of best practice for security management. The most prominent of these standards is **ISO 17799** (ISO stands for International Organization for Standardization). ISO 17799 is not a technical standard for security products or a set of evaluation criteria for products or systems. Instead, the major topics in ISO 17799 are as follows:

▲ **Establishment of organizational security policy:** An enterprise must provide management direction and support on security matters.

▲ **Organizational security infrastructure:** Responsibilities for security within an enterprise have to be properly organized. Management has to be able to get an accurate view of the state of security within an enterprise. Reporting structures should facilitate efficient communication and implementation of security decisions. Security has to be maintained when information services are being outsourced to third parties.

▲ **Asset classification and control:** To know what is worth protecting, and how much to spend on protection, an enterprise has to have a clear picture of its assets and of their value.

▲ **Physical and environmental security:** Physical security measures (fences, locked doors, etc.) protect access to business premises or to sensitive areas (rooms) within a building—for example, only authorized personnel should have access to server rooms. These measures can prevent unauthorized access to sensitive information and theft of equipment. The likelihood of natural disasters can depend on environmental factors—for example, is the area subject to flooding?

▲ **Personnel security:** An organization's employees can be a source of insecurity. There should be procedures for new employees joining and for employees leaving (such as collecting keys and entry badges and deleting user accounts of employees that leave the company). Enforced holiday periods can prevent staff from hiding the traces of fraud they are committing. Background checks on new hires are a good idea. In some sectors those checks may be required by law, but there might also be privacy laws that restrict which information an employer may seek about its employees.

▲ **Communications and operations management:** The day-to-day management of IT systems and of business processes has to ensure that security is maintained.

▲ **Access control:** Access control can apply to data, services, and computers. Particular attention should be applied to remote access, such as through the Internet or dial-in connections. Automated security policies define how access control is being enforced.

▲ **Systems development and maintenance:** Security issues should be considered when an IT system is being developed. Operational security depends on proper maintenance (for example, patching vulnerable code and updating virus scanners). IT support has to be conducted securely (for instance, how does the organization deal with users who have forgotten their passwords?) and IT projects have to be managed with security in mind (who is writing sensitive applications? Who gets access to sensitive data?).

▲ **Business continuity planning:** An organization must put measures in place so that it can cope with major failures or disasters. For example, backups of important data should be kept in a different building. Larger organizations might want to develop reserve computing facilities in a remote location. Organizations must also develop a plan to deal with the unavailability of key staff members.

▲ **Compliance:** Organizations have to comply with legal, regulatory, and contractual obligations, as well as with standards and their own organizational security policy. The auditing process to determine compliance should be efficient while trying to minimize its interference with business processes.

Achieving compliance with ISO 17799 can be quite an onerous task. The current state of your organization vis-à-vis the standard has to be established and any shortcomings identified have to be addressed. There are software tools that partially automate this process, again applying best practices, only this time ensuring compliance with the standard.

1.4.3 Informing Users of the Importance of Security

It is strongly recommended that you organize and publish security responsibilities in an organization in a way that makes it clear that security measures have the full support of senior management. A brief policy document signed by the chief executive that lays down the ground rules can serve as a starting point. This document should be part of everyone's employment handbook. Then, security awareness programs should be organized. Not every member has to become a security expert, but all members should know the following:

▲ Why security is important for themselves and for the organization.
▲ What is expected of each member.
▲ Best practices they should follow.

Trying to force users to follow rules they regard as arbitrary is not an efficient approach. Studies have shown that involving users as stakeholders in the security of their organizations encourages users to voluntarily comply with rules rather than look for work-arounds.

Organizations developing IT services or products have the additional task of providing security training for their developers. There is rarely a clear dividing line between the security-relevant components and the rest of a system. It thus helps if developers in general are aware of the environment that a service will be deployed in and of the expected dangers, so that they can highlight the need for protection even if they do not implement the protection mechanisms themselves. Developers should also be alert to the fact that certain categories of sensitive data (e.g., personal data) have to be processed according to specific rules and regulations. Finally, developers should keep up-to-date with known coding vulnerabilities.

FOR EXAMPLE

Defining a Security Policy

You meet with the owner of the company to plan how you will implement the security requirements you identified. You stress to him the importance of his support when presenting security guidelines to the other employees. You recommend that he create a **written security policy** and that each employee read and sign it.

You explain that some policies, such as requiring that users change their passwords periodically, can be enforced through software policies. But others, such as users not sharing passwords with other employees or with people outside the company, are more difficult to enforce. It is these policies that require user training. You suggest that the company sponsor a security awareness day in which employees receive training about the importance of security and the best practices for protecting company assets.

SELF-CHECK

1. Describe the components that should be included in a security policy.
2. Describe the purpose of ISO 17799.

SUMMARY

In this chapter you were introduced to a number of concepts and terms related to computer and network security. You learned why network security is important. You were introduced to the three key aspects of security: confidentiality, integrity, and availability. Next you learned about risk analysis. You learned that risk analysis involves identifying the assets, vulnerabilities, and threats, and assessing their importance, criticality, and likelihood. Finally, you learned the importance of security policies. You also learned what is required for ISO 17799 compliance.

KEY TERMS

Accountability	Attack script
Analysis paralysis	Attack tree
Appropriate use policy	Availability

Brute force attack

Computer security

Confidentiality

Data integrity

Denial-of-service attack

Dictionary attack

DREAD methodology

Elevation of privilege

External consistency

Fault-tolerant computing

Hypertext Transfer Protocol (HTTP)

Hypertext Transfer Protocol over SSL (HTTPS)

Identity theft

Integrity

ISO 17799

Man-in-the-middle attack

Mitigate

Network security

Nonrepudiation

Nonrepudiation of delivery

Nonrepudiation of origin

Privacy

Qualitative risk analysis

Quantitative risk analysis

Repudiated

Risk

Risk analysis

Risk analysis tool

Script kiddies

Secrecy

Secure by default

Security policy

Shoulder surfing

Smurf attack

Social engineering

Spoof

STRIDE threat model

Threat

TLS

Vulnerability

Vulnerability scanner

Written security policy

ASSESS YOUR UNDERSTANDING

Go to www.wiley.com/college/cole to evaluate your knowledge of computer and network security fundamentals.

Measure your learning by comparing pre-test and post-test results.

Summary Questions

1. An attack in which a person calls on the phone and pretends to be a member of the IT department to obtain a user's password is known as which of the following?

    (a) Attack script

    (b) Brute force attack

    (c) Dictionary attack

    (d) Social engineering attack

2. Which aspect of security is concerned with preventing the unauthorized modification of information?

    (a) Authorization

    (b) Confidentiality

    (c) Integrity

    (d) Nonrepudiation

3. Which aspect of security is threatened by a smurf attack?

    (a) Availability

    (b) Accountability

    (c) Integrity

    (d) Confidentiality

4. Qualitative risk analysis considers the likelihood of threats, but not the value of assets. True or false?

5. Which of the following assets is most difficult to associate with a mathematical value?

    (a) Laptop computer

    (b) Database server

    (c) Reputation

    (d) Web server availability

6. A vulnerability scanner can be used to identify vulnerabilities and rate how critical they are. True or false?

7. Which of the following is not included in the STRIDE threat model?

    (a) Storm damage

    (b) Repudiation

(c) Denial of service

(d) Elevation of privilege

8. When building an attack tree, the generic attack is placed at the root. True or false?

9. The DREAD methodology is an example scheme for quantitative risk analysis. True or false?

10. Which of the following would not be enforceable by an automated security policy?

(a) Firewall settings

(b) Password disclosure practices

(c) Password length restrictions

(d) Access control restrictions

11. ISO 17799 provides the technical standards by which an operating system should enforce security. True or false?

Applying This Chapter

1. You are performing a risk analysis of an existing network. The network is an Active Directory domain with 200 client computers. One server has a modem and allows remote access to the network by dial-in users. The network is connected to the Internet through a firewall.

(a) What type of threat is most likely to compromise the availability of the domain controller? Explain why.

(b) What type of threat is most likely to compromise the confidentiality of the company's data? Explain why.

(c) How can you identify and rate vulnerabilities on the network?

(d) A password policy that requires a new password every 30 days is applied throughout the domain. What effect will this have on social engineering attacks? Discuss the pros and cons.

(e) How can an organizational policy reduce or eliminate the risk identified in question 1(d)?

(f) You identify assets and assign a rating between 1 and 10 based on how long the business could operate if the asset was compromised. What type of risk analysis are you performing?

2. The major topics of ISO 17799 are listed in Table 1-5. Assign the policies listed below to the appropriate topic.

(a) Each employee must swipe his or her own card to be allowed through the front door.

(b) Contractors must be given security training before they begin work.

(c) The "Orders" database must be backed up hourly.

(d) A person who has been terminated must be escorted out of the building by a member of human resources.

(e) Employees can access the company network remotely only if they have been assigned permission by a supervisor.

(f) All client computers should be updated with a security patch within three days of the patch being made available.

(g) A hard drive must be reformatted before it is sent for service.

(h) At the end of each day, the "Accounting" database backup must be taken to a safety deposit box.

(i) Security decisions will be made by a committee composed of one designated participant from each department and the Chief Executive Officer.

(j) The company will comply with local, state, and federal privacy laws.

Table 1-5 Assigning Policies to the Appropriate ISO 17799 Topic

Establishing organizational security policy	
Organizational security infrastructure	
Asset classification and control	
Physical and environmental security	
Personnel security	
Communications and operations management	
Access control	
Systems development and maintenance	
Business continuity planning	
Compliance	

YOU TRY IT

Analyzing the Risks in Your Own Environment

A good place to start practicing risk analysis is by analyzing the risks associated with your own computer and the environment in which it is operating.

1. Identify four assets and rate them in terms of their value. Use a 4-point scale, where 4 is Very Important.

2. Identify any vulnerabilities. Consider the strength of your password, whether you have virus protection, whether your system is running a firewall, whether your operating system is kept up-to-date, the physical environment (who can actually sit down at your system and log on), and how your system is connected to any networks, including the Internet. Rate the vulnerabilities on a 4-point scale, where 1 is the most critical.

3. Identify potential threats. Use the STRIDE threat model and identify one potential threat in each category. Use the DREAD threat model to assign a value.

4. Identify the three most likely risks and describe how you can change your configuration or your security practices to mitigate them. Will you use an automated security policy? How do these mitigation efforts relate to the ISO 17799 categories?

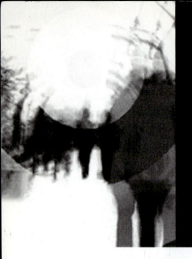

2

NETWORK AND SERVER SECURITY

Starting Point

Go to www.wiley.com/college/cole to assess your knowledge of server security and network borders.
Determine where you need to concentrate your effort.

What You'll Learn in This Chapter

▲ Layers of the OSI model
▲ Layers of the TCP/IP model
▲ TCP/IP protocols and ports
▲ Security by design
▲ Defense-in-depth
▲ How to physically secure a server
▲ How to limit the attack surface
▲ Public, semiprivate, and private networks
▲ Network segments
▲ Firewalls

After Studying This Chapter, You'll Be Able To

▲ Identify the role of each layer of the OSI model and describe how each relates to security
▲ Identify the purpose of key TCP/IP protocols and the layers at which they operate
▲ Describe the role of ports and their impact on security
▲ Describe how the defense-in-depth strategy is applied to network security
▲ List the steps to take to physically secure a server
▲ Identify and disable unnecessary services and limit the permissions of necessary services
▲ Describe how port scanners can be used to compromise a network
▲ Identify the risks associated with input and output devices on a server
▲ Describe the role of border security
▲ Distinguish between packet filtering, stateful packet filtering, and application proxy firewalls

INTRODUCTION

Businesses depend on servers for a number of reasons. Servers can store vital data, manage core business processes, and provide customers with information and services. Servers are also a primary target for attacks. In this chapter, you will learn how to reduce the attack surface for servers and create a segmented network that protects your key resources from attack. The chapter begins with a review of the layers in the networking stack and the TCP/IP protocol. Next, the chapter looks at some best practices for securing servers on your network. Finally, the chapter examines border security and discusses three types of firewalls and how they can be used to protect a network segment.

2.1 Network Protocols Review

To be able to identify and lessen the risk of a data confidentiality or integrity violation during a network data transfer, you must first understand how data is transmitted on a network. It is also essential to understand the role that firewalls play in a network.

2.1.1 Understanding Protocols

The word *protocol* has a number of definitions, based on the context of its use. In the area of computer communications, a **protocol** is a formal set of rules that describe how computers transmit data and communicate across a network. The protocol defines the message format and the rules for exchanging the messages.

Because of the complexity and multiple functions required to initiate, establish, conduct, and terminate communications among computers on a network, these functions are divided into manageable, individual layers. This decomposition is known as a **layered architecture.**

In a layered architecture, the protocols are arranged in a stack of layers in which data is passed from the highest layer to the lowest layer to send a transmission. This stack of layers is called the **network stack** (see Figure 2-1). The protocols and standards supported in each of the layers perform specific functions and attach information to the data as it passes through a particular layer. This process is called **data encapsulation.**

At the receiving computer, the process is reversed and the successive layers of information are stripped as the packet travels through the stack up to the highest layer. Each protocol detaches and examines only the data that was attached by its protocol counterpart at the transmitting computer.

Figure 2-1

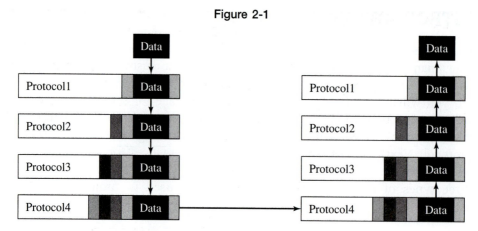

Network stack and data encapsulation.

The layers in the model range from providing application-oriented processes at the highest level to the generation of electrical or optical signals that are injected into the transmission medium (such as wires, optical fiber, or the air), in the bottom layer. The intermediate layers perform additional functions, including setting up the communications session, transferring data, and detecting errors.

2.1.2 The Open Systems Interconnect Model

The **Open Systems Interconnection (OSI) model** was developed around 1981 by the International Organization for Standardization (ISO). The OSI reference model includes seven functional layers, which provide the basis for communication among computers over networks. It's helpful to have a general understanding of the OSI reference model when talking about different security protocols and how they function.

The seven layers of the OSI model, from highest to lowest, are: Application, Presentation, Session, Transport, Network, Data Link, and Physical. You can easily remember them, using the mnemonic phrase "All People Seem To Need Data Processing." Table 2-1 lists the OSI model layers and their general functions.

The following sections discuss each of the OSI layers in turn, explaining their individual functions and the protocols they employ.

The Application Layer

Layer 7, the **Application layer,** is the interface to the user. The Application layer provides services that deal with the communication portion of an application. It

```
*************************************
```
Summit Free Public Library
04/20/2019 12:34:05 PM   908-273-0350
Press option 2 for Circulation
```
*************************************
```

Title:	Raspberry Pi /
Author:	McManus, Sean, 1973-
Item ID:	39547004368390
Due:	05/04/2019

Title:	iOS programming :
Author:	Keur, Christian
Item ID:	39547004387309
Due:	05/04/2019

Title:	
Network security fundamentals /	
Author:	
Item ID:	39547003141400
Due:	05/18/2019

Title:	Albert Einstein /
Author:	Krull, Kathleen
Item ID:	39547003303539
Due:	05/18/2019

Title:	What was D-Day? /
Author:	Demuth, Patricia
Item ID:	39547004068347
Due:	05/18/2019

Title:	
The greatest mathematician :	
Author:	Hightower, Paul (Paul W.)
Item ID:	39547003251597
Due:	05/18/2019

Title:	Tim Duncan :
Author:	Stewart, Mark
Item ID:	39547002150972
Due:	05/18/2019

Title:	Albert Einstein /
Author:	Heinrichs, Ann
Item ID:	39547002398845
Due:	05/18/2019

The items currently checked out on your
card have saved you
$274.33
Have a nice day

Title   Raspberry Pi?
Author   McManus, Sean, 1973-
Item ID   39547004368390
Due   05/04/2019

Title   iOS programming
Author   Keur, Christian
Item ID   39547004387309
Due   05/04/2019

Title
Network security fundamentals /
Author
Item ID   39547003147400
Due   05/18/2019

Title   Albert Einstein /
Author   Krull, Kathleen
Item ID   39547003303539
Due   05/18/2019

Title   What was D-Day? /
Author   Demuth, Patricia
Item ID   39547004068347
Due   05/18/2019

Title
The greatest mathematician
Author   Hightower, Paul (Paul W.)
Item ID   39547003251597
Due   05/18/2019

Title   Tim Duncan
Author   Stewart, Mark
Item ID   39547002180972
Due   05/18/2019

Title   Albert Einstein /
Author   Heinrichs, Ann
Item ID   39547002398845
Due   05/18/2019

Table 2-1: ISO OSI Seven-Layer Model

Layer	Layer Name	Function
Layer 7	Application layer	Provides services such as email, file transfers, and file servers
Layer 6	Presentation layer	Provides encryption, code conversion, and data formatting
Layer 5	Session layer	Negotiates and establishes a connection with another computer
Layer 4	Transport layer	Supports reliable end-to-end delivery of data
Layer 3	Network layer	Performs packet routing across networks
Layer 2	Data Link layer	Provides error checking and transfer of message frames
Layer 1	Physical layer	Defines standards for transmission media, physical connection to the media, and how data should be sent over the network

identifies the desired recipient of the communication and ensures that the recipient is available for a transmission session. Protocols associated with the Application layer include the following:

▲ **File Transfer Protocol (FTP):** provides for authenticated transfer of files between two computers and access to directories; it cannot execute a remote file as a program.

▲ **Trivial File Transfer Protocol (TFTP):** reduced version of FTP; does not provide authentication or accessing of directories.

▲ **Domain name system (DNS):** a distributed database system that matches host names to Internet Protocol (IP) addresses and vice versa. A popular DNS implementation is the **Berkeley Internet Name Domain (BIND)**.

▲ **Simple Mail Transfer Protocol (SMTP):** supports the transmission and reception of email.

▲ **Secure File Transfer Protocol (SFTP):** a protocol that is replacing FTP. It provides increased security because it includes strong encryption and authentication. SFTP is a client that is similar to FTP and uses **Secure**

Shell (SSH) or SSH-2 (a revised version of SSH) to provide secure file transfer. SSH is a remote administration technology for Unix that provides authentication and encrypted transmission, and so is more secure than its predecessor, **Telnet.**

▲ **Simple Network Management Protocol (SNMP):** supports the exchange of management information among network devices through a management entity that polls these devices. It is a tool used by network administrators to manage the network and detect problem areas.

▲ **Remote login (Rlogin):** a command in UNIX that begins a terminal session between an authorized user and a remote host on a network. The user can perform all functions as if he or she were actually at the remote host. The secure version of Rlogin is **slogin** and is used by SSH.

▲ **BootP:** provides a diskless workstation with its IP address based on its Media Access Control (MAC) address; this information comes from a BootP server. Every network adapter is assigned a unique MAC address by the manufacturer. A **MAC address,** defined as part of the Data Link layer (Layer 2), comprises a 6-byte number typically written as six hexadecimal pairs. The first three bytes of a MAC address identify the manufacturer. For example, the hexadecimal value 00AA00 would indicate that Intel® is the manufacturer. The remaining three bytes represent the serial number of the device.

▲ **Multipurpose Internet Mail Extensions (MIME):** enables the use of non–US-ASCII textual messages, nontextual messages, multipart message bodies, and non–US-ASCII information in message headers in Internet mail.

The Presentation Layer

Layer 6, the **Presentation layer,** is so named because it presents information to the Application layer. Layer 6 performs encryption, decryption, compression, and decompression functions, as well as translates codes such as Extended Binary Coded Decimal Interchange Code (EBCDIC) or American Standard Code for Information Interchange (ASCII). **EBCDIC** is a legacy character encoding standard originally developed for IBM servers. **ASCII** is an encoding standard used by Unix, DOS, and Windows® operating systems. Standards associated with Layer 6 include the following:

▲ **Moving Picture Experts Group (MPEG):** the Moving Picture Experts Group's standard for the compression and coding of motion video.

▲ **Joint Photographic Experts Group (JPEG):** standard for graphics defined by the Joint Photographic Experts Group.

▲ **Hypertext Transfer Protocol (HTTP):** a protocol used for sending web pages and information to other locations on the Internet.

▲ **Tagged Image File Format (TIFF):** a public domain raster file graphics format. It does not handle vector graphics. TIFF is platform independent and was designed for use with printers and scanners.

The Session Layer

Layer 5, the **Session layer,** provides services to Layer 4, the Transport layer, to support applications. It sets up communication with other computers, manages the dialog between computers, synchronizes the communications between the transmitting and receiving entities, formats the message data, and manages the communication session in general. The functions of Layer 5 include the following:

▲ Establishing the connection.

▲ Transferring data.

▲ Releasing the connection.

The following are all protocols that operate at the Session layer:

▲ **AppleTalk Session Protocol (ASP):** used to set up a session between an ASP server application and an ASP workstation application or process.

▲ **Network File System (NFS):** supports the sharing of files among different types of file systems.

▲ **Remote procedure call (RPC):** supports procedure calls where the called procedure and the calling procedure may be on different systems communicating through a network. RPC is useful in setting up distributed, client-server based applications.

The Transport Layer

Layer 4, the **Transport layer,** maintains the control and integrity of a communications session. It delineates the addressing of devices on the network, describes how to make internode connections, and manages the networking of messages. The Transport layer also reassembles data from higher-layer applications and establishes the logical connection between the sending and receiving hosts on the network. Transport layer protocols include the following:

▲ **Transmission Control Protocol (TCP):** a highly reliable, connection-oriented protocol used in communications between hosts in packet-switched computer networks or interconnected networks. A **connection-oriented protocol** guarantees the delivery of packets and that the packets will be delivered in the same order as they were sent. There is a large overhead associated with sending packets with TCP because of the tasks it has to perform to ensure reliable communications.

▲ **Stream Control Transmission Protocol (SCTP):** a protocol similar to TCP, except that it transmits multiple streams of messages instead of a single stream of bytes (TCP can only send a single stream of bytes).

▲ **User Datagram Protocol (UDP):** a **connectionless protocol** that transmits packets on a best effort basis. It does not provide for error correction or for the correct transmission and reception sequencing of packets. Because of its low overhead, it is well suited for streaming video/audio applications.

▲ **Sequenced Packet Exchange (SPX):** a protocol maintained by Novell® that provides a reliable, connection-oriented transport service. It uses the **Internetwork Packet Exchange (IPX)** protocol to transmit and receive packets.

The Network Layer

Layer 3, the **Network layer,** sets up logical paths or virtual circuits for transmitting data packets from a source network to a destination network. It performs the following functions:

▲ Switching and routing
▲ Forwarding
▲ Addressing
▲ Error detection
▲ Node traffic control

Network layer protocols include the following:

▲ **Internet Protocol (IP):** provides a best-effort, or unreliable, service for connecting computers to form a computer network; it does not guarantee packet delivery. A computer on the network is assigned a unique IP address. The transmitted data packets contain the IP addresses of the sending and receiving computers on the network, in addition to other control data. The data packets, or datagrams, traverse networks through the use of intermediate routers that check the IP address of the destination device and forward the datagrams to other routers until the destination computer is found. Routers calculate the optimum path for data packets to reach their destination.

▲ **Open Shortest Path First (OSPF):** a shortest-path-first (SPF) routing protocol that selects the least-cost path from a source computer to a destination computer.

▲ **Internet Control Message Protocol (ICMP):** a troubleshooting protocol used to identify problems with the successful delivery of packets within an IP network. It can verify that routers are properly routing packets to the destination computer. A useful ICMP utility is the **ping** command, which can check if computers on a network can communicate.

▲ **Routing Information Protocol (RIP):** a routing protocol that sends routing update messages to other network routers at regular intervals and when the network topology changes. This updating ensures the RIP routers select the least-cost path to a specified IP address destination.

▲ **IP security (IPsec):** a protocol used to ensure data integrity, authentication, and encryption. It can also be used to perform packet filtering.

▲ **Address Resolution Protocol (ARP):** a protocol that maps IP network addresses to the hardware MAC addresses used by a data link protocol. The ARP protocol functions as a portion of the interface between the OSI network and Data Link layers.

▲ **Reverse Address Resolution Protocol (RARP):** a protocol that enables a computer in a local area network (LAN) to determine its IP address based on its MAC address.

The Data Link Layer

Layer 2, the **Data Link layer,** encodes the data packets to be sent into bits for transmission by the Physical layer. Conversely, the data packets are decoded at Layer 2 of the receiving computer. Layer 2 also performs flow control, protocol management, and Physical layer error checking. It is also the layer that implements bridging. The Data Link layer is divided into sublayers: the Media Access layer and the Logical Link layer.

The **Media Access layer** performs the following functions:

▲ Supports the network computer's access to packet data.
▲ Controls the network computer's permission to transmit packet data.

The **Logical Link layer** performs the following functions:

▲ Sets up the communication link between entities on a physical channel.
▲ Converts data to be sent into bits for transmission.
▲ Formats the data to be transmitted into frames.
▲ Adds a header to the data that indicates the source and destination IP addresses.

▲ Defines the network access protocol for data transmission and reception.

▲ Controls error checking and frame synchronization.

▲ Supports Ethernet and token-ring operations.

Data Link layer protocols include the following:

▲ **Serial Line Internet Protocol (SLIP):** a legacy protocol that defines a sequence of characters that frame IP packets on a serial line. It is used for point-to-point serial connections running TCP/IP, such as dial-up or dedicated serial lines.

▲ **Point-to-Point Protocol (PPP):** a protocol used for transmitting data over point-to-point links. It does this by encapsulating the datagrams of other protocols. PPP was designed as a replacement for SLIP in sending information using synchronous modems. IP, IPX, and DECnet protocols can operate under PPP.

The Physical Layer

Layer 1, the **Physical layer,** transmits data bits through the network in the form of light pulses, electrical signals, or radio waves. It includes the necessary software and hardware to accomplish this task, including appropriate cards and cabling, such as twisted pair or coaxial cables. In addition to electronic interfaces, the Physical layer is also concerned with mechanical issues such as cable connectors and cable length. Network cards function at Layer 2 of the OSI Model but connect at Layer 1. This level is addressed in the family of Institute of Electrical and Electronics Engineers (IEEE) 802 LAN/WAN standards, which include the following areas:

▲ 802.1: internetworking

▲ 802.2: logical link control

▲ 802.3: Ethernet (Carrier Sense Multiple Access/Collision Detection, or CSMA/CD)

▲ 802.3u: fast Ethernet

▲ 802.3z: gigabit Ethernet

▲ 802.3ae: 10-gigabit Ethernet

▲ 802.5: token ring

▲ 802.7: broadband technology

▲ 802.8: fiber optic technology

▲ 802.9: voice/data integration (IsoENET)

▲ 802.10: LAN security

▲ 802.11: wireless networking

▲ 802.15: wireless personal area network

▲ 802.16: wireless metropolitan area networks

2.1.3 The TCP/IP Model

The TCP (Transmission Control Protocol) and IP (Internet Protocol) were developed in the 1970s, prior to ISO's OSI model. TCP and IP are part of a layered protocol model that is similar, but not identical to, the OSI model. In fact, the OSI model incorporated some of the concepts of the TCP/IP model. The goal of TCP/IP was to enable different types of computers on different geographical networks to communicate reliably, even if portions of the connecting links were disabled. TCP/IP grew out of research by the U.S. Department of Defense (DoD) to develop systems that could communicate in battlefield environments where communication links were likely to be destroyed. The solution was to send messages in the form of packets that could be routed around broken connections and reassembled at the receiving end. TCP/IP provides this functionality through programs called **sockets** used to access the TCP/IP protocol services.

In the **TCP/IP model**, TCP verifies the correct delivery of data and provides error detection capabilities. If an error is detected, TCP attempts the retransmission of the data until a valid packet is received. This function is based on an acknowledgment that should be sent back to the transmitting computer upon the receipt of delivered packets. If a packet is not acknowledged, the originating computer resends it. The receiving computer then organizes the received packets into their proper order.

The IP portion of TCP/IP is responsible for sending packets from node to node on the network until the packets reach their final destinations.

The routing is accomplished through an **IP address** that is assigned to every computer on the Internet. There are two standards for IP addresses: IPv4 and IPv6. An IPv4 IP address is the 4-byte destination IP address that is included in every packet. It is usually represented in decimal form as octets of numbers from 0 to 255, such as 160.192.226.135. For example, 255.255.255.255 is used to broadcast to all hosts on the local network. An IP address is divided into a portion that identifies a network and another portion that identifies the host or node on a network. Additionally, a network is assigned to a Class from A through E, and this class representation further delineates which part of the address refers to the network and which part refers to the node. Classes A through C are the commonly used categories. The network classes and their corresponding addresses are given in Table 2-2.

IPv6 uses a 128-bit addressing scheme, so it has more than 79 times as many available addresses as IPv4. Instead of representing the binary digits as decimal digits, IPv6 uses 8 sets of 4 hexadecimal digits. IPv6 includes additional security features, including support for built-in authentication and confidentiality. Most current operating systems include support for IPv6 and systems are expected to gradually migrate to the new standard over several years, although some industry experts feel that it unlikely that IPv4 addresses will ever be fully retired.

Table 2-2: IP Address Network Classes

Class	Network address	Host address	Example address
Class A Address range = 1.0.0.1 to 126.255.255.254	First 8 bits define the network address. The binary address of the first octet always begins with 0 (0000-0001011111111). The decimal address ranges from 1 to 126 (127 networks).	The remaining 24 bits define the host address (16 million hosts).	110.160.212.156 Network = 110 Host = 160.212.156
Class B Address range = 128.1.0.1 to 191.255.255.254	First 16 bits define the network address. The binary address of the first octet always begins with 10. The decimal address ranges from 128 to 191 (16,000 networks). 127 is reserved for loopback testing on the local host.	The remaining 16 bits define the host address (65,000 hosts).	168.110.226.155 Network = 168.110 Host = 226.155
Class C Address range = 192.0.1.1 to 223.255.254.254	First 24 bits define the network address. Binary address of the first octet always starts with 110, therefore the decimal address ranges from 192 to 223 (2 million networks).	The remaining 8 bits define the host address (254 addresses).	200.168.198.156 Network = 200.168.198 Host = 156
Class D Address range = 224.0.0.0 to 239.255.255.255	Binary address of the first octet always begins with 1110; therefore, the decimal address ranges from 224 to 239.	Reserved for **multicasting** (sending a message to multiple hosts listening on the same IP address).	

Class E	Binary address of the	Reserved for	
Address range = 240.0.0.0 to 254.255.255.254	first octet always begins with 1111, therefore the decimal number can be anywhere from 240 to 255.	experimental purposes.	

TCP/IP Model Layers

The TCP/IP model has four layers: the **Application layer**, the **Host-to-Host layer** or **Transport layer**, the **Internet layer**, and the **Network Access layer**. These layers and their corresponding functions and protocols are summarized in Table 2-3.

The example protocols listed in Table 2-3 have been discussed under the OSI model, except for the **Post Office Protocol (POP)**. Using POP, an email client can retrieve email from a mail server. The latest version of POP is **POP3**, which can be used with or without SMTP. A security issue with POP3 is that the password used for authentication is transmitted as unencrypted "clear" text.

Table 2-3 TCP/IP Model Layers

Layer	Layer Name	Function	Protocols or Standards
Layer 4	Application layer	Equivalent to the Application, Presentation, and Session layers of the OSI model. In TCP/IP, an application is a process that is above the Transport layer. Applications communicate through ports and sockets.	SMTP, POP (Post Office Protocol), HTTP, FTP
Layer 3	Host-to-Host or Transport Layer	Similar to the OSI Transport layer; performs packet sequencing, supports reliable end-to-end communications, ensures data integrity, and provides for error-free data delivery.	TCP, UDP

(Continued)

Table 2-3 *(continued)*

Layer	Layer Name	Function	Protocols or Standards
Layer 2	Internet Layer	Performs the same function as the OSI Network layer. Isolates the upper-layer protocols from the details of the underlying network and manages the connections across the network. Uses protocols that provide for logical transmission of packets over a network and controls communications among hosts; assigns IP addresses to network nodes.	IP, ARP, RARP, ICMP
Layer 1	Network Access Layer	Combines the Data Link layer and the Physical layer functions of the OSI model. These functions include mapping IP address to MAC addresses, using software drivers, and encapsulation of IP datagrams into frames to be transmitted by the network. It is also concerned with communications hardware, software, connectors, voltage levels, and cabling. Some definitions of the TCP/IP model do not include the Physical layer in the Network Access Layer definition.	IEEE 802.3 IEEE 802.11b IEEE 802.11g

As with the OSI model, encapsulation occurs as data traverses the layers from the Application layer to the Network Access layer at the transmitting node. This process is reversed in the receiving node. Encapsulation in TCP/IP is illustrated in Figure 2-2.

Figure 2-2

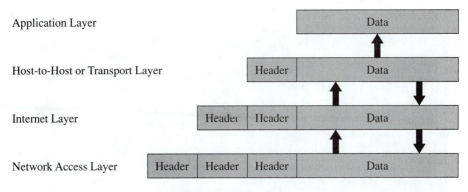

TCP/IP encapsulation.

2.1.4 TCP/IP Ports

A TCP/IP protocol, such as HTTP, uses a specific **port** when transmitting data. A port is a number that is included in a packet's header. The recipient computer uses that number to identify the service that should process the packet. The receiving computer listens for requests on a set of ports. The ports from 0 through 1024 are known as **well-known ports** because they are associated with a specific service. Some well-known ports are listed in Table 2-4.

Ports between 1025 and 65000 can be assigned to custom applications. You can also configure some services that typically use a well-known port to use a different port. For example, you might configure your web server to listen on port 3295 for a specific intranet application. To access this web application, you

Table 2-4: Well-Known Ports

Port number	Protocol
20 and 21	FTP
22	SSH
23	Telnet
25	SMTP
53	DNS
80	HTTP
110	POP3
443	HTTPS

Figure 2-3

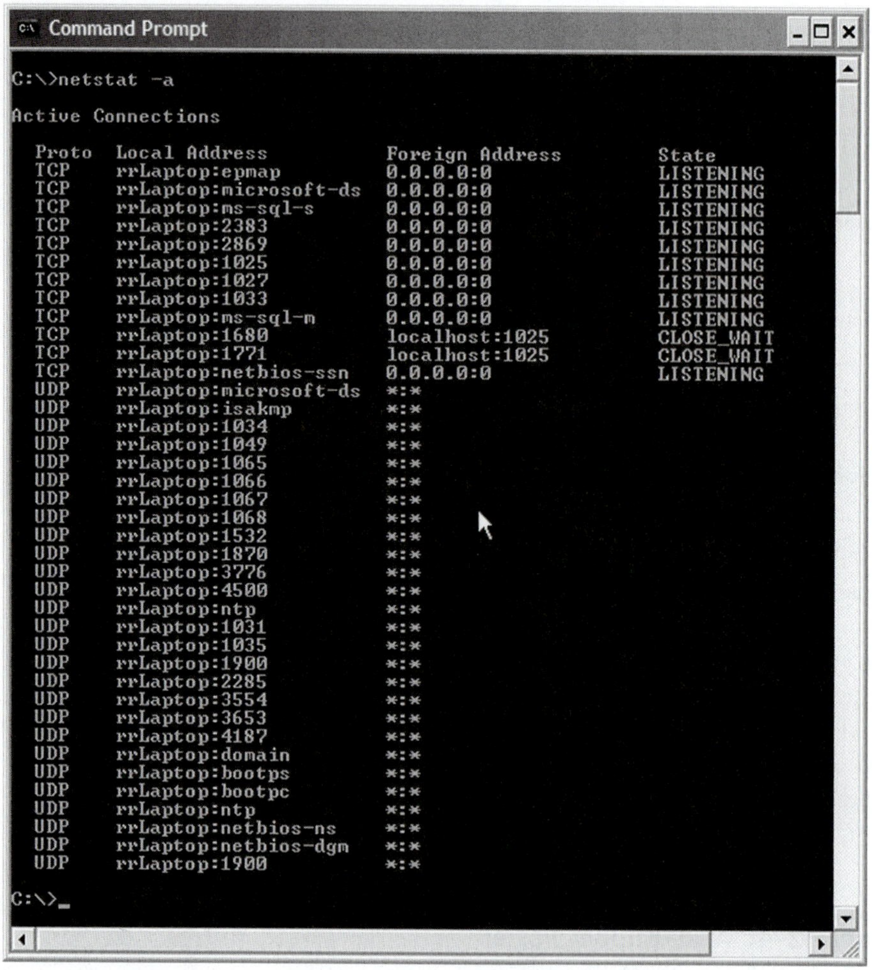

```
Command Prompt                                                        - □ ×

C:\>netstat -a

Active Connections

   Proto  Local Address           Foreign Address         State
   TCP    rrLaptop:epmap          0.0.0.0:0               LISTENING
   TCP    rrLaptop:microsoft-ds   0.0.0.0:0               LISTENING
   TCP    rrLaptop:ms-sql-s       0.0.0.0:0               LISTENING
   TCP    rrLaptop:2383           0.0.0.0:0               LISTENING
   TCP    rrLaptop:2869           0.0.0.0:0               LISTENING
   TCP    rrLaptop:1025           0.0.0.0:0               LISTENING
   TCP    rrLaptop:1027           0.0.0.0:0               LISTENING
   TCP    rrLaptop:1033           0.0.0.0:0               LISTENING
   TCP    rrLaptop:ms-sql-m       0.0.0.0:0               LISTENING
   TCP    rrLaptop:1680           localhost:1025          CLOSE_WAIT
   TCP    rrLaptop:1771           localhost:1025          CLOSE_WAIT
   TCP    rrLaptop:netbios-ssn    0.0.0.0:0               LISTENING
   UDP    rrLaptop:microsoft-ds   *:*
   UDP    rrLaptop:isakmp         *:*
   UDP    rrLaptop:1034           *:*
   UDP    rrLaptop:1049           *:*
   UDP    rrLaptop:1065           *:*
   UDP    rrLaptop:1066           *:*
   UDP    rrLaptop:1067           *:*
   UDP    rrLaptop:1068           *:*
   UDP    rrLaptop:1532           *:*
   UDP    rrLaptop:1870           *:*
   UDP    rrLaptop:3776           *:*
   UDP    rrLaptop:4500           *:*
   UDP    rrLaptop:ntp            *:*
   UDP    rrLaptop:1031           *:*
   UDP    rrLaptop:1035           *:*
   UDP    rrLaptop:1900           *:*
   UDP    rrLaptop:2285           *:*
   UDP    rrLaptop:3554           *:*
   UDP    rrLaptop:3653           *:*
   UDP    rrLaptop:4187           *:*
   UDP    rrLaptop:domain         *:*
   UDP    rrLaptop:bootps         *:*
   UDP    rrLaptop:bootpc         *:*
   UDP    rrLaptop:ntp            *:*
   UDP    rrLaptop:netbios-ns     *:*
   UDP    rrLaptop:netbios-dgm    *:*
   UDP    rrLaptop:1900           *:*

C:\>_
```

"Netstat –a" command.

would append a colon and the port number after the host name in the URL. For example, to access a webpage named "index.htm" on a website listening on port 3295 on a web server named "www.busicorp.com," you would use the URL http://www.busicorp.com:3295/index.htm.

You should not use custom port mappings for Internet applications that need to be accessed by the public because users will not know that they need to append a port number to the server name in the URL.

You can view a list of ports that are listening on a Windows computer by using the "netstat -a" command line utility, as shown in Figure 2-3.

FOR EXAMPLE

Security and the Network Stack

One technique used by attackers is to modify headers so that either the source or the destination address is spoofed. An attacker might modify the destination address to divert packets from their trusted destination to an untrusted destination. One reason to do this is to intercept passwords and other confidential information. An attacker might also modify the source address so that the destination computer thinks the packet originated from a trusted source.

Packet sniffing is another technique frequently used by attackers. A lot of data is sent using clear text. Data sent using clear text can be intercepted by packet sniffers or protocol analyzers. A **packet sniffer** can be software running on a network node or a hardware device that is tapped into the network media. Wireless networks are especially susceptible to sniffing because data is sent as radio waves, and a device operating on the same frequency can intercept those waves. Network administrators can also use protocol analyzers when troubleshooting network problems. A **protocol analyzer** allows you to view the headers added to a message, as well as the data in the message itself. The protocol analyzer included with Windows 2000 Server and Windows Server 2003 is Network Monitor. That version of Network Monitor can only capture traffic destined for or originating at the server where it is running. Some protocol analyzers operate in **promiscuous mode**, which means that they can capture all traffic on the network.

SELF-CHECK

1. Describe the role of the network stack in network transmission using TCP/IP.
2. Describe the purpose of well-known ports. Give an example.

2.2 Best Practices for Network Security

Securing network servers is not limited to the server configuration. Servers are a part of the network and, therefore, the overall security of the network will impact the security of the server. In addition, most servers run applications.

Therefore, it is essential to keep server applications up-to-date with any security patches for known vulnerabilities.

In this section, we'll look at some general guidelines for securing the servers on your network. The section will focus on best practices and methodologies instead of the actual implementation. We'll look at three basic guidelines: designing applications with security in mind, maintaining a security mindset, and defense–in-depth.

2.2.1 Security by Design

In the past, security for server applications has been an afterthought, only to be considered after threats and vulnerabilities have arisen. This led to many instances of security features being retrofitted into an operating system or application. One of the lessons learned from retrofitting is that it is very costly and time consuming to try to put in security after an application and system have been developed and deployed. In most cases, the system cannot be made completely secure.

A conservative estimate is that it is 10 times cheaper to build security into a product than to attempt to retrofit the product after deployment. If the cost benefit is so great, why then is it still difficult for security to become part of the requirements in most software development efforts? Some of the factors affecting security in the design phase of a development effort are as follows:

▲ The software developers and security professionals (network engineers) historically came from different communities. This is still an issue today, although more software developers are attending security training and security conferences.

▲ The security threat was not well publicized. Security has made the front page more often in recent years.

▲ In many cases, the software developers are building an application that they have never coded before. However, a network engineer who designs a network has probably designed dozens of networks in the past.

▲ Until recently, software developers could not justify time spent on security features, because security features did not seem to affect the bottom line from management's perspective.

▲ In the highly competitive marketplace for software, there has been a natural rush-to-market approach to beat the competition.

Even with the heightened attention to security in today's world, it is still an uphill battle to get security rooted into the initial requirements and design of a development effort. Therefore, it is important that you ask questions about security features when deciding on a server application, and if your company develops custom server applications, make sure the development team keeps security in mind during development.

2.2.2 Maintaining a Security Mindset

Having a security mindset is the first step in designing and implementing a strategy for securing your network servers. Security improvements will come at the cost of time, money, and convenience. If an organization does not have a mindset that values security, it will be difficult to implement the needed controls. The following are some approaches to developing a mindset that will help you secure the servers on your network:

▲ Base security decisions on the risk. Security can be like insurance; the risk must be known to determine the coverage needed.

▲ Use defense-in-depth. Many security controls are preferable to a single point of protection.

▲ Keep things simple. Simplicity and clarity will support a more secure environment.

▲ Respect the adversary. Do not underestimate the interest and determination of the threat.

▲ Work on security awareness. Security training is needed at all levels of an organization.

▲ Be paranoid and expect the worst.

2.2.3 Defense-in-Depth

The **defense-in-depth** principle is best thought of as a series of protective measures that, taken as a whole, will secure the environment. The most memorable example is the medieval castle. The king protected his crown jewels (literally) with a series of progressive defenses, including the following:

▲ The chosen site for the castle was on a hilltop. It was and always will be easier to defend the top of a hill.

▲ Trees and underbrush were cut from approaches to make it easier to see and to leave clear lines of sight.

▲ Stone walls and terraces were placed around the approaches to the top of the hill.

▲ Sharp sticks pointing toward an approaching attacker were placed on the hillside. In today's world, these would be mine fields.

▲ A moat was dug around the hilltop.

▲ Vile waste was placed in the moat, sure to discourage the fainthearted from crossing.

FOR EXAMPLE

Defending a Network from Attack

Suppose you are a network consultant. You visit a customer site and talk to the customer about network security. The customer has recently purchased firewall software and is feeling confident that his network is secure. You suggest the possibility that a firewall might not be sufficient protection and compare it to the stone walls placed around the approach to a medieval castle. "What if the attacker climbed the walls or tunneled through them? What if the attacker works for you and walks in every day through the front door?" you ask.

The customer says, "What do you mean? I thought the firewall would keep my network secure."

You explain that it is better to implement security using a defense-in-depth strategy. You describe additional controls that should be put in place, such as strong passwords, access control for assets, virus protection, company security policies, and security awareness training.

"Won't that be expensive?" the customer asks.

"Let's look first at what the risks are," you reply. The customer agrees to a risk analysis—the first step to securing his network.

▲ The outer castle walls were tall and thick.

▲ Rocks and hot oil could be dropped from the outer walls, slowing down the attack.

▲ There was an inner, smaller fortress to which the population could retreat in the event the outer walls were breached.

No one defense of a castle was relied upon for the ultimate protection. The defenses as a whole were designed to weaken and discourage the attackers. Some defenses were easy and cheap to implement (sharp sticks). Others required significant resources (the outer walls). But, taken as a whole, the defense was much stronger than the simple sum of each protective feature.

The defense-in-depth principle applies to network and server security as well. Two important features to note are as follows:

1. All the security resources should not be concentrated on a single protection. The classic case of this mistake is when a company spends its entire security budget on a $200,000 firewall to protect it from the Internet. All of this investment can then be circumvented by a $30 modem because there was no security awareness program to train users as to the risk of connecting to ISPs directly from their workstations.

2. A protective measure (a security control) is worth implementing even if it seems to be a redundant protection. For example, the use of strong passwords is advised even on internal networks in which all users are trusted.

Some specific examples related to server security are covered in the next section.

SELF-CHECK

1. Describe why investing a company's entire security budget in a single defense is not advisable.

2.3 Securing Servers

Even the most securely developed server application must be placed in a secure operational environment. To operate the server securely, an organization must establish a plan with associated procedures. These procedures should include the following key aspects:

▲ **Control the server configuration:** The server must be configured to minimize exposure to an attack. Periodic backups can mitigate the risk if an attack does occur.

▲ **Control users and access:** A need-to-know and need-to-access environment should be established regarding the server's data and access. A **need-to-know environment** is one in which users are only given permissions to read the files that store information they need to do their jobs. A **need-to-access environment** is one in which the only access permissions granted are those users need to do their jobs.

▲ **Monitoring, auditing, and logging:** Security does not stop with deployment of the server. In today's environment, continuous monitoring is required to ensure a server remains safe.

2.3.1 Controlling the Server Configuration

Operating the server safely extends beyond the key application being served up. The host platform must also be secured. The following are three important considerations when securing the host system:

1. Physically secure the system in a locked room and hire a guard, if appropriate. Limit access to the physical server to an as-needed basis only for all personnel.

2. Minimize the risk to the host system by removing unneeded services, closing unnecessary ports, and removing unnecessary input and output devices. This is known as **limiting the attack surface.**

3. Back up the host system to mitigate the risk in the event that an attack does occur.

Physical Security of the System

Any server is vulnerable to an attacker who has unlimited time and physical access to the server. Additionally, physical problems could cause the server to have downtime. This would be a loss of availability. The following should be provided to ensure the availability of the server:

▲ Provide an uninterruptible power supply (UPS) unit with surge protection.

▲ Provide fire protection to minimize the loss of data and equipment.

▲ Provide adequate cooling and ventilation.

▲ Provide adequate lighting and work space for maintaining and upgrading the system.

▲ Restrict physical access to the server. Unauthorized persons should not get near the server. Even casual contact can lead to outages. The server space should be locked and alarmed. Any access to the space should be recorded for later evaluation should a problem occur. Inventory should be tightly controlled and monitored.

The physical protections listed here should extend to the network cables and other devices (such as routers) that are critical to the server operation.

Minimizing Services

As discussed earlier, servers are natural targets for attack. It should be expected that attackers will seek the path of least resistance in an attempt to compromise the server. The attacker will look to break in through any of the services running on the server. For this reason, separation of services is a good security practice.

Separation of services dictates that each major service should be run on its own protected host whenever possible. If any one service or server is compromised, the others are unaffected. In this way, any damage done is limited to the one server.

Most server operating systems will have a number of services enabled or on by default. Care must be taken to ensure that these extraneous services are disabled or even deleted from the system. The following list shows typical services that should be disabled from a host if not needed:

▲ **Telnet:** The secure alternative, SSH, should be used instead, if needed.

▲ **SMTP:** Mail server applications are frequent targets of attacks.

▲ **FTP:** FTP is used to upload files to and download files from a central repository. FTP has a number of vulnerabilities and must be properly configured to be safe.

▲ **TFTP:** TFTP is used to transfer small files and can be used to upload a malicious file to a computer.

▲ **Finger:** Finger allows you to determine the name associated with an email address and the last time the user logged on. However, it can be used to learn information about a computer system that can then be used to launch other attacks.

▲ **Netstat:** Netstat is a Windows troubleshooting tool that allows you to see which ports a computer is listening on, as well as other information about the network. This information can be used by an attacker to locate a door through which to enter the system.

▲ **Systat:** Systat is a Unix® troubleshooting tool. The information it returns can be used by an attacker to determine whether the system is running processes that include vulnerabilities. Systat listens on port 11.

▲ **Chargen** and **Echo:** These services can be used to launch data-driven attacks and denial-of-service (DoS) attacks.

▲ **DNS:** This service requires frequent patches and upgrades to be secure.

▲ **RPC:** Unless the server application explicitly uses RPC to communicate with other systems, this should be disabled.

Managing Windows Services

You can disable a Windows service using the Services utility, shown in Figure 2-4. A service can be configured to start up manually, start up automatically when the system starts, or it can be disabled.

When disabling services, you need to be careful not to disable a service on which another necessary service depends. You can view a list of dependencies by examining the Dependencies tab of a service's Properties dialog box. For example, Figure 2-5 shows the services on which the World Wide Web Publishing service (the service used by Internet Information Services, or IIS) depends.

Another key consideration when managing services is the security context under which the service executes. This is important because an attack might replace the legitimate service with one that performs malicious activities. The attacker's code would execute under the security context of the account specified as the logon account for that service. This means that the attacker's code would be able to access any parts of the computer or network that account is granted permission to access. Therefore, you should use an account with the most restrictive permissions that will permit that service to operate. Windows 2000 (and later) has three built-in accounts that are typically

Figure 2-4

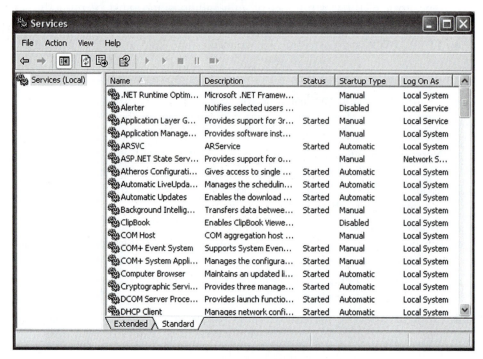

Managing Windows services.

used to run services. In addition, you can create a special user account and assign it the necessary rights and permissions. The three built-in accounts are as follows:

▲ **Local System:** This account has permission to perform any task on the computer and permission to access resources on the network.
▲ **Local Service:** This account has very limited permissions on the computer and cannot access other computers across the network.
▲ **Network Service:** This account has the same local permissions as Local Service, but can also access computers across the network.

You change the security context for a service through the Log On tab of the service's properties, as shown in Figure 2-6.

Blocking Ports

Another important way to minimize the attack surface on a server is to block traffic to all ports except those the computer needs to perform its job. You can

Figure 2-5

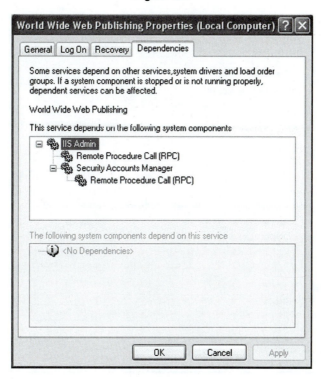

Dependencies of the World Wide Web Publishing service.

block traffic to a specific port by configuring a firewall or, if the computer's operating system supports it, by configuring an IPSec filter. IPSec is a security protocol that allows you to define policies for secure negotiation of traffic based on the source, destination, protocol, and computer authentication.

Some exploits are associated with specific well-known ports and the applications that use them. For example, if a server is listening on port 80, an attacker can assume that the server is running a web server. The attacker can then attempt an attack based on known vulnerabilities of common web server software.

Potential attackers can use **port scanners** to determine whether a specific port is listening, open but not listening, or blocked. A port scanner sends requests to a specific port and records which ports seem to be open. Attackers can use this information to learn about the doorways that are open in a specific server and the attacks to which the server is most vulnerable.

Limiting Input and Output Devices

When evaluating the attack surface of a computer, you should also consider the physical entry points. A **physical entry point** is any interface that allows

Figure 2-6

Setting a service's Log On account.

input or output. Some physical entry points you might consider removing include the following:

▲ **Modems:** Modems should only be enabled on computers that require remote access using a dial-up network or those that act as **remote access servers** (servers that provide network access through a dial-up connection) for dial-up clients. If a modem needs to be used only for outgoing calls, it should not be configured to accept incoming calls.

▲ **Network adapters:** It's essential to remember that as soon as you attach a computer to a network, it becomes vulnerable to attacks through the network interface. Therefore, you should never place a server on the network until you have applied security patches for known vulnerabilities.

▲ **CD-ROM and DVD drives:** In many cases you will need to have a CD-ROM or DVD drive in a server, if only to allow for software installation.

However, keep in mind that if a person gains access to the server room, that person can insert a CD or DVD containing malicious software into the computer.

▲ **Floppy drives:** Many computers today no longer contain floppy drives. However, you might consider removing the floppy drive from a system that does include one. A floppy drive can allow any person with physical access to copy files to or from a server.

▲ **Universal Serial Bus (USB) ports:** USB ports can make a server particularly vulnerable to an attack by a person who obtains physical access. USB hard disks no larger than a pinkie finger with capacities of 1 GB or more are available and can provide an attacker with an easy way to install a malicious file on the server or steal an entire database of customer information. A recent high-profile case involved a number of USB drives containing data about a nuclear power facility found during a drug bust.

▲ **Monitor:** If a server contains critical resources, you might consider running it as a **headless server.** A headless server is one that does not have a monitor and is therefore less susceptible to interactive attacks. However, you need to keep in mind that a headless server must be managed from another system, which in itself can pose a security risk because it requires you to open ports necessary for remote management.

System Backups

System backups are an important security control to mitigate the risk and damage that can be inflicted by an attack. No matter what steps are taken to prevent an attack, attacks should still be expected, and sometimes a backup will be your only chance of recovery. Therefore, every server and server application should have regularly scheduled backups as part of the normal operation of the server.

The frequency of the backups should be determined by how critical the data or service is to the business. The determination should be made based on a risk and business impact analysis. Typically, data is backed up on a daily or weekly basis, however, some servers store data that must be backed up more frequently. If the loss of a day's worth of data cannot be tolerated, a zero-down-time failover system is recommended. A **failover system** is an identical copy of the server and its data that can be used in the event of an attack, natural disaster, or server failure.

Backups can aid in a post-attack reconstruction. The compromised system can be compared with the backup to determine which part of the system was attacked. This might also provide insight into the extent of the damage inflicted by the attacker.

FOR EXAMPLE

Securing a Server

You are network administrator for a hospital. The hospital database server stores confidential medical records of patients. The server is running Microsoft® SQL Server. You need to minimize the likelihood that data on the server will be obtained or modified by an unauthorized user. You also need to ensure that the server is available 24/7. The hospital cannot afford to lose even one day of patient data.

You begin by locking the server in a secure closet. You ensure that there are locks on the closet and that the only way someone can obtain a key is to sign in with a security administrator. You also put the server on a UPS.

Next you determine which Windows services are required for the server to operate. You configure those services to run under an account with only the permissions required. You disable all other services.

Next, you identify the ports that are required for accessing the server. You block all other ports using a personal firewall. A **personal firewall** is firewall software that runs on a server to limit the traffic that server accepts. Windows XP Professional and Windows Server 2003 include Windows Firewall as the personal firewall software.

To mitigate the damage if an attack occurs and to ensure availability if the server fails, you install an identical server as a failover system using the clustering technology included with Windows Server 2003.

SELF-CHECK

1. Describe the steps you should take to ensure the physical security of a server.
2. Explain why separating services onto separate servers can help mitigate risk.
3. Describe the use of a port scanner in launching an attack.
4. Identify the advantages and disadvantages of operating a server as a headless server.

2.4 Border Security

When designing security for your network, you will most likely identify different network segments with different security requirements. For example, some servers will need to be accessible by the public. Others will need to be accessible only by employees. You might also have some servers that should be accessible only by a certain subset of employees. To implement security for different segments, you will erect borders that can only be crossed by certain types of traffic. This is known as **border security.** In this section we'll look at some ways you can segment your network, including perimeter networks and firewalls.

2.4.1 Segmenting a Network

Over the past few years, there has been a heavy integration of network technologies, which has created highly unified and global network architectures. Yet business, government, and military requirements demand segregation of key network segments. These segments can be theoretically classified into the following:

▲ Public networks
▲ Semi-private networks
▲ Private networks

The boundaries of such network segments are established by devices capable of regulating and controlling the flow of packets into and out of the segment, including the following:

▲ Routers
▲ Switches
▲ Bridges
▲ Multi-homed gateways

Public Networks

Public networks allow accessibility to everyone. The Internet is a perfect example of a public network. On public networks there is a huge amount of unsecured data. Typically, security measures for public access networks are quite limited. A one-time password is often all that is required to log into publicly available machines and public access networks. Despite the lack of security, large volumes of unprotected data are transmitted worldwide over public networks because of their convenience and the variety of services they provide.

Semi-private Networks

Semi-private networks sit between public networks and private networks. From a security standpoint, a semi-private network might carry confidential information but under some regulations. Semi-private networks are most often exclusive subnets of large public networks such as the Internet. Large peer-to-peer networks that are designed to handle and share exclusive information (usually multimedia) among its users can also be classified under semi-private networks.

Private Networks

Private networks are organizational networks that handle confidential and proprietary data and are the most common type of network. If the organization is spread over vast geographical distances, the private networks present at each location might be interconnected through the Internet or other public networks. Generally, most commercial organizations prefer not to lay down dedicated lines over vast geographical distances, mainly due to cost factors. Private networks might have exclusive addressing and protocols and do not have to be compatible with the Internet. Address translation schemes and various tunneling protocols can be used to allow incompatible private and public networks to interoperate.

2.4.2 Perimeter Defense

In most cases, networks include various types of servers, including infrastructure servers like domain controllers and DNS servers, database servers, file servers, and application servers.

Securing such enormous processing units often requires security solutions to be highly fortified at the network in addition to using individual server-based security systems. In most common environments, firewalls would be placed at the terminal ends of every network segment. Firewalls (independent or combined with routers) can be ideal choices for securing network perimeters. Specialized application proxies normally placed at the boundaries of network environments can also function as perimeter defense systems. Figure 2-7 shows a comprehensive view of a network protected by perimeter systems (usually firewalls).

A **demilitarized zone (DMZ)** is a noncritical yet secure region generally designed at the periphery of the internal and external networks. A DMZ is also known as a **perimeter network** or **screened subnet.** Normally, the configuration of a DMZ is such that it is either separated by a firewall from the external network or sandwiched between two firewalls, one at the external periphery and the other at the internal periphery. Figure 2-8 shows a DMZ setup for a web server application. You most frequently locate resources that need to be accessed from both the Internet and the internal network on the DMZ. These include, but are not limited to, web servers and FTP servers.

2.4.2 Firewalls

For most enterprises, government institutions, and financial organizations, it is a necessity to safeguard their private networks and communication facilities.

Figure 2-7

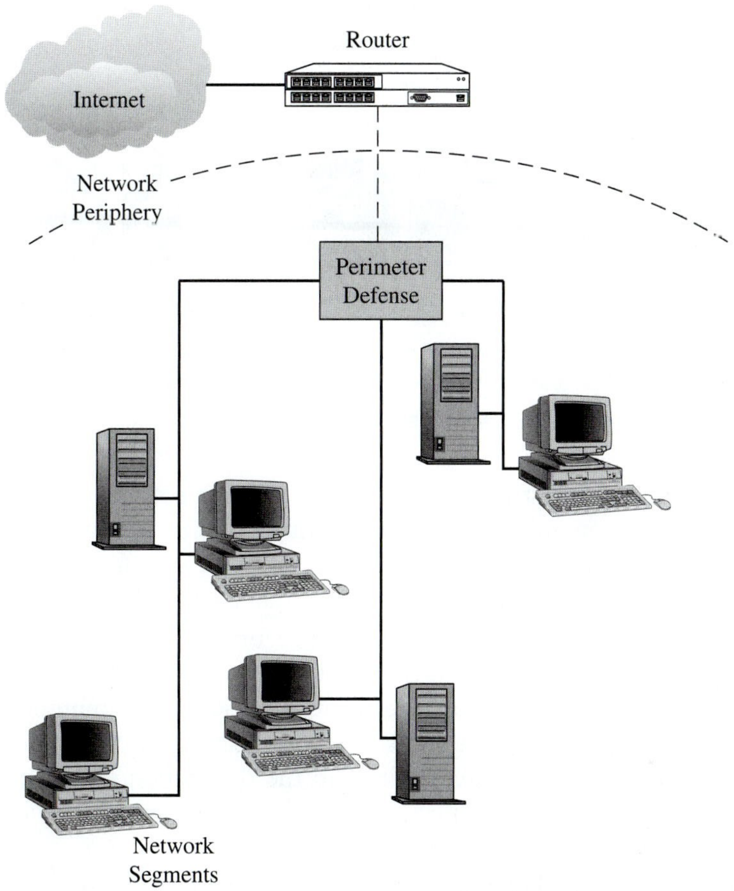

Perimeter defense between a private network and the Internet.

However, many organizations have business demands that require them to connect their private network to the Internet or other large-scale networks that are inherently insecure. Whenever you connect a network to an insecure network, such as the Internet, you open a large doorway for potential attacks. One of the best ways to arm against attacks from the insecure network is to employ firewalls at the connection point of the insecure network and the internal network.

There are many reasons for an organization to employ firewalls to secure their networks from other insecure networks, such as the following:

▲ **Poor authentication:** Most network services and applications do not directly use authentication and encryption features, as they could be too cumbersome or costly. When such applications are accessed from the outside, the applications themselves might not be able to distinguish between legitimate and fake users.

Figure 2-8

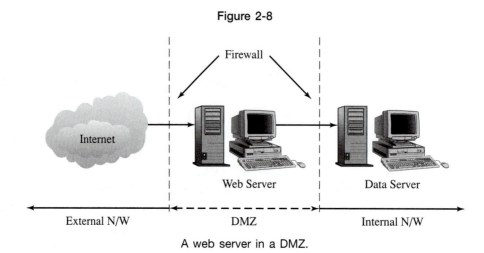

A web server in a DMZ.

▲ **Weak software:** Most purchased software and free software (known as freeware), are not optimized for security features. Using such software could create vulnerabilities in the respective networks. A firewall could be highly effective in scanning and logging Internet traffic using these applications.

▲ **Spoofing:** Address spoofing has been a security problem for a long time. Because routing commonly utilizes both source and destination addresses, it is relatively easy for an attacker to read packets of communication sessions and acknowledge the respective addresses. Once this is done, the hacker can spoof the source address to the destination and vice versa. This can place resources directly under the control of the attacker who could wreak havoc in no time.

▲ **Scanners and crackers:** You have already learned about scanners. **Crackers** are software programs that an attacker uses to launch dictionary attacks on passwords and other sensitive authentication information present on internal networks.

Figure 2-9 shows an example of a firewall placed between the Internet and an internal LAN to guard against attacks from the Internet.

Packet-Filtering Firewalls

Packet filtering is one of the simplest techniques used by firewalls. With packet filtering firewalls, you define a **filter** (a set of rules that determine which packets should be allowed through, rejected, or dropped) and the firewall uses that filter to examine data passing in and out of the firewall. The filter is also called a **rule base** or **ruleset**. In most cases, the rule base is predefined based on a variety of metrics. Rules can include source and destination IP addresses, source and destination port numbers, and protocols used. Packet filtering generally

Figure 2-9

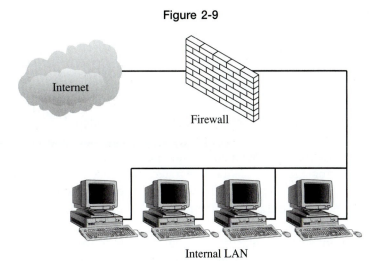

Firewall between an internal network and the Internet.

occurs at Layer 3 of the OSI model and employs some of the following metrics to allow a packet through the firewall, reject the packet, or drop the packet:

▲ **The source IP address of the incoming packets:** Normally, IP packets indicate where a particular packet originated. Approval and denial of a packet could be based on the originating IP addresses. You can usually choose to allow only packets from certain addresses or subnets or to block packets from specific addresses or subnets.

▲ **The destination IP addresses:** Destination IP addresses are the intended location of the packet at the receiving end of a transmission. **Unicast packets** have a single destination IP address and are normally intended for a single machine. **Multicast** or **broadcast packets** are normally destined for multiple machines on the network. Rulesets can be devised to block traffic to a particular IP address on the network to lessen the load on the target machine. Such measures can also be used to block unauthorized access to highly confidential machines on internal networks.

▲ **The type of Internet protocols that the packet might contain:** Layer 2 and Layer 3 packets carry the type of protocol being used as part of their header structure, intended for appropriate handling at the destination machines. These packets could be any of the following types:

　▲ Normal data-carrying IP packets.

　▲ UDP packets.

　▲ Message control packets such as ICMP.

　▲ Address resolution packets such as ARP.

▲ RARP.

▲ Boot-up protocols such as BootP.

▲ IP address assignment packets (Dynamic Host Configuration Protocol, or DHCP).

Filtering can be based on the protocol information that the packets carry. Though packet filtering is accomplished at the OSI model's Layer 3 and below, Layer 4 attributes such as TCP requests, acknowledgment messages, sequence numbers, and destination ports can be incorporated when creating the filters.

Packet-filtering firewalls can be integrated into routers. Such routers route packets and drop packets based on firewall filtering principles. Information about the incoming port and outgoing port in the router of the packet can be utilized to define filtering rules.

The main advantage of packet-filtering firewalls is the speed at which the firewall operations are achieved. Because most of the work takes place at Layer 3 or below in the network stack, a packet-filtering firewall does not require complex application-level knowledge of the processed packets. Most often, packet-filtering firewalls are employed at the periphery of an organization's secure internal networks because they provide a good first line of defense. For example, using packet-filtering firewalls is highly effective in protecting against denial-of-service attacks that aim to bog down sensitive systems on internal networks. The normal practice is to employ additional safety measures inside the DMZ with the packet filtering firewall set up at the external periphery.

Packet-filtering firewalls are not without drawbacks. Because packet-filtering techniques work at OSI Layer 3 or lower, it is impossible for them to examine application-level data directly. Thus, application-specific attacks can easily creep into internal networks. When an attacker spoofs network addresses such as IP addresses, packet filters are ineffective at filtering on this Layer 3 information. Network address spoofing is a primary tool employed by willful attackers on sensitive networks. Many packet-filtering firewalls cannot detect spoofed IP or ARP addresses.

Stateful Packet Filtering

Stateful packet-filtering (also called **stateful inspection**) techniques use a sophisticated approach, while still retaining the basic tenets of packet-filtering firewalls for their operation. As you'll recall, Layer 4 manages connections. The connection pairs can usually be singled out with the following four parameters:

1. The source address
2. The source port
3. The destination address
4. The destination port

Figure 2-10

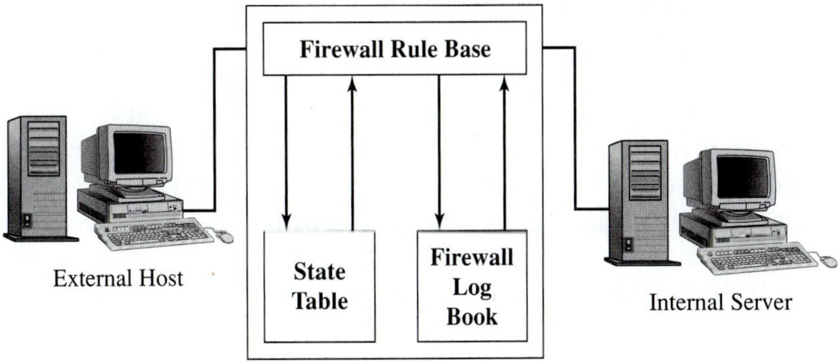

Stateful inspection firewall architecture.

Normally the TCP at Layer 4 of the OSI network stack uses such connection mechanisms for communication and, thus, differs from the connectionless IP present at Layer 3.

Stateful inspection techniques use TCP and higher-layer control data for the filtering process. The connection information is maintained in **state tables** that are normally controlled dynamically. Each connection is logged into the tables, and, after the connection is validated, packets are forwarded based on the rule-set defined on the particular connection. For example, firewalls might invalidate packets that contain port numbers higher than 1023. Similarly, client requests originating from inappropriate ports can be denied access to the server. Figure 2-10 shows the stateful packet-filtering process.

Even though stateful inspection firewalls do a good job of augmenting security features generally not present on packet-filtering-based firewalls, they are not as flexible or as robust as packet-filtering firewalls. Incorporation of the dynamic state table and other features into the firewall makes the architecture of such firewalls complex in comparison and negatively affects the speed of operation. As the number of connections increases (as often is the case on large-scale internal networks), the state table contents expand to a size that causes congestion at the firewall. Users might notice a decrease in performance when accessing resources on the other side of the firewall. Another potential drawback to stateful inspection firewalls is that, like packet-filtering firewalls, they cannot completely access higher-layer protocol and application services for inspection. Most of the higher-level firewalls present in the market are stateful inspection firewalls.

You must also be cautious when designing the filters. When too many restrictions are defined, customers and legitimate remote users might find it exceedingly difficult to get past the firewalls. This can result in loss of business or poor productivity for commercial organizations.

Application Proxy Firewalls

Application proxy firewalls generally aim for the top-most layer (Layer 7, the Application layer in the OSI model) for their operations. A proxy is a substitute for terminating connections in a connection-oriented service. For example, proxies can be deployed in between a remote user (who might be on a public network such as the Internet) and the dedicated server on the Internet. All that the remote user sees is the proxy, so he or she doesn't know the identity of the server he or she is actually communicating with. Similarly, the server only sees the proxy and doesn't know the true user. The proxy can be an effective shielding and filtering mechanism between public networks and protected internal or private networks. Because applications are completely shielded by the proxy and because actions take place at the application level, these firewalls are very effective for sensitive applications. Authentication schemes, such as passwords and biometrics, can be set up for accessing the proxies, fortifying security implementations.

In many cases, dedicated supplementary proxies can be set up to aid the work of the main firewalls and proxy servers. **Proxy agents** are application- and protocol-specific implementations that act on behalf of their intended application protocols. Protocols for which application proxy agents can be set up include the following:

▲ HTTP
▲ FTP
▲ SMTP

Because these firewall activities take place at the Application level and involve a large amount of data processing, application proxies are more expensive and slower than other firewalls. However, application proxies offer the best security of all the firewall technologies discussed here. Figure 2-11 shows a comparison of the firewall technologies.

Disadvantages of Firewalls

There are some inherent disadvantages of installing firewalls. The main disadvantage is the cost involved in installation. A thorough analysis of the protected architecture and its vulnerabilities has to be performed for an effective firewall installation. Moreover, attackers can compromise the firewall itself to get around security measures. When firewalls are compromised by a clever attacker, he or she might be able to compromise the information system and cause considerable damage before being detected. Attackers can also leave back doors that might be unseen by firewalls. These trapdoors become potential easy entry points for a frequently visiting attacker. When improperly configured, firewalls might block legitimate users from accessing network resources. Huge losses can result

Figure 2-11

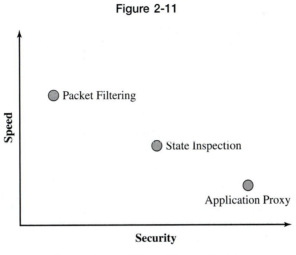

Comparison of firewall technologies.

when potential users and customers are not able to access network resources or proceed with transactions.

2.4.3 Network Address Translation

Network Address Translation (NAT) is the commonly used term for a service that translates private addresses that are normally internal to a particular organization into routable addresses on public networks such as the Internet. Most NAT services actually use Network Address Port Translation (NAPT) or Port Address Translation (PAT) to connect multiple computers to the Internet (or any other IP network) using one IP address.

NAT complements the use of firewalls in providing an extra measure of security for an organization's internal network. Usually, hosts from inside the protected networks (with a private address) are able to communicate with the outside world, but systems that are located outside the protected network have to go through the NAT system to reach internal networks. Many denial-of-service attacks such as SYN flood and **ping of death** can be prevented using NAT technology.

The main feature in NAT is the **translation table.** The translation table maps public IP addresses and ports to internal private IP addresses. Normally, this mapping is not one-to-one. A single public IP address might be mapped to more than one private IP address. Typically, port associations (on the NAT system) are used to map a request for a service to an IP address on the internal network. Any packets from the outside attempting to reach a particular host on the private network use the public IP address and a port number. It is the responsibility of the NAT service to use the translation table to find out the particular private address to

Figure 2-12

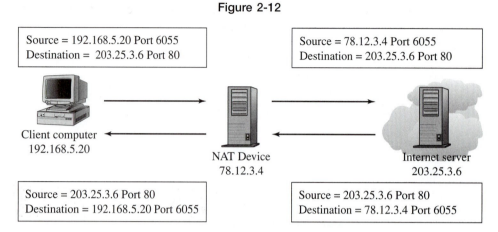

The NAT methodology.

FOR EXAMPLE

Defining Network Borders

You are a network consultant. One of your customers does research and development. When performing a risk analysis, the customer identified three servers that contain highly confidential assets. These servers store data that should only be accessed by thirty employees. The customer has twenty other servers and over three hundred client computers. Client computers need to be able to connect to the Internet. The company also would like to have a web server that can be accessed from across the Internet and by users inside the private network.

You recommend a network with three segments: a DMZ, an internal network, and a highly secure network. You suggest a packet-filtering firewall at the border between the DMZ and the Internet because it will offer the best performance. You also suggest a packet-filtering firewall between the private network and the secure network because it will allow you to limit the users who can access the servers on the secure network by the packet's source IP address. You suggest a stateful inspection firewall at the border between the DMZ and the internal network. A stateful inspection firewall can be configured to prevent unsolicited HTTP traffic from entering the internal network. You also implement NAT to allow users to access the Internet through a single IP address.

which the packet has to be routed. Figure 2-12 shows the technique involved in NAT. Normally, translation tables are built using two methods:

1. **Static:** In this configuration, the relationships among the public and private IP addresses are fixed.
2. **Dynamic outbound packets:** In this mode, the translation tables get updated automatically as outbound packets are processed from the private network.

SELF-CHECK

1. Describe how segmenting a network can help prevent attacks.
2. Identify the three types of firewalls and the OSI model layer at which each operates.

SUMMARY

In this chapter you learned some guidelines for securing the servers on your network. You learned the importance of the security by design and defense-in-depth methodologies. You also learned the steps to take to physically secure a server. Next you learned how to reduce a server's attack surface by disabling services, closing ports, and removing unnecessary peripheral devices. Finally, you learned how to design a segmented network and how to choose the best perimeter defense.

KEY TERMS

Address Resolution Protocol (ARP)

American Standard Code for Information Interchange (ASCII)

AppleTalk Session Protocol (ASP)

Application layer (OSI model)

Application layer (TCP/IP model)

Application proxy firewall

Berkeley Internet Name Domain (BIND)

BootP

Border security

Broadcast packet

Chargen

Connectionless protocol

Connection-oriented protocol

Crackers

Data encapsulation

Data Link layer

Defense-in-depth

Demilitarized zone (DMZ)

Digital Network Architecture Session Control Protocol (DNA-SCP)

Domain Name System (DNS)

Echo

Extended Binary-Coded Decimal Interchange Code (EBCDIC)

Failover system

File Transfer Protocol (FTP)

Filter

Finger

Headless server

Host-to-Host layer

Hypertext Transfer Protocol (HTTP)

Internet Control Message Protocol (ICMP)

Internet layer

Internet Protocol (IP)

Internet Protocol Security (IPsec)

Internetwork Packet Exchange (IPX)

IP address

Joint Photographic Experts Group (JPEG)

Layered architecture

Limiting the attack surface

Local Service account

Local System account

Logical Link layer

Media Access Control (MAC) address

Media Access layer

Motion Picture Experts Group (MPEG)

Multicasting

Multicast packet

Multipurpose Internet Mail Extensions (MIME)

Need-to-access environment

Need-to-know environment

Netstat

Network Access layer

Network Address Translation (NAT)

Network File System (NFS)

Network layer

Network Service account

Network stack

Open Shortest Path First (OSPF)

Open Systems Interconnect (OSI) model

Packet filtering

Packet sniffer

Perimeter network

Personal firewall

Physical entry point

Physical layer

Ping

Ping of death

Point-to-Point Protocol (PPP)

POP3

Port

Port scanner

Post Office Protocol (POP)

Presentation layer

Private network

Promiscuous mode

Protocol

Protocol analyzer

Proxy agents

Public network

Remote access server

Remote login

Remote Procedure Call (RPC)

Reverse Address Resolution Protocol (RARP)

Rlogin

Routing Information Protocol (RIP)

Rule base

Ruleset

Screened subnet

Secure File Transfer Protocol (SFTP)

Secure Shell (SSH)

Semi-private network

Separation of services

Sequenced Packet Exchange (SPX)

Serial Line Internet Protocol (SLIP)

Session Control Protocol (SCP)

Session layer

Simple Mail Transfer Protocol (SMTP)

Simple Network Management Protocol (SNMP)

Slogin

Sockets

SSH-2

Stateful inspection

Stateful packet filtering

State table

Systat

Tagged Information File Format (TIFF)

TCP/IP model

Telnet

Translation table

Transmission Control Protocol (TCP)

Transport layer (OSI model)

Transport layer (TCP/IP model)

Trivial File Transfer Protocol (TFTP)

Unicast packet

User Datagram Protocol (UDP)

Well-known ports

ASSESS YOUR UNDERSTANDING

Go to www.wiley.com/college/cole to evaluate your knowledge of server security and network borders.

Measure your learning by comparing pre-test and post-test results.

Summary Questions

1. Which layer of the OSI model is responsible for routing?
   (a) Data Link
   (b) Network
   (c) Session
   (d) Transport

2. Which TCP/IP protocol is a secure alternative to Telnet?
   (a) ARP
   (b) Finger
   (c) Rlogin
   (d) SSH

3. Which port is associated with POP3 email?
   (a) 25
   (b) 79
   (c) 110
   (d) 445

4. The defense-in-depth security strategy involves implementing multiple controls. True or false?

5. Providing fire protection is one step in physically securing a server. True or false?

6. Which account should be used to execute a Windows service that requires minimal permissions and does not need to access the network?
   (a) Local Service
   (b) Local System
   (c) Network Service

7. A port scanner identifies that port 23 is open. What does this tell an attacker about the computer?
   (a) It is a web server.
   (b) It is running the FTP service.
   (c) It can be accessed by Telnet.
   (d) It can be accessed by SSH.

8. Which of the following devices can allow an intruder with physical access to a server to steal confidential information?

(a) A scanner

(b) A USB port

(c) A modem

(d) A PS/2 port

9. A firewall should only be used on the border between the Internet and the private network. True or false?

10. Which type of firewall operates at Layer 3 of the OSI model?

(a) Application proxy

(b) Packet-filtering

(c) Stateful inspection

11. Which type of firewall can be used to ensure that only responses to a request from an internal host are allowed through?

(a) Application proxy

(b) Packet-filtering

(c) Stateful inspection

Applying This Chapter

1. You are a network administrator at a company. There is a database server that stores accounting data, customer data, and employee data. There is also a web server that must be accessed by customers and employees. Some employees work remotely and need access to an FTP server to upload and download files. The company uses Microsoft Exchange for email.

(a) Describe the justification for running FTP and the web service on different computers.

(b) The table below lists some well-known ports and some servers. Identify whether the ports should be open or closed.

Ports	Exchange server	Web server	FTP server	Database server
20				
21				
23				
25				
80				

(c) Describe the danger port scanners pose to your network.

(d) You decide to segment your network using a DMZ. Which servers should you place in the DMZ?

(e) What is one way you can allow the Microsoft Exchange server to receive email from an SMTP forwarder on the Internet?

(f) What precautions should you take to physically secure the servers?

(g) Which servers should include a modem?

(h) The database servers are in a locked closet on the internal network. How should you apply access permissions to add another layer of depth to the database servers' defense?

YOU TRY IT

Analyzing the Attack Surface of Your Computer

Although typically not as critical as a server, workstations also have an attack surface. Have you thought about the services that are running on your computer? How about your computer's physical security?

1. Make a list of the people who have physical access to your computer.
2. How could you improve the physical security of your computer?
3. If you are running Windows XP or Windows Vista, use the Services utility to view the services running on your system.
4. Does your computer connect directly to the Internet? Is it part of a private network?
5. If it's on a private network, are you using a firewall as border security? If so, what type?

Tools or Threats? You Decide

Packet sniffers and port analyzers can be used as legitimate troubleshooting tools, but can also be used by potential attackers. The ICMP protocol is also useful for diagnosing problems, and several diagnostic tools, such as ping, use ICMP. However, ping can be used to launch a denial-of-service attack.

1. Discuss the impact of the dual nature of packet sniffers and port analyzers on network maintenance and security.
2. Give an example of how you would use each tool for legitimate troubleshooting.
3. Discuss the pros and cons of configuring a packet-filtering firewall to drop ICMP packets.

3

CRYPTOGRAPHY

Starting Point

Go to www.wiley.com/college/cole to assess your knowledge of cryptography and public key infrastructure (PKI).
Determine where you need to concentrate your effort.

What You'll Learn in This Chapter

▲ History of cryptography
▲ Symmetric encryption
▲ Asymmetric encryption
▲ Hashes
▲ Public key infrastructure (PKI)
▲ Certificate Authority hierarchy
▲ Issuing and revoking certificates

After Studying This Chapter, You'll Be Able To

▲ Identify the characteristics of strong encryption
▲ Identify cryptography primitives
▲ Describe how symmetric encryption works
▲ Describe how asymmetric encryption works
▲ Describe the role of a hash in ensuring data integrity
▲ Describe how public key infrastructure (PKI) allows you to securely manage and distribute certificates
▲ Design a Certificate Authority hierarchy
▲ Design a certificate enrollment and revocation strategy

INTRODUCTION

While much of security involves the process of putting up walls to prevent an attack or managing risk when an attack occurs, **cryptography** (the science of changing plain text by substituting or transposing characters) plays an important role in an overall security scheme. Cryptography is an essential part of providing data confidentiality, integrity, and authentication. A basic understanding of cryptographic **algorithms** (step-by-step procedures or mathematical formulas used to solve problems) and their role in providing confidentiality, integrity, and authentication can help you make good decisions about how to use various technologies that are based on them.

This chapter begins with a brief overview of the history of cryptography. Following that, the chapter discusses the four main areas of cryptography: random number generation, symmetric encryption, asymmetric encryption, and hashes. The chapter concludes with a look at public key infrastructure (PKI) and a brief look at designing your own infrastructure for issuing digital certificates.

3.1 Cryptography Overview

In this first section, we'll take a short look at the history of cryptography and the vulnerabilities of a few historical algorithms. Next we'll overview the four key areas of cryptography, known as **cryptographic primitives.** From there we briefly overview how the XOR process is used in cryptography. Finally, we'll introduce the cast of characters that are commonly used when discussing cryptography.

3.1.1 A Brief History of Cryptography

Mankind has had a need to encrypt data since long before computers were invented. Leaders needed to deliver data secretively to generals on the battlefield, and lovers sent messages to each other in code. The earliest forms of cryptography were easy to crack by today's standards. However, before the advent of computers, analyzing and finding the weakness in a cryptographic algorithm (a process known as **cryptanalysis**) could take hours, days, or years because it depended solely on human ingenuity and effort. Today's cryptographic algorithms are broken by computers, which can try millions of combinations each second. As computers become more powerful, the cryptographic algorithms must be made stronger to keep data secure.

But before we discuss the algorithms used today, let's look back at some of the earliest methods of encryption and analyze why they are easy to crack.

Substitution Ciphers

As far back as Julius Caesar, cryptography was used to protect messages. Caesar would encrypt his messages before giving them to messengers, protecting them

Figure 3-1

a	b	c	d	e	f	g	h	i	j	k	l	m	n	o	p	q	r	s	t	u	v	w	x	y	z
d	e	f	g	h	i	j	k	l	m	n	o	p	q	r	s	t	u	v	w	x	y	z	a	b	c

Caesar's encryption scheme.

from being read while in transit. Caesar used a simple method of encryption called a substitution cipher. A **substitution cipher** maps each letter in the alphabet to another letter. For example, the letter *a* might be mapped to *f*, *b* to *g*, and so on through the alphabet. Caesar used to replace each letter in the alphabet with the letter three letters to the right of it, wrapping around at the end of the alphabet. This mapping is shown in Figure 3-1, where the letters in the top row are in **plain text** (data in its unencrypted, readable form), and the ones in the bottom row are the corresponding letters in **cipher text** (data in its encrypted, unreadable form).

Using this encryption scheme, or cipher, if you were to encode the word *cryptography*, you would look up the letter *c* in the top row and find the letter *f* corresponding to it in the bottom row. Applying this process to all the letters yields the following:

> **Plain text:** cryptography
> **Cipher text:** fubswrjudskb

An encryption algorithm requires both plain text and a **key** (a piece of data used with encryption and decryption) to create cipher text. The key in this algorithm is the table shown in Figure 3-1. This table acts as the key for the algorithm, mapping plain text letters to cipher text letters. To determine the table, you need to know the offset used to calculate the cipher text. This value is known as the **shift.**

Without the table, trying to decode *fubswrjudskb* into *cryptography* might seem like an impossible task. However, some **cryptanalysts** (people who analyze and crack cryptographic algorithms) realized that breaking such a cipher was very easy; they needed to try at most 25 different substitutions or rotations of the alphabet before the cipher text would be converted into plain text, making sense of the words.

Another drawback of a simple substitution cipher is that it is prone to **frequency analysis.** Frequency analysis uses the fact that some letters in the English language appear more frequently than other letters. For example, consider the following sentence:

> *The enemy plans to wait until the storm ends to attack.*

When this sentence is encrypted with the Caesar cipher, you obtain the following cipher text:

wkhhqhpbsodqvwrzdlwxqwlowkhvwruphqgvwrdwwdfn

The six most common letters used in English language text are *e*, *a*, *r*, *i*, *t*, and *s*. The most frequent letters in the cipher text are *w* (8 occurrences) and *h* (5 occurrences). So, to determine the shift value using frequency analysis, you would begin by attempting to decode using the most likely shift value, which in this case would be substituting the letter *e* for each occurrence of *w* (a shift value of 18). You only need to decode a few characters to know that this is not the correct shift value.

esppyp

You would then continue with the next most likely shift value, and then next, until you try a shift value of 3 and reveal the correct plain text. Notice that using frequency analysis made it more likely that you would discover the key in the first five or six attempts.

Vigenere Cipher

In the sixteenth century, Blaise de Vigenere proposed a more secure encryption algorithm, the Vigenere cipher. The **Vigenere cipher** works by using a keyword and substituting plain text letters for cipher text letters according to the keyword. However, instead of a simple rotation of the alphabet, Vigenere's cipher assigned a number to each of the letters in the alphabet and then added the value of each letter in the keyword to the value of each letter in the plain text to obtain the cipher text. If the value of the two letters added together was larger than 26, 26 was subtracted from this value to obtain the cipher text character. This process was repeated for each letter in the plain text using the next letter in the keyword, and repeating the keyword as many times as needed to compensate for the length of the plain text. The Vignere cipher uses a method known as **polyalphabetic substitution.**

The numbering for the alphabet was simple and always remained the same: $a = 0$, $b = 1$, and so on until reaching $z = 25$. A different key was constructed for each message, making it more secure. Using the same sample message, *cryptography*, and the keyword *luck*, the plain text is encrypted into *nlazeiibljji* as shown in Figure 3-2.

To obtain the plain text from the cipher text by **brute force methods** (the process of working through all possible keys until the proper key is found that decrypts cipher text into plain text) would take a very long time even with today's computers because the size of the key is not known. To use a brute force method, you would need to try keys of different sizes and all combinations of letters for each key size. For example, you would need to try 26 combinations for each letter in a 2-letter keyword, 26 combinations for each letter in a 3-letter keyword, and so forth.

Figure 3-2

Plain text	C	R	Y	P	T	O	G	R	A	P	H	Y
Key	L	U	C	K	L	U	C	K	L	U	C	K
Plain text values	2	17	24	15	19	14	6	17	0	15	7	24
Key values	11	20	2	10	11	20	2	10	11	20	2	10
Cipher text values	13	11	0	25	4	8	8	1	11	9	9	8
Cipher text	N	L	A	Z	E	I	I	B	L	J	J	I

Encryption with the Vigenere cipher.

The cipher was also not as vulnerable to frequency analysis because a specific plain text letter would not always appear as the same value in the cipher text. The Vigenere cipher was considered unbreakable for 300 years. Then in the 1800s, both Friedrich Kasiski and Charles Babbage independently developed similar techniques for cracking the Vigenere cipher. Their techniques hinge on the weakness that the key is applied repeatedly to generate the cipher text. Therefore, if you can discover the length of the key, you can break the cipher text into multiple simple substitution ciphers. Using our previous example, if you know that the key length is 4 letters, you can independently crack four different simple substitution ciphers, as shown Figure 3-3.

One-Time Pad

The **one-time pad** was used by the military to communicate covertly between field agents. Each agent was given a pad of paper that contained randomly selected numbers between 0 and 25. Two copies of each pad were made. One was given to the agent and the other was kept at the headquarters the agent was to communicate with. To encrypt a message, the agent shifted the position of the first letter of the plain text by the first number in the pad. The second letter of the plain text was shifted by the second number in the pad. This continued until all of the letters in the plain text were encrypted and the resulting

Figure 3-3

Plain text	C	R	Y	P	T	O	G	R	A	P	H	Y
Key	L	U	C	K	L	U	C	K	L	U	C	K
Plain text values	2	17	24	15	19	14	6	17	0	15	7	24
Key values	11	20	2	10	11	20	2	10	11	20	2	10
Cipher text values	13	11	0	25	4	8	8	1	11	9	9	8
Cipher text	N	L	A	Z	E	I	I	B	L	J	J	I
Simple cipher	1	2	3	4	1	2	3	4	1	2	3	4

Breaking the Vignere cipher text into simple substitution ciphers.

cipher text was left. Assuming the numbers were randomly created, the cipher text was completely secure and only the agent and headquarters could decrypt the message. A variation of the one-time pad algorithm was used for encrypting radio communications well into the 1980s. Each unit had a different code book that was changed each day.

While this idea was completely secure, it had logistical flaws. The numbers could not be generated randomly and they would repeat or have patterns that could be detected and reproduced by an agent who carelessly discarded part of the pad. Also, the pads were usually not long enough for more than a few messages. With the agents unable to obtain a new pad, they simply reused the pad starting from the beginning. This reuse of the pad, even across multiple messages, caused the same problem the Vigenere cipher had.

Ciphers that Shaped History

The idea of substituting one letter for another carried on to World War II, where the Germans created a machine called **Enigma** that worked on the same basic principle of substituting each letter for another. However, instead of the substitution being simple, it was a complex set of substitutions that changed while the message was being typed. Rotors in the machine tracked these substitutions. It was the different speeds at which these rotors advanced and the ability to change rotors that provided the machine's security. While the machine was very complex and did a good job of encryption, it was the Germans' belief that letters in plain text should not be substituted for the same letter in cipher text that proved to be its downfall. This poor assumption and design decision greatly reduced the number of possible combinations for substitution, making the machine weak. The United States and Great Britain captured and duplicated the Enigma machine and were eventually able to decrypt messages without the key, essentially breaking Enigma.

Following the Germans' lead, the Japanese created a machine called **Purple**. Purple was modeled after Enigma but used telephone stepping switches instead of rotors to create the character mappings. Purple proved very important in the war because it was used to encrypt diplomatic communications that hinted at the Pearl Harbor attack. The U.S. Government also eventually broke Purple during World War II.

3.1.2 Cryptographic Primitives

Cryptography is best understood by breaking it into four main areas, or primitives. All of cryptography is based on these four primitives, and the primitives are closely connected. With a full understanding of these primitives, you should be able to read any standard that references them and understand protocols built by using them. While the design and construction of cryptographic primitives is usually left to experts, it is important to understand how they work and interact from a high-level perspective.

The four basic cryptographic primitives are as follows:

1. Random number generation
2. Symmetric encryption
3. Asymmetric encryption
4. Hash functions

It is also important to understand the goals of cryptography and how these primitives allow the goals to be achieved. Cryptography has three main goals, often discussed using the acronym **CIA,** which stands for confidentiality, integrity, and authentication. These properties, as they relate to cryptography, are defined here:

▲ **Confidentiality:** Only the parties that should be able to obtain the information are able to obtain it. This relates closely to the decrypting of messages by attackers. If an attacker can decrypt a message without the required key, confidentiality is not achieved.

▲ **Integrity:** Data has not been modified or changed in any way, deliberately or otherwise. Both known and unknown changes are included in the definition of integrity because things such as network errors are considered a breach of integrity even though they are not a deliberate attack.

▲ **Authentication:** The proposed source of the data ideally can be verified to be true. Data that is delivered from one source to another has achieved authentication if the sender of that data can be proven.

Sometimes it is enough to use a single primitive alone to obtain one of the CIA goals; however, most of the time the primitives are used together to obtain the CIA goal. For example, it requires all four of the primitives to complete the task of using a credit card to purchase merchandise from a secure Internet site.

The first of the primitives is discussed here. The other three are presented later in the chapter.

Random Number Generation

The first cryptographic primitive is the generation of random numbers, or, more accurately, random bit strings. While a computer algorithm can never generate completely random numbers, there are algorithms that create **pseudorandom numbers,** or numbers that appear to be random. Even the simplest encryption algorithms, such as the one-time pad, require the generation of pseudorandom numbers.

The numbers created from cryptographic pseudorandom number generators do not have to be 100 percent random—they simply have to be unpredictable to an attacker. If an attacker can recreate the stream of bits used to create the keys for any encryption algorithm, it is as if the attacker has been given the key. By recreating the stream of bits used to create the key, an attacker can recreate the key using the same method because all good encryption algorithms are published.

Because creating truly random numbers is not possible on a computer, many interesting techniques have been used to obtain seemingly random numbers. There are two basic approaches to generating pseudorandom numbers on a computer. The first is to design an algorithm that will create what appears to be random numbers. The main problem with this approach is that at some point the algorithm will cycle and you will start seeing the same numbers in the same order. This is called **depth** and is very dangerous because the repeated bit stream makes it easier to break encryption.

Two pseudorandom number generators that are cryptographically secure are the **Blum-Blum-Shub pseudorandom generator** and the **RSA** (which stands for Rivest, Shamir, and Adleman, its inventors) **pseudorandom generator.** Both of these algorithms rely on a number of theoretical properties that are outside the scope of this text. However, these algorithms are believed to be relatively secure because they require the factoring of large numbers in order to be broken, and this is believed to be computationally infeasible (though not impossible) if the number is large enough.

3.1.3 XOR

Instead of simply rotating characters, a more modern approach to cryptography uses the XOR (exclusive or) function. The **XOR function** is a binary operation performed on two strings of bits, resulting in a third string of bits. Table 3-1 shows the results when the XOR function is applied to two values. In general terms, whenever two bits are not the same, the resulting bit is a 1, and when two bits are the same, the resulting bit is a 0.

Instead of using simple addition, which had the problem of the resulting number being larger than the character set, XOR can be used in the same

Table 3-1: XOR Results

A	B	A XOR B
0	0	0
0	1	1
1	0	1
1	1	0

way as shifting with the same level of security, but without the problem of the result not mapping to a character. XOR also has a very nice inverse property just like addition. For example, A XOR B = C, A XOR C = B, and B XOR C = A. If A represents a plain text character and B represents a key character, then C is the resulting cipher text after encryption using the XOR function. To decrypt, you simply reapply the XOR function to C and B or the cipher text and the key. Without the key it is impossible to know what the plain text was. All possible values can work for the key, but only one returns the proper results. If the key is just as long as the plain text, and the values generated for the key are done so randomly, this method of encrypting is highly secure.

3.1.4 Cast of Characters

Before explaining the other cryptographic primitives, we need to introduce some people that will be used for example purposes throughout the rest of this chapter. The following are used to designate people or computers. The names chosen are not unique to this book; in fact, almost all cryptography explanations use these names. The reason for the names is no more complex than the first letter of their names. Instead of saying, "Computer A sends a message to computer B," "Alice sends a message to Bob" is used instead. The cast of characters is as follows:

- ▲ **Alice:** She is an end user/computer without malicious intentions; one of the main users of cryptography.
- ▲ **Bob:** He is Alice's friend and is also a main user of cryptography, without malicious intentions.
- ▲ **Cathy:** Another user of cryptography; she does not usually have a large role nor malicious intentions.
- ▲ **Eve:** A malicious user that does not interfere with communications. She simply wants to eavesdrop on the conversation between two other characters—typically Alice and Bob—but does not actively try to attack the communication.
- ▲ **Mallory:** The malicious user who is always trying to thwart attempts by other characters to communicate securely.
- ▲ **Trent:** He is a trusted third party. He only communicates with Alice, Bob, or Cathy when they ask for his help. He can always be trusted to do what he says he will do.

These characters are used throughout the rest of this chapter. Familiarize yourself with them because they will often be used to describe a cryptographic protocol without further definition.

FOR EXAMPLE

Windtalkers

Another well-known use of cryptography during war is the cryptographic algorithm used by the code talkers (also called windtalkers) in the Pacific Theater during World War II. The code talkers were Navaho Indians. A group of Navaho Indians developed a cryptographic system that mapped nouns and verbs from the Navaho language to the letters in the English language, as well as a few tactical terms. Multiple words were associated with a single letter.

Native speakers of the Navaho language were deployed as part of the regular armed forces units to encrypt and decrypt the messages. The algorithm was never cracked because doing so would have required a native Navaho speaker to work with a cryptologist.

SELF-CHECK

1. Describe how the Vigenere cipher protects the confidentiality of data better than a substitution cipher.
2. Identify the four primitives of cryptography.
3. Identify the three goals of cryptography.

3.2 Symmetric Encryption

Symmetric encryption, or **single-key encryption,** is the most well understood cryptography primitive. It is where the whole field really started. Caesar and his cipher, the Germans and Enigma, and the Japanese and Purple are all examples of symmetric encryption. The idea behind symmetric encryption is that only a single key is used to both encrypt and decrypt a message. The benefit to using symmetric encryption is that it's very fast. In this section we'll look at how symmetric encryption works, the types of ciphers used by different algorithms, and the main drawback to using symmetric encryption: exchanging keys.

3.2.1 Understanding Symmetric Encryption

Symmetric encryption is used when Alice wants to provide for the confidentiality of a message she sends to Bob. Depending upon the mode of encryption used (modes are explained later in this chapter), symmetric encryption can also provide integrity when used correctly.

The best analogy for symmetric encryption is that of a lockbox. To unlock a lockbox you must have the right key. In the physical world this key is usually a metal object. In the world of cryptography, this key is a set of random bits. Whatever is inside the lockbox is confidential and protected from anyone without the key. Without the key, Mallory is unable to read, modify, or do anything to the data except destroy it (by destroying the lockbox). The same key is used to decrypt the data as is used to encrypt the data.

3.2.2 Encryption Strength

In our lockbox example, Mallory can attempt to open the safe by going through all possible physical configurations for a key until the proper configuration is tried and the safe is opened. In cryptography the same is true. Mallory can try all possible key combinations until one works, and the resulting data or message is understandable. You might be asking yourself, how many combinations would an attacker have to try? The answer to that question depends upon the encryption algorithm or cipher used. An algorithm is considered **computationally secure** if the amount of time needed to compute all possible combinations is so large that it cannot be done in any reasonable amount of time. This definition, "in a reasonable amount of time," is deliberately vague, because the meaning of *computationally secure* is ever-changing as the speed of a computer is ever-increasing. Also, most data does not need to be protected forever. Different types of data have different periods of time during which disclosure is a risk. After that time has elapsed, the data no longer needs to be kept confidential.

One popular symmetric encryption algorithm, **Data Encryption Standard (DES)**, has a key of 56 bits. This means that breaking the algorithm would require 72,057,594,037,927,936 different keys to be tested to exhaust all possibilities. Assuming a computer could try a million keys a second, it would take 2284 years to try all of the keys. That sounds like it is a secure algorithm because we will all be dead by the time the key is discovered. However, a specially built machine was used to crack DES in a little over 36 hours.

3.2.3 Stream Ciphers

A **stream cipher** uses a single key to encrypt a message or stream of data. The message is considered to be a stream of data in that each byte is processed with the bytes preceding it, and the order is important. If you were to change the order of any of the bytes in the plain text, the cipher text, from that point forward, would look different. Figure 3-4 shows what a stream cipher does.

Stream ciphers normally do not require any padding of the message. **Padding** is adding extra bits to the message. Because messages are treated as a stream of data they can be of any length and do not need to be padded in any way except to add randomness to common messages.

Figure 3-4

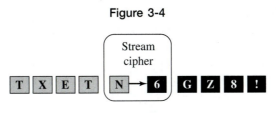

A stream cipher.

You have already learned about one type of stream cipher, the one-time pad. Other stream ciphers include the following:

▲ RC4

▲ SEAL (Software-Optimized Encryption Algorithm)

▲ ISAAC (stands for indirection, shift, accumulate, add, and count)

▲ Panama

▲ A5/1

▲ A5/2

▲ FISH (FIbonacci SHrinking)

▲ Helix

When Alice wants to send a message to Bob using a stream cipher, they must both have the same key and Bob must feed the cipher text into the algorithm in the same order as Alice fed the plain text into the algorithm to encrypt it. Mallory can prevent Bob from decrypting most stream-cipher-encrypted messages by changing the first few bits that Alice sends to Bob. This property of a stream cipher is not always a bad thing. It provides integrity. If any of the cipher text bits are changed, it will be obvious to Bob when he decrypts the message.

There are some stream ciphers that do not propagate errors through the entire message. What this means is that if an error occurs while the message is being sent from Alice to Bob, it will only prevent that section of the message from being decrypted properly. This property is an important one to consider if the message will be sent across an unreliable connection.

3.2.4 Block Ciphers

A **block cipher** is the other kind of symmetric encryption algorithm. Block ciphers also use a single key to encrypt a message, but it is done one block at a time. A block is considered a certain number of bits and is determined by the algorithm. Each block is processed independently, and there is no correlation between the encrypting of one message block and another. Figure 3-5 shows what a block cipher does.

Figure 3-5

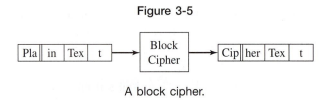

A block cipher.

Because block ciphers have the ability to process a single block of the message independently, they need to include safeguards to prevent someone from gaining information about the message by seeing repeated blocks. For example, if Alice sends the message "yes" to Bob in response to a series of questions, the word "yes" will be encrypted to the same cipher text, assuming the same key is used. Then every time the word "yes" was sent, Eve would know what message was being sent without needing to decrypt it. Worse yet, Mallory could pre-compute the message "yes" with all possible keys and then simply match the cipher text seen to the cipher text of a precomputed message. Assuming the key size was small enough, Mallory would be able to compute the corresponding key and break all further encryptions.

Another attack that Mallory can use is to change the order of blocks. This will not prevent decryption from occurring, as would happen with a stream cipher, because no block depends on any other block. For example, suppose Alice asks Bob what his house number is and his response is "1234," encrypting "12" in one block and "34" in another. Without knowing what house number was actually sent, Mallory can still change the ordering of the blocks and send Alice "3412," the wrong house number. So Mallory can change the ordering of the blocks without Bob or Alice knowing. Although the encryption method provides confidentiality, integrity can be broken.

To prevent the same plain text block always encrypting to the same cipher text block, block ciphers use different encryption modes. The encryption modes are described as follows:

▲ **Electronic code book (ECB):** The message is encrypted one block at a time so that one plain text block maps to one cipher text block. An error in any block only effects the decryption of that block. If an entire block is lost during transmission, none of the other blocks are affected.

▲ **Cipher-block chaining (CBC):** The output block of the previous encryption is XORed with the next block of plain text before being encrypted. If a bit is changed in the plain text of one block, that change is propagated to all subsequent cipher text blocks. If a cipher text bit is changed, the current block will be corrupted and the changed bit will be inverted in the next block. CBC does not allow blocks to be encrypted in parallel. However, they can be decrypted in parallel.

▲ **Propagating cipher-block chaining (PCBC):** Similar to CBC, except that changes to the cipher text are propagated throughout the message. PCBC is the mode of operation used in **Kerberos** (an authentication protocol).

▲ **Cipher feedback (CFB):** The previous cipher text block is XORed with the current encrypted text block. This differs from CBC mode in that the XOR occurs after the encryption of the current text block. If a bit in the cipher text is changed, the current block will have that bit inverted and the subsequent block will be corrupted.

▲ **Output feedback (OFB):** The output of the encryption algorithm is continually fed into the algorithm while the plain text is XORed with this output. This differs from CFB because what is fed into the encryption algorithm does not include the cipher text. If an error occurs in one block, that error is only propagated to those bits that are changed. However, if any of the bits are lost, including a whole block, the error is propagated to all of the remaining blocks and cannot recover.

ECB is almost never used because of the reasons stated. The most popular mode is CBC because errors do not propagate throughout the entire message if bits are lost like they do in OFB. CBC is used over CFB because the error propagation is usually smaller, only two blocks, and because the bit changes that do occur happen in a predictable manor to the later blocks. For example, when using CBC, if Block 1 has bits flipped in it during transmission, Block 1 will be seemingly random, and Block 2 will have the exact bits flipped where they were in Block 1 during transmission. This enables Mallory to cause predictable changes to the message. In CFB mode, bits flipped in Block 1 are the exact bits that are flipped in Block 1 of the deciphered message. The later blocks then appear random. If an attacker is going to flip bits while the cipher text is being transmitted, it is always better to receive a random-looking block on decryption, alerting you that tampering has occurred and to not trust anything that comes after the altered block. This is not true for CFB, because you cannot necessarily tell where the error begins—only that one has occurred.

DES (discussed previously) is only one of many block ciphers. DES was the original block cipher backed by a **National Institute of Standards and Technology (NIST)** publication. NIST is a United States government agency that performs research, develops technical standards, and promotes technological advances. However, because of the small key size involved in DES, 56 bits, it was only thought to be secure for 5 years because computers today can quickly perform a brute force attack against 56 bits. **Triple DES (3DES)** applies the DES algorithm to the plain text three times, for a key length of 168 bits. The primary drawback to 3DES is performance.

In 2001, NIST announced a new algorithm called **Advanced Encryption Standard (AES)**, which was adopted as a standard in May 2002. AES has three key sizes: 128, 192, or 256 bits. The block size is 128 bits. AES has been approved by the **National Security Agency (NSA),** a United States government agency responsible for collecting and analyzing foreign communications and protecting the confidentiality of U.S. government data. AES has gained in popularity and is now a commonly used symmetric encryption protocol. A similar encryption algorithm, **Rijndael,** supports key and block sizes in any multiple of 32 between 128 and 256 bits.

Other block ciphers include, but are not limited to, the following:

▲ Desx

▲ Blowfish

▲ Cast

▲ Skipjack

▲ Twofish

There are many, many more.

3.2.5 Sharing Keys

With strong block ciphers created, the ability to use them is still hindered by the fact that the key must be known by both parties before the algorithm can be used. Often, the other party you are going to communicate with is known, so keys can be created and shared in a secure manner before communication begins. This type of key generation is called using a **pre-shared secret.** The key is shared between parties before communication begins. However, what if Alice wants to communicate with Bob, but she has never met Bob before, so that they do not have a pre-shared secret key? How then can Alice and Bob communicate securely? They could create keys and encrypt them so no one knows the keys, but how are they going to encrypt them without common keys?

One way to solve this problem is to use a trusted third party, Trent. Alice will create a key to be used to communicate with Bob. She will encrypt this key using a pre-shared key that she has with Trent and then send the key to Trent. Trent will then be able to decrypt the key he received from Alice using their pre-shared key and then encrypt it with a key he has pre-shared with Bob and send it to him. Now both Alice and Bob have a common shared key, and only Trent, Alice, and Bob know what the key is. However, this scheme has problems, starting with Trent. What if Trent is really not Trent at all but Mallory? Now she has the key and can decrypt any communication between the two parties. Also, this scheme requires that the sending and receiving parties have a pre-shared key with Trent. Implementing a system like this would be a huge logistical problem.

Another way to share a key between two parties is for the parties to create the key on the fly, in a secure manner. A method for generating keys in this manner is called a **key agreement protocol.** One classic key agreement protocol is **Diffie-Hellman key exchange.** For this protocol to work, both Alice and Bob agree to use a specific prime number (p) and a base number (g). Next, Alice and Bob each choose a secret integer. We'll refer to Alice's secret integer as "a" and Bob's secret integer as "b". Alice sends Bob the value of the following calculation:

$$g^a \bmod p$$

Bob sends Alice the value of the following calculation:

$$g^b \bmod p$$

Alice calculates the key by using the following formula:

$$\text{Key} = (\text{Message}_{bob})^a \bmod p$$

Bob calculates the key by using the following formula:

$$\text{Key} = (\text{Message}_{alice})^b \bmod p$$

Alice and Bob both calculate the same value for the key. However, Eve would need to determine both secrets a and b to arrive at the correct value. This is very difficult to do because it would require Eve to solve the **discrete logarithm problem,** for which efficient algorithms do not exist at this time.

However, a man-in-the-middle attack can be launched against this type of key agreement protocol, as shown in Figure 3-6. In a man-in-the-middle attack, Mallory intercepts the message sent from Alice to Bob and that sent from Bob to Alice. She pretends to be Bob when Alice sends a message to Bob, and pretends to be Alice when Bob sends a message to Alice. With Mallory in the middle of this key exchange, she can create her own two secret keys and exchange communications with Alice and Bob forwarding the messages so Alice and Bob are none the wiser. When Alice sends a message to Bob using what she thinks is the key Bob has, she really uses the one Mallory set up with her. The message is sent; Mallory intercepts it, decrypts it, reads or changes it, and then re-encrypts

Figure 3-6

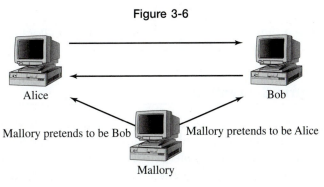

Man-in-the-middle attack.

FOR EXAMPLE

Choosing a Symmetric Encryption Protocol

You are on the team to draft your company's security policy. You need to identify the acceptable algorithms for symmetric encryption. You identify AES as being the preferred symmetric encryption protocol because of its strength, and for highly confidential data, you require a key length of 256 bits. You identify 3DES as an acceptable algorithm when AES is not available, such as on computers running Windows® XP without Service Pack 1. You do some research and find that by installing Service Pack 1 (or later) on computers running Windows XP or upgrading to Windows Vista™ that you can ensure that files encrypted using the built-in encryption feature **Encrypting File System (EFS)** will be encrypted using the AES algorithm. You also discover that Windows Server 2003 uses AES for EFS encryption. However, Windows 2000 uses DESX, which is a variant of DES. You recommend upgrading all computers running Windows 2000 to an operating system that supports AES.

it with the key set up between Mallory and Bob. Bob receives a message he believes to be from Alice when it is really from Mallory. Now Mallory has full control over the communication channel, and both confidentiality and integrity are lost because authentication was never established.

The Diffie-Hellman key exchange is still in use today; however, it is commonly used with authentication mechanisms to help mitigate man-in-the-middle attacks.

SELF-CHECK

1. Describe the block cipher encryption methods.
2. Describe the purpose of the Diffie-Hellman key exchange.

3.3 Asymmetric Encryption

Asymmetric encryption requires the use of two keys: a **private key** that is known only by its owner and a **public key** that is readily available to those who need to use it. It is important to note that asymmetric encryption has the property that figuring out one key from the other should be as hard as decrypting the message without any key. Stated another way, the computational power required to decrypt an asymmetrically encrypted message is approximately the same as deducing one asymmetric key from the other.

In this section we'll look at how asymmetric encryption can be used for ensuring confidentiality and authentication.

3.3.1 Ensuring Confidentiality with Asymmetric Encryption

One of the primary uses of asymmetric encryption is to encrypt a symmetric encryption key. Alice creates the two keys required for asymmetric encryption and publishes one of them to the world. Now everyone in the world, including Bob, has access to this key (Alice's public key). This means Bob, or anyone else in the world, can encrypt data and send it to Alice for only Alice to read. Remember, the only person that can decrypt the cipher text is Alice, or the person with Alice's private key. Now the problem of sharing a symmetric key is easy.

1. Bob creates a symmetric key.
2. He uses Alice's public key to encrypt the symmetric key so no one else can read it.
3. He sends the encrypted symmetric key to Alice.
4. Alice receives the encrypted symmetric key, decrypts it with her private key, and begins communicating with Bob using the symmetric key he created.

But why would you use the symmetric key encryption algorithms at all? If asymmetric algorithms are secure and you already have everyone's public key, why bother with creating a symmetric key and using symmetric algorithms? The answer to that question is simple—for speed. Using **RSA** (a standard asymmetric encryption algorithm developed by Ron Rivest, Adi Shamir, and Len Adleman), assume that your computer can encrypt 35,633 1024-bit messages in 10 seconds. Using AES, the standard for symmetric encryption in CBC mode, on the same computer you can encrypt 69,893 1024-bit messages in only 3 seconds. Using symmetric encryption is more than 6.5 times faster than using asymmetric encryption. Assuming both algorithms are secure, why would you use one that is 6.5 times slower than the other? Asymmetric encryption is slow because it uses properties of number theory to derive its strength. The addition and multiplication of these very large (1024-bit) numbers takes a very long time on computers compared to the binary operations performed in symmetric key encryption.

Even though asymmetric encryption is very slow, it does a very good job of solving the problem of sharing keys. Most symmetric algorithms have a key size somewhere around 128 to 256 bits. These keys can be encrypted in a single asymmetric message block, for most algorithms. This means only one message (the encrypted symmetric key) needs to be sent from Alice to Bob using an asymmetric algorithm before they can communicate using a symmetric algorithm.

3.3.2 Digital Signatures

A **digital signature** encrypts a message with a private key so that anyone can read it, but verify that it came from the holder of the private key because only the person who holds the private key can create cipher text that can be decrypted using the public key.

Using asymmetric encryption is really, really slow. Does this mean digital signatures are really slow as well? If the digital signature implementation encrypted the entire file, it would be slow. To alleviate this problem, the message is represented as a smaller message which is signed by Alice and sent along with the unencrypted original message. This smaller message is so small that it takes only a tiny amount of time to sign. Now anyone can read Alice's message and can also verify that it truly came from her and no one else. You go about making this smaller message that represents the larger one with a hash function. We'll discuss hash functions next.

Figure 3-7

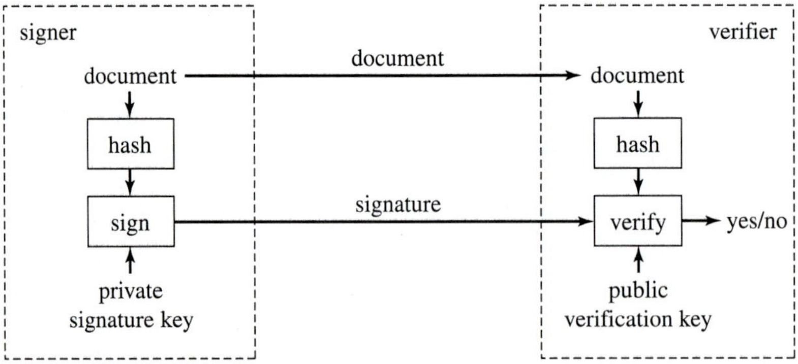

Digital signature of a hash.

FOR EXAMPLE

Using Digital Signatures

You are on the team that is drafting the company's security policy. The policy must describe accepted practices regarding downloading code from the Internet. You know that one option you can select is to enable, disable, or prompt the user before downloading unsigned ActiveX controls. You know that a digitally signed ActiveX control provides you the assurance that the party that signed the control developed the code. You decide to permit users to download signed controls, but prevent them from downloading unsigned controls.

3.4 HASHES

The final primitive of cryptography is hash functions. Hash functions are used to provide better performance when signing large blocks of data using asymmetric encryption, to provide integrity, in authentication protocols, and to create pseudorandom data. In this section, we'll discuss how a hash function works and its uses.

3.4.1 Hash Functions

A **hash function** takes a message of any size and computes a smaller, fixed-size message called a **digest** or **hash** (we will use the term *digest* to refer to the product of a hash function). The computation required to compute a digest is very small. For example, remember in the previous example that with AES in a CBC chain, 69,893 1024-bit messages could be encrypted in 3 seconds. In that same 3 seconds (given the same computer performance), **SHA-1,** the standard for hashing, can hash 224,800 1024-bit messages. SHA-1 can compute digests 3.2 times faster than AES can encrypt those messages. Based on the performance of most modern computers, simply reading a file off of the hard disk requires approximately the same amount of time as computing the hash while doing it. One example of a proprietary hash function is **Message-Digest algorithm 5 (MD5).** The way in which these hash functions compute a digest from an arbitrarily large message is beyond the scope of this course; however, there are three properties of all hash functions that make them very valuable.

1. It is computationally infeasible to find two messages that can hash to the same digest.
2. Given a digest, it is computationally infeasible to find a second message that will create the same digest.
3. Given a digest, it is computationally infeasible to find the original message that created this digest.

These properties not only make hash functions very useful in the application of digital signatures but also in storing passwords. Because the original message cannot be discovered from a digest, when storing a password, only the

---

FOR EXAMPLE

Using Hashes with Digital Signatures

You present the security policy on downloading code to the management team at your company. One of the managers expresses concern that an ActiveX control might be signed and later modified by an attacker in such a way that it does something malicious. You explain that the implementation of code signing creates a hash of the program and signs that. You demonstrate how a change to the code will cause it to hash to a different value. Therefore, signed code guarantees integrity as well as authentication.

---

digest needs to be stored. This way, anyone can read the file containing the passwords, but no one can use this information to figure out someone's passwords.

One issue to consider with hash functions is its resilience to **hash collisions.** A hash collision is the probability that the same hash will be generated from different data. There are two algorithms that attempt to deal with the problem: **Universal One Way Hash Function (UOWHF)** and **Collision Resistant Hash Function (CRHF).** Of the two, CRHF is considered to be more secure.

3.4.2 Using Hash Functions to Ensure Integrity

A message always hashes to the same digest no matter how many times you compute it. The only way to change what digest is created is by changing the message. This property provides the proof of message integrity. If Mallory changes a message while it's in transit, the message's digest will be changed as well. To protect message integrity, Alice must only compute her message's digest, and send the digest encrypted with Bob's public key to Bob along with the message. When Bob receives the message he can compute the digest the same way Alice did, and verify that the message has not been altered in any way.

3.4.3 A Vulnerability When Protecting Passwords

Going back to password storage with a hash function, users do not like passwords and have trouble remembering good ones, such as xSok32$lK329@)O. So instead, they create weak passwords like "fluffy", their cat's name. Mallory, who is looking to attack this type of password scheme, can compute the digest of all the words in a dictionary and compare those digests to the one stored in the password file. If one of the digests from the dictionary matches one in the password file, Mallory has discovered the password.

However, one simple way of preventing this is to randomly salt the password before it is hashed (see Figure 3-8).

Figure 3-8

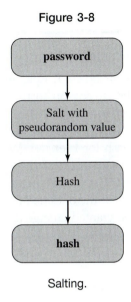

Salting.

Salting is the addition of pseudorandom data to a message before it is hashed so that the aforementioned dictionary attack cannot be carried out. The random data that is added is not too random, though, or no one would be able to verify the password. Instead, the random data is chosen from one of only a few thousand possibilities. This randomly selected piece of data is concatenated to the password and then hashed. To verify the user's password, all combinations of the password and the random piece of data must be computed. If one of them matches, you can verify the password is correct. If none of them match, this password is not correct. This might seem like a lot of work. However, because hashing is a fast computation, computing a few extra thousand digests for a single password is not a big deal. However, computing a few extra thousand digests for all the words in the dictionary makes a brute force attack more difficult to carry out. As computers grow faster, the number of different salting values used is increased.

3.4.4 Creating Pseudorandom Data with Hash Functions

Bringing the discussion of cryptographic primitives full circle, hashing algorithms can be a great source of pseudorandom data. The following is a method for creating pseudorandom data:

1. Seed a hash function with a short random message. The resulting digest will be pseudorandom and the first number generated.

2. Using this number and a combination of the original seed, create a new message. The original seed and the digest must be used together because the digest alone is too small to compute a digest from. Remember, the message is larger than the digest.

FOR EXAMPLE

Using Hashes to Solve a Common Administration Problem

It happens all the time. A user forgets his password or leaves his smart card at home. He needs to be able to log on to the network. What do you do?

RSA®'s Sign-On Manager's IntelliAccess™ uses hashes to solve this problem. IntelliAccess asks the user a number of questions and hashes their answers. It then stores the hash for later use. When the user needs access to the network because he forgot his smart card, PIN, or password, the user can still gain access by answering the questions. Sign-On Manager hashes the user's answers and compares them with the ones he provided previously. If the hashes are the same, the user can be granted emergency access to the network.

3. This new digest is another pseudorandom number. This process is continued for as long as needed.

Like any pseudorandom function, the hashing algorithm will eventually cycle. However, the number of hashes needed to cause the algorithm to cycle is considered computationally infeasible. This same basic method can be used to create a stream cipher. Simply use the key as your seed message. Then use the output of the hash function XORed with the plain text to create the cipher text. This is exactly like a one-time pad, but using a hash function as the random number generator.

3.4.5 Keyed Hash Functions

While most hash functions do not require any sort of key to create their digests, there are hash functions designed to require keys. The idea behind these functions is that they hold all of the same principles as a regular hash function and that they have the additional property of the digest not able to be created without the proper key. Being able to create a message key combination that hashes to the same digest should be computationally equivalent to enumerating through all the keys. Any regular hash function can be turned into a keyed hash function and vice versa. However, it is important to know that such functions exist.

SELF-CHECK

1. Describe the reason password digests are salted.

3.5 Achieving CIA

As a review, let's look at how the four cryptographic primitives can be used to achieve CIA. We'll consider four scenarios in which Alice is sending a message to Bob. She requires confidentiality in the first scenario, message integrity in the second, message authentication in the third, and all three in the fourth scenario. For all four scenarios, assume that Alice and Bob have traded public keys and that they trust these public keys. It is important to note that while these scenarios demonstrate the ability to ensure these properties, they are not the only way to ensure them.

3.5.1 Confidentiality

Alice wants to send a message to Bob without anyone else being able to read it. This can be accomplished using symmetric encryption and asymmetric encryption. To do so,

1. Alice creates a symmetric key and encrypts it using Bob's public key.
2. Alice sends the encrypted symmetric key to Bob.
3. Alice encrypts her message using the symmetric key and a symmetric key algorithm, and sends the message to Bob.
4. Bob, and only Bob, is able to read the message because he has the symmetric key that was sent encrypted with his public key. Confidentiality is ensured.

3.5.2 Integrity

Alice wants to send a message to Bob and ensure the message is not changed during transmission. To accomplish this, she can use a hash function and asymmetric encryption, as follows:

1. Alice hashes her message and encrypts the resulting digest with Bob's public key.
2. Alice sends the message and the encrypted digest to Bob.
3. Bob is able to verify that the message has not been altered because he too can compute the message's digest and verify it with the digest sent with the message.

Mallory cannot change the message because the computed digest would not match the sent one. Mallory cannot change the sent digest because it is encrypted with Bob's public key. Integrity is ensured.

3.5.3 Authentication

Alice wants to send a message to Bob and prove to Bob that she was the sender. She can accomplish this using only a hash function, as follows:

1. Alice hashes her message and digitally signs the digest using her private key.
2. She sends the message and the signed digest to Bob.
3. Bob can verify the signature because he has Alice's public key. He can also verify that the digest belongs to that message because he can compute the digest. The only person that could create such a signed digest is Alice because only Alice has her private key. Authentication is ensured.

3.5.4 CIA

Alice wants to send a message to Bob and in the process make sure that no one else can read the message, ensure that the message does not change, and prove to Bob that she was the sender of this message. To do this,

1. Alice creates a symmetric key and encrypts the key with Bob's public key.
2. Alice sends the encrypted symmetric key to Bob.
3. Alice computes a digest of the message and digitally signs it.
4. Alice encrypts her message and the message's signed digest using the symmetric key and sends the entire thing to Bob.
5. Bob is able to receive the symmetric key from Alice because only he has the private key to decrypt the encryption.
6. Bob, and only Bob, can decrypt the symmetrically encrypted message and signed digest because he has the symmetric key (confidentiality).
7. He is able to verify that the message has not been altered because he can compute the digest (integrity).
8. Bob is also able to prove to himself that Alice was the sender because only she can sign the digest so that it is verified with her public key (authentication).

While the last protocol seems a bit extreme, it ensures confidentiality, integrity, and authentication. This is part of the reason why speed is so important in cryptography. Sometimes, even to send the shortest message, multiple encryptions, hashing, signing, verifying, and decryption must be performed. This is why the fastest algorithm should be used when appropriate. Multiple protocols will ensure any combination of the three CIA properties. Each protocol has its advantages and disadvantages. The protocol used to complete a task is sometimes more important than the primitive used. Always make sure standards are followed when implementing any primitive or protocol.

FOR EXAMPLE

Understanding Pretty Good Privacy

Pretty Good Privacy (PGP) encryption is a freeware encryption program developed by Phil Zimmermann in 1991. It uses symmetric keys, asymmetric keys, and hashes to provide CIA. Users obtain a private key and public key pair. The public key can be distributed to third parties. To ensure confidentiality, PGP uses the following strategy:

1. The sender encrypts a message using a shared key.
2. The sender encrypts the shared key using the recipient's public key.
3. The recipient decrypts the shared key using his private key.
4. The recipient decrypts the message using the shared key.

PGP uses the following strategy to ensure authentication and integrity:

1. The sender creates a digest of the message.
2. The sender creates a digital signature of the digest using his private key.
3. The recipient creates a digest of the message and uses the signature algorithm with the sender's public key to determine whether the digests match.

SELF-CHECK

1. Describe the most optimal way to provide integrity.
2. Describe how you can securely exchange symmetric keys.

3.6 Public Key Infrastructure (PKI)

Now that you understand the key elements of cryptography and why they are important, let's turn our attention to digital certificates and how they can be securely distributed. We'll first define digital certificates and then examine how to design a secure public key infrastructure (PKI) using Microsoft®'s Certificate Services. Finally, we'll overview some certificate management functions.

3.6.1 Digital Certificates

X.509 certificates, also known as **digital certificates** or just **certificates**, are electronic documents that contain information about the owner of the certificate, the public key of the owner, and the signature of the validator of the information in the certificate (the validator is called a **certificate** or **certificate authority**,

Figure 3-9

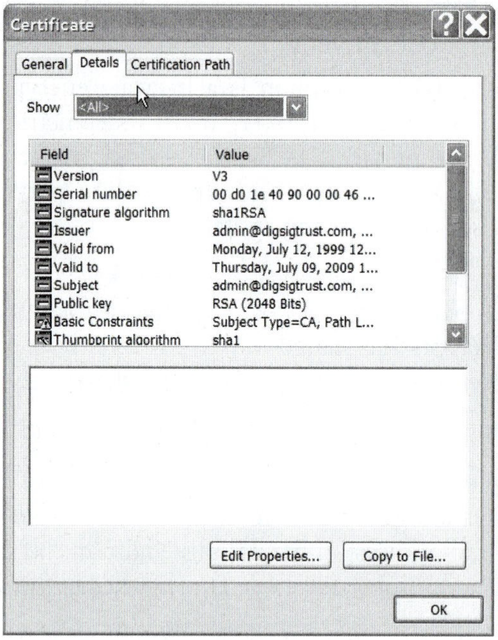

X.509 certificate details.

or **CA**). The X.509 certificate contains a number of fields, including those shown in Figure 3-9, along with their values.

There are different types of certificates for different applications. These applications will use certificates for everything from encrypting email and securing web communications to encrypting files. Windows Server 2003 provides templates for generating certificates for various applications; these templates are called **certificate templates.** They provide the fields necessary for the application that uses the certificate.

The main function of a certificate is to link a public key to the information about a user or computer contained in the certificate. Of course, you cannot trust the information in the certificate because it could have been forged or manipulated in transit. For instance, anyone can create a certificate and say that he or she is from Microsoft or from any other company. The strength of certificates comes from a trusted third party certifying that the certificate information is valid and that the document has not been altered in transit. The creation, verification, and revocation of certificates require an infrastructure to help manage the processes.

3.6.2 Public Key Infrastructure

A **public key infrastructure (PKI)** is the technology, software, and services that allow an organization or organizations to securely exchange information and validate the identity of users, computers, and services. This infrastructure is made up of a variety of services and components, as the following list illustrates:

▲ Digital certificates
▲ Certificate Authority
▲ Certificate revocation list (CRL)
▲ Technology to distribute certificates and certificate revocation lists
▲ Tools to manage the PKI
▲ Software that uses PKI [web browsers, web servers, EFS, Routing and Remote Access Service (RRAS), virtual private network (VPN), Internet Authentication Service (IAS) for authentication, Active Directory, etc.]
▲ Certificate templates

Certificate Authority

At the heart of the PKI is the certificate authority (CA), which verifies the information in the certificate and then digitally signs the certificate with its public key. A CA can be a public third-party CA like Verisign®, Thawte™, or RSA, or you can set up a private CA in your own organization. By signing the certificate, the CA is essentially making a statement that the person sending the certificate is who they say they are based on the proof of identity that the CA required. PKI-enabled applications must be set up to trust the CA, which means that you trust the certificate. There's more on choosing between a public or private CA a little later in this chapter.

A CA needs to perform the following roles:

▲ Maintain a root certificate to distribute its public key.
▲ Identify the certificate requestor and validate its identity. This can vary from simply verifying that the domain is correct to doing a background check and having someone physically verify the identity of the requestor.
▲ Issue certificates to requestors.
▲ Maintain a database of registered users (certificates issued).
▲ Generate and maintain a CRL.

Requesting Certificates

A certificate is created through a separate tool or a tool contained in a PKI-enabled application. The **certificate request** contains the public key of the requestor and the proper fields for the type of certificate requested. The certificate request is then submitted to the CA (through a website, email, or other means), which verifies the information, signs the certificate if the information checks out, and returns the certificate to the requestor. Verification can come in many forms, from confirming that the requestor owns the DNS domain for his or her web application to requiring the requestor to meet in person with a representative and provide two or three forms of identification like a driver's license, Social Security card, or passport. The amount of verification depends on the type and use of the certificate. The requestor then installs the certificate into his or her application to provide identity validation and encryption.

Of course, a certificate can't vouch for the character of the person or company, but at least you know they are who they say they are. If someone tries to alter the certificate, you will be alerted by the PKI-enabled application (like a web browser) that participates in the PKI process because the hash in the signature will not match the one in the certificate.

Configuring Trust

You can view and configure certificates in PKI-enabled applications. The client-side certificates used by Internet Explorer and Outlook® Express can be managed through Internet Explorer on Windows XP. To view a certificate,

1. Start Internet Explorer.
2. Choose Tools and then Internet Options to open the Internet Options dialog box.
3. Click the Content tab, shown in Figure 3-10.

Figure 3-10

The Content tab of the Internet Options dialog box.

Figure 3-11

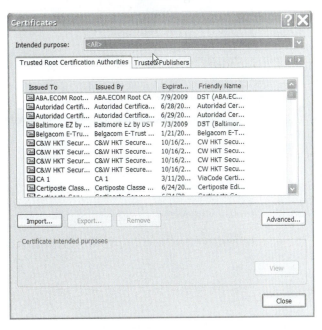

The Trusted Root Certification Authorities tab of the
Certificates dialog box.

4. Click the Certificates button to open the Certificates dialog box.

5. Click the Trusted Root Certification Authorities tab, shown in Figure 3-11. Here, you will see all the certificates that are trusted. Well-known public CAs are listed by default. You can add a trusted CA by clicking Import and selecting the CA's certificate.

6. Double-click any one of the certificates listed in the list box to open the Certificate dialog box, shown in Figure 3-12.

7. Click the Details tab to view the fields that are contained in the certificate (refer back to Figure 3-9).

3.6.3 Designing a CA Hierarchy

When determining how certificates will be used on your company's network, you need to analyze business requirements and make a number of decisions. In this section, we will give you an overview of what you need to consider when designing a certificates strategy.

Determining Certificate Requirements

Applications that use PKI will require a number of types of certificates to be installed. You will need to decide which applications will require certificates and

Figure 3-12

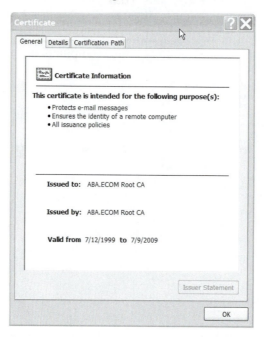

The General tab of the Certificate dialog box.

what types of certificates those applications will require. Table 3-2 lists some technologies that rely on certificates and the ways applications might use certificates.

Choosing Public or Private CAs

After you have determined what applications you need to secure, you will need to decide whether to implement a private CA or use a commercial CA (public CA). There are different reasons you might choose one or the other. You would set up a private CA if you have the need to control and administer your own certificates. You would also do so if you needed to deploy many certificates, because doing so with a commercial CA would be costly.

The disadvantage to implementing a private CA is that it will likely require additional staff and servers to install and manage. You would have to also consider the methods for deploying the certificates. You also need to consider that users who are not employees of your company might not trust a privately implemented CA.

A commercial authority is widely trusted, so clients will not have to complicate things by installing a certificate for your CA. You would use a commercial CA if you need to have a certificate trusted outside your organization. For example, suppose your company has built an application that will be used over the web. Part of the application will require that private or sensitive information

Table 3-2: Common Technologies That Rely on Certificates

Technology	Applications
Client authentication	Validating computers or clients on the network
Digital signatures	Signing a document to verify that it came from the appropriate user
Document encryption	Securing files on the file system of a computer. Microsoft's implementation of file encryption is EFS.
IP security (IPsec)	Securing remote access to a network over a public network through encryption and authentication of machines
Secure email (**Secure/ Multipurpose Internet Mail Extensions,** or **S/MIME)**	Encrypting and signing email messages
Secure Sockets Layer (SSL) and Transport Layer Security (TLS)	Encrypting traffic to and from a website; verifying the identity of the website
Server authentication	Verifying the identity of a server
Smart card logon	Providing authentication with smart card technology. A **smart card** is a special card that contains a digital certificate.
Software code signing	Verifying the source of the code and ensuring the code has not been altered since it was released

be sent over the Internet. You would obtain a certificate from a commercial CA to implement SSL on your website because the commercial CA's certificate will be listed as a Trusted Root CA in the client's browser. The drawback is that you cannot administer your own certificates.

Designing the Roles of Certificate Authorities

When you establish a PKI in your own organization, you will need to choose the roles of the CA servers that you install. You have a choice of three different server roles:

1. **Root CA role:** The first CA you install in your organization is the **root CA.** The root CA server is the ultimate CA in the organization. It is

responsible for signing all other **subordinate CA** certificates. The root CA is the only server role that trusts itself by signing its own certificate and issuing this root certificate to itself, a process known as **self-signing**. The role of the root CA is to authorize other CAs in the organization. Therefore, if your clients trust the root CA, then they trust the certificates issued by the root's subordinate CAs. The root CA is very important and it would be detrimental to network security if it was stolen or compromised, so it is recommended that it be kept offline.

2. **Intermediate CA role:** The root CA can certify the subordinate CAs to accept, approve, and issue certificates on its behalf. The **intermediate CA** can be used to certify requests for certificates. This will reduce the number of times that the root CA's private key is exposed. The intermediate CA is also known as a **policy CA**.

3. **Issuing CA role:** After the intermediate CA, you would install an issuing CA to enroll, deploy, and renew the certificates. The **issuing CA** is the CA that will communicate with the client applications and computers. The issuing CA is the server that needs to be available all of the time for proper CA functionality.

You will want to design for multiple CAs in your organization to provide availability and secure publishing points in your organization. You should not go more than three levels deep with your CA design, and two levels will be adequate for most organizations. With a two-level CA, the same server acts as an intermediate CA and an issuing CA, as shown in Figure 3-13.

A three-tier hierarchy (shown in Figure 3-14) is more secure because it provides an extra layer of isolation between the root CA and the issuing CAs.

Figure 3-13

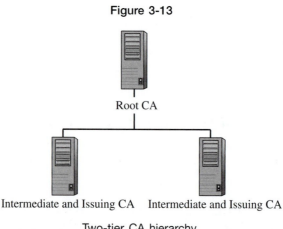

Root CA

Intermediate and Issuing CA   Intermediate and Issuing CA

Two-tier CA hierarchy.

Figure 3-14

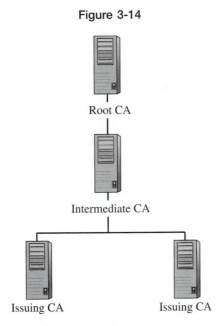

Three-tier CA hierarchy.

You build a **chain of trust,** or a **certificate path,** when issuing certificates. The certificate that a user or a computer receives can be trusted because the issuing CA received its certificate from another CA or directly from the root CA. Because the root CA issues the certificates used by subordinate CAs, as long as you trust the root CA and it is kept secure, you can verify the identity of the certificate. If the root CA is compromised, then all certificates issued by the root CA or any subordinate can be considered invalid because someone can forge them. You should keep the root CA secure.

3.6.4 Security Policy and PKI Implementation

When designing a CA hierarchy, you might find that legal requirements determine the type of hierarchy you choose. Certain industries have requirements about how long documents must be kept, therefore, encryption keys cannot be changed or recycled during that period. Countries have different legal requirements for encryption and you need to make sure issued certificates do not violate these laws. You need to create three documents to help determine the appropriate hierarchy for your organization: the security policy, the certificate policy, and the certification practice statement.

The Security Policy

The security policy is a document that defines the security practices that are used in the organization. The security policy defines the security concerns of the organization, what it needs to protect, and what resources the organization wants to dedicate to security. The security policy should include information about the PKI in use in the organization. You use this information to document procedures and practices with regard to CAs, their certificates, the level of trust that each certificate should have, and the legal liabilities if the different certificates are compromised.

The Certificate Policy

The **certificate policy** defines how a certificate subject (user or computer) is verified before it is assigned a certificate, where the private keys will be stored (separate hardware device or a computer hard drive), the process for responding to lost keys, the enrollment and renewal process, the maximum monetary or intrinsic value that can be protected by this certificate, the types of actions that can be performed with the certificate, and any additional requirements surrounding a certificate that is issued in your organization.

The Certification Practice Statement (CPS)

The **Certification Practice Statement (CPS)** is a document that specifically defines how to implement the certificate policy on the organization's CA hierarchy. It defines the users, computers, and applications that will require certificates. You also can include authentication and identification methods for enrollment and renewal, the obligations and liabilities of the organization with regard to the CA hierarchy, the audit policy for ensuring that the CPS is followed, operational requirements for the CAs in the organization, the types and versions of certificates that will be issued, and the procedures for securing CAs in the organization. The CPS essentially defines the management of the CAs used in the organization, while the certificate policy defines the procedures for managing certificates. On a Windows server, the CPS can be published to the policy CAs through the use of a **CAPolicy.inf file.** The CPS will then be published to all subordinate CAs.

3.6.5 Trusting Certificates from Other Organizations

There are situations in which you need to trust users in other organizations. You could issue certificates from your own CA servers to users in the other organization. If you need maximum control over who gets a certificate or you don't trust the security policies of the other companies, you would issue and revoke certificates from your own CAs. The other organization could be integrated into your CA hierarchy. The drawback to this is that you will need to manage the certificates for the other organization. This means that you need to decide on a method to securely distribute certificates to the other organization. You will also need to revoke certificates for people that leave the other organization or certificates that are lost on a smart card or computer. You will need to have processes in place to manage changes in the organization that will impact the CA hierarchy.

Many organizations will not be ready to take on that much coordination and overhead, which will constitute greater cost. There is an alternative to having to manage the certificates for the other organization: Have the other organization manage their own certificates and trust the certificates that they issue. You can establish **cross-certification** to trust the certificates that are issued in the other organization. Cross-certification will allow two organizations to trust each other and rely on each other's certificates and keys as if they were issued from their own certificate authorities. The two CAs would exchange cross-certificates to enable users in each organization to interact securely with each other.

FOR EXAMPLE

Establishing a Cross-certificate Trust

Jenny is in charge of security at VanderDoes and Fenton, a large law firm in Philadelphia. The law firm takes security very seriously and has a PKI for two-factor authentication and wireless authentication of clients. The law firm is aggressively growing, which means it is merging with other law firms to increase its size and caseload.

VanderDoes and Fenton recently acquired a medium-sized law firm. This law firm has its own PKI in place to support its applications and two-factor authentication.

In addition to the acquisition, VanderDoes and Fenton just purchased a new application that allows its clients to view the progress of a case from a website. The lawyers from both firms are pushing for access to each other's systems and the clients want access to the website, but they want assurances that their transactions will be secure.

Because VanderDoes and Fenton has an existing PKI, Jenny decides that, rather than reissue all the lawyers' and personnel certificates from their CAs, it would be faster to set up a cross-certification so that each PKI trusts the root from the other organization. This means that users will be able to gain access to the information in each domain with the minimal amount of work for Jenny and her staff. She also decides to lease a certificate from a commercial CA to provide SSL to the web application. She decides to require 128-bit encryption to maintain security over the Internet to the application. She authenticates the clients through the web server with basic authentication over SSL.

3.6.6 Creating an Enrollment and Distribution Strategy

You eventually will need to decide how to issue certificates to the users, computers, and services that participate in the PKI. The process of requesting and installing the certificates for the user, computers, or services is called the **enrollment strategy.** There are many types of enrollment methods that you can use, depending on the type of CAs, the client computer operating system, the issuing policy requirements, and where the CAs are located in relation to the clients.

The enrollment strategy you use depends on three factors:

1. **The client's operating system:** The underlying operating systems for the participating clients will affect the means you can use to enroll and renew a certificate. For example, non-Windows operating systems will need to use the web page for enrollment, because autoenrollment by a CA running Microsoft's Certificate Services is supported by only Windows XP and Windows Server 2003.

2. **The type of CA you will be running:** Certificate Services supports two types of CAs: a stand-alone CA and an enterprise CA. The **enterprise CA** is integrated with **Active Directory** (the directory system used by Windows 2000 and Windows Server 2003), and supports autoenrollment for certificates and the use of **Group Policy** (Active Directory's centralized management technology for user and computer configuration settings) and certificate templates to control the request and deployment of certificates. A **stand-alone CA** will only support web-based enrollment or command-line enrollment. A root CA should always be installed as a stand-alone CA because an enterprise CA cannot be taken offline. If you are running different CA software, your enrollment options will be limited to those supported by that software.

3. **The types of user, service, or computer accounts that will receive the certificates:** You need to determine if the accounts or computers are connected to Active Directory. Also, are the accounts contained in your organization or external to your organization?

3.6.7 Renewing Certificates

Certificates are issued for a finite lifetime, which means that they will expire. The lifetime of the certificate will depend on the type of certificate and the policy that the CA has set for the certificates. Certificates will need to be renewed when the lifetime ends. When you renew a certificate, you can choose to keep the same public/private key or generate a new key pair. The longer a key is active, the more vulnerable it is to being compromised. You can reduce the risk of key compromise by renewing the public/private key combination each time you renew a certificate instead of at the maximum lifetime of the key pair. At the least, you should never renew the certificate past the lifetime of the key pair. You can also increase the length of the key when you renew a certificate. This means you can use the renewal process to strengthen the key if you determine that it no longer meets your security policy. It is recommended that the key length be somewhere between 1024 and 4096 bits.

CAs also have certificates that are issued from their parent CA or, in the case of the root CA, to itself. When these certificates expire, the CA can no longer issue certificates and all certificates that the CA issued will expire. You should remember that when a CA's certificate expires, all subordinate CAs' certificates expire. When you renew a CA's certificate, all subordinate CAs' certificates will need to be renewed. You will need to come up with a strategy to renew the CA certificates or any certificate before they expire. When renewing CA certificates, you should always generate a new key pair.

The following questions need to be answered before you can determine a renewal strategy for your certificates:

▲ Which certificates are you allowed to renew?
▲ How often can a certificate be renewed before its key is retired?

You can justify longer lifetimes for certificates if they are infrequently used and have strong keys, because a potential cracker won't have many opportunities to capture them. If the certificate is captured it will be nearly impossible to crack the strong key. You can continue to renew the signature for the certificate up to the issuing CA certificate's lifetime. On the other hand, if the certificate has a weaker key or is used more frequently, you will want a shorter lifetime. You should renew these certificates more frequently but never beyond the lifetime of the CA certificate.

3.6.8 Revoking a Certificate

Sometimes you might have a problem with a certificate—for example, the private key might be compromised or an employee might quit and you no longer want the certificate to be valid. You can invalidate a certificate on the CA and then publish the **CRL (certificate revocation list)** to the root CA and subordinate CAs. This will allow clients to download the revocation list and verify that the certificate is still valid if it is not on the list. There are many situations that can cause you to revoke a certificate, but the following is a list of possible reasons:

▲ The CA has been compromised.
▲ The private key has been compromised.
▲ A new certificate that replaces the previous certificate has been issued. Perhaps you have a need to update information in the certificate.
▲ You have decommissioned or replaced the CA.

FOR EXAMPLE

Designing a CA Implementation

You are designing a CA strategy for your company. The company needs to use a certificate to secure communication on its public web server using SSL. It also needs to issue certificates for EFS encryption and email encryption internally. The company has 500 employees. About half the employees telecommute from various locations around the world.

You recommend that the company install a root CA and two issuing/intermediate CAs for fault tolerance. These CAs will issue EFS certificates and S/MIME certificates. You recommend that the root CA be installed as a stand-alone CA and taken offline. You recommend web-based certificate enrollment to support the telecommuters and allow all users to enroll through a standard mechanism. You publish the CRL to a web site so that it is accessible by the telecommuters.

You recommend that the company purchase the SSL certificate because it needs to be verified by users who are not employees and will not trust the company's CA.

You can configure clients to check the CRL before they accept a certificate. The client can then be configured to either reject the connection or just show a warning box that will state that the certificate has been revoked and ask if the user would like to proceed.

The certificate will include the location of the CRL. If you are running Microsoft Certificate Services, you can publish the revocation list to either the Active Directory or a website. You will need to revoke the certificate(s) before publishing the CRL. The location will be stored in the certificate.

Applications must be configured to check the CRL at the publishing point chosen, so this means that the application will need to support the chosen publication point.

SELF-CHECK

1. Describe the chain of trust.
2. Compare a Certification Practice Statement (CPS) and a certificate policy.

SUMMARY

In this chapter you learned the fundamentals of cryptography and PKI. You learned a little about early cryptographic efforts and their vulnerabilities. Next you learned about the four primitives of cryptography: random numbers, symmetric encryption, asymmetric encryption, and hashes. Finally, you learned about PKI and the things you need to consider when designing a CA implementation.

KEY TERMS

Active Directory

Advanced Encryption Standard (AES)

Algorithm

Asymmetric encryption

Authentication

Block cipher

Blum-Blum-Shub pseudorandom generator

Brute force methods

CAPolicy.inf file

Certificate

Certificate Authority (CA)

Certificate path

Certificate policy

Certificate Practice Statement (CPS)

Certificate request

Certificate Revocation List (CRL)

Certificate template

Chain of trust

CIA

Cipher block chaining (CBC)

Cipher feedback (CFB)

Cipher text

Computationally secure

Confidentiality

Cross-certification

CRHF

Cryptanalysis

Cryptanalyst

Cryptographic primitives

Cryptography

Data Encryption Standard (DES)

Depth

Diffie-Hellman key exchange

Digest

Digital certificate

Digital signature

Discrete logarithm problem

Electronic Code Book (ECB)

Encrypting File System (EFS)

Enigma

Enrollment strategy

Enterprise CA

Frequency analysis

Group Policy

Hash

Hash collisions

Hash function

Integrity

Intermediate CA

Issuing CA

Kerberos

Key

Key agreement protocol

Message Digest-5 (MD5)

National Institute of Standards and Technology (NIST)

National Security Agency (NSA)

One-time pad

Output feedback (OFB)

Padding

Plain text

Policy CA

Polyalphabetic substitution

Pre-shared secret

Private key

Propagating cipher-block chaining (PCBC)

Pseudorandom numbers

Public key

Public key infrastructure (PKI)

Purple

Rijndael

Root CA

RSA

RSA pseudorandom generator

S/MIME

Salting

Self-signing

SHA-1

Shift

Single-key encryption

Smart card

Stand-alone CA

Stream cipher

Subordinate CA

Substitution cipher

Symmetric encryption

Triple DES (3DES)

UOWHF

Vigenere cipher

X.509 certificate

XOR function

ASSESS YOUR UNDERSTANDING

Go to www.wiley.com/college/cole to evaluate your knowledge of cryptography and public key infrastructure (PKI).
Measure your learning by comparing pre-test and post-test results.

Summary Questions

1. The only way to crack a substitution cipher is with frequency analysis. True or false?

2. What are the cryptography primitives?
   (a) Confidentiality, integrity, authentication
   (b) Random number generation, symmetric encryption, asymmetric encryption, hash functions
   (c) Key strength, depth, predictability
   (d) Confidentiality, integrity, availability

3. Which of the following is a symmetric encryption algorithm that can use key sizes of 128, 192, or 256 bits?
   (a) AES
   (b) DES
   (c) 3DES
   (d) RSA

4. A stream cipher requires padding. True or false?

5. A stream cipher provides integrity. True of false?

6. To use the Diffie-Hellman key exchange, both parties agree to use the same prime and base. True or false?

7. What is the primary drawback of asymmetric encryption?
   (a) It is easier to crack than symmetric encryption.
   (b) It does not offer authentication.
   (c) It does not offer confidentiality.
   (d) It is slower than symmetric encryption.

8. Which of the following is a hashing algorithm?
   (a) AES
   (b) DES
   (c) SHA-1
   (d) PGP

9. Which CA has a self-signed certificate?
   (a) Intermediate CA
   (b) Issuing CA

(c) Policy CA

(d) Root CA

10. Which policy defines the process for responding to a user losing a private key?

   (a) Certificate policy

   (b) Certification Practice Statement

   (c) Security policy

11. A cross-certification must be established before a computer will trust a well-known CA. True or false?

12. An enterprise CA can be taken offline. True or false?

13. When a CA's certificate expires, all certificates issued by that CA expire. True or false?

14. At most, you will need to try how many combinations to crack a substitution cipher?

Applying This Chapter

1. You are designing a cryptography and public key strategy for Busicorp. The company has identified some files it considers confidential and others that require integrity. Some users send email that must be authenticated. In addition, the company has a website that customers use to view product information and place orders.

   (a) Why is it preferable to use longer keys when encrypting data?

   (b) Why should you use symmetric encryption to encrypt data instead of asymmetric encryption?

   (c) How can you ensure that emails can be authenticated?

   (d) How can you ensure that the contents of emails are not changed during transit?

   (e) Which requirement should be met by purchasing a certificate from a well-known third-party CA?

   (f) Describe the advantages and disadvantages of a three-tier hierarchy.

   (g) Assuming you are creating a CA hierarchy using Microsoft Certificate Services, how will you configure the root CA?

   (h) Where will you define the company's policy for revoking S/MIME certificates?

Cryptology and PKI in Your Environment

1. Have you ever visited a website and received an error message stating that the certificate could not be verified? Think about how you responded. Would you respond differently now? Why or why not?

2. What are some reasons why a certificate might not be verifiable?

2. Windows XP supports driver signing. The digital signature is created from a hash of the driver. You can locate drivers that do not have signatures using a tool named sigverif. What protections does driver signing provide?

5. Have you ever encrypted a file using EFS? Why is symmetric encryption used instead of asymmetric encryption?

4

AUTHENTICATION

Starting Point

Go to www.wiley.com/college/cole to assess your knowledge of authentication.

Determine where you need to concentrate your effort.

What You'll Learn in This Chapter

- ▲ The purpose of authentication
- ▲ Authentication credentials
- ▲ Authentication protocols
- ▲ Password best practices
- ▲ Limiting logons
- ▲ Authentication auditing

After Studying This Chapter, You'll Be Able To

- ▲ Identify security principals that require authentication
- ▲ Describe how user account information is stored
- ▲ Choose appropriate credentials to meet authentication requirements
- ▲ Choose an appropriate authentication protocol to meet authentication requirements
- ▲ Implement password policies
- ▲ Limit user logon by time and workstation
- ▲ Enable auditing for authentication attempts

INTRODUCTION

A key part of securing a network is ensuring that only users who should access the network can access it. There are really two parts to that process:

1. **Authentication:** the process of verifying an identity (for example, a user).
2. **Authorization:** the process of determining the resources the user can access once authenticated.

In this chapter, we'll focus on authentication. We'll look at the points you need to consider when designing an authentication strategy, including who and what must be authenticated, the credentials users will use to prove their identities, which computers will perform the authentication, and the protocols that will be used to send credentials across the network.

4.1 Authentication Overview

You must consider the authentication requirements of your entire organization when designing the authentication infrastructure. This includes services that your company exposes, such as a website or File Transfer Protocol (FTP) server, and applications that contain their own authentication mechanisms. You must even consider the level of remote access that you intend to support. Obviously, a **heterogeneous environment** (a network environment that runs multiple operating systems) can add a level of complexity to your design considerations, but even on a homogenous network, there might be several different authentication methods used. Users might authenticate locally, remotely, or over the Internet. You also need to consider which computers need to be authenticated. Servers need to be authenticated by clients to mitigate the risk of an attacker setting up a server that impersonates a legitimate resource. An authenticated user or computer is known as a **security principal.** In addition, some applications might have specific authentication requirements.

Before we move on to discuss the details of credentials and authentication protocols, let's look at some potential requirements for authentication on a network, starting with the simplest example, logging on interactively to a computer.

4.1.1 Interactive Logon

Most operating systems today support multiple users. This means that a user must log on to the computer. If the computer is not a network member or is a member of a **peer-to-peer network** (a network without centralized security), the user will supply **credentials** (proof that the user is who he or she claims to be), and the credentials will be validated by the computer where the user is logging on.

Credentials for local user accounts on a computer running Windows® 2000, Windows XP, or Windows Server 2003 are stored in the **Security Accounts Manager (SAM) database.** A user's logon credentials are associated with a **security identifier (SID)**, which uniquely identifies the user. The SID determines the security context under which all the applications the user launches run. Users can change the security context for a specific application by using the Run As command and supplying a different set of credentials. This is known as **secondary logon** and is a good way for administrators to ensure that a security context that has a large number of permissions is used only when required.

If the user is logging on to a computer that is a member of a **domain** (a security boundary in a Windows network that uses centralized or directory-based security), the user is authenticated by the **domain controller** (the server that stores the database or directory of user credentials). When centralized security is used, the logon not only provides the security context that will be used for the interactive logon, but also provides the credentials that will be used for accessing resources on the network. This is known as **single sign-on.** Domain controllers on a computer running Windows NT® store the credentials in the SAM. Domain controllers running Windows 2000 Server or Windows Server 2003 store the credentials in the **Active Directory® database** (a hierarchical database of network objects, including users, groups, and computers).

A Linux computer can authenticate users using a number of different methods. User accounts can be created in the /etc/passwd file or the /etc/shadow file. A Linux computer can also take advantage of several different network authentication protocols to allow for centralized authentication. Some versions of Linux include **pluggable authentication modules (PAMs)**, which are interfaces that provide a standard interface for using a variety of authentication protocols.

4.1.2 Peer-to-Peer Network Logon

In a peer-to-peer network, resources can be shared on any peer. When Windows XP is not a domain member, you can share resources using **simple file sharing** (a type of file sharing in which the Guest account is used to access files and the user is not actually authenticated) or **user-based access control** (a method in which a user is authenticated and the user's SID is used to determine resource access permissions). When a user attempts to access a resource on a peer server, a dialog box like the one shown in Figure 4-1 will prompt the user for logon credentials.

4.1.3 Computer Authentication

Some security architectures also require computers to be authenticated on a network. For example, on an Active Directory network, a domain member must be authenticated by the domain controller. Authenticating a computer ensures that

Figure 4-1

Logon dialog box.

the computer is the computer it claims to be, not an imposter. Although computer authentication is used for all domain members, it is especially important for servers because it helps prevent man-in-the-middle attacks.

When a computer is added to an Active Directory domain, it is assigned an SID and a password. The password is changed automatically, behind the scenes, on a schedule, which is set through the *Domain member: Maximum machine account password age* policy via Local Policies | Security Options. Security Options; this can be managed through Local Security Settings (see Figure 4-2) or centrally, through **Group Policy Objects (GPOs).** A GPO is an Active Directory object that is used to centrally manage user and computer configuration settings, including security settings. It is important to keep in mind that computers running Windows 95, Windows 98, Windows Me, and Windows XP Home cannot be added as domain members.

Another example of when you would use computer authentication is when accessing a secure website. The web server must prove its identity to the browser when using Secure Sockets Layer (SSL) or Transport Layer Security (TLS). It does so by providing a certificate as its credential. The browser checks to make sure the certificate authority is trusted, and, if it is, authenticates the web server.

4.1.4 Mutual Authentication

So far we have discussed only one-way authentication. One-way authentication ensures that one party in the conversation (usually the one requesting access) is who it claims to be. However, the other party's identity is still not known, leaving the network open to spoofing attacks or man-in-the-middle attacks. **Mutual**

Figure 4-2

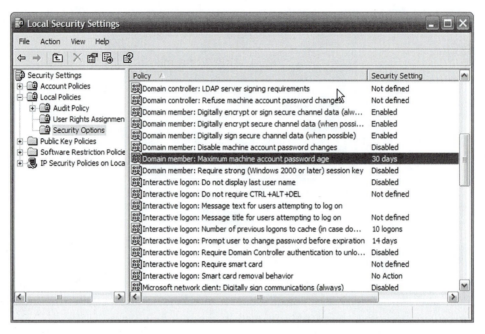

Local security settings.

authentication helps solve this problem by requiring that both parties in the conversation provide authentication credentials.

Let's look at the example of the secure website that uses either SSL or TLS. The example is illustrated in Figure 4-3. Suppose that the website can only be accessed by users who are members of an organization. In this case, you could use a **client certificate** (a digital certificate requested by and issued to a computer that acts as a client in a session) to validate the client computer's membership. Because the server and the client have exchanged certificates and verified that they both trust the respective issuing authorities, the server and client know that they can trust that neither one is an imposter.

Figure 4-3

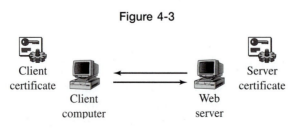

Mutual authentication using SSL or TLS.

4.1.5 Application Authentication

Some applications require users to be authenticated before they can access features of the application. The following are some examples:

▲ Secure websites, such as online banking or a members-only application.

▲ Email servers.

▲ Database servers.

▲ Instant messaging applications.

▲ Online accounting applications.

▲ E-commerce applications.

Applications use a variety of methods to authenticate users. Some use the authentication methods of the operating system on which the application is run. Others might use a public central authentication service, such as **Windows Live™ authentication** (formerly known as **Microsoft® Passport**, or **.NET Passport**). Other applications might use digital certificates to provide authentication. Still others might implement their own authentication by storing credentials in a proprietary database or file.

Sometimes an application needs to access another server, such as a database server. In this case, the application might access that server using its own credentials, or it might **impersonate** the user by passing the user's credentials to the database server.

FOR EXAMPLE

Authentication on Internet Information Services (IIS)

Busicorp would like to provide paid subscribers with access to an online education forum. The forum is a web application running on IIS. The company wants to authenticate users each time they log on. The user accounts will be created and stored in the SAM database on the web server. You need to allow maximum compatibility with different browsers.

The website's authentication methods are currently configured as shown in Figure 4-4.

You determine that you should disable anonymous access because **anonymous access** does not authenticate the user. Instead, it uses the security context of the **IUSR_computername account** to execute the web application. This setting is appropriate for websites with public content.

Your next step is to select one or more authentication methods to use. The authentication methods are described in Table 4-1.

You decide that none of these authentication methods meet your needs and determine that you will need to issue client certificates to

(Continued)

paid subscribers. You purchase an SSL server certificate from a third-party certificate authority. You also install Certificate Services on your web server and provide a link that allows users to request and install client certificates after they have paid. You map the client certificates to user accounts in the SAM database. Users will be authenticated using the client certificates when they log on. The server will be authenticated using the server certificate.

Figure 4-4

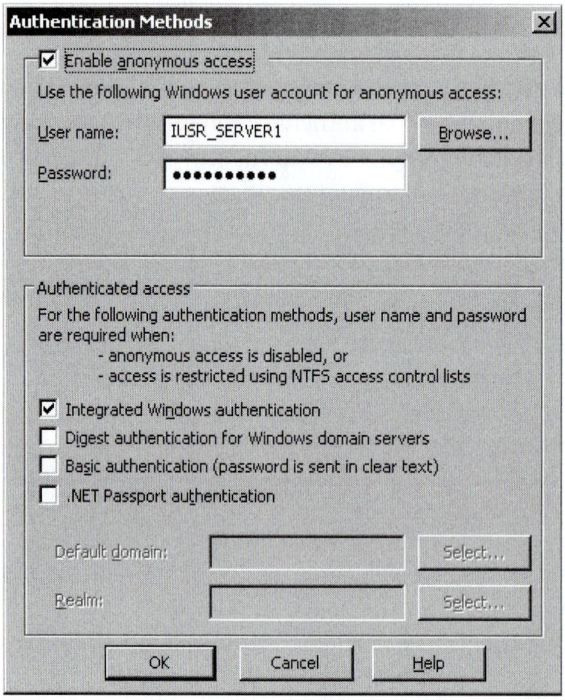

Website authentication methods.

SELF-CHECK

1. Identify the location used to store user credentials on a computer running Windows XP Professional.

2. Describe the purpose of a pluggable authentication module.

3. Identify the type of authentication you can use to help guard against man-in-the-middle attacks.

Table 4-1: IIS Authentication Methods

Authentication Method	Description
Integrated Windows authentication	Authenticates users using either Active Directory or the local account database. Sends credentials as a hash. Requires Internet Explorer.
Digest authentication	Authenticates users using Active Directory. Sends credentials as a hash. Does not require Internet Explorer.
Basic authentication	Authenticates users using either Active Directory or the local account database. Sends credentials as clear text. Works with most browsers.
.NET Passport authentication	Authenticates users using Windows Live.

4.2 Authentication Credentials

The first step in authentication is **identification.** During the identification process, a user or computer supplies credentials that can be used to prove identity. The following are the types of credentials that can be used:

▲ Something you know, such as a personal identification number (PIN) or password; this factor is known as **type 1 authentication.**

▲ Something you have, such as an ATM card, certificate, or smart card; this factor is known as **type 2 authentication.**

▲ Something you are (physically), such as a fingerprint or retina scan; this factor is known as **type 3 authentication.**

Obviously, using more than one factor adds additional credence to the authentication process. For example, **two-factor authentication** refers to using two of the three factors, such as a PIN number (something you know) in conjunction with an ATM card (something you have).

4.2.1 Password Authentication

Passwords are the most common way for users to provide credentials. However, they are also the most vulnerable to attacks, such as social engineering attacks, dictionary attacks, and brute force attacks. A clear written policy on password best practices and an automated policy that requires strong passwords can help mitigate these types of attacks. Some best practices for password-based authentication are provided later in the chapter.

Some authentication systems use a **passphrase** instead of a password. A passphrase is longer than a password and can contain spaces. The passphrase is converted into a virtual password by the system.

Passwords are particularly vulnerable to discovery by network sniffers if they are passed over the network in clear text. The clear text transmission is usually a result of IIS being configured to use basic authentication method when receiving the credentials from the user. Unfortunately, other types of IIS authentication are not supported by most browsers.

If you allow users to log on to your network from outside of the office, you will need to make sure that the credentials being transmitted are encrypted to prevent passwords from being sniffed. You can secure this type of remote access by using SSL to encrypt all of the traffic to your Internet site or by requiring that all access to the network's resources be made through a virtual private network (VPN) connection.

Figure 4-5

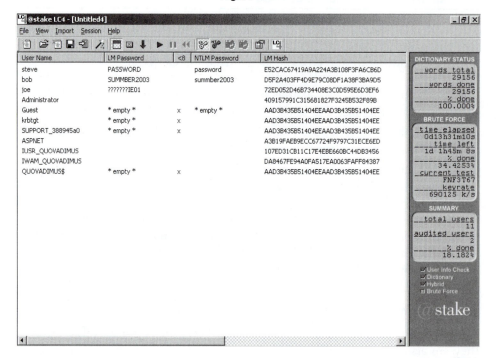

LC4 password recovery.

There are also products that need only the hash of the password in order to break the password. One example of this is **L0phtcrack** (currently called **LC5**), which can sniff the hash on the network and then attack it using dictionary or brute force attacks. To prevent this from happening in your organization you'll want to make sure that the password hashes are not sent across the network. You can see a previous version of LC5 in Figure 4-5 after only a few seconds of processing a typical network password list. Using a utility like LC5, most passwords are broken in the first few minutes. You can minimize its usefulness by not storing passwords on the local machine and by preventing its installation on a machine that has access to your network.

Another potential password vulnerability is that the password could be intercepted by a **keystroke logging program** as the user enters it using the keyboard. There are several **Trojan horse applications** (software that pretends to be a legitimate application, but that is actually performing malicious tasks) or keystroke logging utilities that store and forward passwords to an attacker. You'll need to make sure that you have appropriate policies in place to prevent this type of software from getting installed.

FOR EXAMPLE

Intercepting Passwords Sent in Clear Text

Jim is a traveling salesman for InnaTech banking software and he accesses his email remotely, including from his home, where he has cable modem access. InnaTech has enabled **Outlook Web Access (OWA),** an Internet-facing server that allows access to Microsoft Exchange through HTTP, and has made it available outside the corporate firewall. The IIS web server is configured to use basic authentication through HTTP (port 80) so that Jim and the other salespeople can access their email, calendar, and contacts from anywhere.

Because InnaTech uses both basic authentication and an insecure communications channel, anyone on the network that Jim uses to check his email would be able to sniff his credentials from the network, and the credentials will be in clear text. If Jim uses his home computer, in many cases his neighbors would be able to sniff his network packets traveling to and from his provider. They could also be sniffed from a wireless network at a coffee shop or in an airport.

After a competitor intercepted Jim's password, accessed Jim's email account, and obtained important information about prospective customers, the company changed the OWA server to use SSL. Now the passwords and the email will be sent as encrypted text, making them less likely to be discovered by a competitor.

FOR EXAMPLE

RSA® SecurID® Authenticators

RSA SecurID authenticators use a one-time password, in conjunction with a PIN, to provide two-factor authentication. They are available in a number of different models, including a key fob, credit-card sized device, USB flash drive, and software that can be installed in mobile devices, such as personal digital assistants (PDAs) and smart phones. Some hardware authenticators offer additional features, such as storing digital signatures or storing a username and password.

The RSA SecurID generates a new one-time password every sixty seconds. It is generated using a symmetric key and a pseudorandom number. The user will periodically be required to reenter the current one-time password.

4.2.2 One-Time Passwords

A **one-time password** is a password that can be used only for a short amount of time (generally seconds) or for only a single logon. One-time passwords can be generated using one-way functions that return the next password in a sequence, generated based on the current time, or generated based on a response to a challenge. One-time passwords are normally implemented using a hardware token.

A one-time password generated based on the current time helps to mitigate the risk of man-in-the-middle attacks. However, like any security measure, the risk is not completely eliminated. If the intruder intercepts the password and uses it immediately, the attack will be successful.

4.2.3 Smart Cards

A **smart card** is a card that has a chip in it that securely stores data. This data usually consists of digital certificates and the user's private keys. Smart cards use a two-factor authentication mechanism that requires the user to enter a PIN. Therefore, the certificates and keys are not accessible to someone if they were to steal the smart card without the user's PIN. And knowing the PIN without possessing the smart card will also not allow an attacker to authenticate.

You can require smart card authentication on a Windows 2000 (or later) computer by enabling the *Interactive logon: Require smart card* policy in Security Options. You can also require smart card authentication for a specific user in an Active Directory domain by displaying the Account tab of the user's Properties dialog box and selecting the "Smart card is required for interactive logon" checkbox (see Figure 4-6).

The main drawback to smart card authentication is that each workstation must have a smart card reader. In addition, you need to implement a public key

Figure 4-6

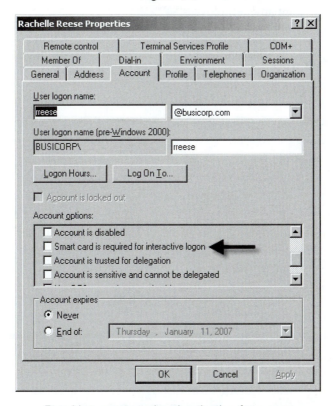

Requiring smart card authentication for a user.

infrastructure (PKI) with a Certificate Authority (CA) that can issue smart card certificates and a certificate enrollment station. You will also need to assign one or more employees the job of verifying credentials and issuing smart cards.

4.2.4 Biometrics

Biometrics is defined as an automated means of identifying or authenticating the identity of a living person based on physiological or behavioral characteristics. Biometrics is a type 3 authentication mechanism because it is based on what a person "is." Biometrics is useful in both identification and authentication modes.

For identification, biometrics is applied as a one-to-many search of an individual's characteristics from a database of stored characteristics of a large population. An example of a one-to-many search is trying to match a suspect's fingerprints to a database of fingerprints of people living in the United States. Conversely, authentication in biometrics is a one-to-one search to verify a claim to an identity made by a person. An example of this mode is matching an employee's fingerprints against the previously registered fingerprints for that employee in a database of the company's employees.

The following are typical biometric characteristics:

▲ Retina scans

▲ Iris scans

▲ Fingerprints

▲ Facial scans

▲ Palm scans

▲ Hand geometry

▲ Voice

▲ Handwritten signature dynamics

Performance measures of a biometric system range from technical characteristics to employees feeling comfortable with their use. The following are examples of performance measures:

▲ **Type I error** or **false rejection rate (FRR):** the percentage of valid subjects that are falsely rejected.

▲ **Type II error** or **false acceptance rate (FAR):** the percentage of invalid subjects that are falsely accepted.

FOR EXAMPLE

Implementing Multifactor Authentication

Your company has a research and development department that performs highly sensitive operations. The company's current network is configured as an Active Directory domain. Users are authenticated using passwords, and a policy is in place to require users to choose strong passwords and change them every 45 days.

Even with all the password procedures in place, a user in the research and development department's password was obtained by a competitor. You suspect the breach occurred as the result of a social engineering attack, but you cannot be sure. Your boss asks you for a recommendation.

You recommend issuing smart cards to the users in the research and development department and changing their user accounts so that they require smart card authentication.

The company implements your suggestion, and there are no more problems with security breaches in the research and development department. The company creates a deployment plan to deploy smart cards to all users within the next three years.

▲ **Crossover error rate (CER):** the percent in which the FRR equals the FAR. The smaller the CER, the better the biometric system.

▲ **Enrollment time:** the time it takes to initially register with a system by providing samples of the biometric characteristic to be evaluated. An acceptable enrollment time is around two minutes.

▲ **Throughput rate:** the rate at which the system processes and identifies or authenticates individuals. Acceptable throughput rates are in the range of 10 subjects per minute.

▲ **Acceptability:** the considerations of privacy, invasiveness, and psychological and physical comfort when using the system. For example, a concern with retina scanning systems might be the exchange of body fluids on the eyepiece. Another concern would be the retinal pattern, which could reveal changes in a person's health, such as the onset of diabetes or high blood pressure.

SELF-CHECK

1. Name the type of credential that provides two-factor authentication.
2. Describe the benefit of one-time passwords.
3. Describe the criteria that are considered when determining the acceptability rating for a biometric authentication.

4.3 Authentication Protocols

The **authentication protocol** defines how the credentials are stored on the authentication server and passed between the client and the server. The authentication protocols supported on your network depend on the operating systems running on the clients and the servers. In this section we'll discuss various authentication protocols. However, our discussion will primarily focus on the authentication protocol that has become a standard, Kerberos.

4.3.1 LAN Manager-Based Protocols

Windows 2000 Server and Windows Server 2003 support both LAN Manager-based protocols and Kerberos. In Windows 2000 and higher, the Security Support Provider Interface (SSPI) will determine which authentication protocol should be used for account validation. The three LAN Manager-based protocols are as follows:

1. LAN Manager
2. Windows NT LAN Manager (NTLM)
3. NTLM version 2 (NTLMv2)

LAN Manager

The **LAN Manager protocol** is used by older Microsoft operating systems such as MS-DOS® and Windows 95. The LAN Manager protocol has a maximum password-length restriction of 14 characters. The one-way function algorithm for LAN Manager passwords is weak and can easily be cracked. Therefore, if your organization does not require LAN Manager, you should remove the LAN Manager password hashes from the account database. You should remove the hashes by enabling the *Network security: Do not store LAN Manager hash value on next password change* policy in Local Security Policy or Group Policy (see Figure 4-7), or simply require that passwords be greater than 14 characters long. LAN Manager authentication protocol is the least secure method supported in Windows 2000 Server and Windows Server 2003 and therefore should be used only if the computers must access resources being served by computers running MS-DOS, Windows 95, or Windows 98 operating systems.

Figure 4-7

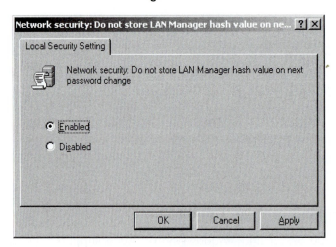

Disabling LAN Manager hashes.

NTLM

The **NTLM protocol** does a better job of storing passwords than LAN Manager, storing them as an MD4 hash. The maximum password length is also 256 characters. NTLM is the default authentication protocol for Windows NT 4.0 domains and for local SAM accounts in Windows 2000 and Windows XP. NTLM hashes are vulnerable to L0phtCrack.

NTLMv2

The **NTLMv2 protocol** is the most secure of the LAN Manager-based protocols in Windows 2000 and Windows XP. This protocol is also available for Windows 95 and newer Microsoft operating systems if the **Active Directory client extensions** are installed. The NTLMv2 protocol can perform mutual authentication. NTLMv2 is the default authentication protocol for Windows Vista™.

Selecting Which LAN Manager Protocols are Supported

You can select how the computers in your environment will use the LAN Manager and NTLM authentication by configuring the LAN Manager compatibility level through the *Network security: LAN Manager authentication level* policy under Computer Configuration\Windows Settings\Security Settings\Local Policies\Security Options\ in Local Security Policy or Group Policy, as shown in Figure 4-8.

The LAN Manager compatibility levels are described in Table 4-2.

There is no way to disable NTLM-based authentication completely in Windows 2000 or Windows XP.

Figure 4-8

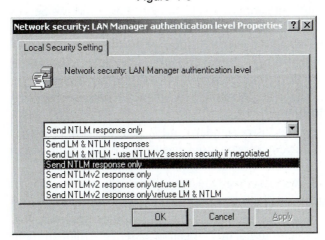

Setting LAN Manager authentication level.

Table 4-2: LAN Manager Compatibility Levels

Level	Clients	Authenticating Servers
0	Use LAN Manager and NTLM only	Accept LAN Manager, NTLM, and NTLMv2
1	Use LAN Manager, NTLM, and NTLMv2	Accept LAN Manager, NTLM, and NTLMv2
2	Use NTLM and NTLMv2	Accept LAN Manager, NTLM, and NTLMv2
3	Use NTLMv2	Accept LAN Manager, NTLM, and NTLMv2
4	Use NTLMv2	Accept NTLM and NTLMv2
5	Use NTLMv2	Accept NTLMv2

4.3.2 Kerberos

Kerberos, named after the three-headed dog that guards the entrance to the underworld in Greek mythology, is an authentication protocol based on symmetric key cryptography. It was developed under Project Athena at the Massachusetts Institute of Technology. It is a trusted, third-party authentication protocol that authenticates clients to other entities on a network and provides a secure means for these clients to access resources on the network.

The Kerberos v5 authentication protocol is the default authentication protocol for computers running Windows 2000 or higher that are in Active Directory domains and authenticating to Windows 2000 or Windows Server 2003 domain controllers. When coupled with strong passwords, the Kerberos v5 protocol is considered the strongest authentication protocol in the Windows arsenal. The Kerberos protocol supports smart cards for multifactor authentication and adheres to RFC 1510. The operation of Kerberos was clarified under RFC 4120, and RFC 1510 is now considered obsolete. A security border in Kerberos is known as a **Kerberos realm.**

Kerberos is an industry standard and is also supported by Unix®-based operating systems, current versions of Novell® NetWare®, and Macintosh® operating systems.

Kerberos allows an Active Directory network to interoperate with Unix-based operating systems by creating a **trust relationship** with a Kerberos realm. A trust relationship is an association that allows computers and users in Domain A to trust computers and users in Domain B based on their authentication by an authentication server in Domain B.

FOR EXAMPLE

Designing Client Authentication

Luke Worrall & Associates is a national accounting firm with over 12,000 employees nationwide. LW&A has offices in Dover, Philadelphia, Miami, Minneapolis, and San Francisco. Each office has its own IT staff that reports to the corporate IT staff located at the corporate headquarters in Dover.

LW&A has upgraded all of its domain controllers to Windows Server 2003. There are several different operating systems that employees use. LW&A is in the process of standardizing on Windows XP Professional. The offices in Dover, Philadelphia, and Minneapolis are all running Windows XP Professional. The office in Miami has mostly Windows XP Professional, but there are still some desktops running Windows 98, Second Edition, and Windows NT 4.0 Workstation. The office in San Francisco was recently acquired from a competing firm and has two Unix servers. The Unix servers run specific software that the employees in the San Francisco office need to access. All other servers in San Francisco are running Windows Server 2003 and all of the workstations are running Windows XP Professional. Each office has its own domain.

Your manager wants to implement NTLMv2 as the least-secure protocol that will be accepted by the domain controllers in your Dover, Miami, and Minneapolis offices to ensure a secure computing environment. She has asked you to identify any potential problems and incompatibilities that might result from this implementation and how would you rectify them.

You tell your manager that there are no issues with regard to Dover and Minneapolis. All servers are running Windows Server 2003 and all workstations are running Windows XP Professional, which natively support NTLMv2. In Miami, however, the Windows 98, Second Edition, and Windows NT 4.0 workstations cannot authenticate using NTLMv2, and requiring NTLMv2 as the least-secure protocol that will be accepted on the servers in Miami will prevent these older operating systems from authenticating to the domain. To resolve the problems stated, you would need to install the Active Directory client extensions on the machines running Windows 98, Second Edition, and Windows NT 4.0 or upgrade their operating systems to Windows 2000 or XP Professional.

You must also incorporate the Unix servers in San Francisco into your network strategy, and you cannot require the users in that office to have more than a single logon. The users at the San Francisco office must be able to access the data and the services published from the Unix servers. To accomplish this, you use Kerberos v5 authentication and create a trust relationship between the San Francisco domain and the Kerberos Unix realm.

How Kerberos Works

A Kerberos authentication server implements three services:

1. **Key distribution center (KDC):** stores credentials in a database and manages the exchange of the keys for the clients and servers on the network.
2. **Authentication service (AS):** responsible for authenticating a user or computer and responding with a session key.
3. **Ticket-granting service (TGS):** responsible for supplying the client with a **Ticket-granting ticket (TGT)**, which can be used to request tickets to access resource servers. It also supplies clients with tickets for accessing resource servers.

Kerberos authentication prevents the replay of the information (a **replay attack**) by using an **authenticator,** which includes a timestamp and other information that proves that the principal requesting access to the application is the same one that was granted the ticket by the TGS. All computers involved in a Kerberos-authenticated session must have their time synchronized within a defined threshold (5 minutes in Active Directory). Kerberos also supports mutual authentication.

SELF-CHECK

1. List the authentication protocols that can perform mutual authentication.
2. List the authentication protocols that can be used by a Windows 98 client computer that does not have Active Directory client software installed.

4.4 Best Practices for Secure Authentication

We have already touched on a few concerns for helping to ensure secure authentication practices. In this final section, we'll look at some guidelines for choosing secure passwords and see how these guidelines can be implemented on a Windows network by using security policies. We'll also look at other considerations, such as limiting the account logon hours or the workstations from which a user can log on. We'll also look at the importance of auditing authentication events. Although we'll look at how to implement these controls on an Active Directory network, keep in mind that similar controls can be implemented through other network operating systems.

Figure 4-9

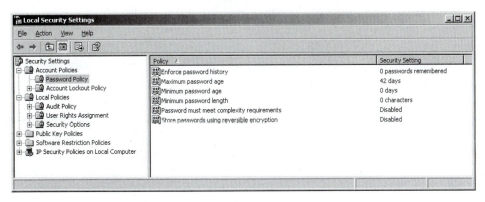

Windows Server 2003 default Password Policy settings.

4.4.1 Password Policies

Windows 2000 and above allow for policies to be set to require **strong passwords** (a password that is difficult to guess or crack using a dictionary or brute force attack). Although we are discussing these guidelines with regards to how you would implement them in Windows 2000 (or later), the same general best practices apply to passwords used for logging on to other operating systems or to applications. When configured in Local Security Policy or in a GPO that is linked at a different level than the domain, these policies apply to local (SAM) user accounts. When configured in a GPO linked to a domain, these policies apply to domain member logon accounts.

Password policies are stored under Security Settings | Account Options. The default policies on a server running Windows Server 2003 that has not been configured as a domain controller are shown in Figure 4-9.

Let's look at each of these policies and how you can configure them to increase security for password authentication.

Enforce Password History

The value you set for the *Enforce password history* policy is the number of unique passwords remembered by the system for the specified account. These passwords cannot be reused, so users will not be able to reuse a password that they have used previously.

Maximum Password Age

The value you set for the *Maximum password age* policy represents the number of days that a password is valid until the user is required to change it. All passwords can be broken given enough time and the correct tool. With that in mind, one of your goals should be to require passwords that are complex and complicated enough so that they will take more time to break than the maximum password age. For example, if you suspect that a user's password can be broken in 40 to 60 days, then the maximum password age should be less than the minimum amount of time that the password could be broken. For example, you could set the *Maximum password age* policy to 30 or 35 and feel confident that it won't be broken before it must be changed.

Minimum Password Age

The *Minimum password age* policy determines the number of days that must pass before the password can be changed. The default value for this option is zero. If *Maximum password age* is set to 30 and *Enforce password history* is set to 12, the policy's goal is to prevent a password from being used again for a year. Many users simply change their password 13 times as soon as it expires, allowing them to keep the original password. The *Minimum password age* policy prevents a user from circumventing the purpose of the *Maximum password age* and *Enforce password history* policies by requiring that a new password must be in place for specified period of time before it can be changed.

Minimum Password Length

The *Minimum password length* policy determines the minimum number of characters that must be used for a password. The default value is zero. Remember that if this value is greater than 14, the LM hashes will not be stored locally.

Password Must Meet Complexity Requirements

The *Password must meet complexity requirements* policy requires passwords that do not contain the user's name or login name, passwords that are at least six characters long, and passwords that contain characters from three of the following four groups:

▲ Uppercase letters
▲ Lowercase letters
▲ Numbers
▲ Special, non-alphanumeric characters such as " < * & > ? /; - _ = | \ ., ` ~ ^ % $ # @ !

Store Passwords Using Reversible Encryption

Enabling the *Store passwords using reversible encryption* policy provides support for applications that use protocols requiring knowledge of the user's password for authentication purposes. Enabling this policy is essentially the same as storing clear text versions of the passwords. Because of this weakness, this policy

Figure 4-10

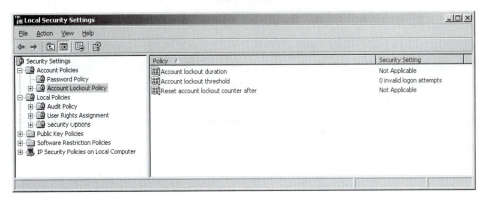

Windows Server 2003 default Account Lockout Policy settings.

should not be enabled unless the specific application's requirements are of greater importance than the need to protect the integrity of the passwords. This policy must be enabled if you are using Digest Authentication in IIS or **Challenge-Handshake Authentication Protocol (CHAP)** authentication for remote access clients. Remote access authentication is beyond the scope of this chapter.

4.4.2 Account Lockout Policy

The *Account Lockout* policy disables an account when the number of failed authentication attempts exceeds a threshold. This policy can increase the number of help desk calls and wind up costing your organization money. For this reason, complex passwords and good auditing should be used to recognize a brute force attack on an account. The default values for the *Account Lockout* policies for a computer running Windows Server 2003 are shown in Figure 4-10. These settings mean that a user will never be locked out from typing the password incorrectly.

Let's look at the policies you can use to configure account lockout for user accounts.

Account Lockout Duration

The *Account lockout duration* policy sets the number of minutes that an account will be locked before it is automatically unlocked. Many environments set this for a short amount of time. The time period is usually in place to minimize calls to the help desk by allowing the user to simply wait and try again after the lockout time period has passed. Obviously this would slow down a brute force attack because the attacker would be able to attempt only a set number of passwords before the account would be locked. Setting the Account lockout duration to 0 causes the account to be locked out indefinitely. A setting of 0 or a setting greater than 30 minutes can actually be detrimental to the availability of your network because it can prevent a user from logging on.

Account Lockout Threshold

The *Account lockout threshold* policy sets the number of invalid attempts that can occur before the account is locked. This value is commonly set to 3, which is typically enough to allow a user to realize that they left his or her Caps Lock key on and still prevent a brute force program from testing a large number of passwords.

Reset Account Lockout Counter After

The *Reset account lockout counter after* policy sets the duration, in minutes, from an invalid logon attempt until the count resets itself back to zero.

The combination of these three account policy options, if used in concert, will minimize the attack surface of many brute force programs. Assuming *Account lockout duration* is set to 30 minutes, *Account lockout threshold* is set to 5, and Reset *account lockout counter after* is set to 15 minutes, an attacker would be able to attempt only 10 passwords per hour as opposed to many thousand per minute if no lockout policy is configured.

4.4.3 Account Logon Hours

A useful account setting that you can and should implement is setting valid logon hours to specify when a user is allowed to access the network. Suppose, for example, that a company has an employee whose job it is to take customer orders over the phone and enter them into an order application during business hours. There should be no reason for this user to be able to log on to the network outside of business hours (since he or she shouldn't be on the phone).

Setting valid logon hours is a feature that exists in most network operating systems, including Windows Server 2003. The setting is configured using the account's Properties dialog box from the Active Directory Users and Computers Microsoft Management Console (MMC). To access it, click the Account tab and then click Logon Hours. The Logon Hours screen is shown in Figure 4-11.

4.4.4 Account Logon Workstation

Another security measure you can take is to restrict a user account to logging on only at specific computers. For example, suppose a user has a dedicated desktop computer in the domain. There is no reason for that user to log on to any other computer on the network. To set this restriction on a Windows Server 2003 computer, open the user's Properties dialog box to the Account tab and click the Log On To button. In the Logon Workstations dialog box, select "The following computers" option button. Then you can enter the computer name(s) for the computer or computers that the user will be allowed to log on to.

Figure 4-11

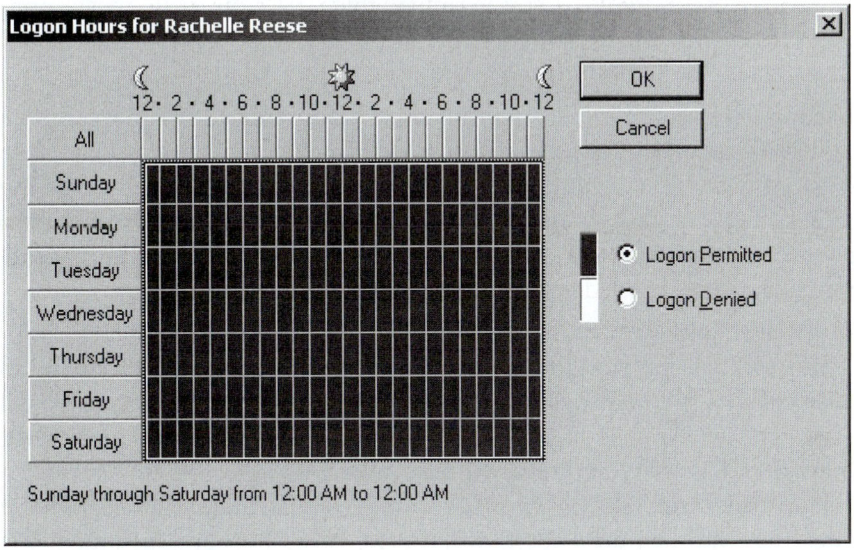

Logon Hours screen.

4.4.5 Auditing Logons

Another key step you can take to mitigate the risk of an attack and to provide an audit trail if an attack occurs is to enable auditing for failed and successful logon attempts. Enabling auditing for failed logon attempts can give you advance warning of an attempted brute force attack. You enable auditing on a Windows computer by enabling the appropriate audit property in Security Settings | Local Policies | Audit Policy. To enable auditing for domain authentication attempts, enable *Audit account logon events*. To enable auditing for interactive logon attempts, enable *Audit logon events*. Events are logged to the Event Viewer Security log.

FOR EXAMPLE

Analyzing Account Risks by Cost Analysis

It has been determined that weak passwords are affecting the overall security of your organization. The organization has estimated that for each incident in which an attacker is able to guess the password that a particular account uses, it costs approximately $12,000. This cost includes all of the resources that are used in determining that an incident has occurred and in reacting to it. Your organization has also estimated that this type of attack occurs about eight times per year.

(Continued)

Your computer security incident response team has proposed three separate solutions, and you must determine which solution is the most appropriate given all of the information involved. The solutions are described as follows:

Solution 1: A security policy will be created and applied to all accounts in the organization. The policy will require complex passwords as defined by a custom filter that guarantees that strong passwords are the only type that are accepted. The help desk determines that it will cost the organization about $2,000 per year to implement this solution and that it will reduce the number of compromised passwords by 25 percent.

Solution 2: Solution 1 will be used, and, in addition, all users and administrators will attend mandatory password training to assure that there are fewer calls to the help desk and that all users affected by an attack will understand what types of passwords are expected when they must select a new one. Password auditing will also take place on random samples of users to make sure that passwords are not easily located. The IT staff estimates that the total cost of this solution is $10,000 per year and that it would reduce the number of password-related security incidents by 50 percent.

Solution 3: Solution 1 will be used, and, in addition, you will require that all users reset their passwords every 25 days. The help desk estimates that this will increase the support calls for password issues by 50 percent, cost $50,000 more per year for increased staff, and reduce the number of password-related incidents by 75 percent.

The company's primary objective is to choose the most cost-effective solution. Which is the most cost-effective solution? With no solution in place, the organization spends approximately $96,000 a year correcting the problem. Solution 1 will add $2,000 to the cost of the correcting the problem but will decrease the quantity of incidents to approximately six per year, which would cost $72,000. Solution 1 makes the total cost of the incidents $74,000 per year. Solution 2 will add $10,000 to the cost and will decrease the quantity of password-related security incidents to approximately four per year. Solution 2 reduces the total cost of the password security incidents to $58,000 per year. Solution 3 adds $50,000 to the cost of the solution and reduces the incidents to two per year, which makes the total cost of password-related incidents $64,000 per year. Based on cost, Solution 2 is the best solution.

SELF-CHECK

1. Describe the steps you would take to make it necessary for a hacker who obtained a password through a dictionary attack to have physical access to a specific client computer on the network to be able to log on.

2. Describe the steps you would take to provide advance notification of a hacker's attempt to use a brute force attack to discover a domain password.

3. Describe how password history can help mitigate an attack.

SUMMARY

In this chapter you learned the fundamentals of authentication. You learned that users and computers can be required to be authenticated. You also learned that some applications must authenticate users. You learned about different types of credentials that can be used to prove a user's identity. Next you learned about four different authentication protocols: LAN Manager, NTLM, NTLMv2, and Kerberos. Finally, you were provided with some best practices for secure authentication on your network.

KEY TERMS

.NET Passport authentication

Acceptability

Active Directory client extensions

Active Directory database

Anonymous access

Authentication

Authentication protocol

Authentication Service (AS)

Authenticator

Authorization

Basic authentication

Biometrics

ChallengeHandshake Authentication Protocol (CHAP)

Client certificate

Credentials

Crossover Error Rate (CER)

Digest authentication

Domain

Domain controller

Enrollment time

False Acceptance Rate (FAR)

False Rejection Rate (FRR)

Group Policy Object (GPO)

Heterogeneous environment

Identification

Impersonate

Integrated Windows authentication

IUSR_*computername* account

Kerberos

Kerberos realm

Key Distribution Center (KDC)

Keystroke logging program

L0phtcrack

LAN Manager protocol

LC5

Microsoft Passport authentication

Mutual authentication

NTLM protocol

NTLMv2 protocol

One-time password

OWA

PAM

Passphrase

Peer-to-peer network

Replay attack

Secondary logon

Security Accounts Manager (SAM) database

Security Identifier (SID)

Security principal

Simple file sharing

Single sign-on

Smart card

Strong password

Throughput rate

Ticket Granting Service (TGS)

Ticket Granting Ticket (TGT)

Trojan horse application

Trust relationship

Two-factor authentication

Type 1 authentication

Type 2 authentication

Type 3 authentication

Type I error

Type II error

User-based access control

Windows Live authentication

ASSESS YOUR UNDERSTANDING

Go to www.wiley.com/college/cole to evaluate your knowledge of authentication. *Measure your learning by comparing pre-test and post-test results.*

Summary Questions

1. Active Directory user credentials are stored in the SAM database. True or false?
2. On a Linux computer, in which file are user accounts stored?
   (a) /etc/users
   (b) /etc/passwd
   (c) /etc/Kerberos
   (d) /etc/credentials
3. Which type of IIS authentication passes the user name and password in clear text?
   (a) basic authentication
   (b) digest authentication
   (c) Windows integrated authentication
4. Which of the following is an example of type 3 authentication credentials?
   (a) password
   (b) PIN number
   (c) smart card
   (d) retinal scan
5. A smart card is an example of two-factor authentication. True or false?
6. Which authentication protocol stores a password using an MD4 hash?
   (a) LAN Manager
   (b) Kerberos
   (c) NTLM
   (d) NTLMv2
7. Which of the following authentication protocols can be used with a Windows 95 client only if Active Directory client extensions are installed?
   (a) LAN Manager
   (b) Kerberos
   (c) NTLM
   (d) NTLMv2

8. Which of the following authentication protocols can be used for Active Directory authentication, but not for SAM authentication?

(a) LAN Manager

(b) Kerberos

(c) NTLM

(d) NTLMv2

9. The *Password must meet complexity requirements* policy is enabled on a computer running Windows XP Professional. Which password is valid?

(a) 123spam

(b) yDo1T

(c) &some1

(d) !@#$%^

10. The *Account lockout duration policy* is set to 0 on a computer running Windows XP Professional. This means the account will never be locked out. True or false?

11. Which of the following can be configured for an Active Directory user account, but not for a local user account?

(a) Account logon hours

(b) Password length restrictions

(c) Password history restrictions

(d) Account lockout policy

12. Which policy would you enable to create a log of all Active Directory users who are authenticated by a domain controller?

(a) Audit account logon events—Success

(b) Audit directory service access—Success

(c) Audit logon events—Success

(d) Audit system events—Success

Applying This Chapter

1. You are designing an authentication strategy for an Active Directory network. The network includes clients that are running Windows 95, Windows 98, and Windows XP Professional. The member servers on the network are all running either Windows 2000 Server or Windows Server 2003. The company is implementing a web application that will be used by employees when they are traveling. The web application will be installed on a server in the perimeter network. You want to minimize administrative effort to manage logons to the web application.

(a) By default, what protocol will be used to authenticate the Windows 98 clients when the users log on to the domain?

(b) What would you need to do to ensure that mutual authentication can be used for all domain authentication?

(c) Which computers will be authenticated by the domain controllers?

(d) What IIS authentication method will be the most secure way to authenticate the users?

(e) What is the drawback to using digest authentication?

(f) What is the drawback to using integrated Windows authentication?

(g) What changes to the network would be required to use smart card authentication?

(h) How can you ensure that users choose good passwords?

(i) Given the current network configuration, what is the largest value you can use for the *Minimum password length* policy?

(j) A kiosk computer in the lobby is often used to log on to the domain. How can you determine which users are logging on to the kiosk computer?

YOU TRY IT

Protecting Your Identity

If you log on to a network at work or use the Internet at work or at home, you most likely must prove who you are and be authenticated by a server. Have you ever thought about the credentials you use and whether they are secure?

1. List some of the servers where you must provide credentials to log on and rate how likely it would be for a hacker to discover your password.
2. Do any of the servers you log on to have password policies?
3. Are the password policies posted?
4. Do you think posting password policies clearly makes a website more or less secure?

Considering a Future of Biometrics

Biometrics offers security, but not without controversy. Many people are concerned that biometric authentica-tion invades our privacy. Others are concerned that devices might not be sanitary. How do you feel about different biometric characteristics and their acceptability ratings? On a scale of 1 to 10, where 1 is least acceptable, rank the following biometric characteristics.

- ▲ Retina scans
- ▲ Iris scans
- ▲ Fingerprints
- ▲ Facial scans
- ▲ Palm scans
- ▲ Hand geometry
- ▲ Voice
- ▲ Handwritten signature dynamics

For any characteristic you ranked lower than 5, describe your concerns.

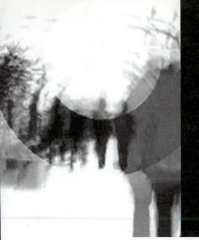

5
AUTHORIZATION AND ACCESS CONTROL

Starting Point

Go to www.wiley.com/college/cole to assess your knowledge of authorization and access control.
Determine where you need to concentrate your effort.

What You'll Learn in This Chapter

▲ Access control models
▲ Access control best practices
▲ Groups
▲ Permissions
▲ Rights and privileges

After Studying This Chapter, You'll Be Able To

▲ Describe the three access control models
▲ Use Windows® groups to assign permissions in an Active Directory® domain
▲ Configure NTFS (NT™ File Systems) and share permissions to meet access requirements
▲ Assign users rights to access a Windows computer
▲ Manage permissions on a Unix® or Linux computer

INTRODUCTION

A key part of securing a network is protecting resources against unauthorized access and preventing users from performing operations they should not be allowed to perform. As you learned in Chapter 4, there are two parts to that process: authentication and authorization.

This chapter will focus on authorization. The chapter starts with a conceptual look at access control by looking at the three access controls models. Next the chapter examines how objects, such as files and printers, are protected in Windows operating systems, particularly in an Active Directory domain. Finally, the chapter looks at how permissions are set on a Unix computer.

5.1 Access Control Models

Access control is designed to mitigate access-related vulnerabilities that could be exploited by threats to a network. In this case, the threat would have the potential to bypass or foil access control mechanisms and allow an attacker to gain unauthorized access to a network. In discussing access control, the terms *subject* and *object* are used. A **subject** is an active entity (such as an individual or process) and an **object** is a passive entity (such as a file). A subject is also called a **principal.** An object is also called a **securable.** Access control involves determining what a subject can do with an object.

Access control models can be classified as discretionary, mandatory, and role-based. In this section we'll discuss each of these. You'll also learn about the principle of least permission.

5.1.1 Discretionary Access Control (DAC)

In **discretionary access control (DAC),** permissions to access an object are assigned by an **authorizing entity** (normally an administrator or an object's owner). One means of specifying discretionary access control is through a table. The table contains the subjects, objects, and access privileges that are assigned to the subjects relative to the objects. This table is sometimes called an **access control list (ACL).** Table 5-1 is an example of an ACL. For example, Windows uses an object's ACL to determine who can access it and how.

Table 5-1 shows that the program named "Salary" can read or write data from the file named "Salary" and has read privileges for the file named "Benefits." Also, the program "Salary" can execute the process called "Evaluation." Ms. Jones can read a file named "Benefits," but cannot access the file named "Salary" or execute the process named "Evaluation." The process named "Average" can read and modify the file named "Salary," but can only read the file named "Benefits."

Table 5-1: Access Control List

Subject	Object 1 (File "Salary")	Object 2 (File "Benefits")	Object 3 (Process "Evaluation")
Program "Salary"	Read/write	Read	Execute
Ms. Jones	None	Read	None
Mr. Tops	Read/write	Read/write	None
Process "Average"	Read/write	Read	None

Resources on a web server can also be secured using an ACL. If a user is not allowed access to the resource, a 403 error occurs.

A user that has the right to alter the access privileges to certain objects operates under **user-directed discretionary access control.** One example of user-directed discretionary access control is peer-to-peer networking. In a peer-to-peer network, each user is responsible for managing access control to his or her own resources. Another discretionary access control type based on an individual's identity is known as **identity-based access control.** With identity-based access control, a user's identity is verified and managed by a different person or organization than the one that manages permissions and privileges.

5.1.2 Mandatory Access Control (MAC)

In **mandatory access control (MAC)**, a subject's authorization or **clearance** is formally matched to an object's sensitivity classification. In the United States, the military classifies documents as unclassified, confidential, secret, and top secret. Similarly, an individual can receive a clearance of confidential, secret, or top secret, and can have access to documents classified at or below his or her specified clearance level. Thus, an individual with a secret clearance can access secret and confidential documents, but with a restriction called the need to know. **Need to know** means that the subject must have a need to access the requested classified document to perform his or her assigned duties. **Rule-based access control** is a type of mandatory access control in which rules determine the access privileges (such as the correspondence of clearance labels to classification labels), rather than the identity of the subjects and objects alone.

A key difference between DAC and MAC is that with DAC, an object's owner can specify the access control list for an object. With MAC, a central authority determines the classification for objects, regardless of who creates or owns them.

Figure 5-1

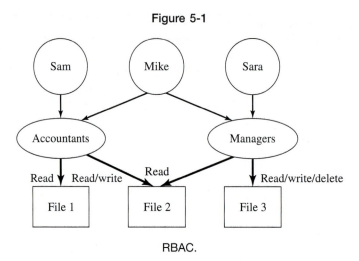

RBAC.

A potential problem with MAC is its lack of flexibility because it segregates access in such large blocks and doesn't provide a good way to group individuals with similar access requirements.

5.1.3 Role-Based Access Control (RBAC)

A **role-based access control (RBAC)** model involves assigning permissions to perform actions on objects based on a person's **role** or job. The model allows for a high level of detail, but the actual implementation of the model will determine how fine a level permissions are granted on and how well roles within the organization are defined.

RBAC requires that you assign users to roles and grant object permissions to roles. This is illustrated in Figure 5-1. As you can see, users are assigned membership in roles and roles are assigned permissions on objects.

In this example, Sam and Mike are Accountants and Sara and Mike are Managers. Accountants are given permission to read File1 and read and write to File2. Therefore, Sam and Mike are granted those permissions because of their membership in the Accountants role. Because Sara is only a member of the Managers role, she can read File2, but cannot write to it. All members of Managers can read, write, and delete File3. Therefore, Sara and Mike have that permission as well.

RBAC can be implemented through the use of **groups** in Windows Server® 2003, Windows 2000 Server, and Windows NT and in Novell® NetWare®. A group is a collection of users that is assigned a specific set of permissions. To implement RBAC, you would create a group for each role. The assumption is that a group's permissions are likely to remain fairly constant. However, the users who are assigned to a specific group might change due to hiring, firing, promotion, and other business requirements. When this happens, the administrator only needs to manage group membership, not individual permissions.

One thing to keep in mind is that all group-based access controls are not necessarily role-based. Sometimes groups are created based on criteria other than the roles performed within the organization. If a company requires role-based access control, it is up to the security team to ensure that the groups created map to organizational roles.

This model is very flexible because it segregates access control based on a user's relationship to the data being secured. It can be used by businesses, and even when securing medical data. For example, you might indicate that patients and doctors can access all patient data, whereas the accounting personnel can access only billing and payment information.

FOR EXAMPLE

RBAC in a Database Management System

A common use of RBAC is to implement access control for the objects in a relational database management system (RDBMS). One example of an RDBMS that implements role-based security is SQL Server 2005.

SQL Server 2005 includes fixed server roles, which are roles mapped to the types of tasks normally performed on a database server. For example, the **serveradmin role** can modify the server's configuration settings, start the server, and stop the server, whereas the **dbcreator role** can create databases on the server. These roles are **fixed server roles,** meaning that their permissions cannot be changed. SQL Server logins can be assigned membership in one or more of these roles.

SQL Server also has database-level roles. These roles are used to assign permissions to the objects in a specific database. Some of these roles are **fixed database roles.** For example, the **db_backupoperator role** has permission to back up a database. A member of the **db_securityadmin role** can create **custom roles,** manage their permissions, and manage membership in those roles. Database-level roles can be used to assign permissions at a very fine level of detail.

SQL Server also supports application roles. An application role is one that is used to allow certain types of access to an application, regardless of who is running it. For example, an accounting application might be granted access to the AccountsPayable table. Any user who runs the accounting application would be able to access that table, but only through the accounting application.

5.1.4 Principle of Least Permission

When designing an access control strategy, you should determine the least amount of access a user or role requires to do his or her job, and you should assign only that amount of access permissions. This is known as applying the **principle of least permission** (also called the **principle of least privilege**). Granting unnecessary permissions can open the doorway to malicious or accidental violations of confidentiality and integrity.

One thing to consider when granting permissions is that the Read permission is used to protect the confidentiality of a file; whereas, the Write permission is used to protect the integrity of a file. With some access control systems, the Write permission implies the Read permission. In others, the permissions are granted independently. The Execute permission is the permission to execute a code file. In most cases, the Execute permission must also imply Read permission.

SELF-CHECK

1. Describe the three access control models.
2. Describe the principle of least permission.

5.2 Implementing Access Control on Windows Computers

Windows Server 2003, Windows Vista™, Windows XP, Windows Server 2000 and Windows NT 4.0 all implement discretionary access control and also allow you to implement role-based access control if you create groups that map to roles within the organization. In this section, we'll look at how to implement access control on a Windows network. Our emphasis will be access control in an Active Directory environment. A discussion of peer-to-peer resource sharing is outside the scope of this chapter, except to note that peer-to-peer resource sharing presents a security risk on your network because access control is put in the hands of the users.

5.2.1 Principals

In Windows 2000/XP/Vista and Windows Server 2003, principals can be local users, domain users, groups, or computers. Principals have a human-readable name (username) and a machine-readable identifier, the **SID (security identifier).**

Local principals (local users and groups) are administered locally and are visible only to the local computer. The human-readable name of a local user has the form `computer_name\principal`, for example, `File-Server1\Administrators`.

Local users and groups can be displayed from the command line with the following commands:

```
net user
net localgroup
```

Figure 5-2 shows the results of running these commands on a computer running Windows XP Professional and SQL Server. Notice that when SQL Server is installed, groups are created. This is something to keep in mind when you install server applications.

Figure 5-2

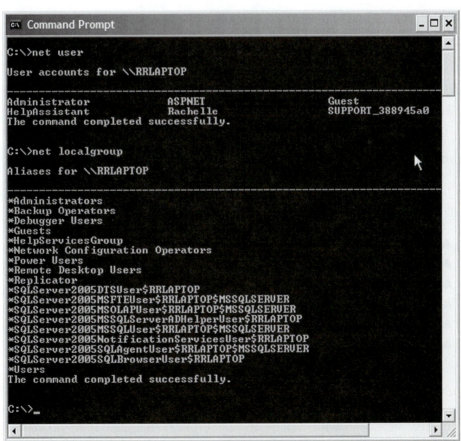

Local users and groups.

Domain principals are administered on a domain controller. They are seen by all computers on the domain. Examples are domain users, Domain Local groups, Domain Global groups, and Universal groups. The human-readable name of a domain user, group, or machine can be written using one of two forms:

1. `principal@domain`
2. `DOMAIN\principal`

For example,

1. `diego@europe.microsoft.com`
2. `EUROPE\diego`

Domain users and groups can be displayed by adding the options switch /domain as follows:

```
net user /domain
net group /domain
net localgroup /domain
```

Figure 5-3 shows the results of running these commands on a domain that includes a server running Microsoft® Exchange Server 2007 and that has a number of role-based groups created, such as the Chefs, Managers, and Temps Global groups and the RecipeReaders and RecipeWriters Domain Local groups.

Security Identifiers (SIDs)

In Windows systems, the SID is a value that uniquely identifies a user, group, or computer. The following are some well-known SIDs (a **well-known SID** is one used on every Windows computer or domain):

▲ Everyone (World): S-1-1-0
▲ LOCAL SYSTEM: S-1-5-18
▲ Administrator: S-1-5-21-<local authority>-500
▲ Administrators: S-1-5-32-544
▲ Domain Admins: S-1-5-21-<domain authority>-512
▲ Guest: S-1-5-21-<authority>-501

The SID is constructed when a user account is created and is fixed for the lifetime of the account. Because a pseudorandom input (clock value) is used in its construction, you will not get the same SID if you delete an account and then recreate it with exactly the same parameters as before. Therefore, the new account will not retain the access permissions assigned to the old account.

Figure 5-3

```
Command Prompt                                                    _ □ ×
Microsoft Windows [Version 5.2.3790]
(C) Copyright 1985-2003 Microsoft Corp.

J:\Documents and Settings\Administrator>net user /domain

User accounts for \\SERVER1

-----------------------------------------------------------------------
Administrator              Christy                Diane
Guest                      IUSR_SERVER1           IWAM_SERVER1
Jane                       jqpublic               krbtgt
SUPPORT_388945a0           test                   Tom
The command completed successfully.


J:\Documents and Settings\Administrator>net group /domain

Group Accounts for \\SERVER1

-----------------------------------------------------------------------
*$C31000-M35U0LF7D6UO
*Chefs
*Designers
*DnsUpdateProxy
*Domain Admins
*Domain Computers
*Domain Controllers
*Domain Guests
*Domain Users
*Enterprise Admins
*Exchange Organization Administrators
*Exchange Recipient Administrators
*Exchange Servers
*Exchange View-Only Administrators
*ExchangeLegacyInterop
*Group Policy Creator Owners
*Managers
*Schema Admins
*Temps
The command completed successfully.


J:\Documents and Settings\Administrator>net localgroup /domain

Aliases for \\SERVER1

-----------------------------------------------------------------------
*Account Operators
*Administrators
*Backup Operators
*Cert Publishers
*DHCP Administrators
*DHCP Users
*Distributed COM Users
*DnsAdmins
*Guests
*HelpServicesGroup
*IIS_WPG
*Incoming Forest Trust Builders
*Network Configuration Operators
*Performance Log Users
*Performance Monitor Users
*Pre-Windows 2000 Compatible Access
*Print Operators
*RAS and IAS Servers
```

Domain users and groups.

When a domain is created, a unique SID is constructed for the domain. When a workstation or a server joins a domain, it receives a SID that includes the domain's SID.

Groups

Windows **security groups** allow you to assign permissions to a large number of users at a single time. This facilitates a consistent assignment of permissions to multiple users with the same access requirements. Using groups to assign permissions makes the management and auditing of users more efficient. There are several types of groups within an **Active Directory forest** (one or more domains that trust each other). Their membership depends on whether the domain is a **native mode domain** or a **mixed mode domain.** A native mode domain is one that consists of only Windows 2000 and Windows Server 2003 domain controllers. A mixed-mode domain is one that contains one or more Windows NT 4.0 domain controllers or one that has not been converted to native mode. Table 5-2 shows the different groups and what can be a member of each of the group types.

Active Directory has the some built-in groups that can be used to manage some permission assignments on the network. All built-in groups are Domain Local groups. The following are some built-in groups you will commonly use:

▲ **Account Operators:** can manage user and group accounts on a domain controller.

▲ **Administrators:** has full control over any computer in the domain.

Table 5-2: Windows Group Types

Group Type	Membership
Universal group	Native mode: Accounts, Global groups from any domain, other Universal groups
	Mixed mode: not available
Global group	Native mode: Accounts or Global groups from the same domain
	Mixed mode: Accounts from the same domain
Domain Local group	Native mode: Accounts, Global groups, and Universal groups from any domain; Domain Local groups from the same domain
	Mixed mode: Accounts and Global groups from any domain

▲ **Backup Operators:** can run backup and restore operations.

▲ **Guests:** more limited than the members of the Users group. Used for anonymous users like the Guest account or the IIS anonymous user account.

▲ **Network Configuration Operators:** has some rights to manage the network configuration parameters for the computers in the domain.

▲ **Print Operators:** can manage printers in the domain.

▲ **Server Operators:** can manage domain member computers.

▲ **Users:** accounts with limited access in the domain.

Some global groups are also created automatically. These include the following:

▲ **Domain Admins:** a member of the Administrators group. Administrator account is a member by default.

▲ **Domain Computers:** all computers that have been added to the domain are members.

▲ **Domain Controllers:** all domain controllers for the domain are members.

▲ **Domain Guests:** a member of the Guests group. The Guest account (which is disabled by default) is a member.

▲ **Domain Users:** a member of the Users group. All users in the domain are members.

You add domain groups through Active Directory Users and Computers. The New Object—Group dialog for a mixed-mode domain is shown in Figure 5-4. As you can see, the Universal Security group option is not available.

The recommended practice for assigning permissions using groups in Windows networks is to follow the practice of AG(G)DLP. The following explains this process:

1. Place (A)ccounts in (G)lobal groups.
2. Optionally, **nest** (G)lobal groups (make a global group a member of a different global group).
3. Place the Global groups in (D)omain (L)ocal groups.
4. Assign (P)ermissions for the resource to the Domain Local group.

Although acronym AG(G)DLP is a great way to remember this process, the last task you should perform is placing the Global groups in the Domain Local groups so that an account can't use a permission until all of the permissions have been assigned.

Universal groups can be used to consolidate groups whose logical membership should span domains. In order to accomplish this, you add the

Figure 5-4

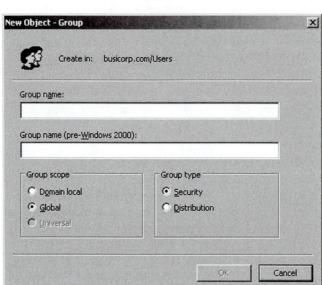

Creating a new domain group.

accounts to Global groups in their respective domain and then nest the Global groups within Universal groups. This is the recommended strategy because changes in the membership of the Global group will not cause changes in the Universal group, which typically would require replication of the global catalog to each global catalog server in the forest. A **global catalog** is a database that contains a subset of Active Directory objects and object attributes for every domain in the forest. A **global catalog server** is a domain controller that hosts a global catalog.

With the addition of Universal groups to the AG(G)DLP guideline, the recommendation becomes AG(G)UDLP, as seen in the following list:

▲ Place (A)ccounts in (G)lobal groups.
▲ Optionally nest (G)lobal groups.
▲ Place (G)lobal groups into (U)niversal Ggroups.
▲ Place Universal groups into (D)omain (L)ocal groups.
▲ Assign (P)ermissions to the Domain Local group.

Computers running Windows Server 2003, Windows 2000 Server and Window NT also support local groups. A local group is created and managed on the local computer. Global groups and universal groups can be members of local groups.

FOR EXAMPLE

Taking Advantage of Universal Groups

Thatcher is the network administrator for a large consulting company. The company's Active Directory is made up of three domains: TJR.lan, east.TJR.lan, and west.TJR.lan. In each domain, there are human resource records that all HR personnel need to be able to modify. There are HR accounts in each of the domains, and Thatcher wants to keep the ACLs short and easy to maintain. In addition, he needs to minimize replication traffic between domains.

Thatcher creates a Global group in each domain—glCorpHR, glEastHR, and glWestHR—and then adds them to the dlHR Domain Local group in each domain. Each time membership changes in any of the Global groups, forestwide replication would be required. Also, the ACL would have three access control entries (ACEs).

To reduce replication, Thatcher creates a Universal group named uHR. He then adds the glCorpHR, glEastHR, and glWestHR Global groups to uHR. Next, Thatcher grants each of the dlHR Domain Local groups (one for each domain) the appropriate permissions on the HR data. Once that step is completed, he adds the uHR Universal group as a member the dlHR groups in each domain. Now as membership changes in the Global groups, replication will only need to occur within each domain and not between them.

5.2.2 Windows Access Control Model

The access control for Active Directory objects relies on the Windows access control model, which is made up of the two basic components:

1. **Security descriptors:** contain the security information that protects an object.
2. **Access tokens:** contain the information regarding a logged-on user. An access token provides the security context for the session.

Security Descriptors

A security descriptor contains two ACLs. An **ACL** (in the Windows environment) is a list of security protections that apply to an entire object, to a set of the object's properties, or to an individual property of an object. Simply put, the ACL contains all of the **permission attributes** regarding an object, including who is explicitly granted access as well as those explicitly denied access to the object. There are two types of ACLs:

1. **Discretionary access control list (DACL):** the part of the security descriptor that grants or denies specific users and groups access to the object. The

owner of an object can modify the DACL, as can administrators and other users who have been granted the Change Permissions permission.

2. **System access control list (SACL):** the part of the security descriptor that dictates which events are to be audited for specific users or groups.

Both the DACL and the SACL consist of **access control entries (ACEs),** which identify the users and groups that are granted or denied a specific type of access. In order to view the DACLs and SACLs, you must enable Advanced Features from the Active Directory Users and Computers tool's View menu.

A security descriptor also includes the object owner's SID.

Access Tokens

When a user logs on successfully, the system will produce an access token that includes the identity and privileges of the user account. The system then uses the token to identify the user when the user's thread interacts with a securable object or attempts to perform some action that requires privileges.

The following is a partial list of the elements that are contained in an access token:

▲ User's SID.

▲ SIDs for the groups in which the user is a member.

▲ Logon SID, which is an SID that persists only for the duration of the active logon session.

▲ List of the privileges possessed by the user or the groups to which the user belongs.

▲ An owner SID.

▲ The SID for the user's primary group.

▲ The default DACL, which includes the creator/owner permissions, that is used when the user creates a securable object.

▲ The source of the access token.

▲ A value that indicates whether the token is a primary or an impersonation token. A **primary token** means the token is associated with the user who is logged on to the computer where the process is running. An **impersonation token** is created when a client accesses a server on behalf of the user.

As a result of this information being assigned when a user logs on, certain conditions might require a user to log off and then back on in order to gain access to a recently modified permission. For example, a user is added to a Security group while they are currently logged on. The access token that they have already received does not contain the SID for the newly assigned group and the user's current thread will not be a member of the group. To rectify this situation, the user must acquire a new access token by logging off and back on again.

5.2.3 Understanding Active Directory Object Permissions

In Active Directory, every object has its own security descriptor that specifies which accounts have permission to access the object as well as what type of access is permitted. The object permissions are what provide you with the capability to control who can access individual objects or an object's attributes within the directory. Typically, you will use permissions to assign privileges to an **organizational unit (OU)**; however, you can assign permissions to any single object. An organizational unit is a container for organizing users, computers, and groups for administration and Group Policy application.

Active Directory has several types of permissions; the standard permissions are composed of those that are the most commonly assigned. Table 5-3 lists the standard permissions.

The standard permissions are a combination of individual (special) permissions. The available special permissions are different depending on the resource that you are attempting to secure. They include Read Attributes, Read Extended Attributes, Write Attributes, Read Permissions, Change Permissions, and so forth.

Table 5-3: Active Directory Standard Permissions

Permission	Description
Full Control	Includes Change Permissions and Take Ownership, as well as all other standard permissions
Write	Provides the ability to change an object's attributes
Read	Provides the ability to view objects, object attributes, the owner, and Active Directory permissions
Create All Child Objects	Provides the ability to create any type of object in a container, typically an organizational unit
Delete All Child Objects	Provides the ability to remove any type of child object from a container

Figure 5-5

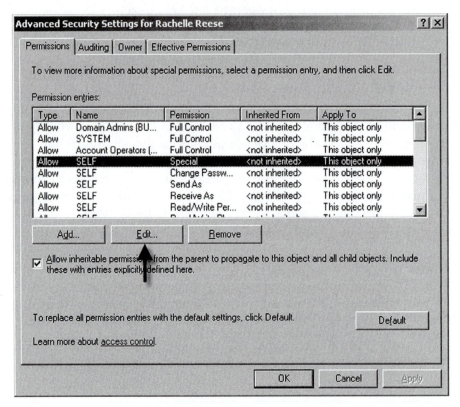

Advanced Security Settings.

You can access the special permissions by clicking Advanced on the Security tab of the object's Properties dialog box, selecting a permission entry for Special permissions (see Figure 5-5), and clicking the Edit button.

The individual permissions granted by that entry will display, as shown in Figure 5-6.

Active Directory object permissions can be granted or denied (either implicitly or explicitly), set as standard or special permissions, and set at the object level or inherited from a parent object. An **inherited permission** is one that is configured at an object higher in the hierarchy and that flows down to the objects lower in the hierarchy. At any level in the hierarchy, a Deny will override an Allow. For example, suppose Tom is a member of the TechSupport group and the Temp group. The TechSupport group is granted the Write permission on the Sales organizational unit. The Temp group is denied the Write permission on the Sales organizational unit. In this case, Tom will not be able to modify the attributes of the objects inside the Sales organizational unit because the Deny in the DACL will override the Allow.

Figure 5-6

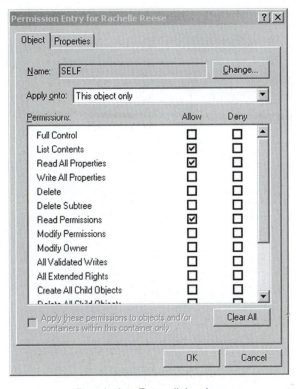

Permission Entry dialog box.

5.2.4 Designing Access Control for Files and Folders

Just as with Active Directory objects, there are different access permissions that apply to files and folders. **NTFS permissions** are permissions configured for a file or folder. They are always checked when an attempt is made to access a resource on the file system locally or when accessing a file or folder across the network. The standard permissions that are provided for an NTFS folder are as follows:

▲ Full Control
▲ Modify
▲ Read & Execute
▲ List Folder Contents
▲ Read
▲ Write

Figure 5-7

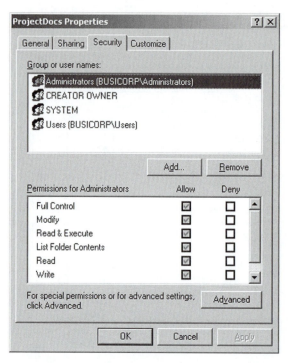

NTFS permissions.

NTFS permissions are managed on the Security tab of a folder's or file's Properties dialog box, as shown in Figure 5-7. The users and groups on the object's ACL are listed. If a box is checked and filled, it means the permissions are inherited from a parent object.

As with Active Directory object permissions, these permissions can be granted (allowed, in the properties dialog box) or denied. These standard permissions are really combinations of special permissions, so when you grant a standard permission, you are really granting one or more special permissions. Although you can grant and deny special permissions individually, you should try to avoid using special permissions and instead use standard permissions to make permissions issues easier to troubleshoot.

Troubleshooting NTFS Permissions

Because a user can be granted or denied permissions in so many ways, sometimes you might need to troubleshoot an issue in which a user has too many or not enough permissions to access an object. The Effective Permissions tab of Advanced Security Settings for an object, shown in Figure 5-8, allows you to determine a user's **effective NTFS permissions** on that object, taking into

Figure 5-8

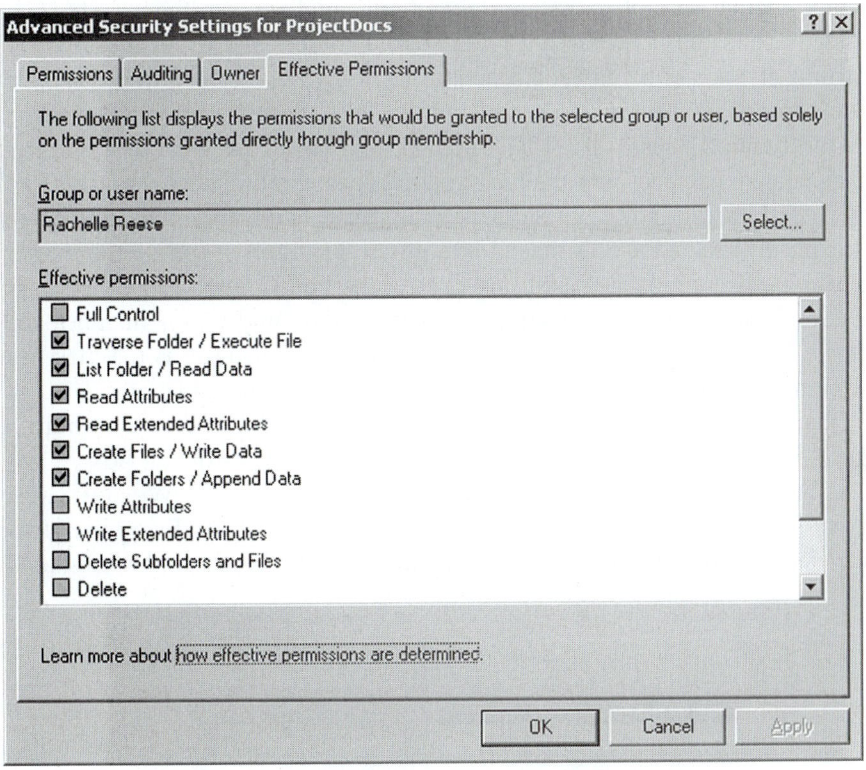

Effective Permissions.

consideration group memberships, inherited permissions, and explicit permissions. This is a good way to start troubleshooting an access control problem.

One thing to keep in mind is that effective permissions consider NTFS permissions only, not share permissions. Therefore, when troubleshooting a permissions problem, if the effective permissions are fine, check the share permissions to see if they are causing the problem.

Default Permissions

In earlier versions of Windows, the default file permissions were inadequate because they gave all users Full Control. As a result of the new focus at Microsoft on security, Microsoft is now implementing secure defaults whenever possible. One example of this is default permissions. In Windows Server 2003, the Users group receives only the Read & Execute, List Folder Contents, and Read permissions by default because it inherits the permissions from the volume root. The Administrators group and the special SYSTEM group inherit Full Control permission.

Share Permissions

There is another level of access control that only applies when the resource is being accessed across the network through a **shared folder: Share permissions.** When designing the access control for files and folders, you will need to remember that Share permissions determine the maximum access that is allowed when the file is accessed through a share. The NTFS permissions that are assigned to the requesting principal are combined with the Share permissions and the most restrictive permission passes through. For example, Server5 is sharing a folder named "myShare" and has explicitly granted the Domain Users group Read permission to the share. The Domain Users group is also explicitly granted the Full Control NTFS permission. If the user is accessing a file using the share (Server5\myShare), members of the Domain Users group will only have Read permission because it is the most restrictive permission when comparing the NTFS to the Share permissions.

Share permissions are managed through the Sharing tab of a resource (see Figure 5-9). Click Permissions to display the Permissions dialog box.

When a folder is shared on Windows Server 2003 or on Windows XP with Service Pack 1 (or later), the Read permission is granted to the **Everyone group** as the default permission, as shown in Figure 5-10. When a folder is shared on

Figure 5-9

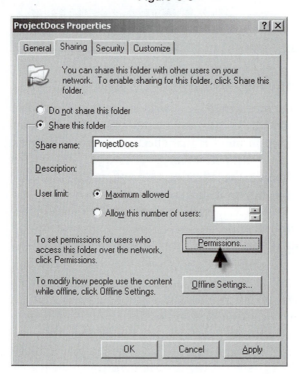

The Sharing tab.

Figure 5-10

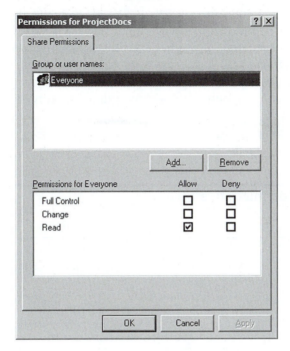

Share Permissions.

Windows XP without service packs, the Everyone group is granted Full control. You will want to remove this and only grant permissions to the required principals. As you grant specific users or groups rights to the share, their default permission is Read. As with NTFS permissions, you can allow or deny permission to a share.

Windows Vista also allows you to create shared folders. However, the available permissions are different. On Windows Vista, you can assign the following permissions:

▲ Reader: allows users to read the files.
▲ Contributor: allows users to read the files, add files, and modify and delete their own files.
▲ Co-owner: allows users to read, add, modify, and delete any files in the folder.

Unlike Windows XP and Windows Server 2003, Windows Vista also allows you to share individual files.

Hidden Shares
You can create **hidden shares** (also called **administrative shares**), which will not be displayed in Windows Explorer if a client navigates to the server using its UNC

(Universal Naming Convention) path. Hidden shares do not add any layer of security, nor should you assume that they are not visible to a potential attacker. You can create a hidden share simply by appending a dollar sign ($) to the name of the share when you create it as you would any other share, such as Accounting$.

Windows Server 2003 has a few hidden shares that are required for certain administrative tasks. By default, the Administrators group is granted Full Control permission to these shares. You cannot modify the permissions of administrative shares.

Table 5-4 shows the administrative shares and describes what they are typically used for.

Table 5-4: Administrative Shares

Share Name	Local Folder	Description
C$, D$, E$	C, D, E	The root of each partition with a drive letter assigned to it is automatically shared. Through this root share, an administrator has remote access to the entire partition tree.
Admin$	**%systemroot%** (C:\Windows)	This is the operating system root. Administrators can use this hidden share to access the Windows installation without knowing the drive or path that Windows was installed to.
Print$	%Systemroot%\System32\ Spool\Drivers	When a printer is shared on the server, this share is created to store the operating system drivers required to print to the printer. The Everyone group has Read permission and the Administrators, Server Operators, and Print Operators all have the Full Control permission. If no printer is shared on a server, this share will not exist.
IPC$		This folder is used when administering the server remotely.

Figure 5-11

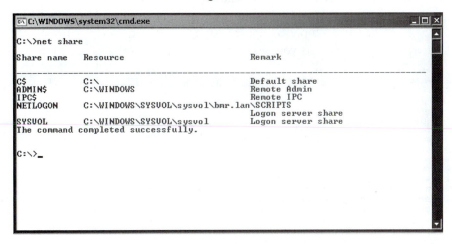

The net share command.

You can view all of the folders that are shared, including the administrative hidden shares, by typing "net share" at the command prompt, as seen in Figure 5-11.

You can also use the Computer Management MMC (Microsoft Management Console), shown in Figure 5-12, to view the shares.

Figure 5-12

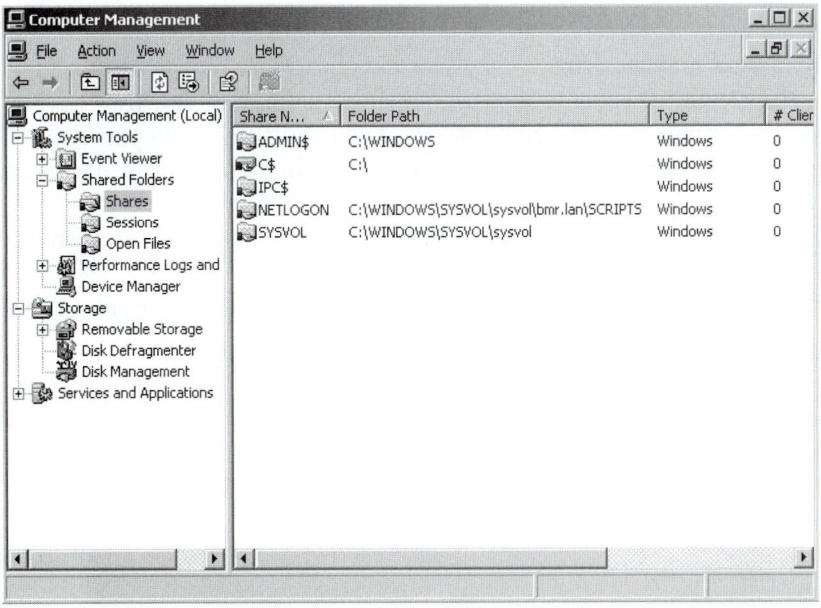

Viewing shared folders in the Computer Management MMC.

Figure 5-13

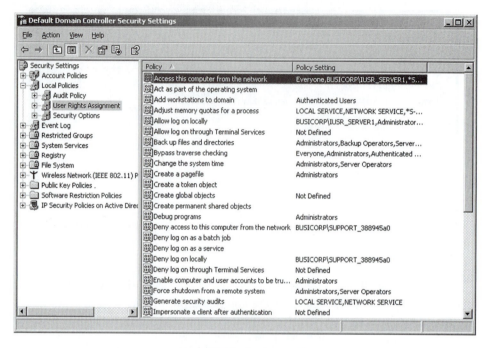

User Rights Assignment.

5.2.5 User Rights Assignment

You can also manage what a user can do on a Windows computer by modifying the DACL of specific user rights. Rights are assigned through the User Rights Assignment policy container in Local Security Policy or in a **Group Policy Object (GPO)**. A GPO is an object in which an administrator can centrally define policies that are applied to users and computers in the domain. The user rights assignments for the Default Domain Controller Security policy are shown in Figure 5-13.

You can assign a user right to a user or to a group. Some rights assignments you might need to modify include the following:

▲ Access this computer from the network
▲ Allow log on locally
▲ Back up files and directories
▲ Deny access to this computer from the network
▲ Deny log on as a service
▲ Deny log on locally
▲ Log on as a service

> ## FOR EXAMPLE
>
> ### Avoiding Deny Permissions
>
> Steve is the network administrator for a large management consulting firm. There are two types of partners that run the firm: equity and nonequity partners. Nonequity partners should have access to everything that equity partners can access with the exception of the firm's financial information. To facilitate this access, Steve decides to create a Global group named All-Partners that has all of the partners' accounts as members. In order to assure that the nonequity partners cannot view the financial information, he creates ACEs on the FinancialData folder for each of the nonequity partner's accounts and denies each one the Read permission.
>
> Over time, the nonequity partners may become equity partners. When this occurs, Steve must remove the ACE denying those individual accounts. In addition to the administrative burden of managing these permissions on individual accounts, the more ACEs on an ACL, the worse the performance will be when accessing the folder.
>
> In order to resolve these problems, Steve creates two additional Global groups: EquityPartners and NonEquityPartners. The EquityPartners group is granted the Read permission to the FinancialData folder and the NonEquityPartners group is not. This makes maintaining these groups in the future easy and it keeps the ACL on the FinancialData folder small.

▲ Restore files and directories
▲ Shut down the system
▲ Take ownership of files or other objects

A detailed discussion of all user rights available is beyond the scope of this chapter.

SELF-CHECK

1. Describe the three types of Active Directory security groups.
2. Describe the impact of hidden shares on security.
3. Describe the default file access permissions when you create a file on a new installation of Windows Server 2003.

5.3 Implementing Access Control on Unix Computers

The access control features available will depend somewhat on the flavor of Unix you are using. However, certain aspects of access control are present in most Unix implementations. In this section, we'll survey some of these aspects to provide you with a general understanding of how access to resources is managed on a Unix system. These same procedures can be used to manage access control on a Linux system.

5.3.1 Principals

The principals on a Unix computer are **user identities (UIDs)** and **group identities (GIDs)**. UIDs and GIDs are 16-bit numbers. Some UID values have special meanings, which might differ between systems, but the **superuser (root)** UID is always 0. The superuser account is similar to the Administrator account on a Windows computer. UID examples are listed in Table 5-5.

User Accounts

Information about principals is stored in user accounts and home directories. User accounts are stored in the **/etc/passwd** file or in the encrypted /etc/shadow file. Only the root user can access this file. Most Linux systems use Message-Digest algorithm 5 (MD5) to encrypt part of the user's information. Entries in this file have the following format:

```
user name:password:UID:GID:ID string:home
directory:login shell
```

The user name is a string up to eight characters long. It identifies the user when logging in but is not used for access control. Unix does not distinguish

Table 5-5: Some Common UIDs

UID	Refers To
-2	nobody
0	root
1	daemon
2	uucp
3	bin
4	games
9	audit

between users with the same UID. The password is stored encrypted. The field "ID string" contains the user's full name. The last two fields specify the user's home directory and the Unix shell available to the user after successful login. Additional user-specific settings are defined in the profile file in the user's home directory. The actions taken by the system when a user logs in are specified in the **/etc/profile** file.

Superuser (Root)

In every Unix system there is a user with special privileges. This superuser has UID 0 and usually the user name "root." The root account is used by the operating system for essential tasks like login, recording the audit log, or accessing I/O devices.

All security checks are turned off for the superuser, who can do almost everything. For example, the superuser can become any other user and can change the system clock. There are also relatively easy ways to circumvent the few restrictions that are imposed on a superuser. For example, a superuser cannot write to a file system mounted as read only, but he or she can dismount the file system and remount it as writable.

Groups

Users belong to one or more groups. Every user belongs to a primary group. The GID of the primary group is stored in the /etc/passwd file. The file **/etc/group** contains a list of all groups. Entries in this file have the following format:

```
group name:group password:GID:list of users
```

For example, the entry "infosecwww:*:209:chez,af" tells you that group infosecwww has the password disabled, has GID 209, and has two members, chez and af.

In System V Unix, a user can only be in one group at a time. The current group is changed with the **newgrp command.** Commands are case sensitive in Unix. Users are free to change into a group where they are already a member. If users attempt to change into a group where they are not members, newgrp will prompt for a password and give temporary membership if the correct group password is entered. In Berkeley Unix, a user can reside in more than one group, so there is no need for a newgrp command.

Subjects

The subjects are processes. Each process has a **process ID (PID)**. Each process is associated with a real UID/GID and an effective UID/GID. The real UID is inherited from the parent process. Typically it is the UID of the user who is logged in. The effective UID is inherited from the parent process or from the file being executed.

5.3.2 Objects

The objects include files, directories, memory devices, and I/O devices. For the purpose of access control, Unix treats all objects as resources. Resources are organized in a tree-structured file system.

The Inode

Each file entry in a directory is a pointer to a data structure called an **inode.** The inode includes the UID of the user who owns the file (normally the person who created the file) and the GID of the group that owns the file (normally either the creator's group or the directory's group).

   You can view the permissions on the files in a directory by using the **ls command,** as follows: `ls -l`.

   A sample listing is shown below:

```
-rw-r--r-- 1 diego staff 1617 Oct 28 11:01 adcryp.tex
drwx------ 2 diego staff 512 Oct 25 17:44 ads/
```

The first character tells you the type of file: "-" indicates a file, "d" a directory, "b" a block device file, and "c" a character device file. The next nine characters show the file permissions. The file permissions (permission bits) are grouped in three triples that define read, write, and execute access for owner, group, and other (also called world), respectively. A "-" indicates that a right is not granted. Thus `rw-r--r--` gives read and write access to the owner and read access to group and other, `rwx------` gives read, write, and execute access to the owner and no rights to group and other.

   The eleventh character is a numeric field that indicates the number of links to the file. Following this value are two fields. The first identifies the owner (diego in this example), and the second identifies the group (staff).

Permissions for Directories

Every user has a **home directory,** such as /home/staff/dieter. This is similar to the My Documents folder on a Windows computer. To put files and subdirectories into a directory, a user has to have the correct file permissions for the directory. The following permissions can be set on a directory:

▲ Read permission allows a user to find which files are in the directory, that is, by executing ls or similar commands.
▲ Write permission allows a user to add files to and remove files from the directory. Deleting a file also requires execute access on the directory.
▲ Execute permission is required for making the directory the current directory and for opening files inside the directory. You can open a file

Figure 5-14

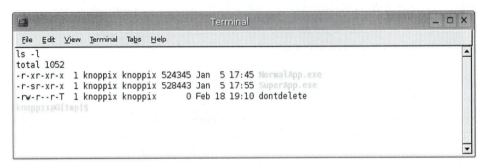

Sticky bit.

in the directory if you know that it exists, but you cannot use ls to see what is in the directory unless you have Read permission.

To prevent other users from reading your files, you could either set the access permission accordingly or you could prevent access to the directory.

One potential problem is that you do not need any permission on a file in order to delete it, even if the file belongs to another user. You only need Read and Execute permission on the directory. You can use the **sticky bit** to restrict the right to delete a file. When a directory has the sticky bit set, an entry can only be removed or renamed by a user if the user is the owner of the file, the owner of the directory, and has write permission for the directory. The one exception to this is that the superuser can delete any file.

When ls -l displays a directory with the sticky bit set, T appears instead of x as the execute permission for world, as shown in Figure 5-14.

Notice that the file named "dontdelete" has the last bit set to T.

Checking Permissions

Unix checks the permission bits in the following order:

1. If your UID indicates that you are the owner of the file, the permission bits for owner decide whether you can get access.

2. If you are not the owner of the file but your GID indicates that your group owns the file, the permission bits for group decide whether you can get access.

3. If you are neither the owner of the file nor a member of the group that owns the file, the permission bits for other decide whether you can get access.

This order means that it is possible to set permission bits so that the owner of a file has less access than other users. This might come as a surprise, but this fact is also a valuable general lesson. For any access control mechanism, you have to know precisely in which order different access criteria are checked.

Set UserID and Set GroupID

Unix requires superuser privilege to execute certain operating system functions; for example, only root can listen at the trusted ports 0–123, but users should not be given superuser status.

To allow users who do not have superuser status to run programs that require access they would not otherwise have, some programs are identified as **SUID (set userID)** programs and **SGID (set groupID)** programs. Such programs run with the effective user ID or group ID of their owner or group, giving temporary or restricted access to files not normally accessible to other users. When ls -l displays an SUID program, then the execute permission of the owner is shown as s instead of x:

```
-rws–x–x 3 root bin 16384 Nov 16 1996 passwd*
```

This is illustrated in Figure 5-15. Notice that the SuperApp program has an s in the user's execute column.

When ls -l displays an SGID program, the execute permission of the group is shown as s instead of x.

If, as is often the case, root is the owner of an SUID program, a user who is executing this program will get superuser status during execution. Important SUID programs are as follows:

▲ /bin/passwd: change password
▲ /bin/login: login program
▲ /bin/at: batch job submission
▲ /bin/su: change UID program

It is important to keep in mind that since the user has the program owner's privileges during execution of an SUID program, this program should only do what it is intended to do. This is particularly true for SUID programs owned by

Figure 5-15

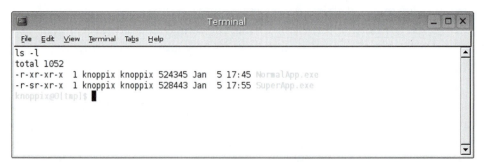

SUID.

root. An attacker who can change the behavior of an SUID program—for example, by interrupting its execution—can not only perform actions that require superuser status during the attack, but might also be able to change the system so that superuser status can be obtained on future occasions.

SUID programs are especially dangerous if they allow user interaction. All user input, including command line arguments (which are case sensitive in Unix) and environment variables, must be processed with extreme care. A particular pitfall is shell escapes, which give a user access to shell commands while running as superuser. Therefore, programs should have SUID status only if really necessary. The systems manager should carefully monitor the integrity of SUID programs.

Changing File Security Attributes

You can change the permission bits with the **chmod command**, but only if you are either the superuser or the owner of the file. This command has four possible formats:

▲ Absolute mode: You identify the permissions using an octal number. A discussion of octal permission values is beyond the scope of this chapter.

▲ Add permissions.

```
chmod [-fR] [who]+permission file
```

▲ Remove permissions.

```
chmod [-fR] [who]-permission file
```

▲ Reset permissions.

```
chmod [-fR] [who]=permission file
```

The option -f suppresses error messages; the option -R applies the specified change recursively to all subdirectories of the current directory. The who parameter can take the values shown in Table 5-6.

Table 5-6: Supported Values for Who

Value	Effect
u	Changes the owner permissions
g	Changes the group permissions
o	Changes the other permissions
a	Changes all permissions

Table 5-7: Supported Values for Permission

Value	Effect
R	Read permission
W	Write permission
x	Execute permission for files, search permission for directories
X	Execute permission only if the file is a directory or at least one execute bit is set
s	Set-user-ID or set-group-ID permission
T	Save text permission (set the sticky bit)

The permission parameter can take the values shown in Table 5-7.

The **chown command** changes the owner of a file; the **chgrp command** changes the group of a file. The chown command could be a potential source of unwelcome SUID programs. A user could create an SUID program and then change the owner to root. To prevent such an attack, some versions of Unix only allow the superuser to run chown. Other versions allow users to apply chown to their own files and have chown turn off the SUID and SGID bit. Similar considerations apply to chgrp.

Some Linux distributions also allow you to change permissions through a file's or folder's properties. For example, Figure 5-16 shows the Permissions dialog for the Knoppix distribution.

FOR EXAMPLE

Beware of Setting Overly Strict Permissions

Tina is a network administrator for a Unix system. She has configured directory and file permissions so that users can access only their home directories. However, some programs that users run need to access files in other directories. Tina works around this problem by making those programs SUID programs and setting the owner to root.

An attack occurs in which a user account is granted superuser status. That account is used by an attacker to perform malicious activities, including reading confidential files. Remember, permissions aren't checked when superuser attempts access.

Tina changes the programs so that they are not SUID programs and modifies the permissions on the files the applications need. This is a much more secure solution.

Figure 5-16

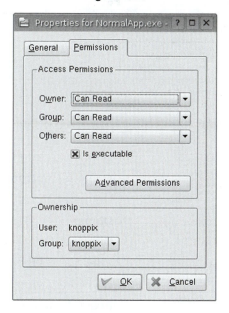

Change Permissions on Knoppix.

Clicking Advanced Permissions allows you to set SUID, GUID, and sticky bit attributes, as shown in Figure 5-17.

SELF-CHECK

1. Identify the three categories of permissions on a file on a Unix computer.
2. Describe an SUID program and how it impacts security.

Figure 5-17

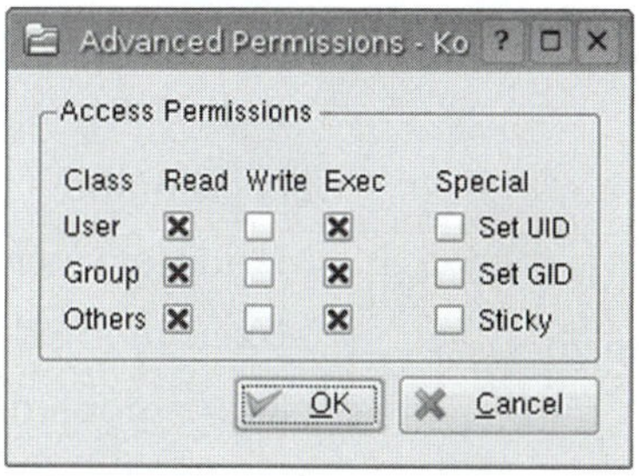

Advanced Permissions on Knoppix.

SUMMARY

In this chapter you learned about three different access control models: DAC, MAC, and RBAC. You also learned how to implement access control for Active Directory objects, file system objects in Windows, user rights assignments in Windows, and file system and device objects in Linux.

KEY TERMS

%systemroot%

/etc/group file

/etc/passwd file

/etc/profile file

Access control entry (ACE)

Access control list (DAC)

Access control list (ACL)
(Windows)

Access token

Account Operators

Active Directory forest

Administrative shares

Administrators

Authorizing entity

Backup Operators

chgrp command

chmod command

chown command

Clearance

Custom role

db_backupoperator role

dbcreator role

db_securityadmin role

Discretionary access control (DAC)

Discretionary access control list
(DACL)

Domain Admins

Domain Computers

Domain Controllers

Domain Guests

Domain Local group

Domain Users

Effective NTFS permissions

Everyone group

Fixed database role

Fixed server role

Global catalog

Global catalog server

Global group

Group identity (GID)

Group policy object (GPO)

Groups

Guests

Hidden share

Home directory

Identity-based access control

Impersonation token

Inherited permission

Inode

ls command

Mandatory access control (MAC)

Mixed mode domain

Native mode domain

Need to know

Nest

Network Configuration
Operators

newgrp command

NTFS permissions

Object

Organizational unit (OU)

Permission attributes

PID

Primary token

Principal

Principle of least permission

Principle of least privilege

Print Operators

Role

Role-based access control (RBAC)

root

Rule-based access control

Securable

Security descriptor

Security group

Security identifier (SID)

serveradmin role

Server Operators

set groupID (SGID) program

set userID (SUID) program

Share permissions

Shared folder

Sticky bit

Subject

superuser

System access control list (SACL)

Universal group

User-directed discretionary access
control

User identity (UID)

Users

Well-known SID

ASSESS YOUR UNDERSTANDING

Go to www.wiley.com/college/cole to evaluate your knowledge of authorization and access control.
Measure your learning by comparing pre-test and post-test results.

Summary Questions

1. Which access control model uses an intermediate layer to determine access?
   (a) DAC
   (b) MAC
   (c) RBAC

2. Which access control model uses an object's classification to determine its access?
   (a) DAC
   (b) MAC
   (c) RBAC

3. The principle of least permission applies only to the RBAC model. True or false?

4. On Windows, each security principal has a unique _____.
   (a) ACL
   (b) ACE
   (c) DACL
   (d) SID

5. Which Active Directory security group type can be created only in a native mode domain?
   (a) Domain local
   (b) Global
   (c) Universal

6. In an Active Directory environment, which group type should be used to grant permissions?
   (a) Domain Local
   (b) Global
   (c) Universal

7. When you deny a group permission to modify an object, you add an ACE to the group's DACL. True or false?

8. Every Active Directory object has a security descriptor. True or false?

9. What is the default share permission when you share a folder on a computer running Windows Server 2003?

   (a) Everyone Full Control

   (b) Everyone Read

   (c) Users Full Control

   (d) Users Read

10. To increase security on a Windows network, you should delete all administrative shares. True or false?

11. What is the UID for the superuser on a Unix computer?

   (a) -2

   (b) 0

   (c) 1

   (d) 2

12. A user on a Unix computer can be associated with 0 or more groups. True or false?

13. Which character indicates that a right is not granted when it appears in a file inode's permission list?

   (a) –

   (b) d

   (c) n

   (d) x

14. Which of the following shows the order in which a Unix computer checks permissions when determining access?

   (a) group, owner, other

   (b) other, owner, group

   (c) owner, group, other

   (d) group, other, owner

Applying This Chapter

1. A file server running Windows 2000 is a member of an Active Directory domain. The file server has a folder named "Projects" that contains a subdirectory for each project. Project managers need to be able to read and modify the files for the projects they manage. One project manager is assigned to each project. The project manager also needs to be able to configure the access control for the files and folders within the project folder. Some folders will be used by everyone working on the project. Others will be accessed only by users working on specific tasks.

(a) What access control model is best suited to meet the requirements?

(b) What are two ways you can grant the project manager the necessary permissions?

(c) What steps can you take to facilitate the project manager's permission management?

(d) Why shouldn't the project manager just assign everyone on the project Modify access to the project folder?

(e) One project manager assigns access permissions, then finds that some of the project team members cannot access the files they need. How can she troubleshoot the problem?

(f) How can you ensure that Share permissions are always enforced when a team member accesses the file server?

2. You are troubleshooting file system permissions for a Unix file server. You run ls -l and the following listing is displayed:

```
-rw-r--r-- 1 steve  hr  1617 Dec  9 13:01 salaries.tex
-rws-x--x 1 root   hr  2399 Dec 10  9:25 payroll.exe
drwx------ 2 mike   hr   512 Dec 12 17:44 hr/
```

(a) What access do members of the "hr" group have to "salaries.tex"?

(b) Who can modify "salaries.tex"?

(c) What is the security vulnerability with the permissions assigned to "payroll.exe," if any?

YOU TRY IT

Configuring Access Control in an Active Directory Network

You are an administrator for an Active Directory forest. The forest has three domains, one for each company location. All accounting is done in the Chicago office. There are members of Human Resources in each office. There are also members of the Executive team and Sales department in each office.

A file server has three shared directories: AR, AP, and HR. It is running Windows Server 2003 and is a member of the Chicago domain.

Users in the Accounts Receivable department need to be able to read and write to files in the AR folder. Members of the Executive team need to be able to read, but not write to, the files in the AR folder.

Users in the Accounts Payable department need to be able to read and modify files in the AP folder. Members of the Sales department need to be able to read the CustomerDelinquency.xls file in the AP folder.

All users in the company need to be able to add files to the VacationRequests and Insurance subfolders of HR. They need to be able to read, but not modify, files in the CompanyInfo folder. Temporary employees should not be able to read information in the CompanyConfidential subfolder of CompanyInfo. Only members of the HR department should be able to read any other files in the HR folder or its subfolders.

1. Design the group strategy to meet the requirements. Use the RBAC security model and apply the principle of least permission.
2. If you chose to use Universal groups, what requirements must be met by the domain in which you create the Universal groups?
3. How would you configure permissions to grant the necessary permission to CompanyInfo and its subfolders?
4. How would you prevent an attacker with physical access to the file server from logging on?

Setting Permissions on a Unix Computer

You are a user on a Unix computer. You own a file named "project.tex." You want to ensure that all users can read the file and that all members of the projectA group can read and modify it.

1. What commands will you run to set the permissions?
2. You run the commands, but members of the projectA group cannot modify the file. They can read the file. What should you do?

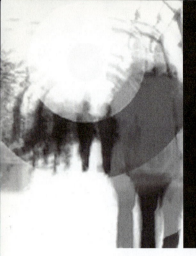

6

SECURING NETWORK TRANSMISSION

Starting Point

Go to www.wiley.com/college/cole to assess your knowledge of designing and implementing a secure network infrastructure.
Determine where you need to concentrate your effort.

What You'll Learn in This Chapter

▲ Types of network attacks
▲ Design considerations
▲ Switches and Virtual Local Area Networks (VLANs)
▲ Secure Sockets Layer (SSL) and Transport Layer Security (TLS)
▲ IP security (IPsec)
▲ Secure Shell (SSH)
▲ Server Message Block signing (SMB signing)

After Studying This Chapter, You'll Be Able To

▲ Identify the threats to data being transferred over the network
▲ Analyze requirements for securing data transmission
▲ Segment a network to improve security
▲ Select the appropriate protocol to secure data being transmitted across a network
▲ Describe how SSL and TLS can be used to secure data on a network
▲ Describe how IPsec can be used to filter and secure data on a network
▲ Describe the security protections offered by SMB signing and SSH

INTRODUCTION

Your network infrastructure is vulnerable to attack at many levels. For instance, you need to be concerned about the data that resides on physical devices and that passes through switches and routers on the network. You also need to consider how to physically secure network devices, because no matter how strong your security, it can be broken by someone who has physical access to network devices.

Physically securing your own devices is one thing, but on a public network like the Internet, you are not in control of the devices that your data might pass over. Even internally, you might want to prevent sensitive types of data from being "accidentally" seen as it travels on the network. You need to come up with a security strategy that reduces the risks associated with moving data across networks.

In this chapter, we will explore the security risks involved in transmitting data over a network and the protocols available for reducing those risks.

6.1 Analyzing Security Requirements for Network Traffic

In this section you will learn about some types of attacks that your network traffic might encounter, as well as the things you should consider when planning a security strategy for your network infrastructure.

6.1.1 Types of Attacks

Attackers can eavesdrop on data by using a network monitoring tool commonly referred to as a **packet sniffer,** which is used for legitimate troubleshooting but can also be used maliciously by being placed on a compromised router or network between you and the data's destination. Attackers can take over the administration functionality of a router, switch, or hub and misdirect packets, causing **denial-of-service (DoS) attacks.** Attackers can exploit flaws in the firmware or take advantage of known default settings in these devices. They can also launch a DoS attack against a device by trying to overwhelm it with large numbers of packets. Table 6-1 lists some common types of attacks to which your data is vulnerable.

Let's take a closer look at what's involved with a session hijacking attack and a special type of DoS attack, the TCP SYN Flooding attack. A detailed look at the other attacks is beyond the scope of this chapter.

TCP Session Hijacking

During a normal TCP/IP (Transmission Control Protocol/Internet Protocol) session between a server and a client, the client initiates a three-way handshake with the server by sending a **SYN message.** A SYN message is used to request sequence number synchronization. The server responds by sending an **ACK**

Table 6-1: Common Attacks on Data Transferred across a Network

Attacks	Description
Packet sniffing	An attacker views confidential data contained in packets from a database application, an email application, or a file transfer. Passwords that travel on the network unencrypted are viewed and used to infiltrate servers.
DoS attack	An attacker sends an unusually large number of packets to the server or exploits a vulnerability that prevents legitimate users from accessing a resource.
Spoofing	An attacker modifies a packet or data to impersonate another resource or person. For example, the attacker forges return addresses on emails or source IP addresses on IP packets.
Data alteration	An attacker modifies data between the source and the destination. This could mean changing the data in the packets, redirecting the packets, or forging information to attack network servers. This is used for man-in-the-middle attacks, **replays** (attacks in which data is captured and replayed with or without modification), session hijacking, and **packet tampering** (an attack in which data packets are modified).

(acknowledgement) message to the client's SYN and a SYN message of its own. The client then responds with an ACK to the server's SYN. The messages contain sequence numbers so that the receiving computer can verify that the message is correct. This exchange is shown in Figure 6-1.

Figure 6-1

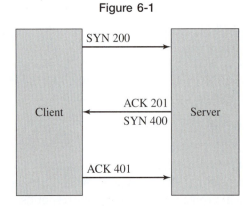

TCP/IP session initiation.

Figure 6-2

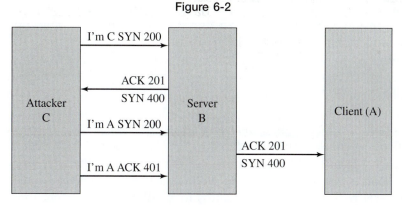

TCP session hijacking attack.

In a **TCP session hijacking** attack, the attacker opens a genuine connection to its target (B) and receives a sequence number. The attacker (C) then impersonates the client (A), sending a packet with the client's (A's) address in the source field and a sequence number consistent with what B expects the sequence number to be. If C guesses the right sequence number, B assumes that it has a connection with A, when in fact C is sending the packets. C cannot see the output from this session, but it might be able to execute commands with A's privileges on the server B. This process is illustrated in Figure 6-2.

This attack could be run in a Unix® environment, where the attacker spoofs messages from a **trusted host** (a Unix host that is trusted because the user name is the same on both the local and remote computers, and thus the user does not need to supply a password for authentication). Protocols such as **remote shell (rsh)** are vulnerable, as they employ address-based authentication, assuming that users logging in from a trusted host have already been authenticated. Remote shell is a Unix utility that allows you to execute shell commands remotely. The attack could also be run in an environment where authentication is not required.

To defend against this attack, a firewall should block all TCP packets arriving from the Internet with a local source address. This scheme works if all your trusted hosts are on the local network. If trusted hosts also exist in the Internet, the firewall has to block all protocols that use TCP and address-based authentication. As a better solution, you could avoid address-based authentication entirely and use cryptographic authentication, such as digital certifications, instead.

TCP SYN Flooding Attacks

After responding to the first SYN packet, the server (B) stores the sequence number so that it can verify the ACK from the client. Most computers limit the number of connections that have not completed the handshake process and are in the SYN_RECV state to prevent these types of connections from consuming system resources. These connections are known as **half-open connections.** In a **TCP SYN flooding attack,** the attacker initiates a large number of TCP open requests (SYN packets) to B without completing the handshake, until B reaches its half-open-connection limit and cannot respond to any new incoming requests.

As part of a TCP session hijacking attack, the attacker (C) could launch a SYN flooding attack against the client (A) so that A does not process the SYN-ACK packet from B and would not close the connection the attacker wants to open. Another way to launch a SYN flood attack is to spoof the source address on the SYN packet (change the address to an IP address different than that of the computer actually sending the packet) so that the SYN-ACK is sent to a wrong or nonexistent address.

Although there are no fail-safe **countermeasures** against a SYN flood attack, you can configure most routers so to reject packets that have a source address on your internal network and that originate on your external network and packets that have a source address outside your internal network but that originate on your external network. SYN filters can also be configured to reject a large number of SYN requests from the same IP address.

6.1.2 Considerations for Designing a Secure Infrastructure

You will need to determine what vulnerabilities will affect a company's network and then consider the importance of the data along with the costs and the technical requirements to secure it. The following sections discuss considerations that will help you in deciding what and how to secure data.

Decide What Network Traffic Needs Securing

Securing network traffic requires the use of CPU and network bandwidth, so you will need to figure out what traffic requires security and the level of security that it requires. This can range from setting up a point-to-point connection from the PC that is sending confidential data to the server to establishing a secure connection or tunnel between routers so all traffic that passes through the routers over the segment is encrypted.

Identify the Compatibility Issues of the Operating Systems You Have Installed and the Applications Running on Them

The version of the operating system or application you are running will affect what security options are available for transmitting data. You will need to weigh the cost of upgrading the operating system or application with the cost of being less secure.

Make Sure that the Hardware Is Secure

If the hardware is not secure, it doesn't really matter what security measures you are taking on the packets moving across your network. Securing the hardware means making sure you lock the wiring closets and control access to the server room. You can also add more security by using switches rather than hubs on the network. A **switch** controls the traffic going out so that it is directed to the device or segment attached to a specific port instead of sending all packets to all devices, making it harder for attackers to sniff packets on your network.

Figure Out What Methods to Use to Secure Data that Will Be Transmitted across a Network

Data is vulnerable as it moves across the physical devices and mediums on the network. You cannot trust devices that you do not exercise full control over, so you will need to take appropriate precautions with your confidential data. Mainly, you will need to figure out the identity of the person and/or computer that is transmitting the data and encrypt the data so it cannot be read on an insecure network. You will also need to take into account laws that restrict encryption strength and exportation to countries where you will do business. This might mean precluding data from being transmitted into these countries or using a separate physical network instead of the less expensive public network.

Once you have decided what types of attacks your data is vulnerable to, you will need to come up with a plan to securely transmit data across the network. This might involve coming up with a method to encrypt the data you are transmitting, verifying that the data has not been manipulated in transit, and choosing which method you will use to authenticate remote clients on the network.

6.1.3 Securely Transmitting Data

If you decide that you need to securely transmit data over a network, there are some actions you need to take to mitigate the risk of an attack:

▲ Make sure that the data will not be read by any unauthorized individual between you and the source.

▲ Verify or authenticate the identity of people (and/or computers) who will send packets.

▲ Verify that the data will not be tampered with, meaning the data in a packet won't be changed by someone in between you and the packet's source (known as a man-in-the-middle attack).

FOR EXAMPLE

Analyzing Traffic Security Requirements

When analyzing data security requirements, you need to consider the type of data being transferred, which computers the data must be transferred between, and the confidentiality, authentication, and integrity requirements for the data. Suppose, for example, that a company's Research department frequently transfers company-confidential data between the researchers' computers and a database server in the department. The company values this data highly and estimates the cost of it falling into the hands of a competitor as very high. In this case, you might decide that you want to allow only members of the Research department to access the database server. You might also decide that you are going to encrypt all traffic that travels on the network within the research department. You have several ways of meeting these goals. For example, you could isolate the Research department on its own network segment and use a firewall to prevent traffic originating outside the segment from being sent to the database server. You could also choose an encryption technology that would encrypt all data sent to the database server or all data on the network. If the database server is running Microsoft® SQL Server 2005, you can choose to encrypt database traffic using SSL. To prevent an attacker from spoofing the database server, you might choose to use certificates for mutual authentication.

You can reduce the risks involved with transmitting data that must be secured by encrypting the data, authenticating the user, and signing the data. You can also segment your network using switches, routers, firewalls, and virtual LANs (VLANs). The rest of this chapter will discuss strategies for securing data on a local area network (LAN) or when accessing a web server. Remote access security, such as security protocols for dial-up networking and virtual private networks are beyond the scope of this chapter.

SELF-CHECK

1. Identify the four types of network attacks.
2. Describe why you need to analyze the types of data being transferred on the network.

6.2 Defining Network Perimeters

One way to secure a network is to isolate segments that have secure data transmission requirements. You can segment a network at Layer 3 using routers and subnets and at Layer 2 using switches and VLANs. Let's take a look at both of these options.

6.2.1 Isolating Insecure Networks Using Subnets

Most organizations have a network perimeter, which is any point that connects the internal network to external networks. Network perimeters include the network connection point to the Internet, links to a satellite office, or a remote access server. A screened subnet is also on the perimeter of a network. One use of a **screened subnet** is as a protected area on the network used to run services that are shared outside of the organization. Business-to-business (B2B) services are typically run from this type of subnet. Other uses of a screened subnet include isolating secure data on a segment or walling off a segment in which unsecure activity is common, such as a software development environment or a test network.

A **DMZ** is a type of screened subnet. DMZ stands for demilitarized zone, which is an isolated network segment at the point where a corporate network meets the Internet. Other examples of network perimeters are wireless access points or virtual private network (VPN) connections.

The network perimeter is the part of any network that is most vulnerable to attack. The attack can be random or targeted. Because of the prevalence of threats that affect public network access points, you should take great care to minimize your internal network's exposure to the public network, also referred to as **"the wild."**

Routers and firewalls can be used to screen the traffic that passes into and out of the screened subnet. There are typically three types of configurations that an organization can implement when securing its network perimeters: bastion host, three-pronged configuration, or back-to-back configuration. Let's take a look at each of these.

Bastion Host

A **bastion host** acts as the only connection for computers on the internal network to use to access the Internet (or other external networks). This configuration is illustrated in Figure 6-3. When configured as a firewall, the bastion host is specially designed to prevent attacks against the internal network. The bastion host uses at least two network adapters: one is connected to the internal network while the other is connected to the external network. This configuration physically separates the internal network from the outside. An example of a bastion host is a computer sharing an Internet connection and providing NAT (Network Address Tramslation) services, such as a proxy server. Its weakness is that it is a single point of failure; should it be compromised, the attacker can gain access to the internal network.

Figure 6-3

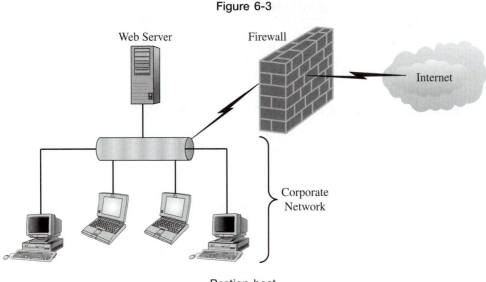

Bastion host.

Three-pronged Configuration

In a **three-pronged configuration,** the firewall system has a minimum of three network adapters. One adapter will be connected to the internal network, one to the external or public network, and the third to a screened subnet. This configuration allows for hosts from the public and internal networks to access the available resources in the screened subnet while continuing to isolate the internal network from the wild. For example, you might want to put a web server in a screened subnet. Figure 6-4 depicts this configuration.

Back-to-back Configuration

The **back-to-back configuration** places the screened subnet between two firewalls. The screened subnet is connected through a firewall to the Internet on one end (similar to a bastion host) and is connected through another firewall to the internal network on the opposite end. This is probably the most secure configuration while still allowing for public resources to be accessed. This would require an attacker to breach both firewalls in order to compromise the internal network. Figure 6-5 shows an illustration of this configuration.

6.2.2 Switches and VLANs

When you segment a network using subnets, you are limited by the IP addressing scheme. In some cases, you might want to group computers into segments that are independent of their IP addresses. One way to do this is by using switches and configuring a **virtual local area network (virtual LAN, or VLAN).**

Figure 6-4

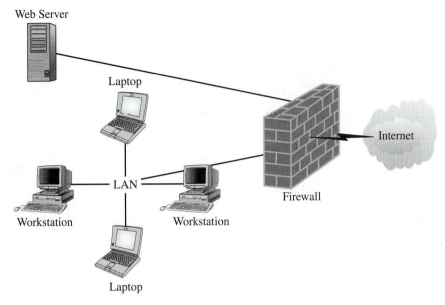

Three-pronged configuration.

Figure 6-5

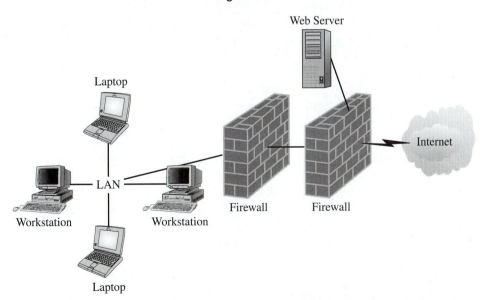

Back-to-back configuration.

FOR EXAMPLE

The Importance of Perimeter Security

Quovadimus Incorporated is a technology firm specializing in biotechnology. The organization frequently works with educational and government institutions. Quovadimus also hosts its own web and mail servers that are accessible from the Internet. The CIO tells the network administrator to provide a partnering organization with access to the company's data. The CIO has promised the partnering organization that the data will be available to them within an hour. As a result of not properly preparing for this type of data access, there is no time to develop a secure perimeter.

Using basic techniques like port scanning, an attacker is able to **footprint** the Quovadimus perimeter network. The attacker learns what operating systems and services are running on the perimeter network. The attacker now has enough information to create an entire diagram of the organization's perimeter. The attacker researches the known vulnerabilities of the services that are running in the perimeter network and can now systematically attack the network.

The attacker now can gain access to some or all of the services that are accessible, including those of the organization's partners. A leak of confidential data causes the company to lose a competitive advantage and creates a loss of credibility with a key partner.

The CIO now tells you that you need to make the perimeter secure for data access by current partners and future partners. One way to do this is to create a screened subnet. You select a back-to-back configuration to ensure that your company's internal network is more difficult for an attacker to access.

You create a VLAN by associating the hosts in a specific VLAN with a **tag** (identifier for a specific VLAN). The tagging protocol specified in **802.1Q** is the most commonly used tagging protocol. VLANs operate at Layer 2 of the OSI model. A host that does not have a tag is associated with the default VLAN, **VLAN 1.**

By isolating computers in a network into separate VLANs, you limit the **broadcast domain.** Communication between VLANs must occur through a router. Because you assign a host to a VLAN through software, the configuration can be based on actual data transfer requirements within the organization. For example, you might create a separate VLAN for the Accounting department. To communicate with members of the Accounting department, computers in other departmental VLANs would have to send requests through a router and be subject to any Layer 3 security measures, such as firewalls.

Like all security measures, a VLAN has potential vulnerabilities. One type of attack, called **VLAN hopping,** allows an attacker to bypass the VLAN boundary by modifying the **VLAN ID** (tag) on a packet. An attacker can also hop to another VLAN by gaining access to a native port.

FOR EXAMPLE

Keeping Your Switches Up-to-Date

Another way you can secure your network is to upgrade your switches to the latest versions. Vendors are constantly making improvements that address vulnerabilities and common attacks. For example, the Cisco® 3560-E series switches include a number of security features designed to make VLANs more secure by providing better isolation between ports and by adding access control lists (ACLs) to ports. You should always consider the security features of a switch before making a purchase.

If your budget does not allow you to upgrade to a new switch, at least visit the vendor sites frequently to look for updates. Most vendors, including Cisco, post security bulletins and updates that resolve issues found in their equipment.

6.2.3 Using IP Address and IP Packet Filtering

As an added layer of protection, you should enable filtering on your servers. There are two types of filters that you can apply to your server: IP address filtering and IP packet filtering.

IP Address Filtering

IP address filtering involves filtering traffic based on the IP address of the client computer. Some web server applications, such as Internet Information Services (IIS), allow you to filter the requests they accept based on a client's IP address. For example, the configuration in Figure 6-6 allows only connections

Figure 6-6

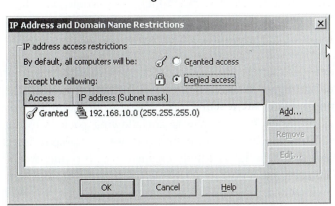

IP address filtering in IIS.

from the 192.168.10.0 subnet and would be appropriate for an intranet website. Another way to filter traffic based on address is by installing and configuring a personal firewall.

You generally have two options for configuring IP filtering: you can enable all traffic except traffic from the IP addresses listed, or you can exclude all IP addresses and allow only the IP addresses listed. If you enable IP address filtering, it is recommended that you filter all traffic except the traffic explicitly specified. You also need to realize that an IP address can be spoofed, so you should still rely on additional forms of authentication for the users.

IP Packet Filtering

If you need a higher level of control than is available by preventing an IP address from communicating with your server, you can use IP packet filtering. **IP packet filtering** prevents specific packets from reaching their destined ports on the server. This can be effective in guarding against packets for specific services that would not represent legitimate traffic to the server. You define a filter based on the protocols or port numbers.

FOR EXAMPLE

Using Filters to Prevent a W32.Slammer Worm Attack

Busicorp had a web server that had some of sample applications installed for development purposes. It had Microsoft Data Engine (MSDE) 2000 installed on it, but the web server did not have the latest SQL Server 2000 patches on the server installed. Therefore, the server was vulnerable to attacks due to security holes that are inevitable in any product. This is usually not much of a problem on a server that is actively maintained. The patches would be installed and the vulnerability would be patched. But this was not the case on this server. Busicorp had installed packet filtering on the box as part of the standard setup of the server. IT knew that the computer would be used for web applications, File Transfer Protocol (FTP) based applications, and Simple Mail Transfer Protocol (SMTP) based applications. The server had filters enabled to allow this traffic, along with the capability to authenticate with Active Directory®. When the Slammer worm hit, the server was protected because it was not allowing packets to communicate with port UDP 1434, so the Slammer worm was not able to infect the computer. These filters, by being totally exclusive of all traffic except the traffic Busicorp allowed, prevented attacks, even though the applications were not properly maintained.

SELF-CHECK

1. Describe the three types of perimeter network configurations.
2. Describe a VLAN.

6.3 Data Transmission Protection Protocols

Several protocols are available for authenticating, encrypting, and ensuring the integrity of data when it is transmitted across the network. In this section, we'll look at several of these: SSL, TLS, IPsec, SMB signing, and SSH.

6.3.1 SSL and TLS

SSL and **TLS** are protocols that provide session encryption and integrity for packets sent from one computer to another. They can be used to secure client-to-server or server-to-server network traffic. They also provide authentication of the server to the client and (optionally) of the the client to the server through X.509 certificates (digital certificates). TLS is an enhancement of SSL, but all of our discussion of SSL relates to TLS as well.

SSL packets can be passed through firewalls, NAT servers, and other network devices without any special considerations other than making sure the proper ports are open on the device. For example HTTP over SSL uses port 443 by default. Therefore, a firewall between the Internet and a web server that uses SSL on its default port would need to allow incoming and outgoing traffic on port 443. Figure 6-7 shows where SSL would typically be used on a network.

Figure 6-7

SSL Between the Web Client and the Web Server

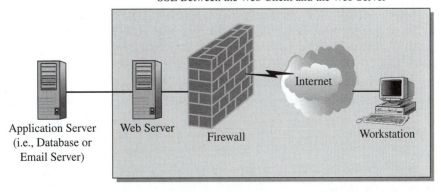

SSL on a network.

Figure 6-8

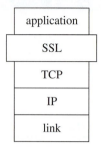

The SSL Security layer.

The most common use of SSL is between a web client and a web server because it is supported by web browsers and web servers on all platforms and has become the standard for encrypting HTTP traffic. However, SSL can also be used to communicate with application or database servers, provided that the application or database management system supports SSL.

SSL works between the Application and Transport layers of the network protocol stack, as shown in Figure 6-8.

SSL Behind the Scenes

SSL has two components, the SSL Handshake Protocol and the SSL Record Layer. The **SSL Handshake Protocol** sets up the cryptographic parameters of the session state, including the session identifier, the cipher that will be used, shared secret keys, certifications, and random values used by protocols, such as Diffie-Hellman. The **SSL Record Layer** takes blocks from an upper-layer protocol, fragments these blocks into **SSL Plaintext records,** and then applies the cryptographic transformation defined by the **cipher spec** in the current session state. Essentially, the SSL Record Layer provides the encryption services.

Figure 6-9 shows the messages exchanged between client and server. Components in parentheses are optional. To illustrate this protocol, we will step through a conversation in which the client authenticates the server. The client initiates the protocol run with a **ClientHello message,** containing a random number, a list of suggested ciphers (ordered according to the client's preference), and a suggested compression algorithm. An example of a ClientHello message is shown in Figure 6-10.

In our example, the server selects the cipher "TLS_RSA_WITH_3DES_ EDE_CBC_SHA" from the suggested suite. This selection means that RSA will be used for key exchange, triple DES (Data Encryption Standard) in CBC (cipher-block chaining) mode for encryption, and SHA as the hash function. The server replies with a **ServerHello** message and a certificate chain, as shown in Figure 6-11.

Figure 6-9

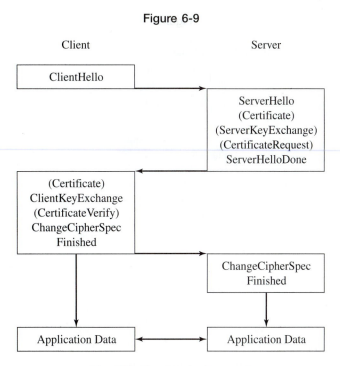

The SSL Handshake Protocol.

If mutual authentication was required, the server would also request a certificate chain from the client. In our example, no certificate is requested from the client. The client verifies the certificate chain to ensure that it trusts the certificate authority (CA) that issued the certificate or its root CA and then locally creates a random 48-byte **PreMasterSecret**. The **MasterSecret** is the first 48 bytes of PRF (PreMasterSecret, "master secret," ClientRandom || ServerRandom).

Here, PRF is shorthand for a more complex function based on MD5 and SHA that takes as inputs a secret, a label, and a seed. The symbol || means that

Figure 6-10

M1:	ClientHello:	ClientRandom[28]
		Suggested Cipher Suites: 　　TLS_RSA_WITH_IDEA_CBC_SHA 　　TLS_RSA_WITH_3DES_EDE_CBC_SHA 　　TLS_DH_DSS_WITH_AES_128 _CBC_SHA
		Suggested Compression Algorithm: NONE

ClientHello message.

Figure 6-11

M2:	ServerHello:	ServerRandom[28]
		Use Cipher Suite: TLS_RSA_WITH_3DES_EDE_CBC_SHA
		Session ID: 0xa00372d4XS

	Certificates:	subjectAltName: SuperStoreVirtualOutlet PublicKey: 0x521aa593 ... Issuer: SuperStoreHQ
		subjectAltName: SuperStoreHQ PublicKey: 0x9f400682 ... Issuer: Verisign

	Server Done:	NONE

ServerHello message.

the ClientRandom is concatenated with the ServerRandom. The MasterSecret serves as input to the construction of a **key block.** All required encryption keys for client and server are extracted from the key block. The keys protecting traffic from client to server are different from the keys protecting traffic from server to client. Thus, the parties can easily distinguish between messages they send and messages they receive, and they are not subject to reflection attacks where a message is replayed to its sender.

The client now transmits the PreMasterSecret to the server, using the key management algorithm specified in the selected cipher suite and the server's certified

FOR EXAMPLE

Designing for SSL on a Windows® Server 2003 Network

Frankfurters, Inc. is a medium-sized company with about 700 employees located in 5 states in the United States. It produces various meat products and is looking to allow access to email for its sales and executive staff throughout the nation. The company is running Windows Server 2003 on its servers and is using Exchange Server 2003 and Active Directory.

During the design process, you conducted the interviews as summarized in Table 6-2.

You decide to enable SSL on the server running OWA. This is a good choice because SSL is supported by most operating systems and devices. Also, it does not require special security settings on the client.

Table 6-2: Interviews

Interviewee	Interview Summary
CIO	We want to provide email access wherever our sales staff or executives might travel and on whatever computer they might be using. We need to keep the cost low, so we are looking at using the Internet and a national ISP to provide Internet access.
Network Administrator	Users might access their email from their home PCs, from laptops issued by Frankfurters's IT staff, or through computers at other locations. The email contains important sales projections, client information, and other confidential information, and you need to protect this information in transit, so we need to make sure the solution can deliver the information securely over various network topologies. We are looking at using the HTTP access in Exchange 2003 called Outlook® Web Access (OWA) because it looks easy to use and comes with Exchange 2003.
Salespeople and Executives	We want a solution that is easy to use. We do not want to deal with setting up software or configuration settings for security on the device we might use.

public key. The client should then immediately destroy the PreMasterSecret. The **ChangeCipherSpec message** indicates that subsequent records will be protected under the newly negotiated cipher suite and keys. The client then ties the third message to the first two through two hashes constructed with MD5 and SHA.

The server decrypts the PremasterSecret and uses it to compute the Master-Secret, the key block, and all derived secret keys valid for this session with the client. The server verifies the hash appended to the client's message and replies with a hashed ChangeCipherSpec response.

The client verifies the hash in the server's message. Both parties have now established shared secret keys which they can use to protect application traffic.

6.3.2 IP Security (IPsec)

IPsec is a security protocol that operates at the Internet layer of the TCP/IP protocol stack (see Figure 6-12), which is equivalent to the OSI Network layer.

Figure 6-12

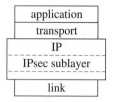

IPsec on the stack.

Because it operates at the Internet layer, it is application-independent. Applications do not need to provide support for IPsec. In fact, they are not aware of it at all. IPsec is optional with IPv4 and is not implemented by all operating systems. IPsec is required by the IPv6 specification.

IPsec can be used to secure traffic on a LAN or on a VPN. IPsec can be configured to offer the following:

▲ Confidentiality
▲ Authentication
▲ Data integrity
▲ Packet filtering
▲ Protection against data reply attacks

IPsec can be configured to use multiple security algorithm options. An administrator can decide which security algorithm to use for an application based on security requirements.

IPsec architecture is described in **RFC 2401**. IPsec includes two major security mechanisms: **Authentication Header (AH)**, described in **RFC 2402**, and **Encapsulating Security Payload (ESP)**, covered in **RFC 2406**.

Authentication Header

AH protects the integrity and authenticity of IP packets but does not protect confidentiality. It was introduced primarily for political reasons. In the 1990s, export restrictions on encryption algorithms created the need for an authentication-only mechanism. These export restrictions by and large have been lifted, and it is now recommended that, in most cases, you use ESP only, to simplify implementations of IPsec.

Encapsulating Security Payload

ESP can be used to provide confidentiality, data origin authentication, data integrity, some replay protection, and limited traffic flow confidentiality. An ESP packet is shown in Figure 6-13.

Figure 6-13

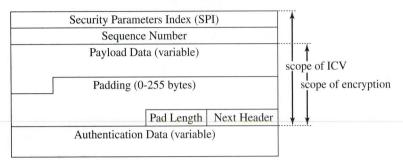

ESP packet.

An ESP packet contains the following fields:

▲ **Security Parameters Index (SPI)** is a 32-bit field that uniquely identifies the security association for the datagram, the destination IP address, and the security protocol (ESP).

▲ **Sequence number** is an unsigned 32-bit field containing an increasing counter value; this value must be included by the sender but might not be processed by the receiver. The sequence number helps to avoid replay attacks.

▲ **Payload data** is a variable-length field containing the transport layer **protocol data unit (PDU)**. A PDU is another word for a network message.

▲ **Padding** is an optional field containing padding data for the encryption algorithm; the length of the data to be encrypted has to be a multiple of the algorithm's block size.

▲ **Pad length** is a value that provides the length of the padding field.

▲ **Next Header** shows the next protocol field on the normal IP packet.

▲ **Authentication data** is a variable number of 32-bit words containing an **integrity check value (ICV)** computed over the ESP packet minus the Authentication Data.

SPI and the sequence number constitute the ESP header. The fields after the payload data are the ESP trailer.

ESP Modes

ESP can be configured to operate in one of two modes:

▲ **Transport mode:** In transport mode, the upper-layer protocol frame [from TCP or UDP (User Datagram Protocol), up the stack] is encapsulated. The IP header is not encrypted. Transport mode provides end-to-end

Figure 6-14

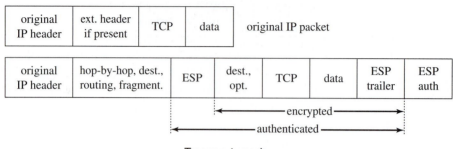

Transport mode.

protection of packets exchanged between two end hosts. Both nodes have to be IPsec aware. This is illustrated in Figure 6-14.

▲ **Tunnel mode:** In tunnel mode (Figure 6-15) an entire datagram plus security fields are treated as a new payload of an outer IP datagram. The original inner IP datagram is encapsulated within the outer IP datagram. IP tunneling can therefore be described as **IP within IP.** This mode can be used when IPsec processing is performed at security gateways on behalf of end hosts. The end hosts need not be IPsec aware. The gateway could be a perimeter firewall or a router. This mode provides **gateway-to-gateway security** rather than end-to-end security. On the other hand, you get traffic flow confidentiality as the inner IP datagram is not visible to intermediate routers, and the original source and destination addresses are hidden.

Security Associations

To generate, decrypt, or verify an ESP packet a system has to know which algorithm and which key to use. This information is stored in a **security association (SA).** IPsec security associations are defined in RFC 2401. The SA is the

Figure 6-15

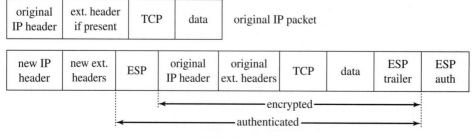

Tunnel mode.

common state between two hosts for communication in one direction. Bidirectional communication between two hosts requires two security associations, one in each direction. Therefore, SAs are usually created in pairs.

An SA is uniquely identified by an SPI (carried in AH and ESP headers), the destination IP address, and a security protocol (AH or ESP) identifier. It contains the relevant cryptographic data, such as algorithm identifiers, keys, and key lifetimes. There can be a sequence number counter and an anti-replay window. The SA also tells whether tunnel mode or transport mode is used.

Internet Key Exchange Protocol

SAs could be created manually. This works if the number of nodes is small, but manually creating SAs does not scale to reasonably sized networks of IPsec-aware hosts. The alternative to manual keying is **IKE**, the **Internet Key Exchange protocol (RFC 2409)**. A new version, **IKEv2**, is defined in **RFC 4306.** At the time this book was written, several implementations of IKEv2 were available. IKEv2 offers enhancements to protect against certain types of DoS attacks aimed at using processor resources for negotiating security associations for a client that does not exist. It also allows each participant to have a different key lifetime. IKEv2 is also designed to allow IPsec to work better through a NAT connection than IKEv1.

Two goals of IKE are entity authentication and the establishment of a fresh shared secret. The shared secret is used to derive additional keys. IKE is also responsible for the secure negotiation of all cryptographic algorithms, for example, authentication method, key exchange method, algorithms for encryption, or hash algorithms.

IKE operates in two phases. Phase 1 sets up an SA as a secure channel to carry further SA negotiation, as well as error and management traffic. This phase involves heavy-duty entity authentication and key exchange. The phase 1 protocol has two variants, a slow main mode (six messages) with more security guarantees, and a faster aggressive mode (four messages). Main mode and aggressive mode each give the choice of multiple authentication mechanisms.

In phase 2, SAs for general use are negotiated. Fast negotiations take place over the secure channel established in phase 1. Each phase 1 agreement can have multiple phase 2 agreements, and multiple pairs of SAs can be negotiated during each phase 2 negotiation.

IPsec specifies authentication and encryption services independently of the key management protocols that set up the SAs and session keys. Thus, IPsec security services are not tied to any particular key management protocol. If a key management protocol were found to be flawed, this protocol could be replaced without further repercussions on IPsec implementations.

Let's wrap up our discussion of IPsec with a look at how you configure IPsec on a computer running Windows Server 2003.

Configuring IPsec on a Windows Network

You can enable and configure the IPsec protocol with Group Policy for Windows 2000 or later computers or through the Network Connection Wizard. You can configure rules that a computer will follow in applying IPsec to outgoing and incoming packets. Windows Server 2003 has three built-in IPsec policies:

1. **Client (Respond Only):** The client will use IPsec if the server requests or requires it.
2. **Server (Request Security):** The server will request that an IPsec session be created with the client but will still establish a connection if the client does not support it.
3. **Server (Require Security):** The server will only allow communication with clients that support IPsec. This means that one of the previous two rules needs to be configured.

These settings are located by navigating to the Security Settings section of the Group Policy console or by launching the Domain, Domain Controller, or Local Security Policy Microsoft Management Console (MMC) from the Administrative Tools section of the Start menu. You can click on the IP Security Policies section to reveal the information shown in Figure 6-16.

The built-in policies are made up of a default set of rules and are mainly provided as examples or for very basic configurations. On a production network, you will most likely need to create a custom **IPsec policy**, which is just a

Figure 6-16

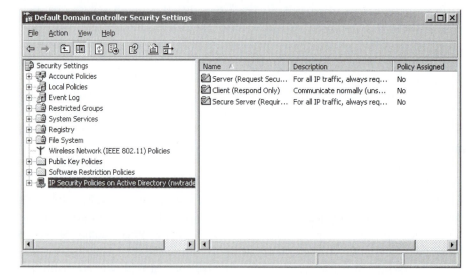

Default IPsec policies on a Windows Server 2003 computer.

collection of rules that define how communication should occur. You can create rules that define the following:

▲ A filter that decides what type of traffic (like HTTP or SMTP) to apply the IPsec policy to and optionally the destination or source address.

▲ A filter action that defines what the policy should do when it matches the traffic type defined in the filter. This could be requiring encryption for a protocol, permitting all traffic, or blocking all traffic from a protocol.

▲ An authentication method that uses one of three mechanisms: Kerberos v5 protocol, public key infrastructure (PKI) certificate, or a preshared key. Kerberos or PKI certificates are the more secure choices but require additional infrastructure. The preshared key does not require Kerberos or PKI infrastructure, but the same key must be entered on each computer. The preshared key option is less secure because it is stored in the policy, which could be compromised. Therefore, you should use preshared keys for testing purposes only.

▲ The type of IPsec connection, which is either tunnel or transport mode.

▲ The network interface that the IPsec policy applies to, such as a VPN connection or specific network interface.

▲ The means for exchanging keys over the Internet via IKE.

The Edit Rule Properties dialog box for configuring IPsec is shown in Figure 6-17.

6.3.3 Server Message Block Signing

If you access files over a network share on a Windows server, you are using the **Server Message Block (SMB)** protocol. By default, the packets sent using SMB are not secure.

Server Message Block (SMB) signing adds a keyed hash to each SMB packet. This allows you to guard your network against man-in-the-middle, replay, and session hijacking attacks. But SMB signing does nothing to protect the confidentiality of the data that is passing over the network connection. Signing requires that every packet be signed and verified, which means that you can expect a slowdown when accessing an SMB resource like a file share.

SMB signing is enabled by default on a Windows 2000 Server, Windows XP, and Windows Server 2003. All Windows clients support it except for Windows 95 without the Active Directory client and Windows NT® pre–Service Pack 3. If SMB signing is not enabled on the client, it will not be able to connect to a server on which SMB signing is enabled. This will prevent access to Group Policy, printing, and file shares on a domain controller or server with SMB signing

Figure 6-17

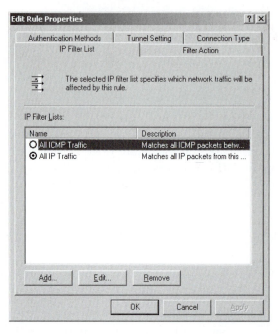

Creating IPsec rules on a Windows Server 2003 computer.

enabled. If you have computers that must run these operating systems, then segment all computers that they need to communicate with in their own organizational unit (OU) and apply the following Group Policy setting to the OU Computer Configuration\Windows Settings\Security Settings\Local Policies\ Security Options\Microsoft Network Server: Digitally sign communications (always) = Disabled (see Figure 6-18).

This can also be applied to a domain, but it will increase the risk of the attacks mentioned earlier. IPsec provides a mechanism to sign all IP traffic and would be a better choice for heterogeneous networks.

6.3.4 Secure Shell

Remote users often rely on remote login programs, such as rsh, ftp, rlogin, rcp, and so on, for attaining connectivity to host machines for application needs. These programs transmit data in clear text. The purpose of each of these utilities is beyond the scope of this chapter.

Secure Shell (SSH), maintained by the Internet Engineering Task Force, addresses this issue with remote login programs such as Telnet and ftp. SSH services have comparatively higher security than services such as Telnet. SSH is

Figure 6-18

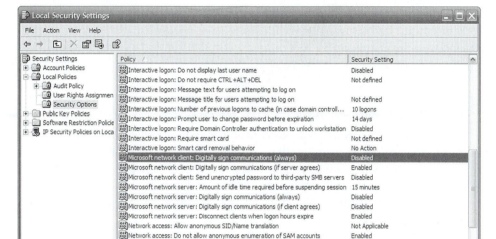

Allowing connections from clients that don't support SMB signing.

now available as the standard for remote computer logins. Typical applications of SSH include remote access to computer resources over the Internet, secure file transfers, and remote system administration. SSH services use public key encryption schemes for providing data confidentiality and authentication. Although SSH services are most suitable and intended for Unix and Linux operating systems, non-Unix operating systems, such as Windows and Macintosh®, also support it.

The SSH service has been released in two different versions. SSH-1 is susceptible to man-in-the-middle attacks and should not be used. Instead, you should use SSH-2 when secure remote login is required.

SSH-2 includes the following features:

▲ Complete replacement of conventional remote login programs, such as ftp, Telnet, rlogin, and so on, with their security-compatible counterparts, such as scp, sftp, sshd, and ssh-agent.

▲ Support for multiple encryption algorithms, including DES, 3-DES, and AES.

▲ High-end security algorithms tailored to detect identity spoofing such as IP spoofing and other security threats.

> ### FOR EXAMPLE
>
> #### Using IPsec to Secure a Subnet
>
> One way IPsec can be used effectively is to block protocols destined for one or more computers. If this is your goal, you would configure a filter for the protocol and optionally the source computers and specify a filter action or block. You would not need to create any security associations because the packets would be rejected.
>
> Another way you can use IPsec to secure data on a network is to secure communication with a server that contains confidential data. You can create a filter that allows only specific client computers to access the server and that requires those communications to be encrypted.
>
> One issue you might encounter is that some operating systems do not support IPsec. For example, Windows 95, Windows 98, and Windows Me support IPsec only for VPN connections, not for LAN connections. In this case, you can use IPsec in tunnel mode to secure communications between a server and another end point.

▲ Authentication through key pairs generated by RSA or **Digital Signature Algorithm (DSA).** DSA is a standard for generating digital signatures.

▲ Multiple sessions for multiple terminal windows through one secure (authentication and encryption) connection.

SELF-CHECK

1. List the network protocols that provide data confidentiality.
2. List the protections offered by SMB signing.
3. Describe the two modes supported by ESP.

SUMMARY

In this chapter you learned how to secure data on the network. First you learned about some attacks that can be launched over the network and some things to keep in mind when securing your network infrastructure. Next you learned about segmenting your network physically using subnets, routers, and firewalls, and logically, using VLANs. You also learned how to protect a server from network attacks by filtering packets based on IP address or protocol. Finally, you learned about protocols that can be used to secure data on the network. These include SSL, TLS, IPsec, SMB signing, and SSH.

KEY TERMS

802.1Q

Acknowledgement (ACK) message

Authentication data

Authentication Header (AH)

Back-to-back configuration

Bastion host

Broadcast domain

ChangeCipherSpec message

Cipher spec

ClientHello message

Countermeasures

Demilitarized zone (DMZ)

Denial of Service (DoS) attack

Digital Signature Algorithm (DSA)

Encapsulating Security Payload (ESP)

Footprint

Gateway-to-gateway security

Half-open connections

IKEv2

Integrity Check Value (ICV)

Internet Key Exchange (IKE) protocol

IP address filtering

IP packet filtering

IPsec policy

IP Security (IPsec)

IP within IP

Key block

MasterSecret

Next Header

Packet sniffer

Packet tampering

Padding

Pad length

Payload data

PreMasterSecret

Protocol data unit (PDU)

Remote shell (rsh)

Replays

RFC 2401

RFC 2402

RFC 2406

RFC 2409

RFC 4306

Screened subnet

Secure Sockets Layer (SSL)

Security Association (SA)

Security Parameters Index (SPI)

Sequence number

ServerHello

Server Message Block (SMB)

Server Message Block (SMB) signing

SSH

SSL Handshake Protocol

SSL Plaintext records

SSL Record Layer

Switch

SYN message

Tag

TCP session hijacking

TCP SYN flooding attack

The wild

Three-pronged configuration

Transport Layer Security (TLS)

Transport mode

Trusted host

Tunnel mode

Virtual local area network (VLAN)

VLAN hopping

VLAN ID

VLAN

ASSESS YOUR UNDERSTANDING

Go to www.wiley.com/college/cole to evaluate your knowledge of designing and implementing a secure network infrastructure.
Measure your learning by comparing pre-test and post-test results.

Summary Questions

1. What type of attack involves an attacker impersonating a legitimate client in order to execute commands on a server?
   (a) TCP SYN flooding
   (b) TCP session hijacking
   (c) brute force
   (d) phishing

2. Which of the following is a denial-of-service attack?
   (a) man-in-the middle
   (b) replay attack
   (c) TCP SYN flooding
   (d) TCP session hijacking

3. When designing security for a network infrastructure, you should plan to use the strongest encryption possible for all data. True or false?

4. Which perimeter configuration requires two separate firewalls?
   (a) back-to-back configuration
   (b) bastion host
   (c) three-pronged configuration

5. A host that is not assigned to a VLAN is automatically assigned to VLAN 1. True or false?

6. In a bastion host configuration, it is not necessary to enable protocol filters on any servers. True or false?

7. Which encryption protocol requires application support on both the server and the client?
   (a) IPsec AH
   (b) IPsec ESP
   (c) SSL
   (d) SMB signing

8. SSL requires a digital certificate on both the server and the client. True or false?

9. Which of the following protections is NOT provided by IPsec AH?

   (a) authentication

   (b) confidentiality

   (c) integrity

10. Which IPsec mode requires that both the source and the destination computer be Ipsec-aware?

   (a) transport mode

   (b) tunnel mode

11. A bidirectional IPsec conversation requires two security associations. True or false?

12. Which default Windows IPsec policy can only be configured if all clients that need to communicate with the server support IPsec?

   (a) Client (Respond only)

   (b) Server (Request security)

   (c) Server (Require security)

13. Which protection or protections is provided by SMB signing?

   (a) authentication only

   (b) authentication and confidentiality

   (c) integrity only

   (d) authentication and integrity

14. SSH is only supported on Unix and Linux operating systems. True or false?

Applying This Chapter

1. Busicorp provides accounting, web development, and marketing services for over 200 small businesses. Busicorp's network is configured as a single sub-net with a bastion host firewall providing perimeter protection between the internal network and the Internet. The CEO is concerned about the company's liability if customer records were obtained. Customers currently upload their records to an FTP server hosted by Busicorp's ISP. After the records have been uploaded, they are downloaded by one of 10 data entry people and entered into a database. The data is then retrieved and manipulated by one of 4 accountants. The accountants handle accounts receivable, accounts payable, reporting, and tax form generation for the companies. No other Busicorp employees should have access to the data.

   (a) Which threat or threats provide(s) the greatest risk to customer accounting data?

   (b) What step could you take to secure the data while it is being transmitted by the customer?

(c) How could you change your network segments to protect the data before it is downloaded by data entry personnel? Choose the most secure option.

(d) Why is a back-to-back configuration more secure than a three-pronged configuration?

(e) What steps involving the network can you take to protect the database server?

(f) What steps can you take to protect the data when it is being transmitted between the database server and the accountants' computers? Select an option that will provide end-to-end confidentiality.

(g) What would prevent you from using SSL?

Designing Network Infrastructure Security

You have been hired by a medical clinic to improve the security of its network. The medical clinic personnel includes doctors, nurses, clerical personnel, and administrators. Only doctors and nurses need access to patient medical data. Clerical personnel need access to patient appointments. Administrators need access to insurance policy data, billing data, and medical inventory data, including the inventory of controlled substances.

The network is currently configured as an Active Directory domain. A single database server stores patient data, including appointments, medical records, and billing data. It is running Windows NT 4.0 with Service Pack 6 and SQL Server 7.0. Client computers are running a mix of Windows XP Professional and Windows 98 with the Active Directory client.

The company wants to enable patients to schedule appointments and submit requests for prescription refills over the Internet.

You must analyze the data transmission security requirements and make suggestions for improving security.

1. Which data requires the best confidentiality protection?

2. Which data requires the best integrity protection?

3. What users need access to the patient medical records?

4. Why might you want to modify the configuration so that patient medical records are stored on a separate database server?

5. Why might you want to modify the configuration so that patient appointments are stored on a separate database server?

6. What upgrades are required to use SMB signing between the database server and the administrators' computers?

7. Could you use IPsec to provide end-to-end confidentiality for when doctors access patient records? Why or why not?

8. What is the most secure network configuration for offering the new Internet services for patients?

9. How can you protect the confidentiality, integrity, and authentication for prescription refill requests?

7

REMOTE ACCESS AND WIRELESS SECURITY

Starting Point

Go to www.wiley.com/college/cole to assess your knowledge of designing and implementing a secure remote access and wireless network infrastructure. *Determine where you need to concentrate your effort.*

What You'll Learn in This Chapter

- ▲ Remote access authentication methods
- ▲ How to limit dial-up access
- ▲ Virtual private networks (VPNs)
- ▲ RADIUS and TACACS
- ▲ Wireless network security

After Studying This Chapter, You'll Be Able To

- ▲ Choose the most appropriate remote access authentication protocol
- ▲ Limit access to a dial-up connection
- ▲ Select a tunneling protocol for a VPN connection
- ▲ Describe how RADIUS and TACACS can centralize authentication policies
- ▲ Implement security for a wireless network

INTRODUCTION

Maintaining data security is becoming increasingly important as more organizations establish network links between themselves to share information and increase productivity, and as more employees are allowed to work from home. In addition, a number of businesses are taking advantage of the convenience offered by wireless networking.

With these conveniences come potential security risks because network links open additional points of entry to your wired local area network (LAN). Another concern, especially with wireless networks, is that data can be intercepted easily unless it is encrypted.

This chapter begins with a look at the most traditional way of accessing a LAN from a computer outside the physical network: the dial-up connection. Next the chapter looks at how to implement a virtual private network (VPN) to allow users to **tunnel** through the Internet to access your company network. From there, the chapter discusses how you can centralize authentication when supporting multiple remote access and wireless entry points to your network. The chapter concludes with a discussion of wireless networking and the protocols available for securely implementing a wireless network segment.

7.1 Dial-up Networking

The traditional way to allow a remote user to access an internal connection is to equip both the client computer and a **remote access server (RAS)** with a dial-up modem. The client computer uses a traditional phone line to dial in a connection to the server. The server attempts to authenticate the user and either allows or refuses access to the network. This section looks at the dial-up protocols that operate at the Data Link layer of the OSI model. The chapter then compares the remote access authentication protocols available. Finally, the chapter discusses some steps that can be taken when configuring a computer running Windows Server 2003 as an RAS to limit which users can access the network through a dial-up connection.

7.1.1 Dial-up Networking Protocols

Early RASs used **Serial Line Internet Protocol (SLIP)** to provide dial-up access. SLIP can only be used to send Internet Protocol (IP) packets and was commonly used to access UNIX servers. SLIP is considered a legacy protocol. Most modern RASs use **Point-to-Point Protocol (PPP)**. PPP allows you to transmit data sent using multiple protocols, including IP and IPX, over a dial-up connection. It does this by **encapsulating** the datagrams of other protocols. The following are some subprotocols that PPP uses:

▲ **Link Control Protocol (LCP):** a protocol that accommodates limits on packet sizes, sets up encapsulation options, and optionally negotiates peer-to-peer authentication.

▲ **Network Control Protocol (NCP):** a protocol for configuring, managing, and testing data links.

This discussion will focus on securing PPP dial-up connections by selecting the most secure authentication protocol supported by both the client and the server.

7.1.2 Dial-up Networking Authentication Protocols

The PPP specification uses no particular authentication protocol as a standard. Which authentication protocol will be used is negotiated using LCP during the **link establishment phase.** During this phase, the two devices establish specific network parameters like the size of a frame, whether to use compression, and the authentication protocol to use for validating the user.

A number of authentication protocols are available. The protocol or protocols you choose will depend on the protocols supported by both the client and RAS operating systems. Let's look first at the individual protocols and then discuss some guidelines for choosing which to use.

Password Authentication Protocol (PAP)

With **Password Authentication Protocol (PAP)**, the user ID and password are transmitted in clear text to the server, where they are compared to the username and password stored on the server. This is not a secure way to authenticate a user and should be avoided in most environments.

Shiva Password Authentication Protocol (SPAP)

Shiva Password Authentication Protocol (SPAP) was developed for the Shiva LAN Rover product. It transmits the password in a **reversible encryption** format. Reversible encryption uses an encryption method that can be decrypted by an application. This means that this protocol is subject to replay and server impersonation attacks. Protocols that depend on reversible encryption should only be used when there is no other option for supporting the remote access clients. The password encryption is also easy to break. This protocol should be enabled only for backward compatibility with devices that support only SPAP.

Challenge Handshake Authentication Protocol (CHAP)

Challenge Handshake Authentication Protocol (CHAP) is the industry standard protocol for performing PPP authentication and is popular among Internet service providers (ISPs). CHAP is defined in **RFC 1994.**

The CHAP protocol uses **challenge-and-response** for validating the user. This process is illustrated in Figure 7-1. When the client and server try to

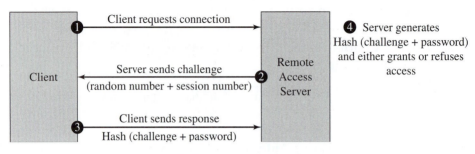

Challenge-and-response.

initialize a PPP session, the server sends a challenge to the client in the form of a random number and a session number. The client concatenates the user's password onto the challenge and hashes it using a Message-Digest 5 (MD5) algorithm with a shared secret to generate a 128-bit response. This response is sometimes referred to as a **one-way hash**. With a one-way hash, there is no way to determine the information in the hash from the hash itself.

The server compares the hash that it receives with the one it generates. In the case of a Windows® Server 2003 **Routing and Remote Access Service (RRAS)** server that is a member of an Active Directory® domain, the server makes a request to the domain controller for the user's password and concatenates it to the challenge it sent to the client. It then hashes the challenge and compares it with the response it receives from the client. If they match, the user is authenticated and a PPP data connection is established to the RRAS server. This process is illustrated in Figure 7-2.

The shared secret for the hash algorithm should not be sent over the network connection, or it should be encrypted by setting up a trust between the client and the server, which would establish a key on both sides through some mechanism not defined in the CHAP protocol. The secret can be variable (just as long as the server and client stay in sync) to discourage replay attacks. The secret can also allow for setting a time limit of use between challenges so that it will expire, and limiting the time of exposure to a single attack because the attacker would need to figure out the new secret.

The advantage to using the CHAP protocol for authentication is that it is a standard supported by many platforms. A disadvantage of CHAP is that it requires you to store the passwords in a reversible encryption format so that the password can be decrypted before it is concatenated to the challenge and hashed for comparison with the client's response. This makes the server susceptible to attackers using tools like l0phtcrack. If you must use reversible encryption, make sure you secure all copies of your accounts database, including backups, and that you limit physical access to the server. Another drawback on an Active Directory network is that the passwords are passed over the network to the RRAS

Figure 7-2

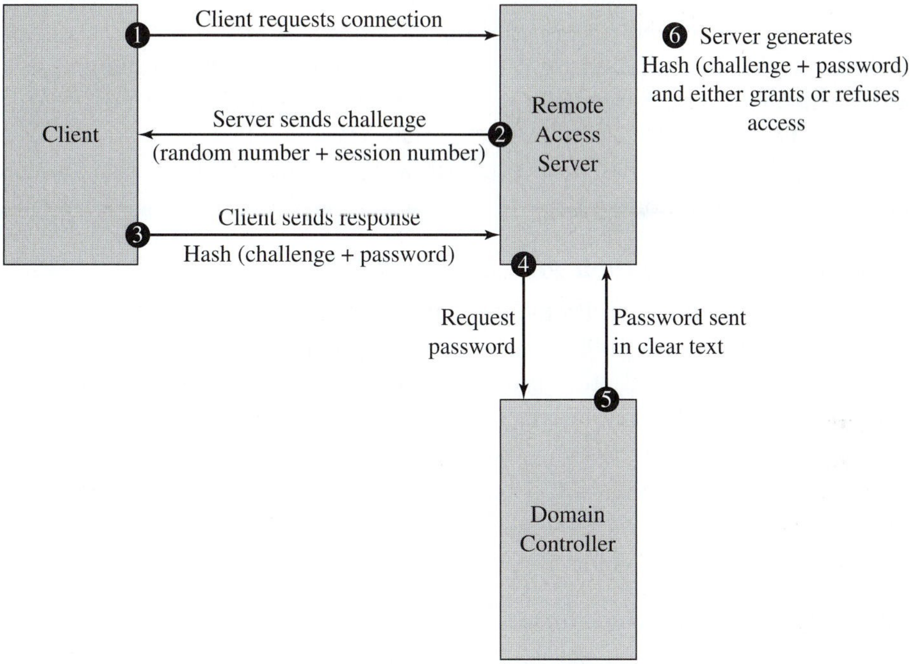

RRAS server in a domain.

server, making them susceptible to attack, so you will need to consider encrypting the connection between the domain controller and the RRAS server.

Microsoft® Challenge Handshake Authentication Protocol (MS-CHAP)

Microsoft Challenge Handshake Authentication Protocol (MS-CHAP) is Microsoft's version of CHAP. It uses the MD4 algorithm to generate the hash. It also provides a mechanism for changing passwords and reporting errors with the authentication process. MS-CHAP was developed for Windows 3.1 and the original version of Windows 95. One drawback to MS-CHAP is that it sends two parallel hashes: LAN Manager and NT LAN Manager (NTLM). The LAN Manager hash is weaker and easily broken. MS-CHAP also does not authenticate the server, so it is subject to man-in-the-middle attacks and replay attacks. MS-CHAP is defined in **RFC 2488**, entitled *Microsoft PPP CHAP Extensions*.

Microsoft Challenge Handshake Authentication Protocol Version 2 (MS-CHAPv2)

In response to security issues discovered in the MS-CHAP protocol, Microsoft released **Microsoft Challenge Handshake Authentication Protocol Version 2 (MS-CHAPv2)**. This is the strongest password-based protocol supported by

Windows Server 2003 for remote access and should be used whenever possible if smart cards or certificates are not an option. MS-CHAPv2 disables LAN Manager Security, which means that the original Windows 95 and older clients will not be able to authenticate. It uses a 16-byte authenticator response to verify that the Windows Server 2003 RRAS server is responding with a SUCCESS message. These and other improvements make MS-CHAPv2 fairly strong, but it still suffers from being based on user password complexity, like other forms of password authentication.

Extensible Authentication Protocol (EAP)

Extensible Authentication Protocol (EAP) is a standard way of adding additional authentication protocols to PPP. EAP provides support for certificate-based authentication, smart cards, and other protocols like RSA's SecurID. It allows third-party companies to provide even stronger authentication protocols to meet your company's security needs. Windows Server 2003 comes with an EAP package for smart cards called EAP-Transport Layer Security (EAP-TLS). It also includes another EAP package, **MD5-Challenge**. MD5-Challenge is a test package used to troubleshoot EAP connections and should not be used in a production environment.

Choosing an Authentication Strategy

There are some things you need to consider when designing authentication security for a remote access infrastructure. You should avoid the use of PAP or SPAP on your RRAS server. Both of these protocols send the password over the wire (PAP as clear text and SPAP using reversible encryption), which means the password can be captured and cracked. You are better off using one of the versions of CHAP or EAP. Due to security problems with MS-CHAP, you should use EAP or MS-CHAPv2 for authentication when possible.

If you need to enable reversible encryption to support CHAP, you should try to minimize the number of accounts affected by enabling it for specific users only. You would also want to make sure that these users have difficult passwords to guard against brute force attacks or dictionary attacks on the passwords. Consider the following when choosing an authentication strategy:

▲ You should choose EAP using smart cards to provide for two-factor authentication. Smart cards validate the user with a certificate in combination with the user's password or PIN. If the person trying to authenticate does not have both, then he or she will not be authenticated. The drawback of EAP is that it requires a public key infrastructure (PKI), which means higher management costs and more complexity in the network infrastructure.

▲ You should choose MS-CHAPv2 in an environment in which you have Windows 98 or more recent clients and do not want to maintain a complex PKI.

▲ You should choose CHAP when you need to support a diverse set of operating systems and devices and do not require strong security.

Enabling Reversible Encryption

If you must use CHAP to integrate with third-party products or non-Windows clients that do not support MS-CHAPv2 or a common EAP mechanism, you need to enable reversible encryption in Windows Server 2003 Active Directory. This is done in one of two ways: by using the Account tab on the user's Properties dialog box or by using the Domain Security Policy snap-in.

To enable reversible encryption from the user's Properties dialog box, open the Active Directory Users and Computers snap-in, right-click the user account and choose Properties from the context menu. In the user's Properties dialog box, select the Account tab. Then select the Store password using reversible encryption option in the Account options list box, as shown in Figure 7-3. Finally, click OK to enable reversible encryption.

To enable reversible encryption from the Domain Policy snap-in, open the Domain Security Policy snap-in (you could also do this in the default domain

Figure 7-3

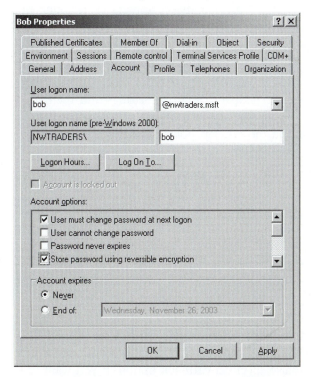

Enabling reversible encryption on the user account.

FOR EXAMPLE

Designing a Dial-up Networking Strategy

Busicorp wants to allow its web developers to work from home three days a week. It also needs to allow salespeople to connect to the network when they travel. All client computers are running Windows XP Professional. Employees need to access various servers on the network. Busicorp also wants to allow customers to dial-in to a server to upload their financial data as an alternative to uploading it to FTP. Some customers have Linux computers. Others are running Windows 98 and Windows XP. The customers have user accounts in the Customers organizational unit in the Active Directory domain. You need to create a secure dial-up solution. The company does not have a PKI.

You install RRAS on two different domain members. You configure one RRAS server to support only MS-CHAPv2 as the authentication protocol. You enable a remote access policy that allows access only to the telecommuters and salespeople.

You configure the second RRAS server to support CHAP and MS-CHAPv2. You enable reversible encryption only for the customers who require connectivity from operating systems that do not support MS-CHAPv2. You disable IP routing to prevent the customers from connecting to any other server on the network.

Group Policy object). Expand Security Settings and then Account Policies and select Password Policy. Then, enable the Store passwords using reversible encryption for all users in the domain policy.

7.1.3 Limiting Dial-up Access

Another way to protect the dial-up server is to limit the users who are allowed dial-in access and the circumstances under which they can connect. The following are some conditions you might use to determine whether a user can connect:

▲ Windows group membership
▲ Day of the week or time of day
▲ Phone number the user is calling from

On an Active Directory network, you can set properties on the Dial-in tab (see Figure 7-4 of a user account to determine whether or not the user is allowed access. You can also specify a **callback** option. If you want to ensure that a user can only dial in from a specific phone number, you would set the option to

Figure 7-4

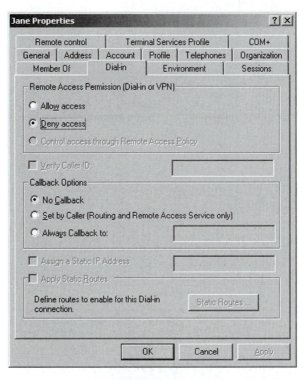

The Dial-in tab.

Always Callback to and enter the phone number. The RRAS server will dial the client back at the specified number. This provides good security protection, provided the client always dials in from a specific number, but is not suitable as a security measure for remote users who travel or who might dial in from multiple phone numbers. An alternate way to ensure that users always call from the same number is to enable the Verify Caller-ID option.

In a native-mode domain, you can define Remote Access policies to determine the circumstances under which a user can connect. For example, you can limit dial-up connections to a specific Windows group, like the Telecommuters group, and allow connections only during specific days and times.

7.1.4 Preventing Access to the Network

You might want to create an RAS that provides resources to dial-in clients but that does not allow access to the rest of the network. With Windows Server 2003 RRAS, you can do this by launching the Routing and Remote Access console, opening the Properties dialog box for the server to the IP tab, and clearing the check mark from Enable IP routing, as shown in Figure 7-5.

Figure 7-5

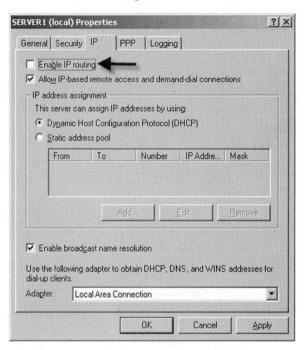

Preventing access to the network.

SELF-CHECK

1. Describe the remote access authentication protocols.
2. What should you consider when choosing an authentication strategy?

7.2 Virtual Private Networks

A **virtual private network (VPN)** is a secure tunnel through a non-secure network, such as the Internet. Companies typically use VPNs to allow access to remote users (see Figure 7-6) or to connect multiple remote locations. Companies might also use a VPN to provide secure access to network resources for its trusted customers or vendors. VPNs offer better performance than dial-up connections because users can take advantage of broadband Internet connections. VPNs offer connectivity between offices without the

Figure 7-6

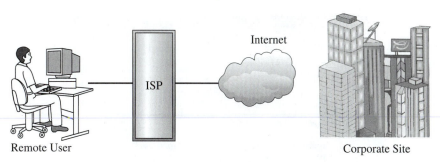

Remote User   Corporate Site

Remote user connecting to a VPN.

expense of dedicated lines because the traffic travels across the infrastructure of the Internet.

In this section, we discuss two protocols for implementing a VPN: Point-to-Point Tunneling Protocol (PPTP) and Layer 2 Tunneling Protocol (L2TP) with IP security (IPsec). Users connecting through a VPN connection are authenticated using the dial-up networking authentication methods already discussed.

7.2.1 Point-to-Point Tunneling Protocol

You can use **Point-to-Point Tunneling Protocol (PPTP)** to enable an encrypted session between two computers. PPTP tunnels PPP over a network like the Internet. This means that you can use the PPP infrastructure and authentication mechanisms to provide secure access to your internal network for partners or employees over the Internet or private connections in much the same way as you can use dial-up access over a modem.

PPTP was developed and standardized by Microsoft to provide a simple mechanism to create a VPN with Windows NT® 4, Windows 9x, and later clients. Microsoft decided to take advantage of the PPP support in the Windows NT 4 RAS to authenticate the PPTP session. The resulting session key from the authentication process is used to encrypt the packets that are sent across the tunnel. Encryption is not enabled by default for PPTP, so you will need to enable it through the Security tab of the user's Properties dialog box, as shown in Figure 7-7.

PPTP is a Layer 2 tunneling protocol that encapsulates PPP packets into IP datagrams by adding a **Generic Routing Encapsulation (GRE)** header and an IP header. The resulting datagram can be routed over IP-based networks and takes advantage of the authentication, compression, and encryption services provided by PPP. PPTP allows you to encrypt traffic using the **Microsoft Point-to-Point**

Figure 7-7

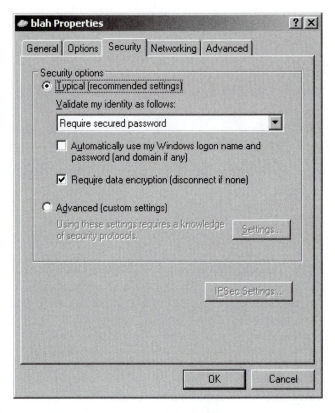

Enabling PPTP encryption on a Windows Server 2003 computer.

Encryption (MPPE) protocol. The session keys for encrypting the traffic are generated from the MS-CHAP or EAP passwords; therefore, you must be using MS-CHAP, MS-CHAPv2, or EAP to support encryption with PPTP. A diagram of PPTP encapsulation is shown in Figure 7-8.

Figure 7-8

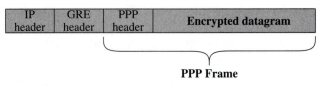

PPTP encapsulation.

The advantages of using PPTP are that it has widespread adoption in Microsoft operating systems and that it is easy to set up on any Windows platform without special downloads. It is also the only way you can set up a VPN connection to a Windows NT 4 RAS server without third-party software. More recent Windows RRAS servers support both PPTP and L2TP. PPTP will traverse all Network Address Translation (NAT) devices because it encapsulates PPP packets inside an IP packet, does not provide IP packet integrity, and does not care if the IP address is changed on the packet. This means that you can use PPTP to establish a tunnel through a NAT server that does not support NAT–Traversal. NAT–Traversal will be described a little later in the chapter.

There are downfalls associated with using PPTP. Although support on the Windows platform is strong, it is not as widely or as well supported by other operating systems and devices. You would need to verify that the device with which you need to set up a PPTP session supports the protocol.

PPTP supports authenticating users but not computers, so you should use it only when you need user authentication and not computer authentication. Another weakness is in the way PPTP handles encryption. Its encryption strength is essentially tied to the strength of the password, so you will want to make sure you have strong password policies if you need to use PPTP. This also means that if an attacker were to obtain a user's password, the attacker might be able to use this information to decrypt the session.

7.2.2 L2TP and IPsec

Layer 2 Tunneling Protocol (L2TP) is an industry-standard tunneling protocol. L2TP provides tunneling and authentication, and utilizes IPsec to provide encryption. The L2TP encapsulation is shown in Figure 7-9. As you can see, L2TP adds an L2TP header and a UDP header to the PPP frame. IPsec then encrypts the resulting L2TP frame and the IPsec Encapsulating Security Payload (ESP) trailer.

L2TP/IPsec is more secure than PPTP because it authenticates both the computer and the user. Computer authentication can be performed through

Figure 7-9

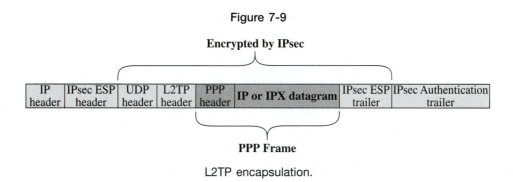

L2TP encapsulation.

either pre-shared keys or certificates. If authentication is performed using certificates, the certificates must be installed on the RAS and the client computers.

L2TP/IPsec also provides stronger encryption than PPTP. However, one problem that might prevent you from using L2TP/IPsec for a VPN tunnel is that some NAT devices are not able to support it. Because NAT needs to alter the IP address in the packet, it will cause the packet to be rejected by the client on the other end. Windows Server 2003 and some other NAT devices support NAT–Traversal of IPsec packets. **NAT–Traversal** is an Internet Engineering Task Force (IETF) draft standard that uses User Datagram Protocol (UDP) encapsulation. This means that the IPsec packet is wrapped inside a UDP/IP header. The NAT device can then change the UDP/IP header's IP address or port number without changing the contents of the IPSec packet; therefore, it will not be rejected on the other end of the connection. You can set up a point-to-point connection with IPSec through a Windows Server 2003 used as a NAT server if the client supports NAT–Traversal also.

L2TP/IPsec is supported natively on computers running Windows 2000 and later. You can support Windows 98 and Windows Me clients by installing the L2TP client software.

7.2.3 Hardware VPN Solutions

Cisco® offers hardware VPN solutions that provide both IPsec and Secure Sockets Layer (SSL) encryption. A number of Cisco routers and switches support VPN features. To determine the appropriate Cisco solution, you need to consider the number of connections requiring support, the throughput requirements, the features required, and the company's budget. Because Cisco devices support both IPsec and SSL, you can determine which clients should be configured to use each protocol. Juniper Networks® also provides both IPsec and SSL VPN appliances.

Your client access configuration choices will be determined by how the VPN user needs to be able to use resources on the network, whether the client software can be preinstalled, if client software can be downloaded, or if clients need to access resources through a browser interface. Let's take a brief look at each option.

IPsec VPN Clients

An IPsec VPN client must be configured using preinstalled client software. This means that IPsec is a good choice when providing VPN access to employees who always access the network from a company computer.

SSL VPN Clients

There are two access methods for SSL VPN clients: via a web browser or via dynamically downloaded client software. Allowing access through a web browser

---

FOR EXAMPLE

Designing a VPN Solution

Many of Busicorp's telecommuters and salespeople have broadband Internet connections. They want to take advantage of the high-speed connections when connecting to Busicorp's network. You use Routing and Remote Access to enable a VPN connection. You configure it and the client computers to support both PPTP and L2TP. You select PPTP because you need to enable salespeople to connect to the network from airport kiosks, and thus you cannot perform computer authentication. You also create a pre-shared key for L2TP computer authentication because the company does not currently have a PKI. You know that pre-shared keys are a risk, but there is currently no money in the budget to implement a PKI.

---

is appropriate when you need to support users who access the VPN through a public computer or when providing access to external users who need limited functionality. A web-based VPN connection can only provide access to resources and applications that support browser-based access.

Dynamically downloaded client software provides users with access to resources as if they were connected to the local area network. However, since it requires downloading and installing software on a computer, it is not appropriate for providing access from a public computer.

SELF-CHECK

1. Compare PPTP and L2TP.
2. What are the two access methods for SSL VPN clients?

7.3 RADIUS and TACACS

If you have multiple RASs, you might want to consolidate the remote access policies onto a single server. Two methods are available for centralizing authentication policies: RADIUS and TACACS. RADIUS is more commonly used and is the centralization option supported for a Windows Server 2003 remote access solution.

Figure 7-10

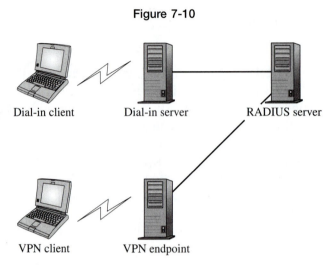

Dial-in client   Dial-in server   RADIUS server

VPN client   VPN endpoint

RADIUS configuration.

7.3.1 Using RADIUS Authentication

Remote Authentication Dial-in User Service (RADIUS) authentication allows the **RADIUS client** (RAS or wireless access point) to authenticate against a **RADIUS server** and has become the standard for integrating various vendors' products. RADIUS is typically used by RRAS to authenticate, authorize, and audit logon requests in a standard way, regardless of whether the user is connecting through a dial-up connection, a VPN, or a wireless access point. Microsoft calls its RADIUS server **Internet Authentication Service (IAS)**. A typical RADIUS configuration is shown in Figure 7-10.

The RADIUS server might use its own authentication database or that of a network operating system, such as Windows Server 2003's Active Directory. IAS can act as an end point to authenticate and authorize requests from the RADIUS client against the Active Directory. The client will connect to the RRAS server or wireless access point and request that it authenticate. The RRAS server or wireless access point, configured as a RADIUS client, will forward the request to the IAS server. The IAS server is installed on a domain controller and will use the Active Directory to attempt to authenticate the user. If successful, it will notify the RADIUS client (RRAS server) and the account will be allowed on the network.

An IAS server configured to forward RADIUS traffic to another server is called an **IAS proxy**. An IAS proxy is most useful when the RRAS and RADIUS infrastructures are maintained by different organizations or where the authentication database (Active Directory) is not directly accessible because the IAS server is located in a perimeter network. This configuration is shown in Figure 7-11.

Figure 7-11

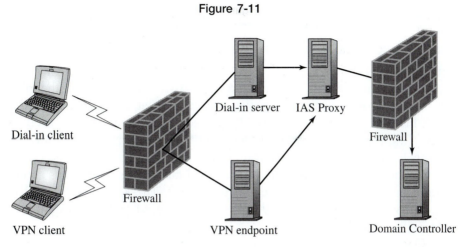

IAS proxy configuration.

You can use RADIUS to manage the accounts of users that connect over a VPN through an RRAS server, so it is often an appropriate choice for allowing network access to partner organizations. Its main benefit is that it provides a standard way to authenticate, authorize, and audit logons, so both organizations don't need to be using the same vendors for their network infrastructures or operating systems.

It also will ease management of duplicating accounts on Internet Information Services (IIS) or in your organization because you can configure IAS to forward RADIUS traffic to the partner organization to verify the account.

7.3.2 Using TACACS and TACACS+

Terminal Access Controller Access Control System (TACACS), which is described in RFC 1492, is an authentication protocol that provides remote access authentication and related services, such as event logging. In a TACACS system, user passwords are administered in a central database rather than in individual routers, which provides an easily scalable network security solution. One important use of TACACS is for securing routers.

A TACACS–enabled network device prompts the remote user for a user name and static password, and then the TACACS–enabled device queries a TACACS server to verify that password. Some TACACS solutions also support authentication using a token card. A TACACS server is usually a daemon that runs on a Unix or Linux computer.

TACACS allows you to support both privileged access, which allows a user to configure a router, and nonprivileged access, which allows a user to monitor a router, but not modify its configuration.

FOR EXAMPLE

Centralizing Remote Access Authentication

Frankfurters, Inc. has decided to expand its business by purchasing a small sausage maker called the Kielbasa Factory. As part of the purchase, the folks in the IT department are integrating the network at the Kielbasa Factory with Frankfurters, Inc.'s network. Employees at Frankfurters will need to access the inventory, accounting, customer, and shipping systems located at the Kielbasa Factory. Frankfurters does not want to spend money on leased lines to the Kielbasa Factory because Frankfurters already has access to the Internet via digital subscriber line (DSL). The Kielbasa Factory has its own Windows Server 2003 Active Directory forest and infrastructure in place.

One of the ways to ensure secure communication between your organization and an external organization is to set up a VPN and use L2TP/IPSec. In addition, you will need to authenticate the users in the external organization, which can be a problem because duplicating user accounts for another organization would surely be a management headache. However, you can use the existing accounts that are in the other (and presumably trusted) organization by setting up a RADIUS client that points to the other organization. You would not need to establish or manage accounts in your organization; all of this would be handled by the other organization.

TACACS does not support prompting for a password change or for the use of dynamic password tokens. TACACS has been superseded by **TACACS+**, which provides for dynamic passwords, two-factor authentication, and improved audit functions. TACACS+ is not compatible with TACACS.

TACACS+ is composed of the following elements, which are similar to those of RADIUS:

▲ **Access client:** a person or device, such as a router, that dials in to an ISP.

▲ A **network access server (NAS):** a server that processes requests for connections. The NAS conducts access control exchanges with the client, obtaining information such as password, user name, and NAS port number. This data then is transmitted to the TACACS+ server for authentication.

▲ The TACACS+ server: a server that authenticates the access request and authorizes services. It also receives accounting and documentation information from the NAS.

SELF-CHECK

1. Identify three types of RADIUS clients.
2. Identify the components in a TACACS+ system.

7.4 Wireless Networks

Wireless networks are everywhere. Mobile phone networks, pager networks, and infrared devices all use wireless networking. Wireless network technology is very beneficial in allowing employees to work from a number of different locations. People use cell phones to check their voice mail from their car or use a device like a Blackberry to check their email on the golf course. Wireless technology allows people to connect notebooks and other portable devices to a network or the Internet without the need to find a physical network port.

But with all of these benefits, wireless technology poses a greater security risk to the data that is transferred because the information is broadcast to anyone within range of the signal. In this section, we'll discuss security concerns when connecting computers to a **wireless LAN (WLAN)**.

7.4.1 Wireless Networking Standards

The general term used to describe a wireless network connecting two or more computers is **Wi-Fi**®, which stands for **wireless fidelity.** There are three major wireless standards for wireless networking defined as *Wi-Fi* by the Institute of Electrical and Electronics Engineers (IEEE):

▲ **802.11a:** 802.11a can transmit data at speeds as fast as 54Mbps but at a shorter range than the other more popular standards. It also uses a different part of the electromagnetic spectrum and so is not compatible with either 802.11b or 802.11g. Its short range and non-overlapping 12 channels means that it is a specification that is more appropriate for densely populated areas. 802.11a is seldom used.

▲ **802.11b:** 802.11b supports speeds up to 11Mbps over a longer range than 802.11a. Devices that support 802.11b tend to be less expensive than those using 802.11a, hence the popularity. Prior to 802.11g, nearly all PC wireless network cards and wireless access points were built to the 802.11b standard.

▲ **802.11g:** 802.11g supports speeds up to 54Mbps and is downward compatible with 802.11b because they both use the same part of the radio spectrum. The majority of PC networking equipment for sale and in current use is based on the 802.11g standard.

Most current Wi-Fi devices support both 802.11b and 802.11g.

7.4.2 Wireless Modes

The 802.11 standards support two methods or modes of communication: ad hoc mode and infrastructure mode. **Ad hoc mode** is a peer-to-peer communication mode, in that clients communicate directly with each other. With **infrastructure mode**, the clients connect to a wireless device called a **wireless access point (WAP)**. A WAP can be used as a bridge to connect a wireless network to a wired network, as illustrated in Figure 7-12. Some WAPs also include a built-in router that can allow you to share a high-bandwidth Internet connection.

An ad hoc mode network is not secure and should not be used when transmitting confidential data.

7.4.3 Preventing Intruders from Connecting to a Wireless Network

People search for unsecured wireless access points through a process called **war driving**, which consists of using a notebook computer or a PDA with a

Figure 7-12

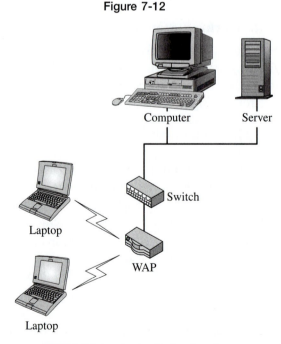

WAP bridging to a wired network.

wireless network card and a utility like NetStumbler or MiniStumbler and driving around looking for unsecured access points. Once an access point is found they publish this information on the Internet or use it for their own purposes. They also might leave a mark on the building or sidewalk to indicate to others that there is an unsecured wireless access point. Leaving such a mark is known as **war chalking**. This means that anybody could be using your wireless access point to access the Internet or your network. They can also capture packets that you might be sending over the wireless network to reveal passwords or confidential information.

There are two security mechanisms that you can implement on any infrastructure-mode Wi-Fi network to guard against unauthorized use of your access point.

Service Set Identifier (SSID)

One security mechanism that the 802.11 standards use is a **service set identifier (SSID)**, which is an identification that recognizes a wireless network. The SSID is used as a means of preventing clients from connecting. Only clients that have been configured with the same SSID as each other or the access point can connect.

Using the SSID to protect your network is not sufficient because most access points will broadcast the SSID to all the clients for ease of configuration. You can turn off the broadcast so that the access point runs in **stealth mode**, which means that the client would have to be configured with the correct SSID before it can connect.

Another concern is that most manufacturers include a default configuration with a well-known SSID. Therefore, you should change the SSID to something difficult to guess. Rules for creating a strong SSID are similar to those for creating a strong password. The longer the SSID, the more difficult it will be for an attacker to guess. You should also avoid obvious SSIDs, such as the manufacturer of the wireless device, the word "wireless", or your company's name.

MAC Address Filtering

You can also use **MAC address filtering** to control which MAC addresses can communicate with the access point. This would require you to set up MAC filtering to specify which clients you want to allow to connect. This can be a management headache if there are a large number of clients. Wireless packets can also be captured, revealing the MAC addresses that are allowed. An attacker can use MAC address spoofing to overcome this restriction.

7.4.4 Wired Equivalent Privacy

You can provide authentication and encryption on any infrastructure-mode wireless network by using **Wired Equivalent Privacy (WEP)**.

Figure 7-13

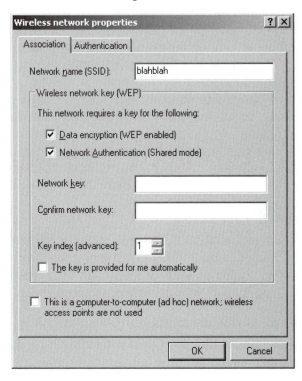

Configuring WEP keys in Windows Server 2003.

WEP Encryption

WEP uses the RC4 symmetric key encryption to authenticate clients and provide for the encryption of transmitted data. WEP uses a symmetric key, which means that the client and the access point require the same shared secret key. There is no standard for providing the shared secret key to the client, and it usually must be done manually, as shown in Figure 7-13. The administrator will also have to rotate the keys on a regular basis to guard against unauthorized use, and, as you can imagine, this will be a tedious process.

The WEP symmetric key is comprised of two components: a variable, 24-bit **initialization vector (IV)** and a fixed 40- or 104-bit secret key. Because the secret key is seldom changed, the purpose of the IV is to thwart cryptanalysis against WEP by having the client use a different IV when encrypting message packets (usually each frame). The packet construction and the key composition are illustrated in Figure 7-14.

Note that the IV is transmitted as clear text in the packet. When the packet is received at the access point, the hardware function retrieves the base secret

Figure 7-14

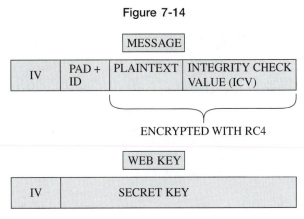

A WEP message and key.

key that it knows, concatenates it with the IV in the transmitted message packet, and uses this key to decrypt the packet.

However, because the IV is relatively short, packet monitoring will show repetitions of the IV and thus enable attackers to obtain the base secret key. On a busy network, the IV might be repeated after only about an hour. One approach an attacker uses is to use the clear text IV and discover WEP RC4 weak keys. A freely available program called **AirSnort** can be used to break WEP encryption and read transmitted messages. WEP is also vulnerable to forgery and replay attacks, wherein an attacker can modify packets and retransmit them or capture packets and retransmit them at a later time.

WEP Authentication

WEP provides for open and shared key authentication. However, each of these types of authentication has vulnerabilities that make WEP a less than perfect solution for securing wireless traffic.

In **WEP open authentication**, a client station provides an SSID that is common to the stations on its network segment and its access point. This SSID authorizes and associates a client station to the access point. A vulnerability exists with this approach in that the access point periodically transmits the SSID as clear text in management frames. Thus, the SSID is easily available to attackers to establish an association with the access point.

WEP shared key authentication was intended to implement secure client authentication through the following steps:

1. The client station transmits an authorization request.
2. The access point returns a challenge string in the clear.
3. The client chooses an IV.
4. Using the IV and secret base key, the client encrypts the challenge string.

5. The client station sends the IV and encrypted challenge string to the access point.

6. The access point also encrypts the challenge string using the transmitted IV and the same secret base key.

7. If the client's encrypted challenge string is identical to the challenge string sent by the client station, the association occurs.

The vulnerability in this process is that cryptanalysis can use the intercepted plain text/cipher text pair and IV to determine the RC4 key. This attack is possible when all the IVs have been exhausted for a session and the IVs have to be reused.

7.4.5 Wi-Fi Protected Access

Wi-Fi Protected Access (WPA) is a standard that was developed to eliminate some of the vulnerabilities of WEP, while still providing backward-compatibility for existing wireless devices. WPA requires the use of EAP for authentication and Temporal Key Integrity Protocol (TKIP) to provide message integrity.

Temporal Key Integrity Protocol (TKIP) is a strategy for managing encryption keys that is built around the existing WEP security algorithm, but it provides some improvements to help protect against the vulnerabilities in WEP. Table 7-1 lists the upgrades provided by TKIP in terms of the security weaknesses addressed.

Let's take a look at each of these enhancements.

Per-packet Mixing Function

The TKIP **per-packet key mixing function** addresses the problem of correlating IVs with weak keys by using a key that varies with time (temporal key) as the WEP secret base key. It then uses the packet sequence counter and temporal key to construct the per-packet key and IV. This process is illustrated in Figure 7-15. These operations hide the relationship between the IV and the per-packet key.

Using the Exclusive Or (XOR) function for the local MAC address with the temporal key results in different client stations and access points generating different intermediate keys. Thus, the per-packet encryption keys are different at every client station. The result of the total process is a 16-byte packet that corresponds to the input that is expected by existing WEP hardware.

Table 7-1: TKIP Upgrades for WEP Vulnerabilities

Vulnerability	Upgrade
Correlation of IVs with weak keys	Per-packet key mixing function
Replay	IV sequencing discipline
Susceptibility to forgery	Message Integrity Code (MIC)

Figure 7-15

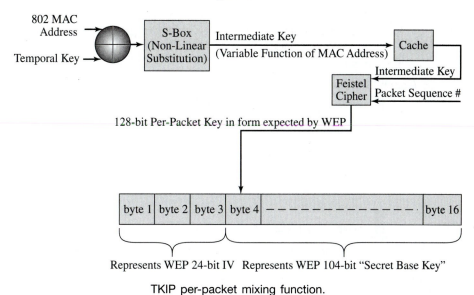

TKIP per-packet mixing function.

IV Sequencing Discipline

As a control against replay attacks, TKIP applies an **IV sequencing discipline** in which a receiver determines if a packet is out of sequence. If that condition is true, the receiver assumes it is a replay and discards the packet. A packet is defined as out of sequence if its IV is less than or equal to that of a packet that was previously received. By using the WEP IV field as a packet sequence number, the procedure for detecting and countering replays is summarized as follows:

1. New TKIP keys are used.
2. Receiver and transmitter initialize the packet sequence number to zero.
3. As each packet is transmitted, the packet sequence number is incremented by the transmitter.
4. The IV sequencing discipline is applied to determine if a packet is out of sequence and a replay has occurred.

This procedure is illustrated in Figure 7-16.

Message Integrity Codes

An ideal **Message Integrity Code (MIC)** is a unique, unambiguous representation of the transmitted message that will change if the message bits change. Thus, if an MIC is calculated by the sender using an authentication key known only to the sender and the receiver and that is sent with the message, the receiver can calculate another MIC based on the message and can compare it to the MIC

Figure 7-16

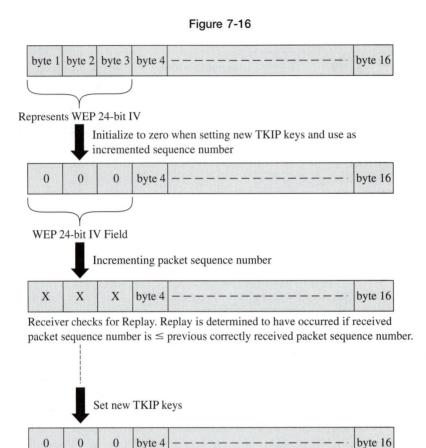

TKIP replay sequence checking.

that accompanied the message. If the two MICs are identical, in theory, the message was not modified during transmission.

An MIC strength of 20 bits satisfies the requirements for WEP, and it is estimated that this level of security will take one year to break. The TKIP MIC is much stronger.

In TKIP, the 64-bit MIC is called **Michael**. The TKIP MIC process is illustrated in Figure 7-17.

7.4.6 Standard 802.1x

The **802.1x** standard was developed to help administrators provide greater security to wireless networks. Standard 802.1x uses TKIP to manage data integrity and EAP-TLS to authenticate the user.

Figure 7-17

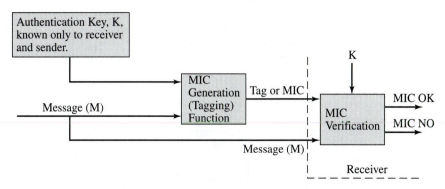

TKIP MIC generation and verification.

EAP-TLS uses certificates on the client and server to provide for mutual authentication. This requires a PKI to manage the creation, distribution, and revocation of certificates. The 802.1x standard also provides for encryption of each connection using TLS. This means that the keys for encryption can be negotiated per session.

Re-keying Against Key Reuse

To protect against key reuse, 802.1x uses a hierarchy of master keys, key encryption keys, and temporal keys. The 802.1x temporal keys are used in the TKIP authentication and confidentiality processes. A temporal key set comprises a 64-bit key for the MIC process and a 128-bit encryption key. A different set of temporal keys is used in each direction when an association is established. The material used to generate the temporal keys must be protected from compromise; this protection is accomplished using key encryption keys. The master key is needed to set up the key encryption keys. This process is summarized as follows:

▲ 802.1x provides that the authentication server and client station share a secret key, the master key.

▲ 802.1x further provides that the authentication server and access point share a secret key, derived by the authentication server and client station from the master key and distributed by the authentication server to the access point.

▲ A new master key is used with each session (a session covers the time from when the user is authenticated to when the key expires, when the key is revoked, or when a client station no longer communicates).

▲ The master key is used to protect the communication of key encryption keys between a client station and the access point.

Figure 7-18

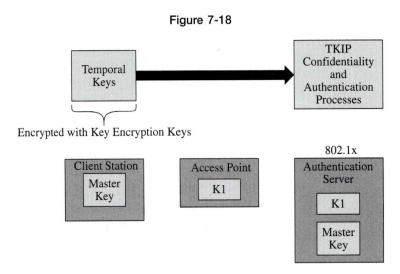

Key hierarchy for re-keying.

▲ The key encryption keys are employed to protect the transmitted keying material used by the access point and client to generate sets of temporal keys.

▲ The pairs of temporal keys are used for integrity protection and confidentiality of the data.

Figure 7-18 shows the relationships and locations of the three types of keys.

Configuring 802.1x in Active Directory

In an Active Directory environment, you can configure 802.1x through Group Policy Security Settings. Doing so allows you to manage many clients at once with Active Directory, which will solve some of the management problems with 802.11. You can get to the Group Policy Security Settings for 802.1x by following these steps:

1. Open the Security Settings section of Group Policy by navigating to the Domain Security Policy Microsoft Management Console (MMC). To do so, open the Start menu, point to All Programs, select Administrative Tools, and then select Domain Security Policy.

2. You can use the Wireless Network (IEEE 802.11) Policies node to configure 802.11 and 802.1x configuration settings (Figure 7-19). Right-click the Wireless Network (IEEE 802.11) Policies node and choose Create Wireless Network Policy from the context menu to configure a wireless policy.

Figure 7-19

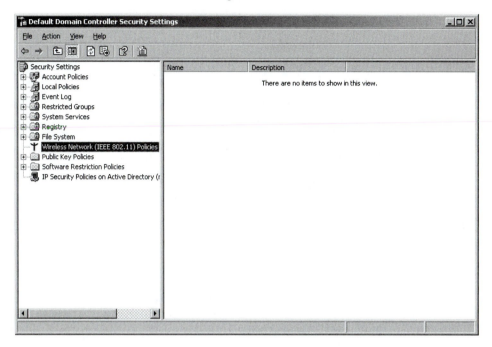

Wireless Network (IEEE 802.11) Policies node.

3. This will launch a Wireless Network Policy Wizard that will ask you to enter the name of the wireless policy and then ask if you would like to edit the wireless policy. Give the policy a meaningful name and then click Next.

4. Click the Finish button to end the Wireless Network Policy Wizard and reveal the Wireless Network Policy Properties dialog box.

You can enable a Windows XP client computer to use 802.1x without using Group Policy by following these steps:

1. Open the Start menu, point to Settings, select the Control Panel, and then select Network Connections.

2. Right-click your wireless network connection and choose Properties from the context menu.

3. In the wireless connection's Properties dialog box, click the Wireless Networks tab to reveal the Properties dialog box for configuring wireless networks for the client, as shown in Figure 7-20.

4. Choose the wireless network configuration in the Preferred Networks list box and click the Properties button.

Figure 7-20

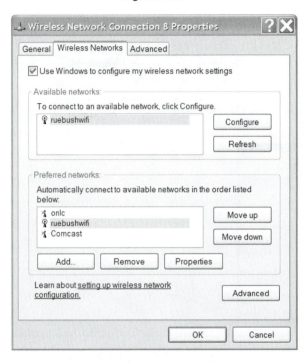

Wireless Networks tab.

5. In the preferred network's Properties dialog box, click the Authentication tab.

6. Click the Enable IEEE 802.1x authentication for this network check box, as shown in Figure 7-21, to enable 802.1x for this client.

Using Protected Extensible Authentication Protocol

Those who don't have the extensive PKI can use a protocol called **Protected Extensible Authentication Protocol (PEAP)**. This protocol is not as strong as smart cards or some other form of certificates used on clients, which is required with EAP-TLS. PEAP can be used with usernames and passwords, one-time passwords, and token cards. PEAP is supported by Active Directory, Novell® NetWare® Directory Service (NDS), Lightweight Directory Access Protocol (LDAP) directory services, and one-time password database systems.

PEAP allows the client to use a password to authenticate the user on the wireless network. This makes it easier to set up 802.1x, but at a cost of degrading security. Remember, however, that you are always weighing the cost of a solution with the loss that would be incurred if security were breached.

Figure 7-21

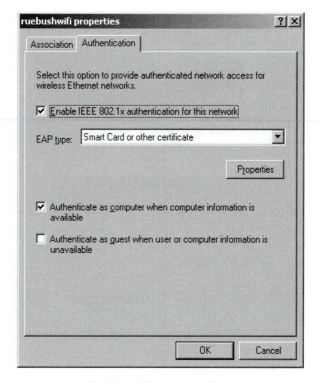

Enabling 802.1x on a client.

PEAP needs to be enabled on the client and the server to support this form of authentication for the network. To enable PEAP on the client side, use the EAP type drop-down box on the Authentication tab in the preferred wireless network Properties dialog box, as shown in Figure 7-22.

RADIUS and 802.1x

Regardless of whether you choose to use certificates or PEAP to authenticate with the wireless access point, 802.1x uses RADIUS to authenticate the requests to connect to an access point. The access point acts as a RADIUS client that will forward all connection requests to the RADIUS server. The RADIUS server will check to see if the client has been allowed access to the wireless access point, which ensures that the client is authenticated to gain access to the network and can prevent unauthorized access points. RADIUS also provides extensive auditing and accounting that can also be used to maintain security. These logs can be reviewed to verify the usage patterns of accounts and to recognize if there has been a security violation.

Figure 7-22

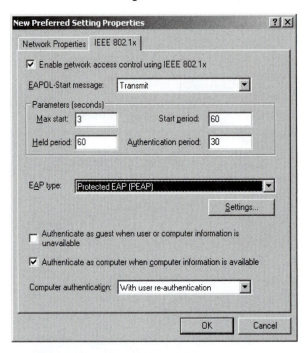

Enabling PEAP for 802.1x authentication.

7.4.7 Standard 802.11i

The **802.11i** wireless security standard incorporates TKIP, 802.1x, and the Advanced Encryption Standard (AES). AES is a block cipher and, in 802.11i, processes plain text in 128-bit blocks. It uses the following set of keys:

▲ A **symmetric master key**: This key is known by the authentication server and client station for the positive access decision.

▲ A **pairwise master key (PMK)**: This key is a fresh symmetric key known by the access point and client station and is used for authorization to access the 802.11 medium.

▲ A **pairwise transient key (PTK)**: This key is a collection of the following operational keys:

▲ **Key encryption key (KEK)**: This key is used to distribute the **group transient key (GTK)**, which is an operational temporal key used to protect multicast and broadcast data.

▲ **Key confirmation key (KCK)**: This key binds the PMK to the client station and access point.

▲ **Temporal key (TK)**: This key protects transmitted data and varies with time.

Standard 802.11i employs a 128-bit key, combines encryption and authentication, uses temporal keys for both functions, and protects the entire 802.11i packet. RADIUS and EAP-TLS are not officially part of 802.11i, but are de facto standards for use in 802.11i.

802.11i provides for pre-authentication for **roaming** (moving between wireless access points) and also for a **pre-shared key (PSK) mode**. In PSK mode, there is no authentication exchange and a single private key can be assigned to the entire network or on a per-client station pair. PSK is acceptable for use in ad hoc and home networks. The PSK mode uses the Public Key Cryptography Standard (PKCS) #5 version 2.0 and the Password-Based Key Derivation Function 2 (PBKDF2) to produce a 256-bit PSK from an ASCII (American Standard Code for Information Interchange) string password. **RFC 2898**, "PKCS #5: Password-Based Cryptography Specification Version 2.0," describes this operation, which applies a pseudorandom function to derive keys. The PSK mode is vulnerable to password/passphrase guessing using dictionary attacks.

7.4.8 Designing for an Open Access Point

Using the 802.1x, standard, you can create a secure private wireless network that will provide for data encryption and integrity, but there are many times that you might want to provide open access to the Internet for clients, consultants, or the general public. To do so, you should use a network that is shielded from your internal network by a firewall. You should also control the types of traffic that could be passed to the Internet on the open wireless access point by using a router, firewall, or an **intrusion detection system** (a system that monitors for network intrusion attempts) to prevent abuse of the public system. A discussion of intrusion detection systems is beyond the scope of this chapter. In addition, you will need to make it clear to those using the open access point that their traffic is not secure and that they should use the open access point at their own risk. Figure 7-23 shows how you would lay out a wireless network with an open access point.

7.4.9 Identifying Wireless Network Vulnerabilities

Wireless networks by their very nature are vulnerable, so you should pay close attention to designing a secure network. The following list includes some of the vulnerabilities you need to consider:

▲ WEP keys must be manually configured in many devices and there is no standard to manage them. You typically have to set them up on the client manually.

▲ **Packet checksums**, which are the result of a mathematical calculation on the packet that is added to it to verify the integrity of the packet, are not encrypted, so an attacker can manipulate the packets in transit.

Figure 7-23

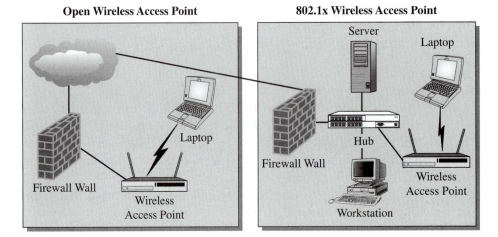

Open access point.

▲ The destination or source of a packet can be changed.

▲ Shared key authentication is all that is available without 802.1x.

▲ There is no user or machine authentication option with 802.11 protocols, so you only need to know the SSID to connect (if WEP is not enabled).

▲ Many access points have a well-known default SSID. For example, a LinkSys® wireless access point's default SSID is LINKSYS. An attacker will guess the defaults on popular devices first to determine if they can gain access.

The following list includes the main threats to a wireless infrastructure:

▲ Attackers can eavesdrop on wireless packets because they are broadcast through the air. You are broadcasting more or less to the world if you don't use encryption.

▲ Employees or attackers can add unauthorized access points to a network to provide access to it. These access points normally will not be secure, opening up a weakness on your network.

▲ Denial-of-service (DoS) attacks can be launched by broadcasting a stronger signal, jamming the air with noise, redirecting packets, or disconnecting clients.

▲ Attackers can figure out your SSID or valid MAC addresses by intercepting wireless packets even if you disable SSID broadcasting or enable MAC filtering.

> ### FOR EXAMPLE
>
> #### Designing a Secure Wireless Access Strategy
>
> A real estate office has agents who are rarely in the office. The agents have laptop computers, and when they are in the office, they want to connect to the network to check email, access the listing database, and submit paperwork. The agents share an open-air conference room, and you want to use a wireless access point to give them access.
>
> The real estate office network has a single domain controller and two servers. You decide to install IAS on the domain controller and configure 802.1x security using PEAP. You plan to upgrade the solution to support EAP-TLS next year, but first you need to convince the board of directors that you need to invest in a PKI.

SELF-CHECK

1. Compare WEP and 802.1x.
2. Define *SSID* and explain how it relates to security.
3. Compare ad hoc mode and infrastructure mode.

SUMMARY

In this chapter, you learned about securing remote access and wireless access. You learned that dial-up users and VPN users are authenticated using the same authentication protocols, and, that of those protocols, your best choices are MS-CHAP v2 for password credentials and EAP-TLS for smart cards. You learned how to limit which users can connect through dial-up or VPN connections. You also learned about the two tunneling protocols available: PPTP and L2TP/IPsec. Finally, you learned about the methods available for securing a wireless LAN, including SSID, MAC filtering, WEP, WPA, 802.1x, and 802.11i.

KEY TERMS

802.11a	802.11i
802.11b	802.1x
802.11g	Access client

Ad hoc mode

AirSnort

Callback

Challenge-and-response

Challenge Handshake Authentication Protocol (CHAP)

Encapsulating

Extensible Authentication Protocol (EAP)

Generic Routing Encapsulation (GRE)

Group transient key (GTK)

IAS proxy

Infrastructure mode

Initialization vector (IV)

Internet Authentication Service (IAS)

Intrusion detection system

IV sequencing discipline

Key confirmation key (KCK)

Key encryption key (KEK)

Layer 2 Tunneling Protocol (L2TP)

Link Control Protocol (LCP)

Link establishment phase

MAC address filtering

MD5–Challenge

Message Integrity Code (MIC)

Michael

Microsoft Challenge Handshake Authentication Protocol (MS-CHAP)

Microsoft Challenge Handshake Authentication Protocol Version 2 (MS-CHAPv2)

Microsoft Point-to-Point Encryption (MPPE)

NAT–Traversal

Network access server (NAS)

Network Control Protocol (NCP)

One-way hash

Packet checksum

Pairwise master key (PMK)

Pairwise transient key (PTK)

Password Authentication Protocol (PAP)

Per-packet mixing function

Point-to-Point Protocol (PPP)

Point-to-Point Tunneling Protocol (PPTP)

Pre-shared key (PSK) mode

Protected Extensible Authentication Protocol (PEAP)

RADIUS client

RADIUS server

Remote access server (RAS)

Remote Authentication Dial-in User Service (RADIUS)

Reversible encryption

RFC 1994

RFC 2488

RFC 2898

Roaming

Routing and Remote Access Service (RRAS)

Serial Line Internet Protocol (SLIP)

Service set identifier (SSID)

Shiva Password Authentication Protocol (SPAP)

Stealth mode

Symmetric master key

TACACS+

Temporal key

Temporal Key Integrity Protocol (TKIP)

Terminal Access Controller Access Control System (TACACS)

Tunnel

Virtual private network (VPN)

War chalking

War driving

WEP open authentication

WEP shared key authentication

Wi-Fi

Wi-Fi Protected Access (WPA)

Wired Equivalent Privacy (WEP)

Wireless access point (WAP)

Wireless fidelity

Wireless LAN (WLAN)

ASSESS YOUR UNDERSTANDING

Go to www.wiley.com/college/cole to evaluate your knowledge of designing and implementing a secure remote access and wireless network infrastructure. *Measure your learning by comparing pre-test and post-test results.*

Summary Questions

1. Which remote access authentication protocol supports using smart cards with a PIN?

    (a) CHAP

    (b) EAP-TLS

    (c) MS-CHAPv2

    (d) SPAP

2. Which remote access authentication protocol requires that you store the password using reversible encryption?

    (a) CHAP

    (b) EAP-TLS

    (c) MS-CHAP

    (d) PAP

3. On a server running Routing and Remote Access as a dial-up server, you can only use policies to determine whether a user can connect if the domain is configured as a native mode domain. True or false?

4. Which VPN protocol(s) provide computer authentication?

    (a) L2TP

    (b) PPTP

    (c) both L2TP and PPTP

    (d) none of the above

5. PPTP traffic can only pass through a NAT server that supports NAT–Traversal. True or false.

6. A RADIUS server can only authenticate users by contacting an Active Directory domain controller. True or false?

7. Which of the following can be a RADIUS client?

    (a) a remote access client

    (b) a wireless client

    (c) a VPN server

    (d) an Active Directory domain controller

8. TACACS+ supports prompting for a password. TACACS does not. True or false?

9. Which wireless networking standard transmits data at up to 11Mbps?

   (a) 802.11a

   (b) 802.11b

   (c) 802.11g

   (d) 802.11i

10. _____ mode wireless networks do not require wireless access points.

   (a) ad hoc

   (b) open authentication

   (c) infrastructure

   (d) shared authentication

11. Which wireless security standard is weak because of the repetition of IVs?

   (a) 802.11i

   (b) 802.1x

   (c) WPA

   (d) WEP

12. Which type of wireless authentication uses knowledge of an SSID as the only credential required for access?

   (a) PEAP

   (b) EAP-TLS

   (c) WEP open authentication

   (d) WEP shared authentication

13. WiFi Protected Access is the only wireless security standard that uses TKIP. True or false?

14. Which TKIP feature helps mitigate replay attacks?

   (a) IV sequencing discipline

   (b) Michael

   (c) per-packet key mixing function

   (d) all of the above

15. Which of the following is required for all implementations of 802.1x?

   (a) PKI infrastructure

   (b) strong password policy

   (c) RADIUS server

   (d) IAS proxy

Applying This Chapter

1. You are analyzing the security for You Buy It Distribution. You Buy It is a wholesale distributor for a variety of products. Its customers are retail

stores that currently dial in to a server to place the order. The dial-in server is a domain member, and all retail stores are authenticated using domain accounts. Their user accounts are shortened versions of the store name, and their passwords are set to their customer account numbers. Account numbers are a letter followed by five numbers. Passwords are set to never expire. The dial-in server is configured to support all authentication protocols. A customer's password was recently discovered by an attacker and the attacker gained access to the company network. You have been asked to mitigate the possibility of such an attack happening at a later time.

(a) Assuming that all customers use Windows 2000 Professional or later, which remote access authentication protocols should you disable?

(b) Which protocol would you need to enable to support Linux clients without changing the credentials used?

(c) Some customers have requested the ability to access the server using their broadband Internet connections. How can you support this functionality?

(d) What are the potential drawbacks of using PPTP?

(e) What are the drawbacks to using L2TP/IPsec?

(f) What additional restriction should you place on the RAS?

(g) What additional step should you take to mitigate the risk of a dictionary attack?

2. You have been asked by Community Health Center to develop a secure wireless networking strategy. Community Health Center wants to offer patients wireless Internet access in the waiting room and activity center. It also wants to provide its doctors and nurses with roaming access to both the Internet and the Health Center's private local area network. Only doctors and nurses should be able to access the local network through the access point. Patient data will be transferred over the local network, so confidentiality and integrity are extremely important.

(a) How will you configure the public access points?

(b) How will you configure the private access points?

(c) What additional server(s) will be required?

(d) What additional requirement should you use to provide stronger authentication?

Designing Remote Access and Wireless Security

You have been hired by NMF Insurance to add remote access functionality to their network. Their adjusters are on 24-hour call and need to be able to submit claims and access customer data through a dial-up connection or through an Internet connection. Adjusters will access the network from home or from a claimant's home. Customer data and claims are stored on different file servers on the network. In addition, the company is moving to a new location. The owner of the new building will not allow them to run cable. All insurance adjusters have laptop computers running Windows 98 or Windows XP Professional. All other employees have desktop computers running Windows XP Professional. The network is currently configured as an Active Directory domain. Aside from the domain controller, there are two file servers and a database server. The network is not currently connected to the Internet.

The company is very concerned about the security of data on the network. They are willing to invest the capital for additional servers, if necessary.

1. What change to the current network will you sugggest?
2. What will you recommend as the most secure VPN protocol and why?
3. What changes to the client computers will be required to support the VPN protocol?
4. What, if any, are the justifications for installing a PKI?
5. What, if any, are the justifications for installing a RADIUS server?
6. What restrictions might you place on dial-up and VPN access?
7. Is there any need to store passwords using reversible encryption?

8

SERVER ROLES AND SECURITY

Starting Point

Go to www.wiley.com/college/cole to assess your knowledge of designing server security based on a server's role.
Determine where you need to concentrate your effort.

What You'll Learn in This Chapter

▲ Security baselines
▲ Security templates
▲ Network infrastructure server security
▲ Domain controller security
▲ File sharing security
▲ Print server security
▲ FTP server security
▲ Web server security

After Studying This Chapter, You'll Be Able To

▲ Develop and implement a secure baseline
▲ Secure network infrastructure servers, such as DHCP, DNS, WINS, RAS, and NAT servers
▲ Secure a domain controller
▲ Secure a file, print, and FTP server
▲ Identify the steps to take to secure a web server
▲ Secure a web, application, and database server

INTRODUCTION

Each server in an organization has a specific role. Some roles are filled by multiple servers, and occasionally a server will perform multiple roles. It is important that you consider a server's role when determining how that server should be secured. This chapter begins with an overview of server roles and a discussion of how to create a security baseline. The chapter then looks at the security concerns associated with various server roles, including network infrastructure servers, domain controllers, file and printer sharing servers, web servers, application servers, and database servers.

Although most of these roles exist in non-Windows® networks, we will use an Active Directory® domain environment in most of our examples. Keep in mind that although the implementation of security policies will be different in other environments, the security concerns are similar.

8.1 Server Roles and Baselines

A **server role** is the job that a server performs on your network. Although in most cases it is recommended that a server perform only a single role, there are a few exceptions to this rule. In addition, some critical roles will be performed by multiple servers in order to provide **fault tolerance** (protection in case one of the servers fails), better performance, or support for multiple geographic areas.

For each server role, you need to define a **trusted computing base**, which is the total combination of protection mechanisms in a computer system. A **secure baseline** is a plan for applying the pieces of this trusted computing base to computers. In this section, we'll discuss the elements of a trusted computing base and describe how to implement a secure baseline on a Windows 2000 Server or Windows Server 2003 network using security templates. A **security template** is a file that is used to configure specific security settings on a computer.

8.1.1 Trusted Computing Base

Before you start identifying the settings that should be configured in the templates for your organization, you should first document the default settings for each role. Then you can proceed to create a trusted computing base for each server role. The trusted computing base includes the following components:

▲ The detailed configuration and procedure of each component: Each option should have a required setting.

▲ Elaborate documentation: Each configuration step should documented.

▲ Change and configuration management: Procedures must be defined for applying changes, such as service packs and security updates.

▲ Procedural review: All procedures should be reviewed regularly to identify potential weaknesses.

8.1.2 Secure Baseline

A secure baseline is a detailed description of how to configure and administer a computer. The secure baseline will define how to implement the components of the trusted computing base on an individual computer. A secure baseline contains the elements described in the remainder of this section.

Service and Application Settings

You should specify the settings that need to be configured for each service that runs on a computer, as well as the settings and business rules for each application. An example would be a business rule that specifies that only users in the human resources department can run the human resources application. You could also include a rule that dictates that a particular server should accept only connections coming from a specific computer or network segment.

Operating System Component Configuration

You will also want to specify the settings for the operating system components. For example, your organization might specify that the Internet Information Services (IIS) home directory must be %systemroot%\IISApp\WebROOT. Changing the default directory that IIS uses as its home directory can prevent intrusion by Internet worms that have the path of IIS hard-coded in their code.

Having a policy in place for the configuration of each of the operating system components should lower the **total cost of ownership** (or **TCO**, the cost of the computer, including hardware, software, and administrative costs) of the servers in your organization because you will know, based on the role of the computer, how it is configured.

Permissions and User Rights Assignments

You should also create a policy that specifies the standards that your organization will follow as it relates to permissions and user rights assignments. One example is having a rule that states that only members of the Domain Admins security group will be able to log on locally to the domain controllers. You also should have a written guideline for resource permissions—for example, only auditors can access client financial data for their clients remotely.

Administrative Procedures

The business that your organization is in will determine the importance of administrative procedures. An example of an administrative procedure is a rule stating that the password must be changed on all administrative accounts every 30 days.

8.1.3 Preparing to Implement the Baseline

Before you can define a template for the computers in your organization, you need to audit your environment by completing the following steps:

1. Record all applications and services on the computer. You must make an inventory of all of the hardware and software components on the system. Without this inventory, you might fail to properly secure an essential component or you might not notice a hardware change that will require a change to be made in the baseline.

2. Record the required security configuration for the operating system and its applications and services. Each security-related setting and configuration task, including administrative procedures, must be documented clearly.

3. Decide how to automate the application of these settings for all computers. Consider using Group Policy or some other automated technique to apply these settings to the computers in your environment. This will minimize errors, ensure consistent configuration settings, and save time.

4. Establish procedures to audit computers in order to detect changes to the baseline. Regular audits will detect changes in the computer settings in addition to changes in the baseline that haven't been applied.

8.1.4 Security Templates

One way to automate the application of baseline settings on a Windows computer is to use a security template. A security template can be imported directly to Local Security Policy or it can be deployed to a number of computers by importing it into a Group Policy Object (GPO) and linking that GPO to the organizational unit (OU) containing those computers. An example of a role-based OU hierarchy is shown in Figure 8-1.

In most cases within an organization, the security settings for a specific role will be the same on multiple computers. For example, the security settings for one Microsoft® SQL Server (a relational database management system) computer in your organization are likely to have the same configuration requirements as those of another Microsoft SQL Server computer running in your organization. You can create a template for all of the servers running Microsoft SQL Server and a different template for another computer role, such as DNS servers. You can utilize Group Policy to automate the assignment of the templates to the different computers. This implementation strategy guarantees that the security settings on all computers of a specific role will be identical. Group Policy will also automatically reapply the template settings should any of the settings be modified in Local Security Policy on a computer.

A good way to design a security template hierarchy is to create a **baseline template** that contains settings relevant to all member servers and to import that template into a GPO linked to the servers' OU, then apply role-specific settings to

Figure 8-1

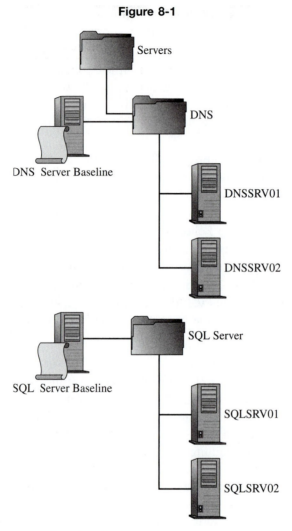

Sample OU design for Group Policy.

role-based templates and deploy those templates through GPOs linked to the OU for each role. The role-based templates are sometimes called **incremental templates**.

Predefined Templates

Windows Server 2003 provides several predefined security templates that contain the Microsoft-recommended security settings for some of the more common configurations. Table 8-1 lists each of the predefined templates that come with Windows Server 2003.

Table 8-1: Predefined Security Templates

Name	Filename	Description
Default Security	Setup security.inf	Default security settings that are applied when the operating system is installed
Domain Controller Default Security	DC security.inf	Default security settings on files, Registry keys, and services. This template is applied when a server is promoted to a domain controller, and if reapplied to an existing DC, it may overwrite permissions on new files, Registry keys, and services that were created by other applications. The **Registry** is a database on a Windows computer that stores hardware and software configuration settings.
Compatible	Compatws.inf	A template containing more lenient access control settings than those defined in the default security configuration. Some legacy applications require users to have more access permissions than are granted by the default Windows configuration.
Secure	Securedc.inf and securews.inf	The secure templates for enhanced security with a low likelihood of conflicting with application compatibility. The secure templates limit the use of LAN Manager and NT LAN Manager (NTLM) authentication by configuring workstations to use NTLMv2 and servers to refuse LAN Manager; therefore, for this to work in your organization, all domain controllers must be running Windows NT® 4 Service Pack 4 or higher. The securedc.inf file is used for Domain

(Continued)

Table 8-1: (*Continued*)

Name	*Filename*	*Description*
		Controllers, and the securews.inf file is used for workstations and member servers.
Highly Secure	Hisecdc.inf and hisecws.inf	A superset of the Secure templates. Even more secure configuration settings than those defined in the Secure templates. The highly secure templates will impose higher restrictions on LAN Manager authentication. In order to apply the hisecdc.inf template on a domain controller, all of the domain controllers in all trusted or trusting domains must be running Windows 2000 or later. The hisecdc.inf file is used for Domain Controllers, and the hisecws.inf file is used for workstations and member servers.
System Root Security	Rootsec.inf	Default root permissions for the operating system partition. Applies the permissions and propagates them to child directories and files that are inheriting from the root.

Creating Custom Templates

As you can see, there is not a predefined template for a Microsoft SQL Server or any other application server role. Therefore, you will need to define them yourself. The templates that you create are referred to as **custom templates**, and it is usually a good idea to use a predefined template as a starting point for them. You can use the Microsoft Management Console (MMC) **Security Templates snap-in** to create, view, and modify security templates. Figure 8-2 shows the snap-in within a custom MMC console.

All computers running Windows Server 2003 store the security templates in the %systemroot%\security\templates folder, and by default, authenticated users can read all of the settings within a GPO. You will want to make sure that your production templates are secured so that only authorized administrators have the

Figure 8-2

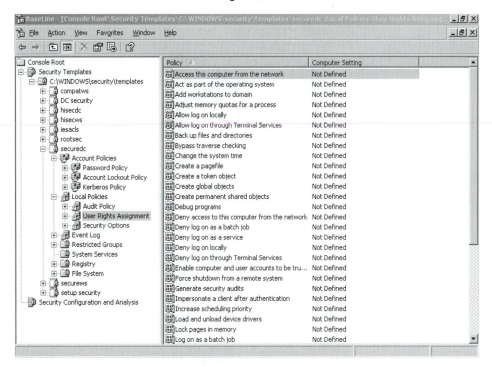

Security Templates snap-in.

ability to view and modify them. It is also considered best practice to designate a single domain controller to hold the master copies of the templates to prevent versioning problems that can occur with multiple copies being modified at the same time.

Using Security Templates to Audit Configurations

You can monitor changes to the baseline using the Security Configuration and Analysis MMC snap-in. The **Security Configuration and Analysis snap-in** is used to analyze and configure the security of the local computer. It will detect any conflicts that exist between the settings defined in a specified template file and those that are in effect on the computer. After it analyzes the two, it can be used to apply the template's settings to the computer. However, remember that settings applied through Group Policy will override those applied through Security Configuration and Analysis. Figure 8-3 shows the report generated when you analyze a computer using Security Configuration and Analysis.

Figure 8-3

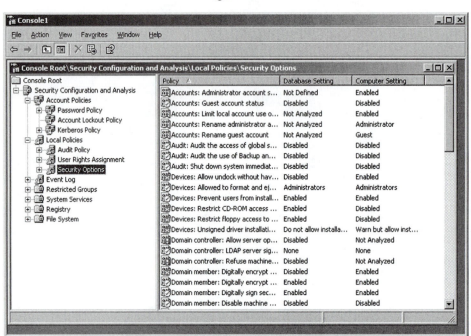

Analyzing a computer's security configuration.

8.1.5 Security Configuration Wizard

If you are securing servers running Windows Server 2003 with Service Pack 1 (or higher), you can use the **Security Configuration Wizard (SCW)** from Microsoft's website to simplify the configuration of a server that hosts one or more roles. Before you can use the tool, you must install it through Add or Remove Programs.

SCW includes an Extensible Markup Language (XML) database of recommended security settings for various roles (see Figure 8-4).

After selecting the roles, SCW examines the system and asks you to confirm or select the following:

▲ Client features.

▲ Options that enable services or open ports.

▲ Additional installed services.

▲ Information to determine appropriate Server Message Block (SMB) signature settings.

Figure 8-4

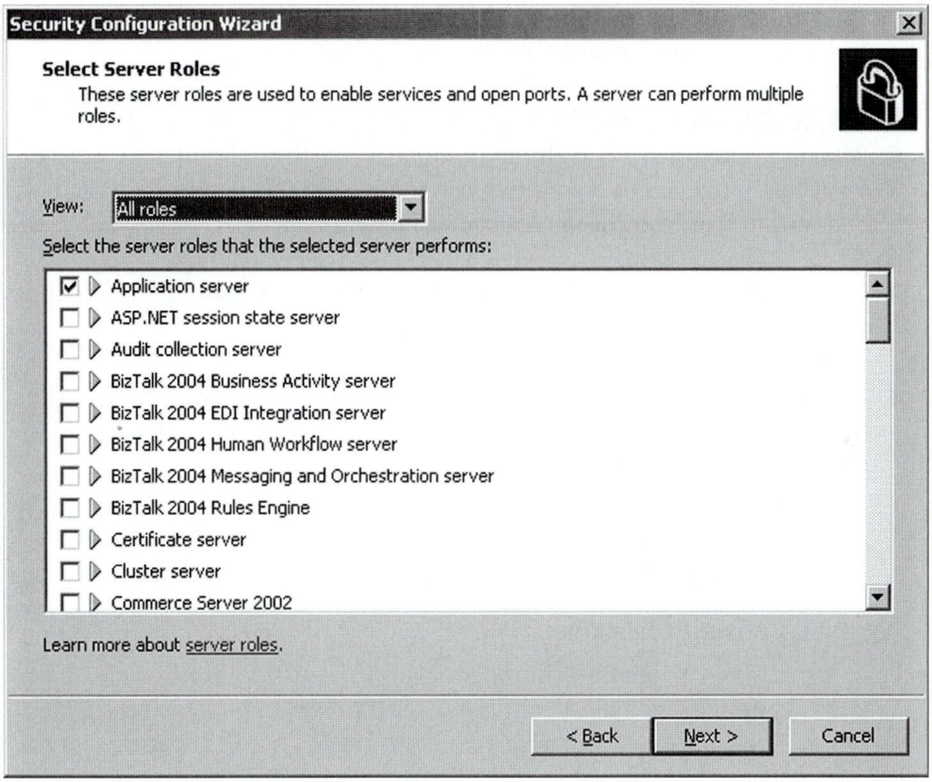

Server roles.

▲ Information to determine Lightweight Directory Access Protocol (LDAP) signing settings.

▲ Information about how the computer authenticates to other computers.

▲ Audit configuration settings.

▲ Application-specific information if the server is running an application covered in the SCW database.

When the wizard is finished, it generates a policy file which you can apply to one or more computers.

The SCW also allows you to import application-specific XML files. For example, you can import an XML file that contains the recommended settings for an Exchange 2007 server. You can also create custom XML files to support the security settings required by in-house applications.

8.1.6 Secure Baseline Configuration for Linux Servers

There are some best practices you should use when establishing a secure baseline for a Linux server. These include the following:

▲ Ensure that the root is protected with a strong password.
▲ Prevent CTRL+ALT+DEL from shutting down the computer. You perform this modification by editing the inittab file in the etc directory and adding a "#" in front of the following line:
```
ca::ctrlaltdel:/sbin/shutdown -t3 -r now
```
▲ Next, you need to cause the system to load the new setting by executing the following from the command prompt:
```
/sbin/init q
```
▲ Prevent unnecessary daemons from running. Daemons are stored in the /etc/r.d directory. The procedure for configuring which daemons load is distribution-specific.

FOR EXAMPLE

Deploying Security Baselines

Busicorp has two domain controllers and fifteen member servers. The domain controllers are also configured as domain name system (DNS) servers. Of the fifteen member servers, five are file servers, two are print servers, one is a Network Address Translation (NAT) server, one is a Dynamic Host Configuration Protocol (DHCP) server, two are database servers, and four are web servers. Two of the web servers are on the perimeter network. One is used by development and the other is used for Quality Assurance testing. Client computers include Windows 98 and Windows XP Professional computers.

You create an OU hierarchy like the one shown in Figure 8-5.

Because there are legacy clients in the environment, you decide to use the Secure templates as a basis for creating the baseline templates you will import into GPOs linked to the domain controllers and servers OUs respectively. Next, you will create five incremental templates, which you import into GPOs linked to the OUs of the file servers, web servers, database servers, print servers, and NAT servers.

Another administrator asks you why you created a NAT servers OU and a DHCP servers OU if there is only a single NAT server and a single DHCP server. You reply that creating OUs for each role enables you to use Group Policy to deploy the security settings, which will ensure that the settings cannot be changed on the local computer.

Figure 8-5

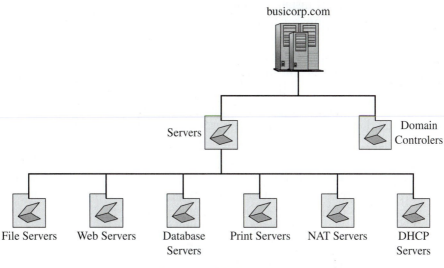

Busicorp OU hierarchy.

▲ Disable unnecessary services. Depending on the distribution, services will be stored in /etc/inetd, /etc/xinetd, or /etc/inet.d.

▲ Filter TCP/IP (Transmission Control Protocol/Internet Protocol) traffic. You can limit the computers that can access the computer by editing the /etc/hosts.deny file and the /etc.hosts.allow file. The syntax for allowing and denying access to a host will vary by distribution.

▲ Disable anonymous FTP (File Transfer Protocol) access. The procedure for doing this will differ by distribution.

▲ Make sure passwords are shadowed. Most current Linux distributions hash user passwords using an MD5 (Message-Digest algorithm 5) hash and store the hash in the /etc/shadow file. To verify that your Linux distribution is shadowing passwords, view /etc/passwd. The second file should contain an *x*, as shown below:

```
root:x:0:0:root:/root:/vin/bash
daemon:x:1:1:daemon:/usr/sbri:/bin/sh
```

▲ Set permissions to limit access to files to only those users or groups that require access.

▲ Verify that programs are configured as SUID programs only when necessary.

8.1.7 Virtualization

In many cases, a company does not have the necessary hardware to segregate server roles so that each server runs only a single role (or in the case of an Active

Directory–integrated DNS server, two roles). One emerging trend is to use **virtualization** (the process of installing multiple virtual machines on a single physical host). A **virtual machine** runs an operating system and one or more applications. To network clients, it is accessed as if it is a physical server.

Segregating application servers, web servers with different purposes, or infrastructure servers that do not require significant resources using virtualization can allow you to reduce the attack surface of each virtual server. For example, if you run an FTP server in one virtual server and a web server in another virtual server, the web server is not vulnerable to security breaches through FTP and vice versa.

One potential drawback to virtualization is that all virtual servers share the same hardware resources of the physical computer. This means that virtualization is not appropriate when you need to support an application that consumes a lot of resources, such as processor time and memory.

VMware® is a popular virtual server software package that has been around for a long time. If you need a free virtual server that runs on Windows Server 2003, you can download Microsoft's Virtual Server 2005 from the Microsoft website.

SELF-CHECK

1. Define *trusting computer base*.
2. Compare baseline templates and incremental templates.

8.2 Securing Network Infrastructure Servers

A **network infrastructure server** is a server that provides a specific service to allow other computers on the network to communicate. The following are some network infrastructure roles in a typical network:

▲ **Dynamic Host Configuration Protocol (DHCP) server:** a server responsible for automatically assigning IP addresses and TCP/IP configuration settings.

▲ **Domain name system (DNS) server:** a server responsible for maintaining a database of, and resolving host names to, IP addresses. A **host name** is the name of a computer on a TCP/IP network.

▲ **Windows Internet Name Service (WINS) server:** a server responsible for maintaining a database of, and resolving NetBIOS names to, IP addresses. A **NetBIOS name** is the name of a computer that is compatible with NetBIOS applications and legacy Windows operating systems.

▲ **Remote access server (RAS):** a server responsible for providing network access to dial-up or virtual private network (VPN) clients.

▲ **Network Address Translation (NAT) server:** a server responsible for acting as a gateway between the Internet and computers on the internal network.

8.2.1 Securing DNS Servers

One of the most important services running on your network is the DNS service. There are a number of ways your organization's DNS infrastructure can be compromised by attackers.

The first thing you should consider is your DNS namespace. A **DNS namespace** is the name of the domain for your network. You should use a different domain name for your public network and your private network. For example, busicorp.com might be your public namespace and busicorp.local might be your private namespace. An alternative is to create your private namespace as a subdomain of your public namespace. For example, the private domain name might be corp.busicorp.com.

You should also have a separate DNS infrastructure for your public or Internet presence and your internal network. You might use an Internet service provider (ISP) to perform your public DNS name resolution, but you will need to implement your internal network's name resolution on a DNS server. Also, by default the DNS service will listen on all interfaces on the computer. If the DNS service is running on a **multihomed computer** (a computer with multiple IP addresses assigned to one or more interfaces), you should specify which interfaces the DNS service should be listening and responding to.

As with any software, you should make sure your DNS server software is kept up-to-date with any updated versions and security patches.

Problems Caused by Incorrect Zone Data

Records on a DNS server are stored in **zones**. Each zone corresponds to a DNS namespace. A zone contains the records of the hosts in that namespace and special records that identify the services run by those hosts. When a zone stores incorrect data, either because of an accidental misconfiguration or an attack, it can lead to a variety of problems, including the following:

▲ **Service redirection:** The site "downloads.com" is a popular location to acquire free and shareware software applications. If DNS requests to this site were instead redirected to the IP address of a malicious attacker's site, a user might download tainted software without realizing it. If the user trusts the site and does not verify the authenticity through cryptographic signature hashes, the consequences could be monumental. Unscrupulous companies could also use the same approach to redirect traffic from a competitor's website to their own. Similarly, name servers with **MX records** (records that identify email servers) can be modified to redirect email from one domain to another.

▲ **Denial of service:** An incorrect record on a DNS server can also be used to launch a denial-of-service (DoS) attack. Instead of redirecting records elsewhere, they can be redirected to 10.1.1.1 or another address range that does not exist. Changing a record to a nonexistent IP address means every time someone tries to resolve the host name he or she is sent to a server that does not exist.

▲ **Information leakage:** DNS servers maintain significant amounts of information about the architecture of a network. For example, many server naming conventions in companies are descriptive of the services provided by the server. For example, mail.company.com is likely the mail server and www.company.com is the web server. Obtaining DNS records can provide an attacker with a complete database of these names along with their associated IP addresses. This database can provide the attacker with recognizance information needed to target specific hosts without actively scanning the network itself.

Zone Transfer Vulnerability

One of the simplest exploits occurs when insecure zone transfers are allowed. A **zone transfer** is a method of sharing DNS records with one or more other DNS servers. Insecure zone transfers allow an attacker to request your entire DNS zone, thereby giving the attacker all of the names and TCP/IP addresses of the hosts in your network. In addition to the names and addresses of the hosts, the attacker knows which servers are running which services if your DNS server supports SRV records. **SRV records** are DNS records that are used to locate a server running a particular service, such as a domain controller.

In Figure 8-6, you can see that having an entire zone returned to a server that you don't control allows an attacker to view, among other things, the SRV record for the Global Catalog server, the Kerberos server, and so on. Once the attacker has this information, he or she knows enough to direct attacks at the servers that host the services he or she wants to hijack. The attacker could spoof the DNS data so that a DNS query returns his or her server's address when a request is made for a trusted server.

If zone transfers must be allowed, you should limit the servers that can receive a zone transfer. On a Windows DNS server, you accomplish this by specifying which servers are allowed to receive the zone data. These settings can be

Figure 8-6

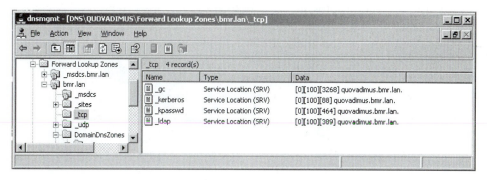

DNS zone SRV records.

modified in the Zone Transfers tab of the DNS server Properties window, shown in Figure 8-7, from the DNS Management MMC snap-in.

The "Only to servers listed on the Name Servers tab" setting requires a DNS lookup to determine the IP address of the server. This setting would be susceptible to DNS spoofing. To mitigate the risk of DNS spoofing affecting your zone transfers, you should select the "Only to the following servers" option and manually add the IP addresses of the appropriate servers, eliminating the need for a DNS lookup.

A better solution in an Active Directory domain is to use Active Directory–integrated zones. An **Active Directory–integrated (ADI) zone** uses Active Directory replication, which is encrypted on the network. You can only create an Active Directory–integrated zone if DNS is installed on a domain controller. Therefore, this is a good example of when it is appropriate for a computer to hold multiple roles.

A **BIND name server** is a type of DNS server that runs on Unix® or Linux computers. BIND name servers can also be used on Windows networks. A BIND name server uses the field "allow-transfer" in the zone statement to allow you to limit the servers that can receive a zone transfer to those listed. An example of the allow-transfer field is shown here:

```
zone "sytexinc.com" {
type master;
file "data.sytexinc.com";
allow-transfer { slave-1-IP-addr; slave-2-IP-addr; };
}
```

The preceding master statement specifies that it is allowed to transmit zone information to (and only to) the IP addresses of slave-1 and slave-2 DNS servers.

Alternatively, a slave should not transmit to anyone in most configurations. An example of an appropriate configuration for a slave follows:

Figure 8-7

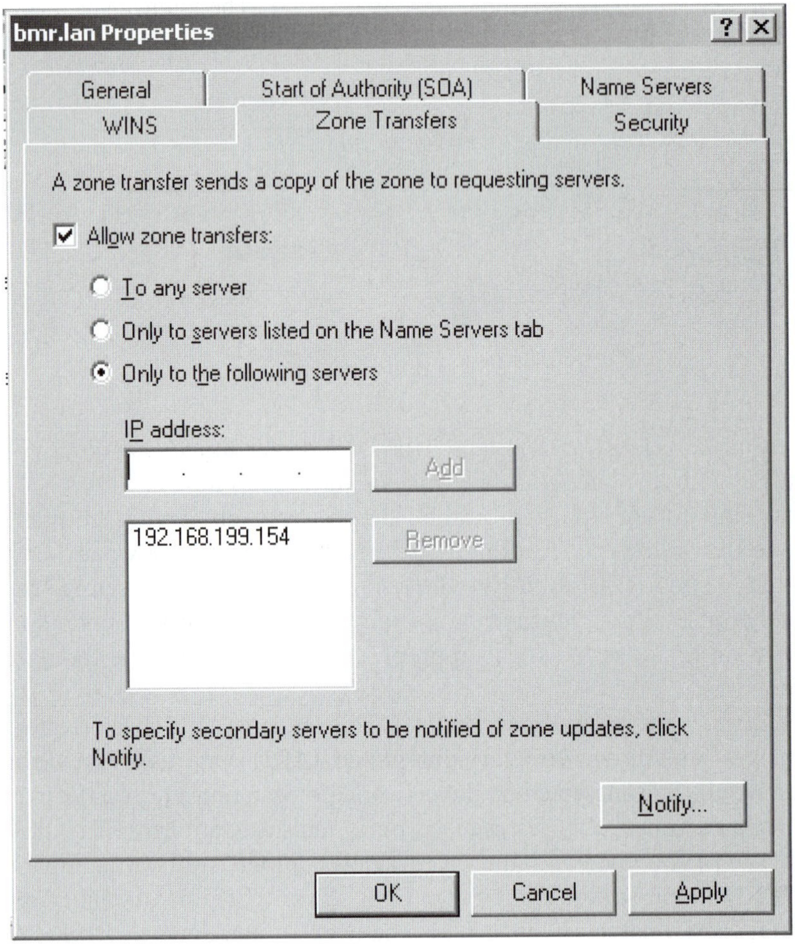

The Zone Transfers tab.

```
zone "sytexinc.com" {
type slave;
file "copy.sytexinc.com";
allow-transfer { none; };
}
```

Transaction Signatures (TSIGs) can provide additional security for conventional zone transfer services. Instead of limiting transfers purely based on IP address, sites can maintain cryptographic signatures that further guarantee their authority.

Starting with BIND 8.2, this can be implemented using a shared secret key. This key is stored in a record for each allowed transfer site. The following is an example:

```
key "rndckey" {
algorithm hmac-md5;
secret "k6ksRGqf23QfwrPPsdhbn==";
};
zone "sytexinc.com" {
type master;
file "data.sytexinc.com";
allow-transfer { key "rcdnkey"; };
};
```

In this example, only DNS zone transfer requests that have been signed with the shared secret key "k6ksRGqf23QfwrPPsdhbn==" are processed.

The benefit of this approach versus the previous IP address restriction is that it allows for more flexibility. Name servers configured with dynamic addressing schemes (that is, DHCP) will not operate using the IP address approach, but as long as they are knowledgeable of the shared key they will operate using TSIGs.

On the slave, the configuration file would include the following entry:

```
key "rndckey" {
algorithm hmac-md5;
secret "k6ksRGqf23QfwrPPsdhbn==";
};
zone "sytexinc.com" {
type slave;
file "data.sytexinc.com";
allow-transfer { none; };
};
server master-IP-addr {
keys { "rndckey"; };
};
```

This identifies that all requests destined for the IP address of the master name server should be signed with the shared secret key "rndckey".

The weakness of this design is that shared secret keys are used between the two servers, which means that if one server is compromised, the key has been exposed and all are vulnerable.

Several popular alternatives exist to conventional zone transfers. The secure copy program, scp, is one example. By default, this program is manual, but it can be combined with scripts and automated distributed file maintenance methods.

The Dynamic Updates Vulnerability

Another DNS–specific vulnerability that can be exploited is the **dynamic updates** feature, which allows clients and DHCP servers to automatically update the host (A) and PTR records on a DNS server. The **host record** (or **A record**) is used to determine the IP address when a client knows the host name, a process known as **forward lookup**. The **PTR record** is used to determine the host name when the IP address is known, a process known as **reverse lookup**. The most secure solution is to simply disable dynamic updates; however, this would require much more administrative effort. To disable dynamic updates completely, you would set the Dynamic Updates drop-down list on the General tab to None, as seen in Figure 8-8.

Figure 8-8

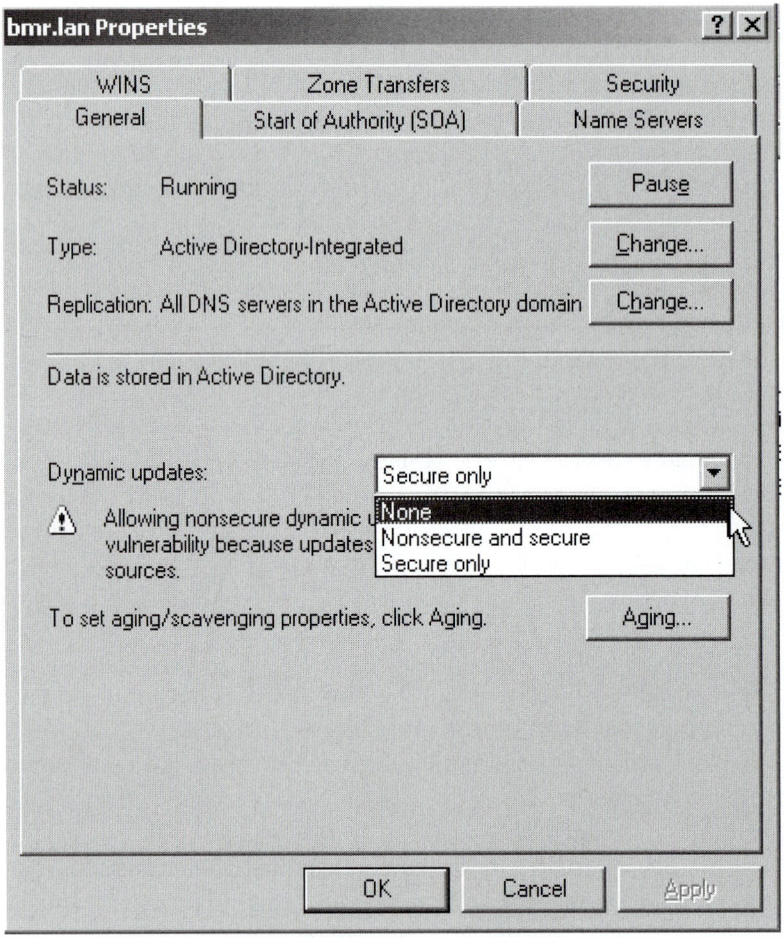

Configuring dynamic updates.

If you decide to support dynamic updates on a DNS server running on Windows 2000 Server or Windows Server 2003, you will want to make sure that only **secure updates** are allowed, which prevents unauthenticated computers from creating entries. If you allow unsecure updates, anyone could create a record in your DNS zone that points to the server of their choice. To support secure updates, the zone must be an Active Directory–integrated zone to provide discretionary access control lists (DACLs) on the DNS data.

Cache Poisoning

The last major attack to DNS that we'll discuss is accomplished by poisoning the **DNS cache**. When a DNS server must query another DNS server to resolve a name, the DNS server caches that information for future requests. **Poisoning the cache** refers to changing the data in the cache on the downstream DNS servers such that they are pointing to bogus or malicious addresses instead of

---

FOR EXAMPLE

Preventing Attacks by Securing DNS Updates

Jim is the security architect of a small financial institution that processes market trades for its customers. The employees answer calls in a call center and process the trades using a web application. In addition to the line-of-business application that processes the market trades, all applications are run from an internal web server, including the human resources and accounting applications.

Because all of the applications are run from the finbank.net domain, it has been added to the **trusted zones** (DNS domains for which Internet Explorer® enforces fewer restrictions) for all workstations in the domain. When employees enter the web address into their browser, a DNS lookup will return the address of the server—which might change—that is running the web application.

An attacker is able to modify the DNS entries by updating the DNS server and changing the record of the trusted server so that it points to a server that the attacker controls. Now when employees navigate to the site that they believe is running their business applications, they are in fact navigating to the attacker's website. The site is considered trusted by the users' browsers and will be given the permissions as such. This might allow certain applets to run and access sensitive information on the workstations of the users.

After discovering the attack, Jim changes the permissions on the DNS server so that it supports only secure updates.

Figure 8-9

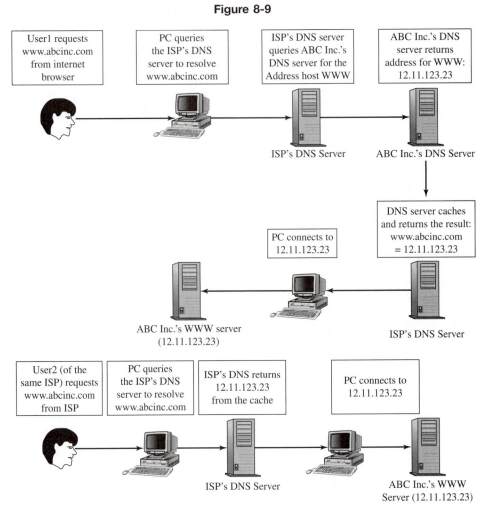

Proper DNS caching process.

the proper address. This can occur because of a malicious or invalid update to the master (upstream) server that gets propagated to a downstream DNS server, where it is considered to be valid until the cache expires. Figure 8-9 shows the correct process of DNS caching.

If a hacker can modify the cache on the ISP's DNS server, any requests for that cached data will be serving the malicious information. In Figure 8-10, the malicious information is an attacker's IP address.

You can minimize the poisoning of the DNS cache to a certain extent by selecting the "Secure cache against pollution" option (the default setting) on the Advanced tab in the DNS server Properties dialog box (see Figure 8-11).

Figure 8-10

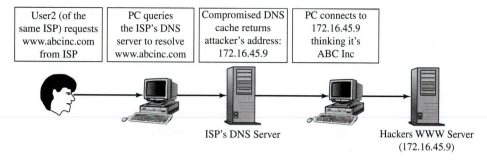

| User2 (of the same ISP) requests www.abcinc.com from ISP | PC queries the ISP's DNS server to resolve www.abcinc.com | Compromised DNS cache returns attacker's address: 172.16.45.9 | PC connects to 172.16.45.9 thinking it's ABC Inc |

ISP's DNS Server

Hackers WWW Server
(172.16.45.9)

Name resolution request with a poisoned cache.

Figure 8-11

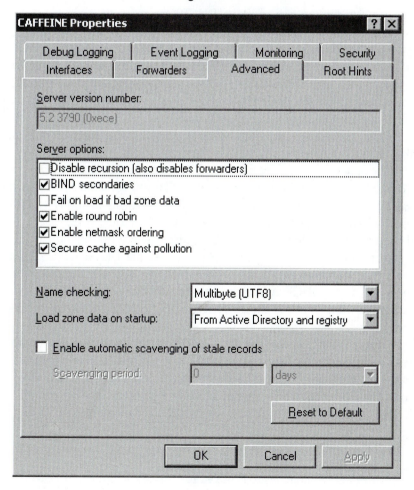

Secure cache against pollution option.

8.2.2 Securing DHCP Servers

Another important infrastructure server in most networks is the DHCP server. A DHCP server is configured with one or more **DHCP scopes**, which are ranges of addresses to assign to DHCP clients. Possible threats against a DHCP server include the following:

- ▲ **Rogue DHCP servers** (unauthorized DHCP servers) assigning invalid addresses.
- ▲ Denial of service by using all addresses in the DHCP scope.
- ▲ Modification of the DHCP scope information.
- ▲ When dynamic DNS updates are used, the DHCP server can make invalid entries in the DNS zone.

You can mitigate the risk of rogue DHCP servers on an Active Directory network by using Windows 2000 or Windows Server 2003 DHCP servers and authorizing them in the domain. A Windows 2000 or Windows Server 2003 DHCP server that is a domain member will send a **DHCPINFORM message** to verify that it is authorized to run and will not start the service unless authorized. Although this protection helps prevent rogue DHCP servers on the network, it does not eliminate the risk. Some DHCP servers, including Windows NT 4.0, do not send a DHCPIN-FORM message. Another important consideration is that **Internet Connection Sharing (ICS)** operates as a DHCP server and always assigns addresses in the 192.168.0.x range. ICS is a very simplified NAT service that can run on Windows 2000 Professional or Windows XP computers. You can sometimes tell that there is a rogue DHCP server on the network when clients begin to receive incorrect IP addresses or when duplicate addresses are assigned on a network.

To mitigate the risk of modification of DHCP scope information, you should make sure to limit who has permission to modify the DHCP scope. On a Windows 2000 or Windows Server 2003 DHCP server, you can do this by limiting membership in the DHCP Administrators group and (of course) the Administrators group. On a Unix or Linux DHCP server, you need to limit who has permission to modify the dhcpd.conf file.

One way to mitigate the risk of a DHCP attack is to use DHCP to assign addresses only to clients. Server IP configuration should be manually configured. You can configure a DHCP scope to always assign a static address to a server. On a Windows DHCP server, you do this by creating a client reservation. On a Linux or Unix DHCP server, you add a static configuration to the dhcpd.conf file as follows:

```
host securesvr {
      hardware ethernet 07:fa:32:87:92:13;
      fixed-address 192.168.1.180;
   }
```

Another way attackers might use DHCP in an attack is to assign the addresses in the DHCP scope using manual configuration. When DHCP attempts to issue the address, an error will occur because the IP address is already in use. You can be warned of this type of attack by auditing the DHCP server, as shown in Figure 8-12. The "Enable DHCP audit logging" is enabled by default. On a Windows 2000 or Windows Server 2003 DHCP server, you can view the audit logs in %windir%\system32\dhcp.

When **dynamic DNS updates** are enabled, the default settings allow clients to register the A record and the DHCP server to register the PTR record. Because only the owner of a record can modify it using dynamic updates, this configuration ensures that the client can update its A record when its address

Figure 8-12

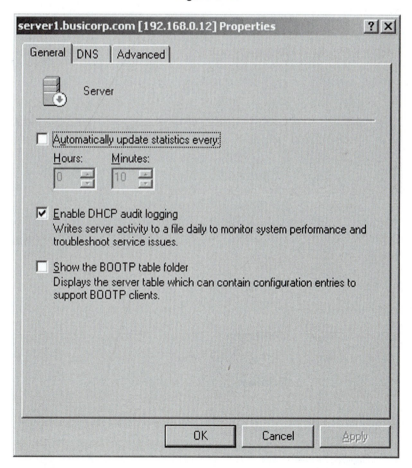

Enabling auditing on a Windows Server 2003 DHCP server.

changes. For legacy clients that do not support dynamic updates, you can change a Windows 2000 or Windows Server 2003 DHCP server's configuration so that the DHCP server updates (and owns) both the A and PTR records belonging to legacy clients, as shown in Figure 8-13. This is a dangerous configuration if there are multiple DHCP servers or rogue DHCP servers. If you need to support legacy clients, add the DHCP servers to the **DNSUpdateProxy group** to prevent the DHCP server from taking ownership of the records it creates. Another precaution is to avoid installing DHCP on a domain controller because it might prevent the domain controller from owning its A records and SRV records, especially if the DHCP server is a member of the DNSUpdateProxy group.

Figure 8-13

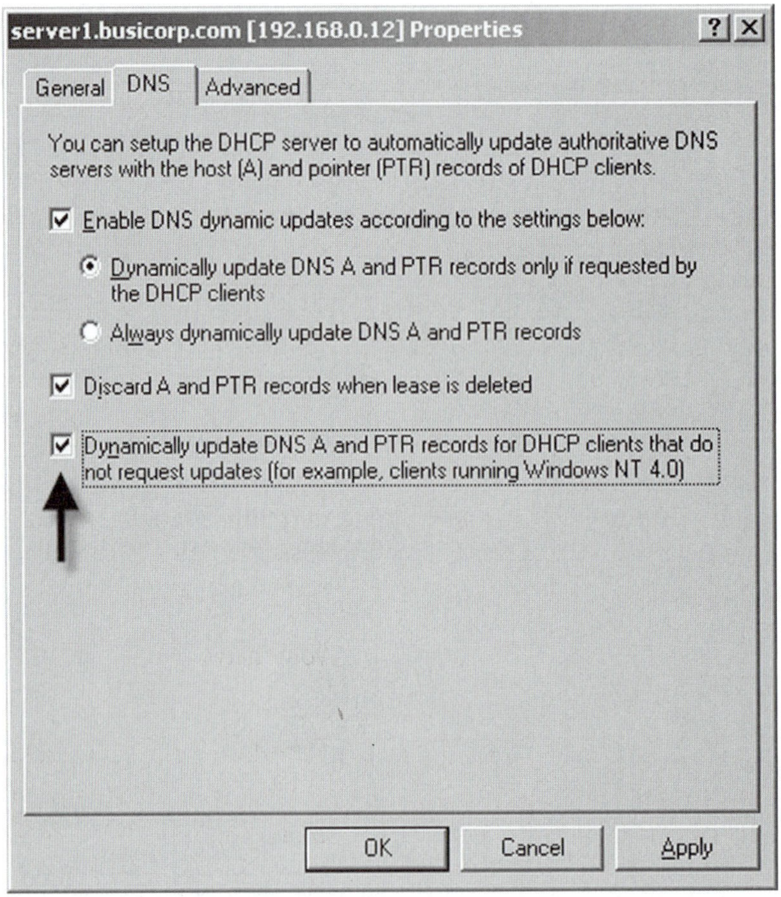

Supporting dynamic updates for legacy clients.

Dynamic updates are controlled on a Linux or Unix computer by the ddns-update-style parameter in the dhcpd.conf file. To prevent dynamic updates, enter the following line:

```
ddns-update-style none
```

8.2.3 Securing WINS Servers

WINS uses dynamic registration to allow computers to create and update records in the WINS database. Most attacks against a WINS server are DoS attacks that prevent clients from locating resources on the network. These attacks can include the following:

▲ Preventing WINS replication from occurring. **WINS replication** copies the records registered at one WINS server to the other WINS servers on the network. If records do not exist on a client's primary WINS server, the client will not be able to locate the other computers on the network.

▲ Registration of invalid records. Registering an invalid record for a server can cause clients to connect to the wrong server or be unable to connect to resources on the network. One vulnerability of the WINS server is that if a host record has the same name as a group record (such as for a domain), the group record will not be found.

The best way to mitigate attacks against WINS servers is to eliminate the need for them by replacing legacy operating systems and **NetBIOS applications** (an application that uses the NetBIOS application layer protocol to communicate on the network). Keep in mind that NetBIOS broadcasts can be used for lookup instead of WINS if all computers that require NetBIOS names are on the same subnet. Another option is to use an **LMHosts file** to provide for NetBIOS lookup if only a few computers need access to NetBIOS resources on a different subnet. However, keep in mind that the LMHosts file must be manually created and maintained, so if there are significant NetBIOS clients that need to resolve names across subnet boundaries, it is best to use WINS.

If you must include WINS servers on your network, you should do the following:

▲ Minimize the number of WINS servers to reduce the need for replication.
▲ If replication is required, monitor the configuration periodically.
▲ Limit the membership in the WINS Admins group.

You should also configure IPsec (IP security) filters to allow the following services:

▲ WINS Resolution server (if a WINS server).

▲ WINS Replication client (to a WINS Replication partner only).

▲ WINS Replication server (to a WINS Replication partner only).

▲ All ports and protocols for domain member communication with domain controllers (to domain controllers only).

You would also create an additional filter that blocks inbound traffic from any unnecessary services and protocols not included in the preceding list. All traffic rules should be mirrored to allow for two-way communication.

8.2.4 Securing RASs

Each RAS on your network provides an additional entry point. An unauthorized RAS can bypass network protections, such as firewalls, leaving your network vulnerable to attack.

The best way to guard against such an attack is to ensure that only authorized computers can be configured as RASs. On an Active Directory network, you can use Group Policy to prevent the Routing and Remote Access service from being started on any computer except the designated remote access or VPN servers.

Another important consideration is keeping the authentication policies and authorization policies consistent throughout the RASs in your organization. A good way to do this is to make all RASs Remote Authentication Dial-In User Service (RADIUS) clients.

FOR EXAMPLE

Securing a DHCP Server

You must configure the incremental security baseline for Busicorp's DHCP server. The server is currently configured to allow the DHCP server to make dynamic updates on behalf of clients. The company has also had a problem with rogue DHCP servers, usually because an employee enables ICS.

To prevent rogue DHCP servers on the network, you disable the DHCP Server service in the baseline server template and in the organizational unit that contains the client computers. You then enable the DHCP Server service for automatic startup in the incremental template that will be imported into the GPO linked to the DHCP Servers OU.

To prevent a DHCP server from owning the A records, you add the DHCP server to the DNSUpdateProxy group. You also recommend that Windows 98 client computers be replaced with Windows XP Professional computers as soon as the budget allows.

8.2.5 Securing NAT Servers

You should install servers that allow clients access to the Internet on a perimeter network and make sure the appropriate firewall rules are configured to prevent unwanted network access over the Internet. You should also prevent unnecessary services from running on the NAT server and ensure that confidential files are not stored there. It is a good idea to disable file sharing on the NAT server.

SELF-CHECK

1. Identify the risk involved with zone transfer on a DNS server.
2. Describe how a rogue DHCP server can cause a DoS attack.
3. Identify the steps you need to take before you can decommission the WINS servers on a network.

8.3 Securing Domain Controllers

A server that performs authentication on your network is one of the most critical resources to secure because it contains the database of user credentials. If an authentication server is compromised, the attacker has access to user accounts or can create an account and assign it administrative permission on the network. In this section we'll look at the steps you should take to secure domain controllers in an Active Directory network.

The domain controller role is the most important server role to secure in an Active Directory environment. Because these servers are so critical to the domain, you should make sure that they are physically stored in a secure location and are only accessible to qualified and authorized administrative staff. If you must store a domain controller in an unsecured location, such as a satellite office, there are several security settings that can be configured to minimize the potential damage from physical threats.

You control the configuration of domain controllers by creating a **Domain Controller Baseline Policy (DCBP)** and linking it to the Domain Controllers OU. You should make sure that the DCBP takes precedence over the Default Domain Controllers Policy. Linking an improperly configured GPO to the Domain Controllers OU could severely impact the operation of the domain.

Depending on the environment you are using, the DCBP will specify additional settings for the various sections of the template. One of the sections you can use to provide a higher degree of security is the User Rights Assignment

section under the Local Policies heading. It is in this portion that you can specify who is permitted to perform certain tasks. The following is a partial list of
the user rights assignments you might want to configure:

▲ **Access This Computer From The Network:** This user right gives the
users granted the right the ability to communicate with the server and
access shares and services over the network.

▲ **Add Workstations To Domain:** This user right gives the user or group
the ability to join the computer to the Active Directory Domain.

▲ **Change The System Time:** This user right allows the user or group to
change the time on the computer.

▲ **Log On Locally:** This user right allows a user or group to log on interactively on the computer. On a domain controller, this right should be
granted to Administrators only.

▲ **Log On As A Service:** This user right grants a user or group the ability
to register a process as a service.

▲ **Manage Auditing And Security Log:** This user right grants a user or
group the ability to configure the audit and security log.

According to the Windows Server 2003 Security Guide, your domain controllers should have the following rights configured in the template:

▲ **Deny Access To This Computer From The Network:**
  ● Built-In Administrator
  ● **Support_388945a0** (a built-in account used by the Help and
    Support service and normally disabled)
  ● Guest
  ● All Non-Operating System service accounts

▲ **Deny Log On As A Batch Job:**
  ● Support_388945a0
  ● Guest

▲ **Deny Log On Through Terminal Services:**
  ● Built-In Administrator
  ● All Non-Operating System service accounts

When configuring the template in an environment that does not include
Windows 9x computers, you will want to enable the "Network security:
Do not store LAN Manager hash value on next password change" setting.
Figure 8-14 shows this setting being configured from the Security Templates
MMC snap-in.

Figure 8-14

Preventing storage of LAN Manager passwords.

All domain controllers have the following services configured to start auto-matically in the System Services section of the predefined templates:

▲ **Distributed File System (DFS):** a service that manages the Windows Server feature that allows multiple file shares to be represented as a sin-gle logical volume.

▲ **DNS:** required for Active Directory–integrated zones.

▲ **File Replication Services (FRS):** service responsible for transferring files and the directory database between domain controllers.

▲ **Intersite Messaging service (IsmServ):** allows communication between domain controllers at different Active Directory sites. A **site** is a grouping of computers that usually represents a geographic location.

▲ **Kerberos key distribution center (KDC):** required on all domain controllers to perform authentication.

▲ **Remote Procedure Call Locator (RpcLocator):** service that allows computers to find a server running the **remote procedure call (RPC)** service. RPC is used to allow some applications to communicate across the network.

You should disable any unnecessary services. For example, if you are not using DFS on your network, you should disable it.

SELF-CHECK

1. Describe how you should deploy a DCBP.

8.4 Securing File and Print Servers

Servers that share files and printers to the network need to be secured against an attacker gaining access to confidential information or violating the integrity of data. In this section we'll look at some steps to take to secure a file server and a print server. We'll also discuss how to mitigate the risk involved with deploying FTP servers.

8.4.1 Securing File Servers

The security required on a file server will depend on the confidentiality and integrity of the files being stored on the file server. Access control is essential to securing a file server. In addition, you should enable auditing for access to files with confidentiality or integrity requirements. Enabling auditing for file access on a Windows computer is a two-step process. First, you must enable the Audit object access policy under Local Policies | Audit Policy. This is shown in Figure 8-15.

Next, you need to enable auditing on the specific folder or file. To enable auditing on a folder or file, do the following:

1. Open the object's Properties dialog box to the Security tab and click "Advanced."
2. Select the Auditing tab, as shown in Figure 8-16, and then click "Add."
3. Type the name of the user or groups whose access attempts you want to audit and click "Check Names." For example, if you want to audit all access attempts, type "Everyone," then click "OK."

Figure 8-15

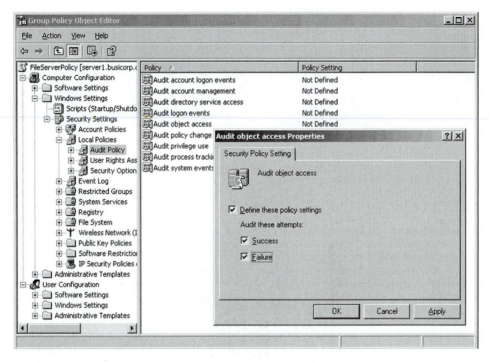

Enabling the Audit object access policy.

4. Select "Success" and/or "Failure" for each permission you want to audit access for, as shown in Figure 8-17. In this case, you are auditing successful and failed deletion attempts.

5. After you have selected the appropriate permissions, click "OK," and then close all open dialog boxes.

8.4.2 Securing Print Servers

The incremental template for a print server must include enabling the **Print Spooler service** and configuring it to start automatically.

When securing a print server, you should first ensure that the appropriate permissions are set on the printer. On a Windows network, printers support the following permissions:

▲ **Print permission:** Users with the Print permission can send documents to the printer.

▲ **Manage Documents permission:** Users with the Manage Documents permission can manage the print queue, including deleting documents

Figure 8-16

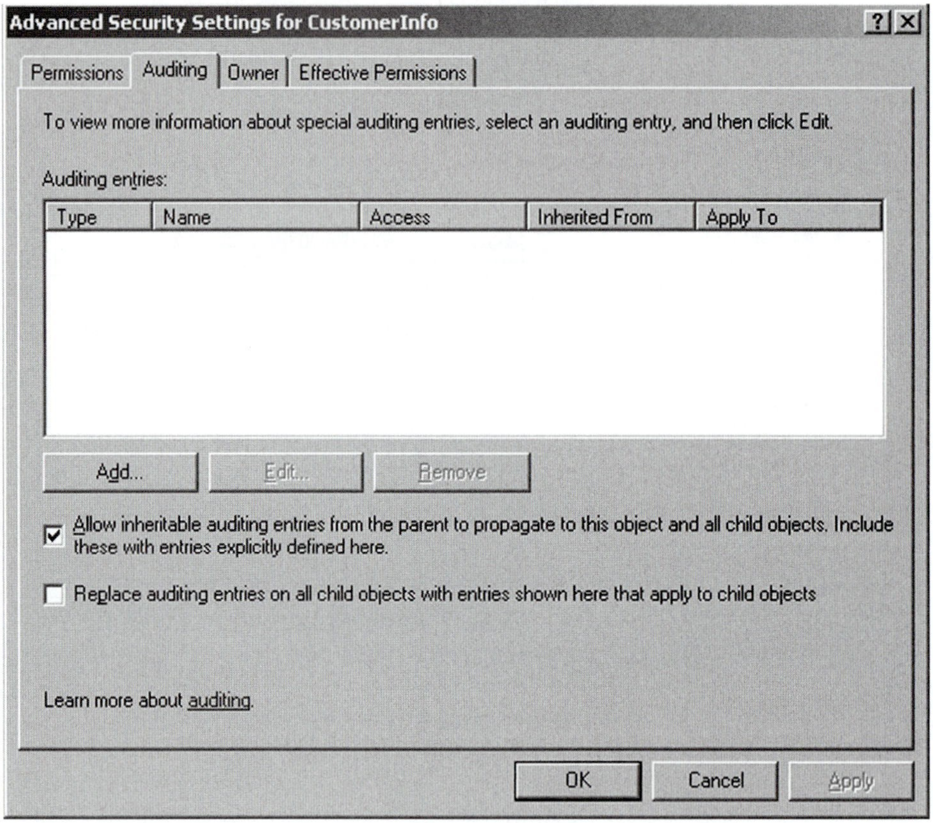

Advanced Security Settings for CustomerInfo   ? ✕

| Permissions | Auditing | Owner | Effective Permissions |

To view more information about special auditing entries, select an auditing entry, and then click Edit.

Auditing entries:

Type	Name	Access	Inherited From	Apply To

Add...   Edit...   Remove

☑ Allow inheritable auditing entries from the parent to propagate to this object and all child objects. Include these with entries explicitly defined here.

☐ Replace auditing entries on all child objects with entries shown here that apply to child objects

Learn more about auditing.

OK   Cancel   Apply

The Auditing tab.

that were sent to the printer by other users. A **print queue** is a list of documents **(print jobs)** that have been sent to the printer.

▲ **Manage Printer permission:** Users with the Manage Printer permission can change printer settings and install drivers.

Another concern is that documents are **spooled** to the hard disk of the print server (stored in a file in a designated folder until it has been printed). If the print server is configured to keep documents that have been printed, this presents a security risk because an attacker who can gain access to the spooler folder might be able to obtain confidential data from the spooled files.

Another potential risk is with printers that have been shared through IIS. These printers can be located and accessed through a browser. Therefore, it is especially important to secure these printers by setting permissions.

If you want a record of printer use, print queue modification, or printer configuration modification, you can enable auditing. You configure auditing

Figure 8-17

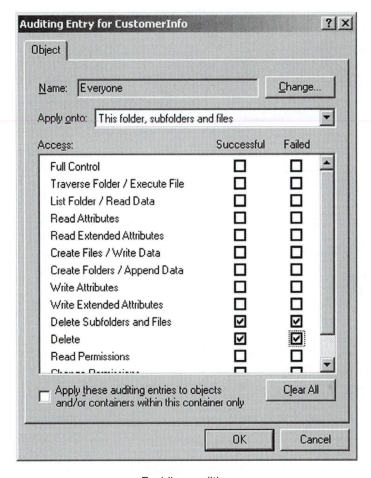

Enabling auditing.

for printers on a Windows network the same way you configure auditing for files.

8.4.3 Securing FTP Servers

Exchanging files with the public or with unknown users will often involve the use of FTP. Many server operating systems will come with FTP as a means for transferring files to the server, but it is usually not enabled by default. If not locked down, an FTP server can be a point of compromise for the server and network as a whole.

Anonymous FTP is particularly risky and open to various attacks. As the name implies, anyone can transfer files without being authenticated with a password.

When prompted for a username, the word *anonymous* is provided. When prompted for a password, the user is expected to enter his or her email address. Most FTP sites do not check that the email address is valid or even that the domain in the email matches the domain being used by the user.

Some sites configure their anonymous FTP servers to allow writable areas (for example, to make available incoming or **drop-off directories** for files being sent to the site). If these files can be read by anonymous FTP users, the potential for abuse exists. Abusers often gather and distribute lists describing the locations of vulnerable sites and the information these sites contain. The lists (known as **warez lists**) commonly include the names of writable directories and the locations of pirated software; they can also include password files or other sensitive information. These drop-off sites are used as data repositories for the abusers to share information.

Unfortunately, in many cases, system administrators are unaware that this abuse is taking place on their FTP servers. They might be unfamiliar with this type of abuse (and so haven't taken steps to prevent it), or they might think that they have configured the FTP server to prevent abuse when, in fact, they have not. System administrators at the sites being used to place or pick up items from the drop-off area might also not be aware that their users are participating in this activity.

FOR EXAMPLE

An FTP Server Exploited by Elevation of Privilege

Busicorp has provided its clients with a more secure method of uploading financial data by deploying a VPN server. However, you discover that the developers had been using the FTP server on the perimeter network to allow members of the development team to transfer files back and forth when they were telecommuting. The developers need to continue to use the FTP server for this purpose. Several of the developers have complained about poor performance when accessing the FTP server and they say the server is running out of disk space. You examine the files on the server and realize that there is a hidden directory that contains a large volume of pirated software. You also notice that a customer's account that you had not deleted has been added to the Administrators group.

You delete the hidden directory and all user accounts except those belonging to developers. You configure permissions so that the developer accounts can access only a single folder on the server and verify that they are all members of the Users group. You also enable auditing for failed and successful account management events so that you can be warned of a future elevation of privilege attack.

An FTP server can be run securely but requires constant monitoring. Following are recommendations to minimize the risk when using an FTP server:

▲ Lock down the server's host. The server should not run any other services. If possible, place the server behind a firewall that only permits FTP access to the server. Other hosts on the same network should not consider the FTP server trusted.

▲ Turn off the FTP server when it's not actually needed. In many cases, the server's administrator expects one or more users to access the FTP server in a certain window of time. The administrator should let the users know the window of time for which the server will be up so the users can get the files they need.

▲ Do not allow anonymous access to the FTP server. Anonymous FTP has a number of vulnerabilities. If anonymous FTP is enabled, any files on the root directory would be available for downloading. Also, malicious applications might be uploaded.

▲ If anonymous FTP is required, set up a separate server to handle this traffic.

▲ Do not put any sensitive files on the same host as the anonymous FTP server.

▲ Turn on extensive logging on all the FTP servers.

▲ Closely monitor the logs and activity to the FTP server. Be prepared to stop and isolate the server in the event it exhibits any unusual behavior.

FTP transfers files in clear text. Therefore, you should consider using Secure FTP (SFTP) or secure copy protocol (SCP) instead. Another option is to encrypt the FTP traffic using IPsec.

SELF-CHECK

1. List the steps required to enable auditing for file access on a computer running Windows Server 2003.
2. Identify the change to System Services you will make when creating an incremental template for print servers.
3. Describe the credentials used by tradition on an anonymous FTP server.

8.5 Securing Application Servers

The final type of server we'll discuss are servers that run applications. Our focus will be on web servers and database servers. Email servers and issues related to email security are discussed in Chapter 9.

The security measures you decide to implement on an application server depends on the criticality of the service the server provides and the confidentiality and integrity requirements of the data stored on the server and the data that can be accessed across the network by the application. Servers in this category are especially vulnerable to attack because you do not have control over vulnerabilities that might exist in the applications running on the servers.

8.5.1 Securing Web Servers

A web server is a target for attack because of its high value and the high probability of weakness. As it turns out, the web servers that provide the highest value often also provide the highest probability of weakness because they rely on multiple applications. Let's look at some of the common attacks on web servers and some steps for mitigating them.

Enumerating Directories

A common mistake made by website administrators is to allow directory listings. By default, a website's default page will be displayed if the **Uniform Resource Locator (URL)**, the path to the web page, does not include a filename. On a server running IIS, this would usually be a page named "default.asp," "default.aspx," or "default.htm," but you can specify a different filename for the default page. On most other web servers, this would be a page named "index.html" or "index.htm." If the default page does not exist and directory listings are allowed, the website will display the subdirectories and files in the folder, and might accidentally leak sensitive information, such as files that an administrator does not intend to be available to users.

Investigative Searching

Pieces of information posted on the Internet are rarely forgotten (even years after being identified by a caching search engine). As a form of reconnaissance against a site, attackers will often harvest usernames by using websites to search for email addresses. For instance, simple searching on the partial email address @maia.usno.navy.mil quickly turns up over a dozen email newsgroup postings, each of which provides a unique username that can be used in an attack. In addition, web administrators often place email addresses of employees and web masters on a web page, which can provide an attacker with additional ammunition against a site.

Faulty Authorization

Mistakes in authentication and authorization can lead to account harvesting or, even worse, impersonation. One example of this is using Basic authentication on a computer running IIS. Basic authentication allows usernames and passwords to be passed as clear text.

Defacing a Website

Another common attack launched against web servers is to deface the website by adding content or modifying a **hyperlink** (clickable area on a web page that loads a different URL) so that it redirects a user to a site with malicious content. You should ensure that content directories are protected by permissions to prevent unauthorized users from modifying the content. It is also a good idea to use server-side programs so that the website's programming logic cannot be seen by viewing the source in a browser. A **server-side program** is code that executes on the web server and returns **HyperText Markup Language (HTML)** to the browser. Server-side programming technologies include **Common Gateway Interface (CGI)**, **Active Server Pages (ASP)**, **Internet Server Application Programming Interface (ISAPI)**, and **ASP.NET**. HTML is the standard language used to create web pages.

Steps for Securing a Web Server

Now that you are aware of some of the dangers with web servers, let's look at some general steps you can take to prevent unauthorized access. These steps include the following:

▲ Set suitable access control lists (ACLs) on web content. You should consider the minimum permissions with regard to content. You will need to pay attention to permissions on log files to prevent alteration or revealing too much information. You will need to make sure the scripts and executables have the necessary permissions to run.

▲ Install only components that are being used by the web server. Software that is installed but not used is usually not secured, maintained, or set up properly. This makes it a great target for attacks. Having extra services running also increases the odds that you will be attacked through a bug in one of the components. If the web server supports multiple websites, make sure that each website has only the necessary services and extensions enabled to run its content.

▲ Use secure communication mechanisms where appropriate. Determine what connections are vulnerable to eavesdropping and use appropriate encryption mechanisms over the connection. The most common mechanism for Hypertext Transfer Protocol (HTTP) applications is Secure Sockets Layer (SSL).

▲ Decide what protocols you need and filter anything else. You will need to evaluate the protocols you are using on the server. This means not only evaluating the application's protocols, but also looking at the protocols used to manage the application and to update the content of the application. You will then apply TCP\IP packet filtering or, for more security, IPSec filters to deny access to the server for protocols that are not used. Filtering on the server should not take the place of a good firewall—it is an added precaution.

▲ Remove any samples or demonstration applications. The sample applications are meant to show a developer how to solve some particular problem or use a certain technology. As a result, they are generally not secure and can be the source of attacks. They should be removed from production servers.

▲ Enable logging on the server. Logging is how you track what is happening on the server. You will be able to use logging information to report trends about usage and performance. It can also be used after a security incident to determine the damage done to the server or as evidence to prosecute the attacker.

▲ Install and configure UrlScan if your web server is running IIS. **UrlScan** is an ISAPI filter that screens and analyzes URLs and requests before IIS has a chance to process them. IIS 6 incorporates features that make UrlScan less necessary than with previous versions of IIS. However, you still need UrlScan if you want to do the following:

● Filter URLs based on their length.

● Filter HTTP commands, which are called **verbs** (GET, POST, PUT, SEARCH, BPROP, to name a few).

● Remove the server header to conceal the identity and version of the web server and operating system.

▲ Create a plan to keep the server up-to-date. Keeping up with security updates on a web server is very important. As new vulnerabilities are discovered, security patches are released to address them.

▲ Create a plan to back up all of the server content. The successful implementation of a backup plan can help you recover the server quickly in case of a security breach, like website defacement. You will need to consider a plan for backing up the log files on a regular basis and determine how much information you will need to keep.

▲ Create a plan for updating content on the server. You will need to decide how new content will get moved to the server. Moving content can introduce security issues if it is not carefully considered. You should understand what protocols are available and what the network infrastructure will allow.

8.5.2 Securing Database Servers

Because database servers are used to store data, they are often the subject of attacks that seek to breach the confidentiality or integrity of the data they store. Therefore, when planning security for a database server, it is important to determine the cost of an attacker gaining access to the data on the site.

A network administrator is often not the person responsible for securing the relational database. That job usually belongs to a database administrator. However, a network administrator does need to ensure that the server the database management system runs on is secure. As with most servers, this involves minimizing the server's attack surface by physically securing the server, disabling services, limiting user rights, and creating IPsec filters to limit and secure the traffic to the server.

A database server is usually accessed from a client/server application or a web application. It is important that you work with the database administrator and application developers to understand who needs to be able to access the database and the protocol or protocols they will use to access it.

A common attack launched against a database server is an SQL injection attack. Let's take a look at how it happens and how to mitigate it.

SQL Injection Attack

Structured Query Language (SQL) is the American National Standards Institute (ANSI) standard for database query languages. Implemented in a number of database management systems, including Microsoft Access™, Microsoft SQL Server, Oracle®, and Sybase®, this standard has been accepted industrywide. Statements written in SQL are capable of adding, removing, editing, or retrieving information from a relational database. The sample database provided in Table 8-2 is an example of a database.

The following SQL command (**query**) will return the entries for customers Molly and Margaret Carroll:

```
select * from customerinfo where last='Carroll';
```

A **SQL injection attack** occurs when a malicious user purposefully enters data into this table that will cause an error in its processing. For example,

Table 8-2: Sample Database

First	Last	Location	Organization
Molly	Carroll	22305	University of Science
David	Michaels	45334	International Sales Corporation
Barbara	Richards	35758	Tungsten Tidal
Margaret	Carroll	44506	Association of Metallurgical Science

suppose that this information was collected through online registration for the International Metallurgical Convention. If David Michaels had been a malicious user, he might have tried to inject SQL into his input by entering the following:

```
First Name:  David
Last Name:  Mi'chaels
```

Now the query string for this element has become the following:

```
select * from customerlist where last='Mi'chaels'
```

However, with the added single quote, this statement is syntactically incorrect and will result in an error:

```
Server: Msg X, Level X, State 1, Line 20
Line 20: Incorrect syntax near 'chaels'
```

This error would be even more serious if the malicious user were to add a semicolon and a command following the single quote that would be executed by the server:

```
First Name:  David
Last Name:  Mi'; shutdown
```

If the web application does not validate the data entered and the server supports the shutdown commands, the server will execute a shutdown after performing the query.

Websites that use SQL as a means of authentication are just as vulnerable. Take the following authentication query, for example:

```
Var login="select * from users where username = '"+
username + "' and password = '" + password + "'";
```

The user can simply add another condition to the query string, which makes it always true to grant access:

```
First Name:  David
Last Name:  ' or 1=1
```

To guard against SQL injection attacks, website and database developers need to be educated about the danger and add code to their applications to validate all user input before it is concatenated onto an SQL query.

FOR EXAMPLE

Code Red worm

The **Code Red worm** was the first big worm to attack IIS and has inspired many derivatives, such as the **Nimda worm** and **Code Red 2**. This virus took advantage of a buffer overflow error in the **Index Server service** (a Windows service that indexes files on a hard disk for faster search access). A **buffer overflow attack** attempts to exploit a program that does not validate a text value, like a URL, for length and allows a larger value to be placed in memory than the amount of space allocated. For example, the Code Red virus uses the following URL to exploit IIS:

```
/default.ida?NNNNNNNNNNNNNNNNNNNNNNNNNNNNNNNNNNNNNNNNNNNNN
NNNNNNNNNNNNNNNNNNNNNNNNNNNNNNNNNNNNNNNNNNNNNNNNNNNNNNNNNN
NNNNNNNNNNNNNNNNNNNNNNNNNNNNNNNNNNNNNNNNNNNNNNNNNNNNNNNNNN
NNNNNNNNNNNNNNNNNNNNNNNNNNNNNNNNNNNNNNNNNNNNNNNNNNNNNNNNNN
N%u9090%u6858%ucbd3%u7801%u9090%u6858%ucbd3%u7801%u9090%u68
58%ucbd3%u7801%u9090%u9090%u8190%u00c3%u0003%u8b00%u531b%u5
3ff%u0078%u0000%u00=a
```

The N in the URL is taking up space to overflow the **string buffer** (a memory location set aside to store a specific number of characters), and the %u represents **hexadecimal commands** (commands represented in base 16) that the sender wants to execute. Subsequently, the program will not allocate enough space in memory to store a text value, which means that the additional information will "**break the stack**" and insert the value starting at the %u9090 as the next command on the **stack** to execute. The stack is an internal structure where the operating system places the commands that should execute in a **last-in-first-out (LIFO)** order. This value represents code that will run with the permissions of the service running the code (administrator equivalent).

As a result of the buffer overflow, the sender of the Code Red worm is allowed to execute arbitrary code with the Local System Account privileges. This is dangerous because it means that the attacker has complete control over the infiltrated system. If you have IIS 4 or IIS 5 servers that have Index Server installed, they will be affected by this vulnerability unless they are patched. The Code Red exploit can occur even if the Indexing Server service is installed but stopped or disabled. You will need to make sure that you do not have the indexing service installed. This is an example of why you need to make sure that you install only the products you are using. If you don't need it, don't install it. You can also avoid the Code Red worm by keeping your server up-to-date with security patches, which would be appropriate if you depend on Index Server.

SELF-CHECK

1. Describe how using server-side programming logic can help protect a website.
2. Describe how you can protect a database server from an SQL injection attack.

SUMMARY

In this chapter you learned some general guidelines for designing and implementing security baselines for your member servers. You also learned some best practices for securing a server based on its role in the network. The roles covered included infrastructure servers, domain controllers, file servers, print servers, web servers, and database servers.

KEY TERMS

A record

Active Directory–Integrated (ADI) zone

Active Server Pages (ASP)

Anonymous FTP

ASP.NET

Baseline template

BIND name server

Break the stack

Buffer overflow attack

Code Red 2

Code Red worm

Common Gateway Interface (CGI)

Custom template

DHCPINFORM message

DHCP scope

Distributed File System (DFS)

DNS cache

DNS namespace

DNSUpdateProxy group

Domain Controller Baseline Policy (DCBP)

Domain Name System (DNS) server

Drop-off Directory

Dynamic Host Configuration Protocol (DHCP) server

Dynamic DNS updates

Dynamic updates

Fault tolerance

File Replication Services (FRS)

Forward lookup

Hexadecimal commands

Host name

Host record

Hyperlink

HyperText Markup Language (HTML)

Incremental template

Index Server service

Internet Connection Sharing (ICS)

Internet Server Application Programming Interface (ISAPI)

Intersite Messaging service (IsmServ)

Kerberos key distribution center (KDC)

Last-in-first out (LIFO)

LMHosts file

Manage Documents permission

Manage Printer permission

Multihomed computer

MX record

NetBIOS application

NetBIOS name

Network Address Translation (NAT) server

Network infrastructure server

Nimda worm

Poisoning the cache

Print job

Print permission

Print queue

Print Spooler service

PTR record

Query

Registry

Remote access server (RAS)

Remote procedure call (RPC)

Remote Procedure Call Locator (RpcLocator)

Reverse lookup

Rogue DHCP server

Secure baseline

Secure updates

Security template

Security Configuration and Analysis snap-in

Security Configuration Wizard (SCW)

Security Templates snap-in

Server role

Server-side program

Site

Spooled

SQL injection attack

SRV record

Stack

String buffer

Structured Query Language (SQL)

Support_388945a0

Total cost of ownership (TCO)

Transaction Signature (TSIG)

Trusted computing base

Trusted zones

Uniform Resource Locator (URL)

UrlScan

Verb

Virtualization

Virtual machine

Warez list

Windows Internet Name Service (WINS) server

WINS replication

Zone

Zone transfer

ASSESS YOUR UNDERSTANDING

Go to www.wiley.com/college/cole to evaluate your knowledge of designing server security based on a server's role.

Measure your learning by comparing pre-test and post-test results.

Summary Questions

1. A secure baseline is a plan for applying the pieces of a trusted computing base to the appropriate computers. True or false?

2. In an Active Directory domain, how can you automate deployment of security settings to a large number of computers?
   (a) Import a security template into a GPO and link the GPO to an OU.
   (b) Link a security template to an OU.
   (c) Import a security template into a GPO and link the GPO to a Windows group.
   (d) Grant a Windows group containing the computers the Execute permission on the security template.

3. What is the biggest risk of zone transfer?
   (a) An attacker can modify host records to spoof a server.
   (b) An attacker can perform a DoS attack against your DNS server.
   (c) An attacker can gain information about your network.
   (d) An attacker can poison the DNS cache.

4. A DNS server is configured to query an Internet DNS server to resolve names it cannot resolve. What is the biggest risk of this configuration?
   (a) An attacker can modify host records to spoof a server.
   (b) An attacker can perform a DoS attack against your DNS server.
   (c) An attacker can gain information about your network.
   (d) An attacker can poison the DNS cache.

5. Active Directory authorization can completely protect your network against rogue DHCP servers. True or false?

6. A WINS server is only needed if you have legacy Windows operating systems in your environment. True or false?

7. Which operating systems cannot communicate with a domain controller when the "Network security: Do not store LAN Manager hash value on next password change" security policy is enabled?
   (a) Windows NT 4.0 only
   (b) Windows 95, Windows 98, and Windows Me
   (c) Windows 95 only
   (d) Windows NT 4.0 and Windows 95

8. You enable the Audit object access policy and select "Success." However, no file access events are audited. Why not?

   (a) You need to enable auditing on the individual folders and files you want to audit.

   (b) Your account is not a member of the Administrators group.

   (c) You need to enable the Audit system events policy.

   (d) You need to enable the Audit privilege use policy.

9. Which printer permission allows users to delete print jobs that were sent to the printer by other users?

   (a) Print

   (b) Manage Documents

   (c) Manage Printer

   (d) all of the above

10. Which is NOT a risk of an anonymous FTP site?

    (a) An attacker might list the site on a warez list.

    (b) An attacker might upload pirated software to the site.

    (c) An attacker might upload malicious code to the site.

    (d) An attacker might use a packet sniffer to obtain logon credentials.

11. When securing a web server, you should enable support for all server-side extensions the web server software supports. True or false?

12. How can you guard against an SQL injection attack?

    (a) Set the query buffer size to unlimited.

    (b) Instruct developers to validate user input before using it in a dynamic query.

    (c) Grant the right to modify a database only to administrators.

    (d) Encrypt all databases.

13. How can you prevent a host from accessing a Linux server?

    (a) Add an entry for the host to the /etc/hosts.deny file.

    (b) Add an entry for the host to the dhcpd.conf file.

    (c) Add an entry preceded by a "#" to the /etc/hosts.allow file.

    (d) none of the above

Applying This Chapter

1. You are configuring security for a company with six locations. The network is an Active Directory network and there are a total of seven domain controllers: two at the main office and one at each other office. There is currently a BIND DNS server at each location. Most

workstations are running Windows XP Professional, but around a dozen computers at one of the offices are still running Windows 98. A NetBIOS application at the main office must be accessible by all users. A server running WINS and DHCP is also running at each office. There are between four and ten file servers at each location, two print servers at the main office, and one print server at each other office. The offices connect through a VPN connection, with a VPN endpoint configured at each office.

(a) What server roles are there on the network?

(b) What changes should you make to reduce the likelihood of an attack on a WINS server?

(c) How can you reduce the likelihood of an attacker learning about the hosts on your network?

(d) Does the network need to support LAN Manager hashes? If so, which accounts require them?

(e) How can you ensure that a network administrator at a branch office won't loosen the security on a domain controller?

(f) At minimum, what security templates should enable the Audit object access policy?

(g) How can you ensure that the VPN servers all use the same authentication policies?

2. A development team at your company is building an application that will be used by customers to obtain product availability information and automated support. The service will be a web application and will use a database on a different server. At first, the application will be installed on only a single web server. However, as performance requirements increase, it will be installed on multiple web servers. You are responsible for implementing security on the web server and the database server.

(a) Why is it important for you to work with the development team?

(b) The development team has told you that the application will be an ASP.NET application. What are the security ramifications?

(c) The development team wants to use FTP to transfer files to the server. What are some security concerns and how can you mitigate them?

Identifying Risks and Securing Servers

You have been hired by a company to identify security vulnerabilities in their existing server infrastructure and to recommend changes. The company's network is configured as a single Active Directory domain. There are domain controllers at each of four offices. An administrator at each location is a member of Domain Admins. All client computers are running Windows XP Professional. Three files servers are running Windows NT 4.0 Server. They are located at location C. Twenty file servers are running Windows 2000 Server. Five file servers are running Windows Server 2003. The company has three print servers at each office. The company has a server running WINS, DNS, and DHCP at each office.

DNS supports dynamic updates. The company has an RAS at location A that provides access to telecommuters. The same server is also configured as a VPN server and an FTP server. The FTP server has a drop-off directory that is configured to use anonymous FTP. A database server stores accounting information, which must be accessed through a web application, and a traditional client/server application. The web application was developed in-house and will replace the client/server off-the-shelf application within two years.

1. Identify the vulnerabilities in the current configuration and describe how you could mitigate them.

9

PROTECTING AGAINST MALWARE

Starting Point

Go to www.wiley.com/college/cole to assess your knowledge of protecting a computer against viruses, worms, and other malicious programs.
Determine where you need to concentrate your effort.

What You'll Learn in This Chapter

▲ Viruses
▲ Worms
▲ Trojan horses
▲ Spyware
▲ Web browser security
▲ Spam
▲ Email security

After Studying This Chapter, You'll Be Able To

▲ Identify various types of malicious code
▲ Mitigate the risk of a malware infection
▲ Configure web browser security settings
▲ Mitigate the risk of spam
▲ Identify safe email practices

INTRODUCTION

As software has become more powerful and users around the world have become more interconnected, the threat of a computer being infected with malicious code has ballooned. In this chapter you will learn about the types of malicious code you need to guard against and some steps for mitigating the threat. This chapter pays particular attention to two venues frequently used to spread malicious code: web pages and email.

9.1 Viruses and Other Malware

Before you can understand how to mitigate the threat of malicious code, you need to understand the types of malicious code being **propagated** (spread from computer to computer) and the methods of propagation. In this section, we'll look at various types of malicious code, which is also known as **malware** or **malcode**.

9.1.1 Viruses

A **virus** is a piece of code that inserts itself into legitimate software. As with a biological virus, the computer virus is not viable without a host. The virus needs the **host** software or file to propagate and carry out its mission. A virus is able to **replicate** (reproduce) itself and attach itself to a host file, a technique known as **self-propagation**.

Early viruses infected boot sectors of floppies and were spread by the sharing of applications on floppies. Today, floppies are too small to be practical for sharing applications, so **boot sector viruses** that are transmitted through floppy disks are not common anymore.

If the virus has attached itself to an application, the code in the virus is run every time the application runs. The virus code will have the same privileges as the host application. A typical example of a host for this kind of virus is a self-extracting video clip. When the unsuspecting user launches the file to extract the video, the virus code runs. This virus spreads by people sending the self-extracting video clip to their friends.

Some viruses are able to attach to data files such as spreadsheets and word processor files. These viruses are **scripts** that execute when the file is loaded. A script is code written in a scripting language, so it does not need to be **compiled** (converted from human-readable source code to binary machine language) into an executable. Instead, it is run by an application that supports such scripts.

One of the first widespread viruses to exploit scripts was **Melissa**, which spread by infecting Microsoft® Word files. When the Word files were opened, the virus code would run and infect the Normal.dot template file used by the word processor. After Normal.dot was infected, any Word document saved would have the Melissa virus. Melissa used the **autorun macros** in a Word document to run a **Visual Basic® script (VBScript)** when an infected Word document was first opened. Microsoft now has a feature called **Macro Virus Protection** that can stop macros from running. This protection should not be disabled.

Email viruses move from PC to PC as part of the body of a message. When the virus code is executed, a message with the virus embedded is sent to other mail clients. The virus can either be an attachment that must be opened or an embedded script. Scripts can access the user's address book, and can use those addresses to propagate the virus-infected message.

One example of a virus that propagates through email is the **ILOVEYOU virus**. The ILOVEYOU virus first appeared in the spring of 2000 and was simply an attachment that users launched. Once launched, the virus's Visual Basic script sent out an infected message to everyone in the user's address book.

9.1.2 Worms

A **worm** is code able to replicate itself and propagate to other hosts by exploiting a vulnerability in a program. Most worms exploit previously identified vulnerabilities that are correctable with patches or upgrades. Therefore, the best protection against worms is to stay current with patches and upgrades for Windows® as well as for other major applications.

Another way to protect against worms is to minimize the services and applications running on a computer. For example, worms often target common, high-visibility applications, such as the Microsoft web server, Internet Information Server (IIS). If a computer does not need to serve web pages and it is not being used to develop an application that relies on IIS, IIS should be disabled on the computer.

9.1.3 Trojan Horses

A **Trojan horse** is a program that masquerades as a legitimate application, while also performing a covert function. Users believe they are launching a legitimate application, such as a screen saver. When the Trojan horse runs, the user has every indication that the expected application is running. However, the Trojan horse also runs additional code that performs a malicious activity.

The best way to detect a Trojan horse is to identify executable files that have been altered. This is most easily done by creating a baseline of **cyclic redundancy check (CRC)** values for all executable files on a workstation. A CRC calculates the file size and divides by a number, then stores the remainder of the operation. If an executable file is later altered to include a Trojan horse, it can be detected by comparing the current CRC value with the baseline value.

Trojan horses are more difficult to distribute than viruses and worms. They do not propagate on their own. They rely on users accepting questionable executables from untrusted sources.

Trojan horses are very powerful threats to the security of a computer, network, and organization. They bypass most security controls put in place to stop attacks. Trojan horses are not stopped by firewalls, intrusion detection systems (IDS), or access control lists (ACLs) because a user installs them just as they would any other application.

Logic Bombs

A **logic bomb** (also called **slag code**) is a type of Trojan horse that lies in wait until some event occurs. The most common trigger for a logic bomb is a date, in which case the code is known as a **time bomb**. The **Michelangelo** virus was an early logic bomb, created in 1991. Its trigger was March 6, Michelangelo's birthday. It was a particularly destructive logic bomb because it was designed to overwrite the hard disk. The **Nyxem Worm** is a more recent time bomb that activates on the third of each month. It disables file sharing security and virus protection and deletes certain file types, including Microsoft Office files, .zip files, and .rar files. The files with extensions .zip and .rar are compressed files.

The use of Trojan horses to launch **distributed denial-of-service (DDoS) attacks** is common. The attacker installs a logic bomb Trojan horse on a number of computers. When the triggering event occurs, those computers launch a denial-of-service attack against the target. The more computers hosting the Trojan horse, the more devastating the attack. The fact that the packets are coming from a number of locations also makes it more difficult to track down the source of the attack. When a computer is controlled to launch a DDoS attack, it is known as a **zombie**.

9.1.4 Browser Parasites

A **browser parasite** is a program that changes some settings in your browser. The parasite can have many effects on the browser, such as the following:

▲ Browser plug-in parasites can add a button or link add-on to the user's browser. When the user clicks the button or the link, information about the user is sent to the plug-in's owner. This can be a privacy concern.

▲ Browser parasites can change a user's start page or search page. The new page might be a "pay-per-click site," where the owner of the browser parasite earns money for every click.

▲ Browser parasites can transmit the names of the sites the user visits to the owner of the parasites. This can be used to formulate a more directed attack on the user.

9.1.5 Spyware

Spyware is a software application that gathers information about the computer and user. This information is then sent back to the developer or distributor of the spyware and is often used to serve ads to the user.

Targeted marketing has long been a part of a good sales program. The classic example is marketers that use census data to direct more effective mass-mailing campaigns. Census data is used to find certain zip codes that have the best demographics (characteristics such as age, number of children, and annual income) for the particular product being advertised. The use of census data and data compiled by companies that conduct market research is not as controversial because specific names and addresses have been removed, and the data is a summary of statistics for the zip code.

Spyware does not provide the developer with summarized data, but instead includes specifics on a named individual. Therefore, it is a violation of privacy and might make it possible for the person who receives the data to steal the victim's identity.

Typical information that can be reported includes the following:

▲ **User keystrokes:** User keystrokes can be used to capture passwords and other very sensitive data entered by the user.

▲ **Copies of emails:** Emails sent or received can be forwarded to the person wanting to monitor the user, unbeknownst to the user.

▲ **Copies of instant messages:** Essentially, any communications to and from the PC can be copied and sent to the spyware's owner.

▲ **Screen snapshots:** Even encrypted communications will at some point be displayed in clear text on the screen. At this point, the spyware can take a screen shot and send the image to whoever has developed or distributed the spyware.

▲ **Other usage information:** Login times, applications used, and websites visited are examples of other data that can be captured and reported back.

9.1.6 Backdoors

A **backdoor** (also called a **trapdoor**) is way for an attacker to access a computer without being detected or blocked by usual security measures. Often, the initial attack on a computer is potentially detectable by a firewall or IDS. So the attacker will install an application that will allow him to get back into the computer quickly and easily. These backdoors are often stealthy and difficult to detect.

If a Windows computer has been connected to the Internet for more than a day without any security protections in place, it most likely has been **rooted** and

> ## FOR EXAMPLE
>
> ### Social Engineering at Work
>
> In January 2007, a worm called the Storm Worm was propagated through email attachments. The subject line of the email related to current news stories, a social engineering technique used to entice users to launch the attachment. One of the headlines used as the subject was "230 dead as storm batters Europe," giving the worm its name. The worm is a Trojan horse that can be used to launch a DDoS attack and send data.
>
> As you can see, sophisticated attacks often do not fit into a specific category. Instead, they use a combination of methods to launch the attack. In this case, a social engineering attack was used to encourage users to launch malicious code, which then installed a Trojan horse and propagated itself as a worm.
>
> Almost immediately, other variant subject lines began to emerge, making it impossible to identify the worm by subject line alone. In fact, within three days, the worm began appearing in emails with matchmaking subject lines instead of news stories. This example illustrates the fact that malware detection is a moving target. In this example, user education and attachment filtering helped prevent the worm from becoming even more of a problem than it was. The attachments were .exe files, so they were easily identified as executable code.

has a backdoor installed. In such a case, the best thing to do is wipe the system clean and re-install the Windows operating system. Although you can delete the application, you can never be sure that other changes have not been made on the computer. Some operating system and driver modifications are difficult to detect.

SELF-CHECK

1. Identify the types of malware that are self-propagating.
2. Describe a logic bomb.

9.2 Protecting the Workstation

Now that you have a basic understanding of the types of programs you are up against, let's look at some ways you can protect the computers on the network against these threats. Malware protection should focus on the following:

Figure 9-1

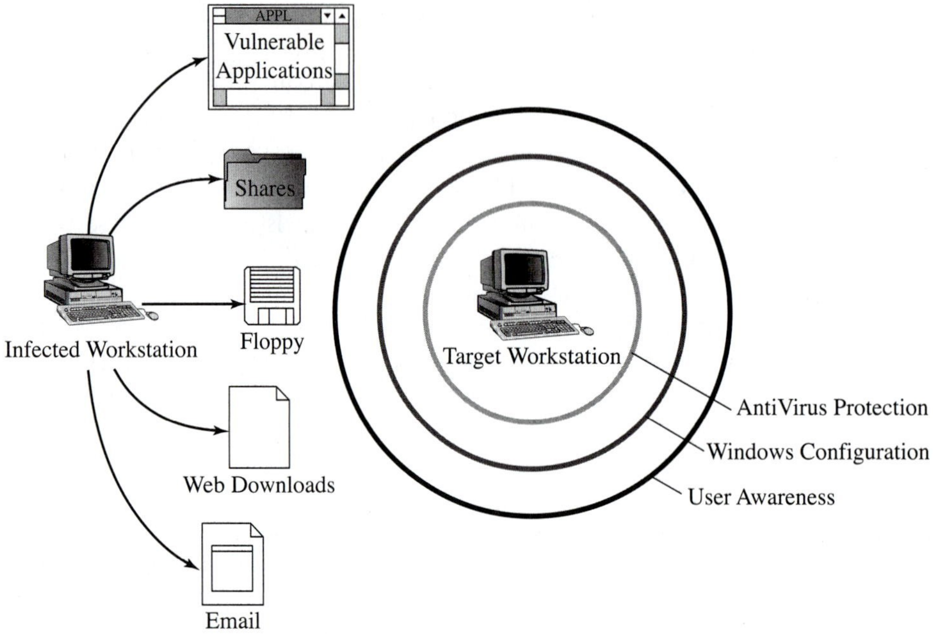

Protecting against malware.

▲ The use of antivirus and anti-spyware applications.
▲ Hardening the computer's configuration.
▲ User training and awareness.

This multilevel defense against viruses and worms is shown in Figure 9-1. Because new viruses and worms are constantly being created, the best protection is to run antivirus software, properly configure Windows, and educate users on safe practices.

It is important to note that anti-malware protection is also important on Linux-based computers, as well as on computers running Windows. Although currently a larger number of viruses and other malware programs are developed to target Windows computers, the number of malware programs that target Linux and Mac® OX is increasing. As these operating systems become more popular, they will become more desirable targets, and the number of malware attacks will increase even more.

This section will focus on protecting the workstation by looking at some general guidelines. The next two sections will look at defending against the two most common methods of propagation: web pages and email.

9.2.1 Antivirus Software

In today's threat environment, virus protection applications (**antivirus** programs) are no longer optional. A number of good antivirus products are available today, such as those from Symantec™, McAffee®, and Computer Associates™.

An organization should have protection on every computer where people are saving files, storing email messages, or browsing web pages. The antivirus software should be configured to provide real-time protection as well as routinely scheduled scanning. Without continuous protection, a virus can spread throughout an organization before the next routine scan is scheduled.

Keep Current with Antivirus Signatures

Because new viruses are always being released, antivirus software relies on periodic updated virus signature files to provide protection against the latest threats. A **virus signature** is the pattern of bits inside a virus that allows the antivirus software to recognize it.

Most signature updates are obtained by accessing the antivirus vendor's site and pulling down the latest update. Most antivirus packages will allow the administrator to choose to have the new signatures downloaded automatically on a regular schedule. Automating the process ensures that critical updates are not missed.

If the new antivirus signature is downloaded to be redistributed throughout a large organization, it should be tested first and deployed from a server within the organization. The local server, in turn, gets its files from a master server that distributes the tested update. There are four key steps to deploying updated signatures in a large organization:

1. Download new signatures.
2. Test new antivirus downloads.
3. Deploy new signatures.
4. Continue to monitor.

Finally, it is important that the computers be monitored periodically to ensure that the new antivirus signatures are being distributed properly. When the next big virus or worm hits is not the time to find a flaw in the system.

9.2.2 Anti-spyware

Anti-spyware software monitors a computer for spyware and allows you to remove it. There are a number of anti-spyware applications. In fact, some companies like Symantec and Microsoft sell an integrated package that includes antivirus and anti-spyware software. A term describing software that protects against a variety of malware is **anti-malware**. As with an antivirus application, you must keep your anti-spyware software up-to-date.

Some Internet service providers (ISPs) are so concerned about preventing malware that they offer security suites to their subscribers free of charge.

9.2.3 Computer Configuration Guidelines

Another important way to guard against malware is to make sure client computers are hardened. Many of the same guidelines apply as for hardening servers, including the following:

▲ Remove unnecessary services and applications.
▲ Filter traffic.
▲ Implement access control.

In this section, we'll look at a few specific precautions: personal firewalls, limiting user rights, and disabling hidden file extensions.

Personal Firewalls

A **personal firewall** is software that runs on the user's computer and blocks incoming and outgoing traffic. When used properly, a personal firewall can be very effective. For instance, a properly configured personal firewall can be very specific to a user's need for LAN traffic. A good way to configure a personal firewall is to start by blocking all traffic in and out of the computer. As the user encounters warnings of attempted activity that has been blocked, the user can choose to permit that traffic. In a short period of time, the user will have unblocked the majority of traffic he or she needs and the firewall will be configured to the user's very specific requirements.

Windows XP Professional with Service Pack 2 includes Windows Firewall. Other personal firewalls are available for Windows, Linux, and Mac OX from a variety of software distributors.

Limiting User Rights

Remember that malware usually runs under the security context of the user who is logged in. Therefore, you should consider the rights and permissions a user has on his or her computer. For example, if a user does not need to install applications, the user should be prevented from doing so.

A **managed computer** is one that is configured through an automated policy. On an Active Directory® network, the policy is deployed through Group Policy Objects (GPOs). A large number of templates are available for configuring computers, as shown in Figure 9-2.

Some things you can do include the following:

▲ Prevent users from creating automated tasks through Task Scheduler.
▲ Disable services.

Figure 9-2

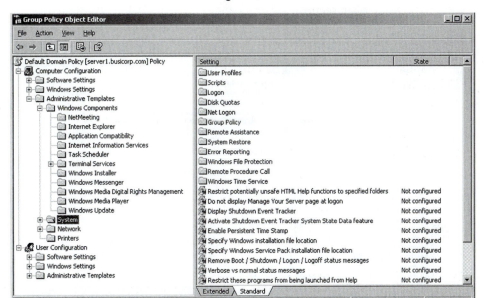

Computer configuration policies.

▲ Prevent users from installing applications.

▲ Set permissions on directories.

▲ Restrict the software that can run based on file type, publisher, and location.

▲ Restrict membership in specific groups.

You can also create policies that apply to user accounts, as shown in Figure 9-3. For example, you might want to prevent users from accessing the Control Panel or from running applications unless they meet specific criteria.

On a NetWare® network, you can use ZENworks® to create managed computers and restrict the features available on a desktop. ZENworks patch management can also be used to ensure that desktop computers are kept up-to-date.

File Extensions

Windows has a feature that allows file extensions to be hidden from the user. Although this feature is designed to make the system more convenient and user friendly, this convenience comes at a security price. By hiding the extensions, malicious code is able to masquerade as something benign. For example, a user might be tempted to open a file named readme.txt, knowing that simple American Standard Code for Information Interchange (ASCII) text files cannot

Figure 9-3

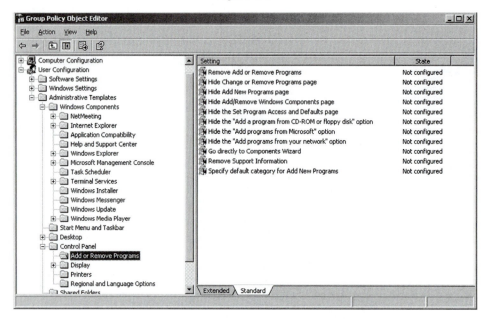

User configuration policies.

contain malicious code. However, the user will be at risk if the real file name is readme.txt.bat, because Windows hides the true extension, .bat. If the user opens the file by double clicking it, the malicious code in the BAT file will run with the same permissions as the user. File extension hiding should be disabled on Windows systems. You disable file extension hiding by removing the check from the "Hide file extensions for known file types" check box on the View tab of the Folder Options dialog box, as shown in Figure 9-4.

9.2.4 User Training

Windows users can also take steps to minimize the spread of viruses, worms, and Trojan horses on their systems. Remember, many malware schemes depend on social engineering to propagate. Some good practices for users include the following:

▲ Configure the email client to not download graphics and audio automatically. Some malicious email includes links that will let the attacker know that the file was opened. An attacker is more likely to continue to send malicious emails to addresses on which they are opened. A graphic or audio file embedded for this purpose is known as a **web beacon**.

Figure 9-4

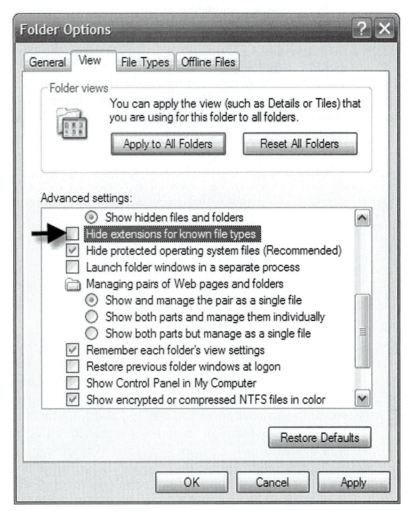

Showing file extensions.

▲ Don't open any email from strangers that contain attachments.

▲ Only accept or open expected attachments. The user should have prior knowledge that the attachment was going to be sent. Many viruses today will at first appear to be legitimate messages. However, upon scrutiny, a user will be able to catch unexpected messages.

▲ Do not open attachments on email that seems vague or out of character. Watch out for nondescript messages such as "Check this out." The sender should include information in the message that helps the recipient trust the attachment. For example, instead of "Check this out," the message should be "Bobby's graduation pictures," where the sender, Bobby, and a graduation are familiar or expected.

▲ If questionable email must be received and read, use a separate email client that is less susceptible to viruses. There are circumstances when a user is part of a public mailing list in which the members routinely share files. If attachments from this mailing list are routinely opened, an email client that does not run scripts should be used.

▲ Use macro protection in spreadsheet applications and word processors. Macros should be enabled on a case-by-case basis.

In many cases, the preceding procedures require a judgment call on the part of the user. Security awareness training is essential to help users recognize dangerous code before installing it on their computers.

FOR EXAMPLE

Adding a Computer to a Network Securely

When adding a new computer to the network, it is important that you harden the computer before attaching it to the network. Otherwise, you run the risk of installing malware before the computer has been completely configured and the latest security updates installed. Consider this scenario. You install Windows XP Professional on a computer and add it to the network. Next, you browse the Web to locate an anti-malware program. While browsing the Web, you unintentionally download spyware. When you reach the website distributing the anti-malware, you are asked to type in your email address, mailing address, phone number, and credit card information. The spyware monitors the data you enter and sends it to an advertiser, who then knows too much information about you. You install the anti-malware program and it detects and removes the spyware. However, your private data has already been compromised.

When setting up a new computer, you should always install the latest service packs and security updates, along with anti-malware software *before* connecting the computer to the Internet.

Another important consideration is to make sure you use a trusted source for anti-malware applications. A particularly annoying browser parasite called **SpyBlast** claims to locate and eradicate spyware, but in actuality it displays pop-up advertisements. A type of malware that displays pop-up ads or other advertisements is known as **adware**.

SELF-CHECK

1. What should malware protection focus on?
2. What is a *virus signature*?
3. What is the function of a personal firewall?

9.3 Web Browser Security

Web browsers today provide a lot more features than simply rendering images and HyperText Markup Language (HTML) code. Their convenience is greatly enhanced by their capability to do the following:

▲ Run Common Gateway Interface (CGI) scripts on the web server.
▲ Run scripts written in JavaScript® or VBScript on the web browser.
▲ Run executables such as Java™ and ActiveX® on the web browser host.
▲ Launch various plug-ins such as an audio player or movie player.

The convenience, productivity, and popularity of web browsers make them a prime target for hackers and would-be attackers. The hacker who develops an attack for a common web browser is sure to find many susceptible targets. This section looks at some of the risks associated with web browsers and how to mitigate them by configuring browser security settings and educating users.

9.3.1 Web Browser Risks

The security risks associated with browsing the Internet can be grouped into several categories:

▲ The web server might not be secure. All the data that users enter into their browsers is ultimately processed on the web server. In most cases, this information is stored in a database of some sort. Most typical users trust businesses to make sure their data is secure. However, the opposite is probably true. The best defense a user can have against an unsecure web server is to limit the sensitive data that is transmitted to the server.
▲ The browser runs malcode in the form of scripts or executables. Web applications often have dynamic elements that execute on the client. When used legitimately, these technologies improve the browsing experience. However, when used maliciously, client-side code can do a lot of harm to a computer.

▲ An attacker might eavesdrop on network traffic. Users should be aware that the security of the data transmitted to and from the web server is no more secure than the security of the network on which it travels. This risk can be reduced when the web server uses Secure Sockets Layer (SSL) to encrypt the data transmitted and received.

▲ A website might add browser parasites to your browser.

▲ An attacker might employ a man-in-the-middle attack. Web-based applications are **sessionless**, meaning that each request is sent independently, and are potentially susceptible to man-in-the-middle attacks, such as hijacking and replay.

9.3.2 Web Browser Technologies

Browsers support several types of client-side code. These features come with security risks, but are essential to many web-based applications. Therefore, it is important that you understand what these features are and why they present a risk so that you can configure the browser to limit or provide support for them according to a user's requirements and the organization's security policy.

Plug-ins

A **plug-in** or **add-on** is an addition to the browser that allows you to open a specific type of content. For example, the Adobe® Reader® plug-in allows you to view **Portable Document Format (PDF)** files in the browser window. The Macromedia® Flash® plug-in allows you to view and interact with Flash animations.

ActiveX

ActiveX is a technology developed by Microsoft for creating reusable content that can be distributed over the Internet or through an application installation. **ActiveX controls** are user interface elements that are embedded in a web page and must be downloaded to the client.

The use of ActiveX is a security risk because the browser places no restrictions on what an ActiveX control can do. To mitigate the risk of using ActiveX, each control can be digitally signed. The digital signatures can then be certified by a trusted certifying authority, such as VeriSign®. The developer can also indicate whether the control is safe for scripting and/or safe for executing. A control that is **safe for execution** should not modify files on the computer or perform other harmful tasks when it is added to a web page. A control that is **safe for scripting** should not allow parameters that could be used for harmful purposes to be set in script. For example, if a control is safe for scripting, it should not allow a web page developer to set a path to a file. It is up to the developer to be honest about the safety level of the control. Figure 9-5 shows some of the security settings you can configure to control how ActiveX controls are downloaded and executed by Internet Explorer® 7.

Figure 9-5

ActiveX control settings.

If the browser encounters an ActiveX control that hasn't been signed (or that has been signed but certified by an unknown certifying authority), the browser presents a dialog box warning the user that this action might not be safe. At this point the user can elect to accept the control or cancel the download. Few users that accept an unsigned control appreciate the risk involved. This is an area where user education is essential to preventing the installation of malevolent code.

Java

Java applets are programs written in the **Java** programming language that are run on the user's workstation. Java has a large number of security safeguards intended to avoid attacks. A **security manager** monitors what the applet does and prevents it from performing tasks that are known to be risky. The following security features are part of the Java design:

▲ The security manager does not ordinarily allow applets to execute arbitrary system commands, to load system libraries, or to open up system device drivers such as disk drives.

▲ Applets are generally limited to reading and writing to files in a user-designated directory.

▲ An applet is only allowed to make a network connection back to the server from which it was downloaded.

▲ The security manager allows Java applets to read and write to the network and to read and write to the local disk but not to both. This limitation was created to reduce the risk of an applet spying on the user's private documents and transmitting the information back to the server.

JavaScript

JavaScript is a scripting language that can be executed by most browsers. The designers of JavaScript built security into the language itself. The basic approach was to eliminate the possibility of JavaScript code doing insecure activities by not providing commands or objects for those activities. The following are some examples of the security protections with JavaScript:

▲ JavaScript cannot open, read, write, create, or delete files. The language does not have any objects for managing files. A script cannot even list files and directories.

▲ JavaScript cannot access the network or network resources. The language does not have any objects for connecting or listening to the network interface.

▲ JavaScript can only access the domain from which it was downloaded. The script cannot access any other domain other than the one from which it originated.

Over the years, a number of security vulnerabilities have been discovered when using JavaScript. Patches and updated browsers have eliminated most of the security problems. However, the general concept that JavaScript is a potential avenue for the loss of private data still exists. For instance, JavaScript can access information available to the browser, such as URLs, cookies, names of files downloaded, and so on, and can make Hypertext Transfer Protocol (HTTP) requests. Scripts can request URLs and send other HTML information such as forms. This means the scripts could hit CGI programs that run on the web server.

Cookies

A **cookie** is an ASCII file created by a website to store information about the user visiting that site. This information is stored for the convenience of the website or for the convenience of the user. When a new request is made, the server can ask the browser to check if it has any cookies and, if it does, to pass those cookies back to the server. The browser can potentially pass any cookie to a web server. This could include cookies from completely different websites.

The contents of the cookie are under the control of the web server and might contain information about you or your past and present surfing habits, and when used maliciously can present a threat to a user's privacy.

There are two general types of cookies: persistent and nonpersistent. A **persistent cookie** is one that will survive reboots and last for a predetermined period of time. Persistent cookies are traditionally stored on the hard drive in a file such as "cookies.txt." This file can be read and edited by the user or system administrator. Some marketing companies have attempted to exploit user behavior by trying to capture these persistent cookies.

More and more people are becoming wary of cookies, especially those that can be used to track users over time. Therefore, many sites are starting to use nonpersistent cookies. A **nonpersistent cookie** (also called a **session cookie**) is stored in memory, so when the computer is turned off or rebooted, the cookie information is lost. Some browsers delete nonpersistent cookies when the user closes the browser, navigates to a different website, or after an elapsed period of time. There is no assurance that every browser will handle nonpersistent cookies the same way. The web server has no control over how the browser stores or disposes of the cookies; it merely tells the browser whether the cookie is meant to be persistent or nonpersistent.

9.3.3 Specific Threats to a Browser Session

Now that you are familiar with some of the web technologies and the general risks they present, let's look at some specific attacks that target web browsers and sessions with web servers.

Hijacking Attack

Session hijacking occurs when an HTTP session is observed and captured by a network sniffer. The attacker modifies the captured traffic to allow the attacker to impersonate the client. All future traffic in the session is then channeled between the web server and the attacker.

The hijacking is usually done after the legitimate user has authenticated to the web server. Therefore, the attacker does not have to re-authenticate (usually for the remainder of the session). In this way, the attacker bypasses one of the major security features of the web-based session, the initial authentication.

Figure 9-6

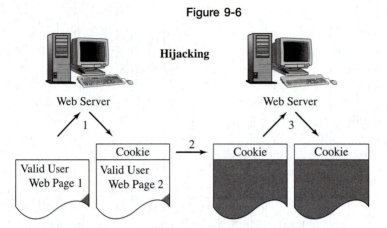

1. A valid user does some web activity that results in him or her acquiring a cookie.
2. The cookie is stolen or captured by an attacker.
3. The cookie is transmitted with the attacker's attempt to access the application. The cookie authenticates the attacker as a valid user. The attacker gets access to the application.

Hijacking when cookies maintain state.

The hijacking attack exploits a weak method of maintaining **state** (information about the current session). If the attacker can understand how state is maintained, they might be able to inject themselves into the middle of the session by presenting the intercepted authentication cookie or credentials. This is illustrated in Figure 9-6.

The attack involves the following steps:

1. A valid user performs some web activity that results in him or her acquiring a cookie.
2. The cookie is stolen or captured by an attacker.
3. The cookie is transmitted with the attacker's attempt to access the application. The cookie authenticates the attacker as a valid user. The attacker gets access to the application.

Replay Attack

As with a hijacking attack, the first step in a **replay attack** is to capture HTTP packets for a session. Some aspect of the session is then modified (certain replays, such as transferring bank funds, might not require modifications). The modified session is then fed back onto the network. If the replay is successful, the web server will believe the replayed traffic to be legitimate and will respond accordingly. This could produce a number of undesirable results. Figure 9-7 illustrates session replay.

Figure 9-7

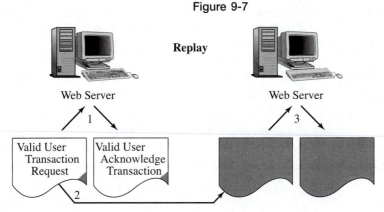

1. A valid user does some web activity such as "Transfer $5,000 from account A to account B". There might or might not be a cookie.
2. The web page holding the transaction request is stolen or captured by an attacker.
3. The web page is retransmitted. The transaction is repeated—an additional $5,000 is transferred. The attacker can retransmit numerous times.
4. Depending on whether the attacker had to do spoofing, the final acknowledgment transaction might go back to the valid user's IP address where it is dropped beccause no session is open.

Replay attack.

The responsibility is on the web server to prevent replay attacks. The web server should be able to recognize replayed traffic as no longer being valid.

The following steps are involved in a replay attack:

1. A valid user performs some web activity such as "Transfer $5,000 from account A to account B." There might or might not be a cookie.

2. The web request is stolen or captured by an attacker.

3. The web request is retransmitted. The transaction is repeated; an additional $5,000 is transferred. The attacker can retransmit numerous times.

4. Depending on whether the attacker had to do spoofing, the acknowledgment might go back to the valid user's IP address, where it is dropped because no session is open.

9.3.4 Browser Configuration

Web browsers, like most Internet applications, respond to emerging security threats. In the early years, web browsers were very vulnerable. They had features making them convenient and productive but had no means for the user to make them more secure. Web browsers have evolved (due to the security threat), and users are now able to set various configuration settings to improve the security of their web browsers.

The problem with relying on the user to make security configuration decisions is that most users are not sophisticated and savvy when it comes to securing a web browser or even understanding the threat. Often users will not change any of the browser's security configuration settings, or even know they exist. The customization, for security purposes, is then left to the system or network administrator. However, as discussed earlier, browsing has become such an accepted norm for convenience and productivity that few users will tolerate less than total functionality. As a result, administrators who initially attempt to secure browsers are often beaten back by the onslaught of complaints and requests for help. In the end, the administrator must relax the web-browsing security settings.

In this section, we'll look at some areas where you can configure a browser to help mitigate the risks.

Secure Socket Layer

The Secure Socket Layer (SSL) protocol provides for the encryption of traffic between the web browser and server. SSL uses public-key encryption to exchange a symmetric key between the client and server; this symmetric key is used to encrypt the HTTP transaction (both request and response). Each transaction uses a different key. If the encryption for one transaction is broken, the other transactions are still protected.

Some of the settings related to digital certificates in Internet Explorer 7 are shown in Figure 9-8.

Settings related to digital certificates when using the Firefox® web browser on a Linux computer are shown in Figure 9-9.

A properly configured web browser will warn the user of a certificate problem if any of the following occur:

▲ The certificate was not signed by a trusted certificate authority.

▲ The certificate is currently invalid or has expired. Legitimate websites will keep their certificates up-to-date. This could indicate that the certificate has been stolen and is being used by a third party.

▲ The certificate or the certificate of the server that issued it has been revoked.

▲ The common name on the certificate does not match the domain name of the server. The host name of the web server is a fixed part of the site certificate. If the name of the web server doesn't match the name on the certificate, the browser will report the problem.

If a problem has been identified with the certificate, the user is prompted whether or not to accept the certificate.

Figure 9-8

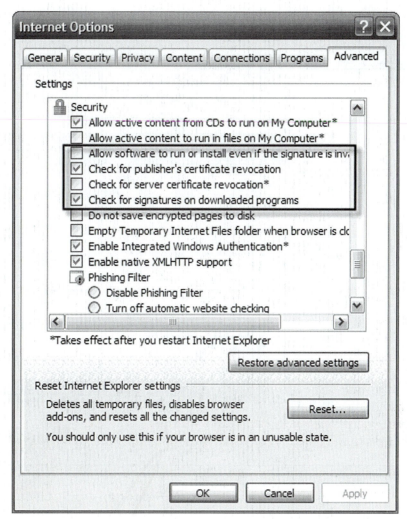

Certificate settings in Internet Explorer 7.

Configuring Support for Cookies

Some configuration settings that can be set on the web browser to mitigate the risk of a loss of privacy due to cookies are as follows:

▲ Turn off all cookies.
▲ Limit the websites that can download cookies. The browser can be set to ask the user if any particular cookie should be accepted. In this way, the user can decide in each case if the information put into the browser for

Figure 9-9

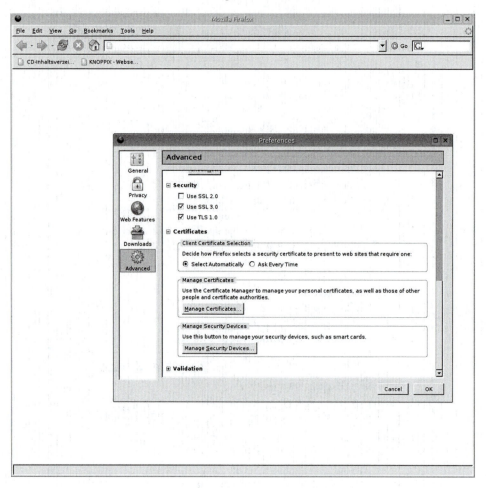

Certificate settings in Firefox.

that particular site poses a privacy risk. In most cases, when prompted to accept or reject a cookie, the user has the option to accept all future cookies from this website.

▲ Only return cookies to the **originating domain**. Cookies originate (are sent to the browser) from a web server. The browser can refuse to send these cookies back to any website other than the one that created the cookie in the first place. This will mitigate the risk of a third-party site trying to get private data about a user. A cookie that sends data to a different domain is known as a **third-party cookie**.

▲ Force all cookies to be nonpersistent.

Figure 9-10

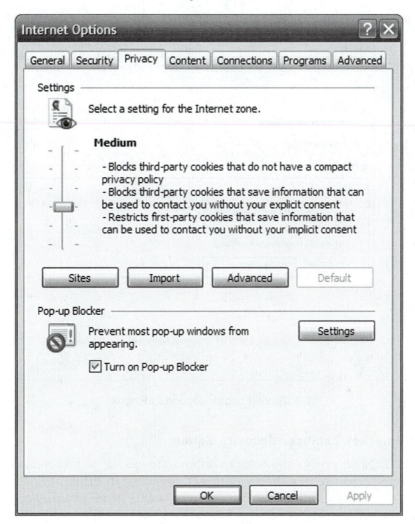

Configuring cookie support in Internet Explorer 7.

▲ Clean out persistent cookies. Periodically, go into the browser settings and delete any persistent cookies.

In Internet Explorer 7, cookie policies are defined on the Privacy tab of the Internet Options dialog box, as shown in Figure 9-10. As you can see, you can set a general policy level, but configure individual sites as exceptions.

Firefox allows you to configure cookies by displaying the Preferences dialog and clicking Privacy. The Cookies options are shown in Figure 9-11.

Figure 9-11

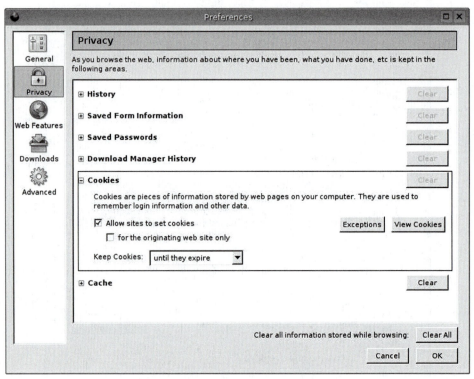

Configuring cookie support in Firefox.

9.3.5 Internet Explorer Security Zones

Internet Explorer orients the Security settings around the web content zone of the site to be accessed by the web browser, as shown in Figure 9-12. In other words, the security settings the browser uses will depend on which zone the website being requested resides in. The zones are as follows:

▲ Internet
▲ Local intranet
▲ Trusted sites
▲ Restricted sites

Internet Zone

The **Internet zone** contains all websites the user hasn't placed in any other zone. In a sense, this is the default zone. Unless security is relaxed for a particular site, it will be put into the Internet zone and have default security settings. This is one zone to which you cannot add sites. By default, all websites that are not

Figure 9-12

Internet Explorer zones.

added to the local intranet zone, the trusted sites zone, or the restricted sites zone, are placed into the Internet zone.

Local Intranet Zone

The **local intranet zone** is intended to contain all websites that are on the intranet of the user's organization. These sites are considered to be more trusted than those that default to the Internet zone. The local intranet zone contains local domain names, as well as the addresses of any proxy server exceptions you might have configured. To be effective, the local intranet zone should be set up

> ### FOR EXAMPLE
>
> #### Flaw in Acrobat Reader Plug-in
>
> Many companies and government offices post PDF files on their websites to provide users with information and even to allow users to fill out and print or submit forms. It has long been regarded as a secure way to distribute information on the Internet. However, in December 2006, researchers discovered a flaw that will allow attackers to execute malicious code when a user clicks a PDF document link.
>
> The attack is performed by modifying the link to a PDF document on a website. The modified link includes code that exploits the vulnerability in the plug-in. According to researchers, this vulnerability could be used to create a number of attacks, including installing Trojan horses and accessing data. The flaw exists when the plug-in is used in Internet Explorer 6.0 (and earlier) and in Mozilla's Firefox browser.
>
> What do you do to mitigate the attack? If you are using one of these browsers, you need to avoid opening PDF documents within the browser. Instead, download them to the hard disk and open in them in Acrobat Reader. Or better yet, upgrade your browser to one that does not have the flaw.

in conjunction with a local area network (LAN) proxy server or firewall. The intent is that all sites in the local intranet zone are on the local network and inside the firewall.

Trusted Sites Zone

The **trusted sites zone** contains websites that the user trusts will not damage the computer. The user should also trust this site with sensitive or personal data. The Security settings can require SSL for all the sites in this zone. This zone should rarely be used. Few websites need the added features of this zone. Most web sites that might be put in this zone will probably operate equally well in the local intranet zone. Be cautious when adding sites to the trusted sites zone. If the site is compromised at some point in the future, your computer will be vulnerable.

Restricted Sites Zone

The **restricted sites zone** contains websites that could potentially damage your computer or data. The default security level for the restricted sites zone is High.

9.3.6 Configuring Web Features in Firefox

The Firefox browser allows you to configure feature support for pop-ups, installing software, loading images, Java, and JavaScript. As you can see in Figure 9-13, you can allow pop-ups, installed software, and images from only specific sites.

SELF-CHECK

1. Compare persistent and non-persistent cookies with regards to the security risk.
2. Identify and describe the four security zones in Internet Explorer.

9.4 Email Security

Along with web browsing, email has made the Internet popular, widespread, and indispensable for most users. Despite its critical role in the typical Internet user's life, email is comparatively insecure.

Email is widely used and has well-defined and universally implemented protocols. Therefore, it is a prime target for hackers developing attacks. Attacks on email focus on two areas: the delivery and execution of malcode and the disclosure of sensitive information. In this section we'll look at how to mitigate both types of attacks.

9.4.1 Attacks that Disclose Data

For many years, the popular email protocols **Post Office Protocol (POP3)** and **Simple Mail Transfer Protocol (SMTP)** have transmitted email in clear text. Figure 9-14 shows a captured IP packet from an SMTP session. The text of the email can be clearly seen in the raw packet.

Because email is transmitted in ASCII text, the words typed into an email message are easily viewed and read at the IP packet level. In the preceding sample packet, the text "My passcode is S0nnyB0y" can clearly be read. It is only slightly more difficult to modify the text in the email by modifying the packets.

The capturing and modifying of email can be done via either a man-in-the-middle, replay, or phishing attack. In this section, we'll look at each of these types of attacks.

Email Man-in-the-middle Attacks

In some man-in-the-middle attacks, the attacker must have control of one of the many firewalls, routers, or gateways through which the email traverses. Other man-in-the-middle attacks do not require control of a device; rather, the attacker merely needs to reside on the same local area network (LAN) segment

Figure 9-13

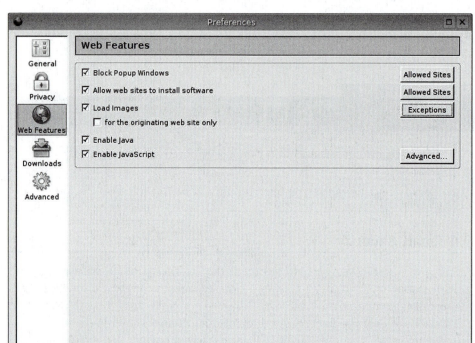

Web Features settings in Firefox.

as one of the computers sending or receiving the email. In this case, the attacker can use an **Address Resolution Protocol (ARP) spoofing tool**, such as **ettercap,** to intercept and potentially modify all email packets going to and from the mail server or gateway. In an **ARP spoof attack**, the attacker gets between any two hosts in the email transmission path. There are four possible locations to attack:

1. **Between the email client and server:** This situation assumes that the client and server are on the same LAN segment.
2. **Between the email client and the gateway:** The gateway must be in the path to the mail server.
3. **Between two gateways:** The gateways must be in the path between the client and the server.
4. **Between the gateway and the mail server:** This option assumes the client and the server are not on the same LAN segment, and therefore the email traffic must reach the server via a gateway.

Figure 9-14

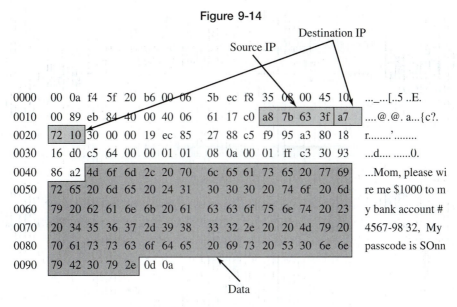

A captured IP packet clearly shows email text.

Figure 9-15 illustrates the network configuration for the ARP spoofing attack. In the ARP spoofing man-in-the-middle attack, the email's IP packets are intercepted on their way to or from the mail server. The packets are then read and possibly modified. The attacker has some minor limitations when modifying the packets. For example, the total length of the packet cannot grow to a size larger than the maximum allowable for transmission on the network.

Man-in-the-middle attacks can be avoided by using encryption and by digitally signing messages. If the encryption is sufficiently strong, the attacker will not be able to decrypt and alter the email. Digital signatures ensure the integrity of the body of the email message. The recipient is able to decrypt the hash with the sender's public key and verify the email to have been unaltered. An attacker could not alter the message or the hash (digital signature) without being detected. Figure 9-16 illustrates how a digital signature is created and attached to the email.

Email Replay Attack

An **email replay attack** occurs when an email packet (or set of packets) is captured, the email message extracted, and the message put back on the network at a later time (replayed). This causes a second, identical email to be received. The danger or damage occurs when the second email is accepted as legitimate and causes unforeseen consequences.

Replay might be used if an attacker discovers a business that sends financial transactions over email. The attacker then arranges for a nominal transaction

Figure 9-15

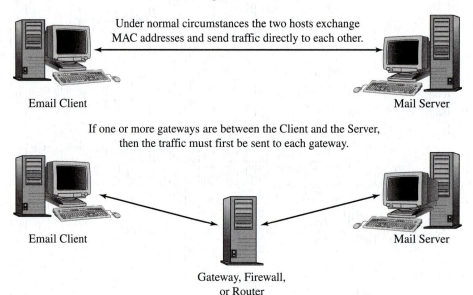

Under normal circumstances the two hosts exchange
MAC addresses and send traffic directly to each other.

Email Client   Mail Server

If one or more gateways are between the Client and the Server,
then the traffic must first be sent to each gateway.

Email Client   Mail Server

Gateway, Firewall,
or Router

No Attack

- -

Man-in-the-Middle ARP Spoofing Attack

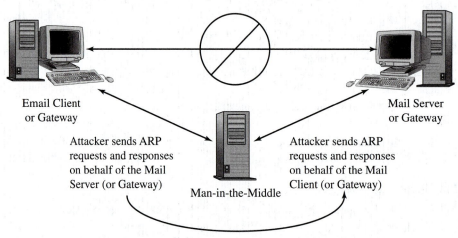

Direct communications do not occur—the Man-in-
the-Middle interrupts the ARP request/response

Email Client   Mail Server
or Gateway   or Gateway

Attacker sends ARP   Attacker sends ARP
requests and responses   requests and responses
on behalf of the Mail   on behalf of the Mail
Server (or Gateway)   Client (or Gateway)

Man-in-the-Middle

All traffic between the email client (or gateway) and the email
server (or gateway) passes through the Man-in-the-Middle

ARP spoofing attack.

Figure 9-16

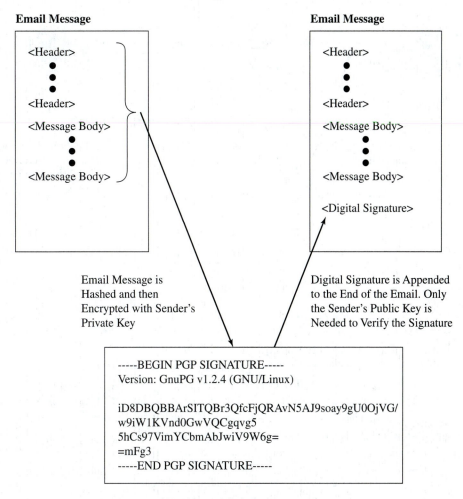

Attaching a digital signature.

(perhaps a $100 refund). The attacker captures the email authorizing the refund and replays it several times, causing several refunds to occur.

In the case of a replay attack, shown in Figure 9-17, the attacker does not have to use the gateway or ARP spoofing. The attacker merely needs to be on one of the many segments that the email packets traverse on their way to or from the mail server.

Phishing

A **phishing attack** is one in which a user is tricked into clicking a link in an email and divulging confidential information, such as a bank account number or logon credentials for an online banking website. To launch a phishing attack,

Figure 9-17

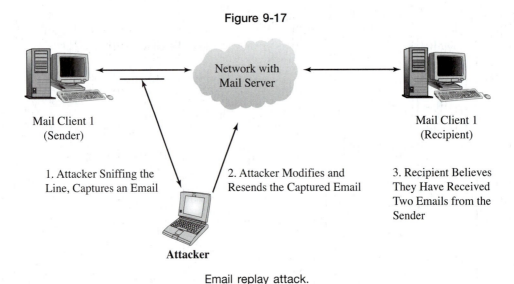

Mail Client 1
(Sender)

Network with
Mail Server

Mail Client 1
(Recipient)

1. Attacker Sniffing the
Line, Captures an Email

2. Attacker Modifies and
Resends the Captured Email

3. Recipient Believes
They Have Received
Two Emails from the
Sender

Attacker

Email replay attack.

an attacker sends email that pretends to be from a legitimate company, such as a bank, PayPal®, or eBay®. The email includes a link that appears to be to the legitimate site, but that actually goes to an imposter site.

Internet Explorer 7.0 provides a **phishing filter** that attempts to determine whether a site is legitimate. However, the best way to mitigate the risk of phishing attacks is to train users to never click on a link in an email or to verify the actual address of the link before clicking it. Figure 9-18 shows an example of an email sent in a phishing attack. Notice that when you mouse over the link, an address appears that is different from that of the legitimate website.

In this case, the spoofed email does a good job of impersonating an actual email that might be sent by eBay. However, notice that the email does not originate from ebay.com, but from ebay.eu. Also, the ISP's spam filter was able to identify the message as spam and marked it as such in the Subject line. We'll talk about spam next.

9.4.2 Spam

Spam is an unwanted email. Spam has become a serious problem in today's networking environment. It is a major irritant and consumer of resources. It has been estimated that for some of the large email providers, over half of the email they service is spam. In gross terms, this means that these providers could get by with half of their current resources to handle their customers' email. From a security perspective, spam is a potential denial-of-service (DoS) problem.

Spammers (people who send spam) make money by getting their advertising message out to thousands or millions of people. Very few will respond positively

Figure 9-18

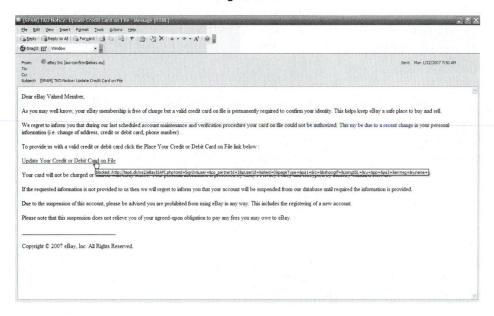

Phishing attack email.

to the message, but even a very small percentage of responses will produce enough activity to make the spamming profitable because it is very cheap to send email.

Spammers put their advertising message into the body of the email and view email headers as a necessary encumbrance needed to get the body delivered. Spammers view email headers as a possible Achilles heel that can hurt them. If users and ISPs are able to trace the spam back to the source, the spammers could be tied up in legal proceedings, fined, or blacklisted. Blacklisting is discussed a little later.

Spammers take steps to hide their originating (From:) address. This is easily done if spammers run their own email servers. This address can be either fake (such as "yourfriend.spam") or a legitimate address that is not owned by the spammer. Some spam even uses your own email address as the sender.

Spam DoS Attacks

Spam DoS attacks can be launched by spammers using false domains in the emails they send. If a spammer does not use a valid domain, the spam can be blocked by testing that the email was sent from a legitimate domain. In this case, a domain is legitimate if it returns a value when a domain name system (DNS) lookup is done.

The most prevalent DoS attack that occurs due to spam is when a spammer forges an address on thousands or millions of mail messages. The result is tens of thousands of bounces, complaints, and a few responses. This results in a flood of email traffic to the forged address, essentially shutting down the address for legitimate use.

Another DoS situation occurs when the spammer forges a valid email address, and this address then gets blacklisted. When this occurs, the user of the valid email can experience obstacles to sending legitimate email to users whose ISP uses blacklists.

Blacklisting

A **blacklist** is a database of known Internet addresses (by domain names or IP addresses) used by spammers. Often, ISPs and bandwidth providers subscribe to these blacklist databases to filter out spam sent across their network or to their subscribers. Lists of IP addresses to be added to the blacklist are collected in different ways, including the following:

▲ The email user community sends samples of spam to the blacklist site. The site parses out the offending originating email IP addresses and adds them to the blacklist.
▲ The blacklist provider runs its own mail server and fake email address. Any email received is automatically unsolicited and therefore spam.
▲ Blacklist providers exchange lists.

Some blacklists are implemented by placing offending IP addresses in a DNS database. When a spammer's email arrives, a DNS lookup is conducted to verify that the sender's email address is legitimate. However, blacklisted addresses return invalid responses so the server rejects the email.

Spam Filters

Spam filters attempt to identify spam from the content of the message subject and body, based on identifying words that frequently appear in spam. This is known as the **naive Bayes classifier**. However, this method of classification often results in non-spam being classified as spam. Also, spammers have begun to use various methods of preventing spam filters from working. One method is to insert **word salad** (a set of random or pseudorandom words) into the text of the message. Another is to use **letter salad** to disguise words in the subject that are frequently associated with spam. For example, here are two letter salad subject lines:

▲ Why seek? Choose any love pill you want!
▲ Re: primar VIAttGRA

Figure 9-19 shows an example spam email that uses both word salad and letter salad. It includes an attachment, which should not be opened under any circumstances. In this example, the ISP did not identify it as spam, but the Norton AntiSpam™ application did. This is a good illustration of why multiple layers of defense should be used to protect against malware.

Figure 9-19

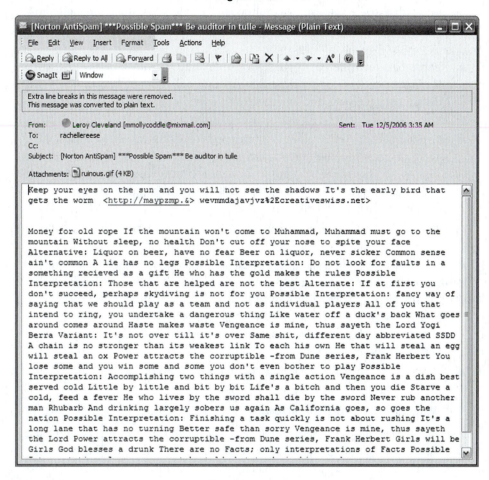

Sample spam.

9.4.3 Protecting Against Malcode Propagated by Email

Most malcode transmitted by email is not activated unless a user opens the email or the attachment. Therefore, user education can go a long way toward thwarting such an attack. The following are some guidelines users should keep in mind:

▲ Be paranoid. You can avoid most email-propagated malcode attacks by properly using your email.

▲ Keep your email address private. Avoid providing it whenever possible on websites and other interactive forums such as chat rooms.

▲ Set up one or more sacrificial email addresses. When an email address must be provided to a website, the user should have a sacrificial email address to use. When an email is received on this account, the user knows that there is a high likelihood that it will be spam or malicious in nature. The user should resist the temptation to browse through the emails received on this account.

▲ Keep email for different organizations separate. In most cases, this will mean one account for work and a separate account for home. The ramifications of receiving and propagating malicious code in a work environment might be more damaging than at home.

▲ Do not open any email that is not expected. Common sense can be a strong deterrent to the spread of malicious code. An unexpected "Read This" or "Try This Game" should be ignored until the user can verify the sender's intentions. The verification can be in person, by phone, or by a second email (initiated from the user).

▲ Never save or open attachments from strangers. All curiosity must be resisted.

▲ Never save or open attachments that are not absolutely needed. The fact that a friend wants to send a user an attachment does not obligate the user to open it. Some users would be surprised to find how easily life proceeds without opening risky emails and attachments. If it is really important or of special interest, the friend will follow up and explain what is in the attachment.

▲ If supported, turn off the preview function on your email client.

9.4.4 Mail Client Configurations

Microsoft Outlook® uses the same security zones as Internet Explorer to allow users to customize whether scripts and active content can be run in HTML messages.

Scripting capabilities of the email clients should be disabled whenever possible. As discussed earlier, if scripts are executed by the email client, the user will be vulnerable to worms and viruses. If scripts must be passed around, they should be compressed when they are sent, saved to a file, and examined before being executed.

You can also determine whether elements in HTML pages, such as pictures, are downloaded automatically. The default is to not download automatically unless the site is included in the trusted sites zone or if the sender has been added to the Safe Senders or Safe Recipients list, as shown in Figure 9-20. You should not turn on automatic download for all senders.

Some mail clients, including Outlook and Outlook Express, are configured to block attachments with risky file extensions. This protection should be kept enabled and you should add file extensions to the list as attacks emerge.

You can configure email encryption and digital signatures to protect the confidentiality and integrity of the messages you send. These settings are shown in Figure 9-21.

Figure 9-20

Automatic Picture Download Settings dialog box.

9.4.5 Architectural Considerations

A number of system- and network-related architectural considerations ensure safe use of email:

▲ Check for viruses. Every computer should have virus protection installed.

▲ Use a mail relay or mail proxy. Medium- to large-size organizations benefit from having all their mail received first by a **mail relay** or **mail proxy**. The mail relay will usually sit in the perimeter network. If configured properly, the relay can check for unwanted scripts, viruses, and questionable attachments. Mail relays are also a good place to put spam protection, such as blacklist monitoring and spam filtering.

▲ Buffer against attacks. If possible, risky email should be read on computers that can better afford to be attacked. Generally, this would be a computer that has little or no personal and sensitive data. This computer also should not contain critical applications that can't be lost or re-installed. It should

Figure 9-21

Outlook security settings.

be expected that a computer that is buffering this way might have to be rebuilt every 3 to 6 months.

▲ Back up frequently. Even the best security measures will occasionally fail to stop a new and emerging threat. To minimize the impact when that happens, backups should be done frequently. The frequency of backups depends on the level of critical data involved. A book author will back up a few times a day, although the typical home user might get by with backing up once a week or once a month.

▲ Control scripting capabilities. Some mail clients will provide collaboration capability and run scripts automatically. Usually, this feature can be disabled to reduce the risk of worm and virus attacks.

FOR EXAMPLE

Microsoft Exchange 2007

In response to the increasing prevalence of spam, phishing schemes, and malware distributed through email, software developers are creating solutions that can help protect against email-propagated threats. One such enhancement is the **Edge Transport** server role in Microsoft Exchange 2007. When a server is installed as an Edge Transport server, it can perform spam filtering based on the sender's reputation and usage patterns, the safe sender lists compiled by users, content filtering, and an Outlook postmark. The **Outlook postmark** is a puzzle of varying complexity that is attached to the email. The Edge Transport server can also implement virus scanning and attachment filtering, including examining the contents of a .zip file, to determine whether email contains file types that should be filtered.

The Edge Transport role is meant to be assigned to a dedicated server on the perimeter network. It does not need to be a member of the Active Directory domain because it can receive encrypted directory data through **Active Directory Application Mode (ADAM)**.

The Edge Transport server can quarantine suspect messages, allowing the administrator to selectively send them to users or even to convert them to plain text before sending them.

▲ Limit attachments. Attachments can contain scripts and executable code. When the user runs these scripts or executables, they will have all the privileges and access that the user enjoys. Unless the user is diligent and fully appreciates the risk, it is not safe to allow attachments on email.

▲ Quarantine attachments. In many cases, an organization can benefit from **quarantining attachments**. A mail relay or mail proxy strips attachments off of emails before they are delivered to users. If the user needs the attachment and can verify that it has been sent by a legitimate sender, the user can recover that attachment.

SELF-CHECK

1. Compare ARP spoofing and replay attacks.
2. Compare blacklisting and spam filtering.

SUMMARY

In this chapter you learned about various types of malware, including viruses, worms, Trojan horses, and spyware. You also learned how to protect yourself against these threats. Threats, such as spam, phishing attacks, man-in-the-middle attacks, and replay attacks were also covered.

KEY TERMS

Active Directory Application Mode (ADAM)

ActiveX

ActiveX control

Add-on

Address Resolution Protocol (ARP) spoofing tool

Adware

Anti-malware

Anti-spyware

Antivirus

ARP spoof attack

Autorun macro

Backdoor

Blacklist

Boot sector virus

Browser parasite

Compiled

Cookie

Cyclic redundancy check (CRC)

Distributed denial-of-service (DDos) attack

Edge Transport

Email replay attack

Ettercap

Host

ILOVEYOU virus

Internet zone

Java

Java applets

JavaScript

Letter salad

Local intranet zone

Logic bomb

Macro Virus Protection

Mail proxy

Mail relay

Malcode

Malware

Managed computer

Melissa

Michelangelo

Naive Bayes classifier

Nonpersistent cookie

Nyxem worm

Originating domain

Outlook postmark

Persistent cookie

Personal firewall

Phishing attack

Phishing filter

Plug-in

Portable Document Format (PDF)

Post Office Protocol 3 (POP3)

Propagated

Quarantining attachments

Replay attack

Replicate

Restricted sites zone

Rooted

Safe for execution

Safe for scripting

Scripts

Security manager

Self-propagation

Session cookie

Session hijacking

Sessionless

Simple Mail Transfer Protocol (SMTP)

Slag code

Spam

Spam DoS attack

Spam filter

Spammer

SpyBlast

Spyware

State

Third-party cookie

Time bomb

Trapdoor

Trojan horse

Trusted sites zone

Virus

Virus signature

Visual Basic script (VBScript)

Web beacon

Word salad

Worm

Zombie

ASSESS YOUR UNDERSTANDING

Go to www.wiley.com/college/cole to assess your knowledge of protecting a computer against viruses, worms, and other malicious programs.

Measure your learning by comparing pre-test and post-test results.

Summary Questions

1. Which of the following requires a host file to propagate?
   (a) worm
   (b) spyware
   (c) virus
   (d) logic bomb

2. Which of the following uses the autorun macro to attach itself to the Normal.dot file?
   (a) Michelangelo
   (b) Melissa
   (c) Nymex worm
   (d) SpyBlast

3. A logic bomb can be used to launch a DDoS attack. True or false?

4. A browser parasite is an annoyance, but it cannot do any actual damage. True or false?

5. SpyBlast is an effective anti-spyware program. True or false?

6. An effective antivirus program with updated signatures is the only protection you need against viruses and worms. True or false?

7. Which of the following is a computer that is centrally configured through an automated policy?
   (a) managed computer
   (b) rooted computer
   (c) host
   (d) zombie

8. Which statement best describes the dangers of automatically downloading graphics in an HTML message?
   (a) The graphics might contain macros that will perform a malicious task.
   (b) The graphics might be web beacons.
   (c) The graphics might be Trojan horses.
   (d) There is no danger involved.

9. An ActiveX control that is marked safe for execution has been certified by Microsoft not to do anything harmful. True or false?

10. Code written in JavaScript cannot access any file on the hard disk. True or false?

11. What type of cookie sends data to a different website than the one from which it originated?

    (a) nonpersistent cookie

    (b) persistent cookie

    (c) session cookie

    (d) third-party cookie

12. Which Internet Explorer zone contains any computer not included in the other zones?

    (a) internet

    (b) local intranet

    (c) restricted sites

    (d) trusted sites

13. What type of attack can be mitigated by using digital signatures?

    (a) ARP spoofing

    (b) email replay

    (c) phishing

    (d) spam DoS

14. Which type of attack relies on social engineering techniques?

    (a) ARP spoofing

    (b) email replay

    (c) phishing

    (d) spam DoS

15. Which of the following attempts to identify spam by looking at the content of the message?

    (a) blacklist

    (b) anti-malware program

    (c) spam filter

    (d) web beacon

16. A mail proxy should be installed in the perimeter network. True or false?

Applying This Chapter

1. Busicorp is concerned about the possibility of malware propagating through the organization. They are currently using their ISP to manage email. Users connect to the Internet using a shared Internet connection

on the company network. Some users have laptop computers and also connect to the Internet from home or when traveling. There are three file servers on the network. You have been asked to devise a plan for mitigating the risk of malware.

(a) Identify the potential sources of viruses.

(b) What questions should you ask the ISP?

(c) What additional protections would be offered by an anti-malware program that are not offered by an antivirus program?

(d) Why might you want to limit ActiveX controls to only trusted sites?

(e) What benefits are provided by issuing digital signatures to be used on email?

(f) Why should security awareness training be a necessary part of the plan?

(g) Describe how the company could be a victim of a Spam DoS attack.

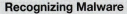
Recognizing Malware

Understanding how to identify a risky download, attachment, or phishing email is an essential part of mitigating the threat of malware. Automated scanners have limitiations—they can only identify known attacks. Identifying new or unpublished attacks requires a sharp eye and a keen nose for trouble. Users can develop those over time, but they need training. Of course, before you can train users in what to look for, you have to know yourself. Think about the following situations and determine whether the action is safe, moderately safe or moderately risky, or risky. Explain why.

1. You access an online shopping site. A dialog is displayed that reports the site's SSL certificate has expired. How risky is it to provide your credit card on this site?

2. You access an online shopping site. A dialog is displayed that reports that the site's SSL certificate was not issued by a trusted certificate authority. How risky is it to provide your credit card on this site?

3. You access a vendor's website and a yellow bar appears asking you to download an ActiveX control. When you attempt to install it, you receive an error that the control is not signed. You have been working with this vendor for a few years and have not had a problem. How risky is it to download the control?

4. You receive an email from your bank asking you to verify your address and phone number. The email contains a link with a different domain name than your online banking site. When you click the link, you are prompted for a username and password. How safe is it to enter the information?

5. You receive an email from a former business acquaintance who you haven't heard from in several years. The subject of the message is Hello. The message contains an attachment. How risky is it to open the attachment?

6. You have antivirus software installed, but you are connecting to the Internet through a dial-up connection until your broadband service is restored. How risky is it to ignore the virus signature update message?

7. An online training website uses a nonpersistent cookie to track your progress in a session. How risky is it to accept the cookie?

8. You are creating a website for your business and need to publish your email address so that customers can contact you. How risky is it to use your regular email address?

10

ONGOING SECURITY MANAGEMENT

Starting Point

Go to www.wiley.com/college/cole to assess your knowledge of ongoing security management.

Determine where you need to concentrate your effort.

What You'll Learn in This Chapter

▲ Configuration management
▲ Importance of keeping computers up-to-date
▲ Windows Update
▲ Software Update Services (SUS)
▲ Systems Management Server (SMS)
▲ Auditing
▲ In-bound remote management
▲ Out-of-bound remote management

After Studying This Chapter, You'll Be Able To

▲ Design a configuration management policy
▲ Choose a method of keeping Windows® computers up-to-date
▲ Implement auditing
▲ Choose an in-bound remote management method
▲ Choose an out-of-bound remote management method

INTRODUCTION

After you have designed and implemented security policies on your network, your job has really just begun. Now begins the day-to-day work of ensuring your network stays operational and secure. This chapter examines three areas you must consider to keep your network operating securely. The chapter begins by looking at the importance of keeping your computers up-to-date with the latest security patches. Next, the chapter discusses ways to audit your network to verify that attacks are not occurring. Finally, the chapter examines how to set up a secure infrastructure to allow you to manage your servers remotely.

10.1 Managing Updates

Attackers are constantly searching for ways to exploit systems. In 2007, a study conducted by Michel Cukier from the University of Maryland revealed that a computer on the Internet is hacked every 39 seconds. Therefore, it is important to remain vigilant in keeping your network up-to-date against the latest security threats.

There is much more to updating the security of your infrastructure than just applying new patches. In addition to applying security-related patches, you will need to make configuration changes as new information and attacks become known or as new services or applications are installed. In this section, we will show you the different tools that you can use to solve your security update woes, as well as the benefits and drawbacks of each potential solution. Our focus will be on the tools provided for updating the computers in a Windows network. However, first we'll look at configuration management in general terms.

10.1.1 Configuration Management

Configuration management is the process of tracking and approving changes to a system. It involves identifying, controlling, and auditing all changes made to the system, including hardware and software changes, networking changes, or any other changes affecting security.

The primary security goal of configuration management is to ensure that changes to the system do not unintentionally diminish security. For example, configuration management might prevent an older version of a system from being activated as the production system. Configuration management also makes it possible to accurately roll back to a previous version of a system in case a new system fails or you discover that it has a vulnerability not present in the previous version. Another goal of configuration management is to ensure that system changes are reflected in current documentation to help mitigate the impact that a change might have on the security of other systems.

Configuration management requires the following tasks:

▲ Identify and document the functional and physical characteristics of each configuration item for the system.
▲ Manage all changes to these characteristics.
▲ Record and report the implementation status for each change.

Configuration management involves process monitoring, version control, information capture, quality control, bookkeeping, and an organizational framework to support these activities.

Primary Functions of Configuration Management

The primary functions of configuration management or **change control** are

▲ To ensure that the change is thoroughly tested before being implemented.
▲ To ensure that users are informed of the impending change.
▲ To ensure that the change is implemented in such a way that disruption to the business is minimal.
▲ To analyze the effect of the change on the system after implementation.
▲ To reduce the negative impact that the change might have had on the computing services and resources.

The change control process generally consists of five tasks:

1. Proposing a change.
2. Cataloging the intended change.
3. Scheduling the change.
4. Implementing the change.
5. Reporting the change to the appropriate parties, such as those who are affected by the change and those who need to document the change.

10.1.2 Understanding the Components of Configuration Management

The five major components of configuration management and their functions are as follows:

▲ Configuration identification
▲ Configuration control
▲ Configuration status accounting

▲ Configuration auditing

▲ Documentation control

Let's look at each of these components.

Configuration Identification

Configuration management entails decomposing a system's configuration into identifiable, understandable, manageable, and trackable units known as **configuration items (CIs)**. The decomposition process is called **configuration identification**. A CI is a uniquely identifiable subset of the system that represents the smallest portion to be subject to independent configuration control procedures.

CIs can vary widely in size, type, and complexity. Although no hard-and-fast rules exist for decomposition, the ability to create CIs of various sizes can have great practical importance. A good strategy is to designate relatively large CIs for elements that are not expected to change over the life of the system, and small CIs for elements likely to change more frequently.

Configuration Control

Configuration control is a means of ensuring that all system changes are approved before being implemented and that the implementation is complete and accurate. This activity involves strict procedures for proposing, monitoring, and approving system changes and their implementation. Configuration control should be directed by personnel who coordinate analytical tasks, approve system changes, review the implementation of changes, and supervise other tasks such as documentation.

Configuration Status Accounting

Configuration status accounting documents the status of configuration control activities and, in general, provides the information needed to manage a configuration effectively. It allows managers to trace system changes and to establish the history of any problems and associated fixes. Configuration accounting also tracks the status of current changes as they move through the configuration control process.

Configuration Auditing

Configuration auditing is the quality assurance component of configuration management. It involves periodic checks to determine the consistency and completeness of accounting information and to verify that all configuration management policies are being followed.

Documentation Control

Documentation control is a cornerstone of configuration management. It's important to update all relevant documentation when system changes occur. Such changes could include the following:

▲ Changes to the system infrastructure.

▲ Changes to security policies or procedures.

▲ Changes to the disaster recovery or business continuity plans.

▲ Facility environment changes, such as office moves or HVAC (heating, ventilation, and air conditioning) and electrical changes.

10.1.3 Importance of Automating Updates

As new vulnerabilities are discovered, operating system and application vendors release **security updates** (one type of **patch**) that remove those vulnerabilities. However, those updates are useless unless they are applied.

Although you can (and should) periodically check informational sites to see what new vulnerabilities have been reported and check vendor sites for information about security patches and new threats, it is easy to forget to do so or to put it off because you have so many other things to do. And even if you read about a patch, there's still the issue of deploying it. Will you visit each user's computer to ensure the patch is applied? Will you send an email to users and trust them to download and apply the patch?

One way to help prevent your systems from becoming out-of-date and to automate the effort of applying patches is to create a **security update infrastructure** that automates the deployment of patches throughout the organization.

10.1.4 Creating a Security Update Infrastructure

To create a security update infrastructure, you must be able to determine what needs to be updated and how the updates will be accomplished. Unfortunately, as far as security updates go, no single solution solves all of the problems. The solution you devise will depend on the automatic update methods supported by the operating systems and applications you must update. For our discussion, we'll focus on the methods available for updating computers in a Windows network.

Table 10-1 lists the different methods of updating computers in a Windows network, including the operating system that the method supports and whether or not it supports software patches, configuration changes, or both.

When deciding which security update method to use, you should consider how many client computers need to be updated. The Microsoft Windows Update website is useful when only a small number of computer systems require updating because it requires each computer to download updates, which can really use up bandwidth on even a medium-sized network.

Table 10-1: Methods of Updating a Windows Network

Update Method	Description	Operating Systems Supported
Windows Update	The Microsoft Windows Update website is a wonderful utility for keeping individual computers and the computers for a small business up-to-date. Windows Update allows users to update their own systems or, for Windows XP Service Pack 1 and higher, to configure updates to be downloaded and installed automatically using **Automatic Updates**.	Windows 98 and higher
Software Update Services (SUS)	Microsoft SUS gives an administrator the ability to selectively deploy updates and services packs. The updates can be synchronized from the Microsoft Windows Update website and saved to an SUS server, where an administrator can test the update to see if it is compatible with the configuration and applications that are currently running in the network environment. The client computers, running the Automatic Updates component, will download only approved updates from the SUS server and apply them.	Windows 2000 and higher
Windows Server Update Services (WSUS)	WSUS 3.0 is the newest version of SUS. It includes a Microsoft Management Console (MMC) snap-in instead of a web-based management interface. It can also be used to deploy updates for Microsoft Exchange, Microsoft Office, and Microsoft SQL Server, Windows Defender, and a number of other products.	Windows 2000 Service Pack 4 and higher
Systems Management Server (SMS)	Microsoft SMS 2003 is a comprehensive change management and configuration solution. It is capable of deploying applications, managing security and software patches, and managing assets. Unlike SUS, SMS 2003 is not free and requires SQL Server.	Windows 98 and Windows NT® 4.0 and higher

An SUS or WSUS server can update a relatively small number of client computers or several thousand. WSUS has the added advantage of updating some applications.

Microsoft SMS 2003 can be used to update a practically limitless number of client computers. It is usually reserved for the larger enterprise organizations because it is expensive and requires its own administrative staff to configure, deploy, and manage its infrastructure.

There will also be some situations in which Automatic Updates is not the best solution. For example, most servers should not be updated automatically because some updates cause a reboot. Also, you should never update servers directly from the Windows Update website because you should test patches before installing them on servers, especially mission-critical servers.

In most cases, a configuration made up of both WSUS and Group Policy will solve most update and configuration management issues. The remainder of this section will focus on WSUS, but most of the same considerations would apply to SUS.

10.1.5 A WSUS Solution

There are two parts to the WSUS solution:

▲ The server (or servers) running WSUS and that downloads updates from the Microsoft Windows Update servers or from other internal WSUS servers.

▲ The Automatic Updates client that downloads the updates from an SUS server in your network. Before applying the updates, WSUS will check the digital signature to make sure that it bears Microsoft's signature. If the update package is not signed, it will not be applied.

Each WSUS server can handle updating about 15,000 client computers; you should add additional WSUS servers as needed. You can still make sure that only one of the WSUS servers in your hierarchy retrieves the updates from Microsoft and then configure the other WSUS servers to download the updates from the WSUS server that receives the updates directly from Microsoft.

One reason you might need multiple WSUS servers is to support multiple geographic locations. This design is illustrated in Figure 10-1.

With SUS, you had to deploy a different SUS server for each computer configuration that might need a different set of updates. With WSUS, this is no longer a requirement because you can create groups of computers on the WSUS server or through Group Policy.

10.1.6 Configuring SUS Clients

You will also need to configure the Automatic Updates client on the computers in your organization to look to their respective WSUS server to retrieve and apply

Figure 10-1

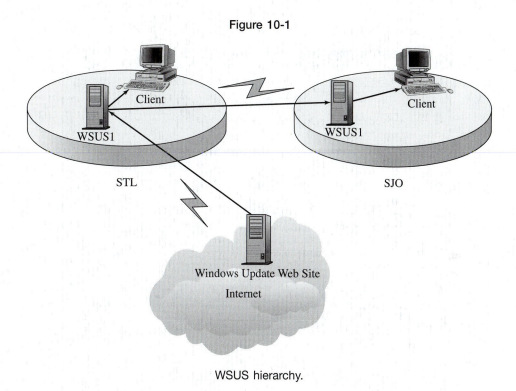

WSUS hierarchy.

the updates. In the following sections, we will look at the different techniques that you can use to configure a computer to use your WSUS infrastructure.

Using Group Policy Objects to Configure SUS Clients

The recommended method of configuring WSUS clients is to use Group Policy. As is the case with any other configuration options being set in a Group Policy Object (GPO), Group Policy allows an administrator to configure a policy once and have it be applied consistently throughout the directory.

Windows Update settings are configured under Computer Configuration | Administrative Templates | Windows Components | Windows Update. If you do not have the Windows Update section under the Windows Components container, right-click "Administrative Templates" and select "Add/Remove Templates" and add "wuau.adm."

The Configure Automatic Updates Properties dialog box is shown in Figure 10-2. Here you can enable Automatic Updates and set the appropriate schedule for the client computers to check for updates. You might want to apply a different schedule to various organizational units (OUs) to distribute the load on the WSUS server across time.

Figure 10-2

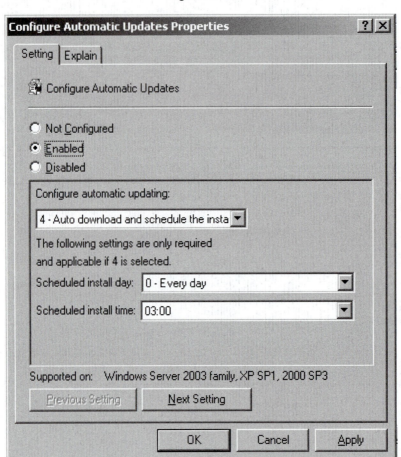

The Configure Automatic Updates Properties dialog box.

You will also need to enable and configure the Specify intranet Microsoft update service location policy to point to the WSUS server, as shown in Figure 10-3.

Manually Configuring SUS Clients

In addition to using a GPO, you can configure the settings manually on the client using any one of the following techniques:

▲ Use the Local Security Policy on each workstation. The steps are identical to when configuring a GPO, but applied only to the computer that you configure it on.

Figure 10-3

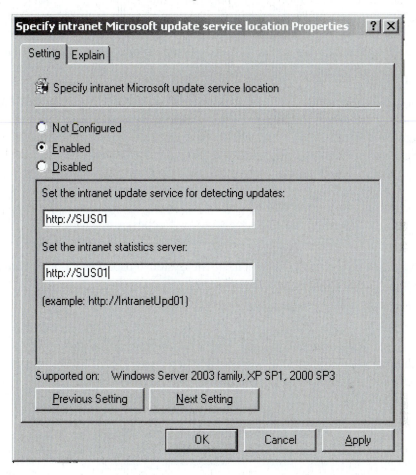

Specify intranet Microsoft update service location Properties dialog box.

FOR EXAMPLE

Designing a Software Update Infrastructure

Busicorp has four locations. Most of the IT staff is located in Chicago. The company has two domain controllers at each location, a Microsoft Exchange 2003 server at each location, and a computer running Microsoft SQL Server 2005 in Chicago and Detroit. All servers are running Windows Server 2003. There are over 1000 client computers at each location. All client computers are running Windows XP Professional with Service Pack 2. All client computers run Microsoft Office XP. There are between 50 and 100 application

(Continued)

developers at each location. Developers use Visual Studio® .NET, Java™, and Macromedia® Flash®. Some application developers run SQL Server 2005.

Busicorp wants to ensure that applications and operating systems are kept up-to-date, but they do not want to invest more money than necessary. They also want to ensure that only tested patches are applied to client computers.

You install a WSUS server at each office. You configure the one in Chicago to download updates for Windows Server 2003, Windows XP Professional, Microsoft Exchange 2003, Microsoft SQL Server 2005, and Microsoft Office XP from the Windows Update website. You configure the WSUS servers at the other offices to download updates from the WSUS server in Chicago. You use Group Policy to configure automatic update policies for clients using WSUS groups. You also create GPOs to deploy software not supported by WSUS to the developers' computers and to manually monitor these applications for security patches.

▲ Use the Automatic Updates tab of the System Properties Control Panel applet, as seen in Figure 10-4.

▲ Manually modify the Registry on each client.

As you can see, the only realistic option is to use a GPO when there are a moderate or large number of client computers involved. You will want to make sure that your OU structure is designed in such a way that software updates and patches can be deployed with a minimum of administrative effort.

Figure 10-4

The Automatic Updates tab in the System Properties Control Panel.

10.2 Auditing and Logging

Auditing and monitoring procedures for networks are used to ensure that security controls are operating and providing effective protection for the information systems. An **audit** is a one-time or periodic event to evaluate security, and **auditing** or **monitoring** refers to an ongoing activity that examines either the system or the users.

10.2.1 Security Audits

An audit is conducted by either a group internal to an organization or by third-party auditors. Third-party auditors are usually certified professionals such as Certified Information Systems Auditors (CISAs). Internal auditors normally evaluate security practices and compliance with standards, and recommend improvements to safeguards and controls.

Standards

The Information Systems Audit and Control Association (ISACA) has developed standards and guidelines for auditing IT systems. The following are examples of some of the guidelines:

▲ The audit function must be sufficiently independent of the area being audited to permit objective completion of the audit.

▲ The information systems auditor must adhere to the Code of Professional Ethics of the ISACA.

▲ The information systems auditor must maintain technical competence through the appropriate continuing professional education.

▲ During the course of the audit, the information systems auditor obtains sufficient, reliable, relevant, and useful evidence to achieve the audit objectives effectively.

▲ The information systems auditor provides a report, in an appropriate form, to the intended recipients upon the completion of the audit work.

Auditors evaluate contingency plans, development standards, audit trails, and other procedures related to the business and its assets.

Audit trails (also called **audit logs** or **event logs**) are logs of events that provide a history of occurrences in the IT system. They are used for tracing sources of intrusions, recording results of intrusions, and, in general, summarizing the history of activities that took place on a system. An audit trail associated with information system security might record the following:

▲ Internal and external attempts to gain unauthorized access to a system.
▲ Patterns and history of access.
▲ Unauthorized privileges granted to users.
▲ Occurrences of intrusions and their resulting consequences.

Because of their importance, audit logs should be protected at the highest level of security in the information system.

10.2.2 Monitoring

Monitoring is an active, sometimes real-time, process that identifies and reports security events that might be harmful to the network and its components. Examples of such potentially harmful events or situations include unauthorized network devices, unauthorized personal servers, and unprotected sharing of resources. Examples of items monitored include LAN and Internet traffic, LAN protocols, inventories of network devices, and operating system security functions.

Intrusion detection mechanisms, penetration testing, and violation processing are used to accomplish monitoring. **Intrusion detection (ID)** is applied to detect and analyze intrusion attempts. By using threshold or **clipping levels**, below which activities are deemed benign, the amount of information that has to be analyzed can be reduced significantly. A detailed discussion of intrusion detection systems is beyond the scope of this chapter.

Penetration testing probes and tests a network's defenses to determine the state of an organization's information security. Penetration testing employs many of the same tools used by attackers, including scanners, **war dialers** (equipment that looks for an unauthorized remote access server), **protocol analyzers** (packet sniffers), and social engineering to determine the security status of the organization.

Violation analysis uses clipping levels to detect potentially harmful events. For example, clipping levels can detect excessive numbers of personnel with unrestricted access to the system, personnel exceeding their authorization privileges, and repetitive mistakes.

Monitoring responsibility in an organization usually falls under the CIO or equivalent officer.

10.2.3 Auditing on Unix®

Some security-relevant events are recorded automatically in Unix or Linux log files. These log files are as follows:

▲ **/usr/adm/lastlog:** The **lastlog command** records the last time a user has logged in; this information can be displayed with the **finger command**.

▲ **/var/adm/utmp:** The **utmp command** records accounting information used by the **who command**.

▲ **/var/adm/wtmp:** The **wtmp command** records every time a user logs in or logs out; this information can be displayed with the **last command**. To prevent this file from taking over all available memory, it can be pruned automatically at regular intervals.

▲ **var/adm/acct:** The **acct command** records all executed commands; this information can be displayed with the **lastcomm command**.

The precise name and location of these files might be different depending on the flavor of Unix or Linux you are running. Accounting, turned on by the **accton command**, can also be used for auditing purposes.

Most of these events refer to a user, so the log entry should include the user identity (UID) of the process causing the event. How is auditing then affected by **set** userID (SUID) programs? Such a program runs with the UID of its owner, not with the UID of the user running the program. Hence, the log entries should also include the real UID of the process.

10.2.4 Auditing in Windows

You can enable auditing on a Windows 2000 (or later) computer through Local Security Policy or Group Policy. Audit policies can be configured so that successful, failed, or both successful and failed attempts are audited.

The audit policies, shown in Figure 10-5, are as follows:

▲ **Audit account logon events:** audits attempts to authenticate. This event occurs on the computer that is authenticating the user.

▲ **Audit account management:** audits attempts to create, delete, or modify a user account.

▲ **Audit directory service access:** audits specific types of directory service access. Each Active Directory® object has a **security access control list (SACL)** that defines which types of access are audited for that object.

▲ **Audit logon events:** audits attempts to log on interactively to a computer.

▲ **Audit object access:** audits file system or printer object access. Each directory, file, and printer has an SACL that defines what types of access attempts should be audited.

▲ **Audit policy change:** audits changes to security policy, such as user rights assignments, trust relationships, auditing policies, Kerberos policies, and IPsec agent events.

▲ **Audit privilege use:** audits attempts to exercise a user right.

Figure 10-5

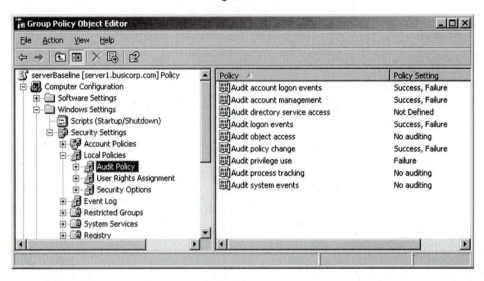

Audit Policy node.

▲ **Audit process tracking:** audits detailed events about activities in the system, including each time a program is started or a user tries to install a service or create a task scheduler job. Enabling this audit policy can result in a large number of events being written to the Security log.

▲ **Audit system events:** audits shutdowns, startups, clearing the audit log, changing the system time, and other operating system security events.

FOR EXAMPLE

A Hacker Doesn't Leave Breadcrumbs

Although a script kiddie might not think to delete the evidence of an attack, a professional hacker will try not to leave behind evidence. One way to do this is by deleting the audit trail. It is essential to keep the audit files on each computer secure so that an attacker does not have an easy way to delete or modify them.

On a Windows 2000 (or later) computer, the right to manage the security log and to generate security audits is managed through User Rights Assignment. By default, only Administrators have the right to manage the security log and only the Local System and Network Service built-in accounts have the right to generate security audits. You should think long and hard about extending these rights to any other users or groups.

Figure 10-6

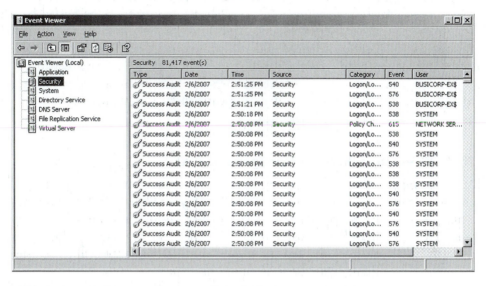

Security log.

You can view audited events through the Security log in Event Viewer, as shown in Figure 10-6.

SELF-CHECK

1. Identify the Unix log file that stores information about each time a user logs on and logs off.
2. Identify the Windows audit policy that tracks each time a system is restarted.

10.3 Secure Remote Administration

A network needs constant maintenance and administration to keep it running successfully. You will need to use tools to manage the network, but these tools can put your network at risk for attack, especially if you need to be able to manage one or more computers remotely.

The most secure way to manage a server is by sitting down at the console and keyboard and logging in to it. But there will be times when this is inconvenient or impossible. For example, you might not have access to the server room where the equipment is housed; you might be required to have access to the system seven days a week, twenty-four hours a day; or your computers might be hosted by a remote company like an Internet service provider (ISP) or an offsite data center. You will need to decide whether you will allow remote administration of each server and the extent to which you will need to remotely manage the network.

In this section, you will learn about the security risks associated with managing the network remotely. You will also learn about various tools that can be used for remote network management.

10.3.1 Creating a Remote Management Plan

A **remote management plan** ensures that the proper tools and configuration you choose for managing your servers are in line with your security policy and infrastructure. Your remote management plan will help you understand what type of management each server needs, whether they need to be managed locally or remotely, the location of the servers in your organization, who will administer them, and the requirements for security on the servers.

You should use the following steps to develop the remote management plan:

1. Evaluate remote management needs.
2. Determine the tools and hardware needed to meet your remote management needs.
3. Design the hardware and software configuration.
4. Configure the network infrastructure to accommodate remote management.
5. Plan remote management deployment.

Evaluating Remote Management Needs

When developing your remote management plan, the first thing you need to do is determine which servers you will manage remotely. You need to consider the cost savings, convenience, and availability requirements and weigh them against the company's security policy requirements. You might find that the cost of remote management within the security guidelines outweighs the benefits of remote management. Some benefits of remote management include the following:

▲ Reduced total cost of ownership.
▲ Increased availability of servers.
▲ Increased convenience and productivity of administrators.

For example, suppose your company's security policy requires that data on sensitive database servers be protected by an expensive authentication and data encryption system if the servers are to be remotely accessed. The system might contain per-server and yearly subscription fees that make remote administration more expensive than just using local administration of the server as the only administrative option.

You also need to decide whether you need to allow remote administration from the internal network only or from an external network as well. For example, if you need around-the-clock uptime, you might need to allow an administrator to connect to a server from home. If you need to provide access from an external network, determine whether remote administration will be permitted through a virtual private network (VPN), Hypertext Transfer Protocol (HTTP), or dial-up connection.

Threats of Remote Management

Remote management introduces new threats to your servers. When you remotely manage a server, you need to consider additional security measures. Remotely managing computers will potentially allow sensitive information to be transmitted across the network. You must ensure that the management tool provides the necessary means to prevent eavesdropping of the data it sends, or you must provide this service yourself (usually through VPN, IPsec, or Secure Sockets Layer).

Some of the threats posed by remote management include the following:

▲ Increased attack surface because attackers can use the tools to gain access.

▲ Security holes in remote administration tools or services that are not patched or kept up-to-date.

▲ Sensitive data sent across the network.

Determining the Tools and Hardware Needs

Remote management tools make it possible to perform any management action on the server remotely except for hardware installation. You can take advantage of in-band and out-of-band remote management tools.

In-band remote management tools are tools that you use to manage a server that is functioning correctly and can communicate with the network. Some in-band remote management can be used only on a Windows server. Others can be used on servers running various network operating systems. In-band remote management tools are discussed a little later in the section.

Out-of-band remote management tools are used if the server is not responding to standard network communications. This could be because the server is hung up or a network device has stopped functioning. Using out-of-band management tools combined with the appropriate hardware, you will need to locally manage a server only for hardware upgrades and maintenance.

Out-of-band connections usually involve using the serial port on the server to administer the server. This connection can be established remotely through specialized hardware or a dial-up connection.

Out-of-band management services in Windows Server 2003 are provided by the **Emergency Management Services (EMS)**. To effectively use EMS, you might need to purchase additional hardware and you'll need to weigh the cost of additional hardware with the benefit of the service.

10.3.2 Remote Management Security Considerations

It's important to secure the hardware and software used for remote management. With in-band remote management, you must pay attention to requirements of how the administrators will authenticate to the server and mechanisms for encrypting communications with the server. You will also need to consider the impact of in-band remote management on your firewall configuration. Out-of-band communication cannot be secured using operating system security features, so you will need to plan for the physical security of the serial connections required.

You will also need to design the appropriate rights and folder permissions to protect the remote management tools, so that only the appropriate administrators can access them. In general, your security strategy for remote management should include the following:

▲ **User authentication:** The server should allow remote management only by the appropriate administrator.
▲ **Machine authentication:** The server should allow remote management from only the appropriate computer. Computers can be authenticated using IP address restrictions or (preferably) computer certificates.
▲ **Physical security:** The hardware should be physically secure, especially in the case of out-of-band remote management.
▲ **Encryption:** Information sent over the network because of remote management needs to be confidential.
▲ **Auditing:** All access due to remote administration should be logged in a secure fashion.

Configuring the Network for Remote Administration

Configuration changes must be made to the network infrastructure to support remote administration. There are a few things to consider:

▲ Types of connection.
▲ Changes that will need to be made to firewall configurations.
▲ Changes to IP packet filtering settings to support remote management.

The type of connection you use will depend on which type of connection will support the remote management tool you are using. Beyond that, the type of connection you choose will determine whether you need additional security in terms of establishing a VPN connection first to encrypt the traffic that passes over the connection.

If you need to manage a server through a firewall, you should verify the firewall settings to determine if the management tool can work through the firewall. If it will not, you must determine the port numbers used by the management tool. Some common ports for management tools include 3389 for the Remote Desktop Protocol (RDP), 135 for remote procedure call (RPC), 23 for Telnet, 22 for Secure Shell (SSH), 80 for HTTP, and 443 for HTTPS (HTTP over SSL). After you identify the ports required for the remote management tool, you should decide whether the risk of opening the ports is worth the benefits of using the management tool through the firewall. You might determine that it is not, in which case you should look for an alternative tool to manage the server.

You will also need to consider any IP packet filtering you might be doing on the firewall, routers, or servers. IP packet filtering allows you to control which packets can pass through a network device. This is useful for controlling the applications that can communicate with the server or through a router or firewall. You might need to reconfigure these settings for the remote management tool to work properly.

Using a Secondary Network for Remote Management

One way to increase remote management security is to establish a **secondary network** specifically designed for remote management traffic. A secondary network can improve the performance, security, and availability of your remote management solution by separating the traffic for remote management to its own network, accessed using a secure router. Administrators would be allowed to remotely administer computers only if they had access to this network, along with having the correct user and machine credentials and user rights.

10.3.3 Planning Remote Management Deployment

After you have designed security for remote management, you should test the design in a lab setting that simulates your production environment. You will need to verify that your configuration is secure and meets the organization's needs for remote management. You should also verify network connectivity, hardware and software configurations, and the security settings of your servers for remote administration.

You will need to verify that you can connect to network resources for the required remote management tools. The following is a list of some of the things you should configure and test according to your design:

▲ Configure and test a secondary network for remote management if one is included in your design.

▲ Configure and test the dial-up settings over a VPN connection if you plan to support secure remote management through dial-up.

▲ Configure and test the firewall settings if you will use remote management tools through the firewall.

▲ Configure and test the IP packet filter settings if you have configured the servers or routers to filter for specific applications.

▲ Configure and test the IPsec and SSL settings to the servers if you plan to use IPsec or SSL to encrypt remote management traffic. Verify that the traffic is encrypted using a network monitoring utility.

Verify the hardware and software configurations in your design, particularly your out-of-band hardware configuration and auditing settings. The following is a list of some of the items that you will need to do:

▲ Verify out-of-band remote management configuration and hardware settings.

▲ Install and test EMS.

▲ Configure auditing and verify that it collects the information that you need.

▲ Verify any additional software or hardware settings that your design calls for.

▲ Verify that you can accomplish your remote management needs through the chosen tools.

You will need to verify the security settings that you have configured for remote administration. You should verify the following settings for your remote management configuration if they are applicable:

▲ Verify the authentication protocols used to access the server remotely.

▲ Verify that physical security is adequate for the servers and out-of-band remote management components.

▲ Verify that the proper encryption protocols are being used with your design.

▲ Verify any Group Policy settings that you are using to manage the security settings of your servers, including control of remote management.

▲ Verify that the security groups and user rights assigned to perform administration of servers only permit the necessary remote management tasks.

▲ Verify the shared folder and NT File System (NTFS) permissions for your remote management plan.

10.3.4 Securing Windows Inbound Management Tools

If your remote management plan calls for inbound remote management, you will need to choose the tool or tools you will use. In this section, we examine several management tools that can be used for inbound remote management on a Windows network and the security implications of each.

Using MMC

MMC is the standard administrative tool in Windows Server 2003. MMC is really a framework to host various management tools. It provides administrators with a standard environment from which they can manage their servers and network.

MMC can be used to manage a local server or a remote server by adding snap-ins. Not all snap-ins support remote management. Figure 10-7 shows the dialog box for Computer Management that allows you to select to manage the local computer or a computer on the network.

You will need to verify the remote management capabilities and the security features of the snap-ins you want to use for remote management. You will need to determine whether the snap-in supports the following security options:

▲ **Encryption capabilities:** Does the snap-in support encryption internally and what strength is the encryption? If it does not support encryption, you need to determine how to encrypt its network traffic or not use it for remote management.

Figure 10-7

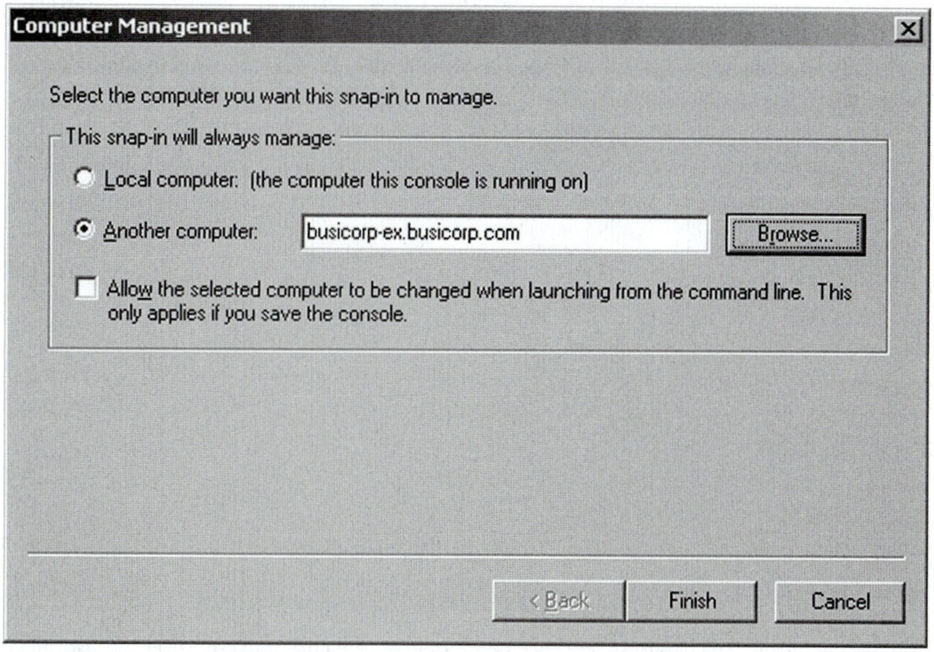

Selecting the computer you want to manage.

> ## FOR EXAMPLE
>
> ### Using Snap-ins that Support DCOM
>
> Many snap-ins use **Distributed Component Object Model (DCOM)**. DCOM uses **remote procedure calls (RPCs)** to communicate between the client and server. DCOM supports encryption by using the **Packet Privacy** option in the **dcomcnfg** tool used to configure DCOM. This encryption supports the RC4 public key encryption algorithm with a symmetric key strength of up to 128 bits. DCOM also supports the use of other algorithms implemented through the cryptoAPIs of Windows. DCOM authentication is integrated into Windows and supports NT LAN Manager and Kerberos authentication.
>
> Because DCOM uses RPCs, it can support various network protocols, but generally you will be using TCP/IP. The TCP port 135 and UDP port 135 used for RPCs would need to be opened on the firewall if you will be using the tool through a firewall. Due to the danger to your network of these ports being opened (all RPC traffic uses these ports, so it would be difficult to differentiate between programs), your security administrator might not allow you to use the tool directly through the firewall. You could use the tool over a VPN connection to prevent needing to open the port.

▲ **Authentication capabilities:** Are passwords encrypted or passed as clear text? What authentication protocols can be used? Does the snap-in support integration with Windows authentication or do you have to manage a separate password database and policies for the application? Does the management tool support two-factor authentication, like smart card authentication?

▲ **Network communications technology:** What protocols does the snap-in support for network communication?

Since most snap-ins will support TCP\IP, you should determine the ports that it uses for communication in case you will need to manage a server through a secured router or firewall.

Using Remote Desktop for Administration

Remote Desktop for Administration (**Remote Desktop** for short) provides a graphical user interface (GUI) to remote computers over local area networks (LANs) and wide area networks (WANs). All application processing happens on the server—just the display, keyboard commands, and mouse motions are sent over the network to and from the client. The Remote Desktop does all of this through the **Remote Desktop Protocol (RDP)**. Remote Desktop for Administration was known as **Terminal Services** in Windows 2000.

Using Remote Desktop has become one of the most popular ways to remotely manage Windows servers on a network. Remote Desktop provides the following features for administering servers equipped with Windows Server 2003 and Windows 2000 Server:

▲ Remote reboots of servers.

▲ Encryption of up to 128 bits in strength.

▲ Support for low-bandwidth connections.

▲ Support for 2 remote administrators sharing remote sessions for collaboration.

▲ Local printing, clipboard mapping, and serial device redirection.

▲ Support for smart card redirection (only supported in Windows 2003).

▲ **Roaming disconnect support**, which means that if your connection is disconnected, programs will continue to run, which will prevent interrupted installs or long-running tasks.

Remote Desktop for Administration is installed on a Windows Server 2003 computer by default, but it is disabled. You enable it through the Remote tab of System properties (see Figure 10-8) or through Group Policy.

When you enable Remote Desktop, you will be warned that any accounts that do not have a password will not be able to create a Remote Desktop session with the server, as shown in Figure 10-9.

You have the option of connecting through the Remote Desktop client in Windows or through the web version of the Remote Desktop, which provides an ActiveX® control that will allow you to connect over an HTTP connection. You would need to install Internet Information Services (IIS) on each server that you want to support web-based Remote Desktop connections.

By default, Remote Desktop for Administration requires 128-bit encryption for the connection. This is supported by the Remote Desktop client in Windows XP and Windows Server 2003. If you have an older version of the Terminal Services client, you will not be able to connect to a Windows Server 2003 computer with the default settings for RDP. You can configure RDP by navigating to Administrative Tools and clicking the Terminal Services Configuration utility. Expand the Connections folder and then right-click the RDP-TCP protocol and select "Properties." On the General tab, select the Client Compatible option to support clients that do not support 128-bit encryption, as shown in Figure 10-10.

It is recommended that you use the highest possible encryption for remote management tools, so you should leave the RDP protocol setting set to "High" and upgrade the client tools if possible. Only change this option if it is necessary to support an older client that cannot be updated. For example, you might

Figure 10-8

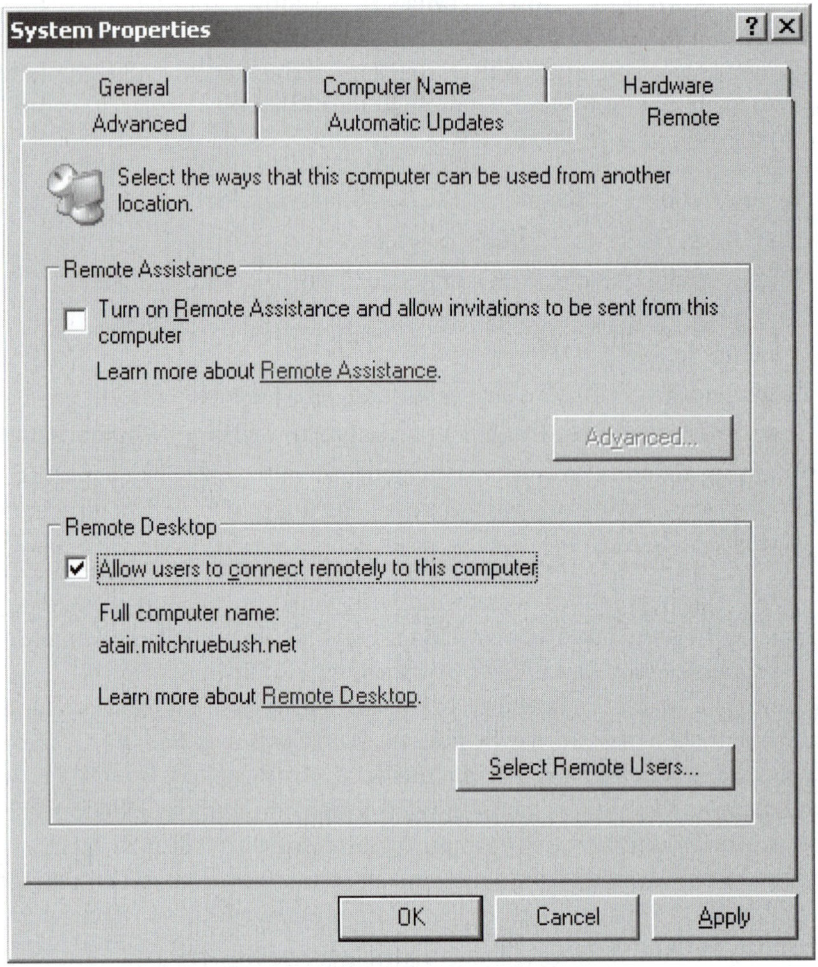

Enabling Remote Desktop.

have a Remote Desktop client that runs on a Linux workstation or a Windows CE device that does not support 128-bit encryption and cannot be upgraded.

You also will need to consider allowing administrators to connect to the console session of the Windows Server 2003 computer. Using the console session is the same as if you were physically sitting in front of the server. You can connect to the console session by launching the mstsc.exe (Remote Desktop client) with the /console switch or by launching the Remote Desktop MMC snap-in and choosing to connect to the console. This means that you can view all messages and use applications that only work with the console session. Whenever you connect to the console session, the physical console will lock for security so that

Figure 10-9

Remote Sessions warning.

nobody can watch what the remote administrator is doing by physically sitting at the console.

Using Remote Assistance

Remote Assistance was designed to allow someone to connect to a Windows computer to provide assistance. It is used primarily by help desk staff to help users solve their problems. When a Remote Assistance session is established, both users will see the same screen and can chat with each other through the Remote Assistance chat program. You can even allow the remote user to take control of your computer. Remote Assistance does not use the RDP protocol, like Remote Desktop, but is based on the technologies and protocols of Microsoft **NetMeeting**®, an online conferencing application.

Figure 10-10

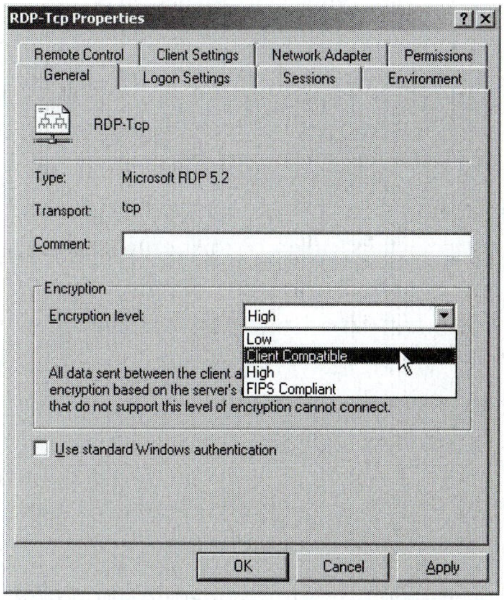

Setting the RDP protocol encryption level.

Remote Assistance is installed, but disabled, on Windows XP and Windows Server 2003 computers by default. You should enable it only on clients where it is needed.

One security issue you will need to determine is whether you should change your firewall configuration to support Remote Assistance. Remote Assistance requires that TCP port 3389 be opened on a firewall to pass through it.

You should set a short invitation period for Remote Assistance and use a password that is at least eight characters long and that is a mixture of symbols, numbers, and letters.

10.3.5 Securing TCP/IP Remote Management Tools

If you are managing a non-Windows computer or need to manage a Windows computer from a non-Windows computer, you might need to use a command-line tool, such as Telnet or SSH. These tools are supported on any computer that supports TCP/IP. Let's look at each.

Using Telnet

Telnet is a **terminal emulation** program that runs a command console on the client computer. The commands you execute do not run on the client but on the server you are connected to. This is similar to the capability provided by Remote Desktop for Administration except that it is command line only.

On a Windows computer, you can run Telnet by opening the Start menu, selecting "Run" and typing "telnet" to launch the client. You would then type the following to connect to the remote server running Telnet:

```
open server_name
```

You can then issue commands that run on the server, as shown in Figure 10-11.

Telnet is not a secure management tool and should not be used across an unsecured network, especially over a WAN. It requires you to log on using a username and password, but these are passed in clear text over the network. Authentication is limited to passing the username and password in clear text without support for smart cards or other forms of authentication. Also, all commands and data are sent over the network without any form of encryption. Therefore, if you require Telnet, you will need to implement another means of encryption, like establishing a VPN using L2TP (Layer 2 Tunneling Protocol) and IPSec for providing a stronger means of authentication and encryption of network traffic. If this is not possible, you should use SSH as an alternative to Telnet.

Secure Shell (SSH)

Secure Shell (SSH) is a technology that was developed by SSH Communications Security, Ltd. to provide for secure authentication and communications for remote shells and file transfers. SSH provides for strong authentication mechanisms,

Figure 10-11

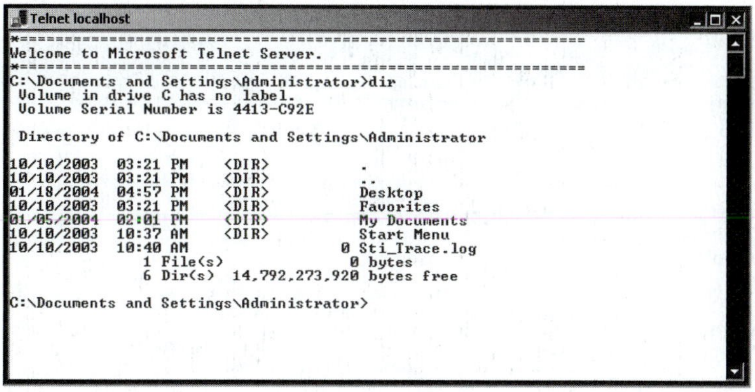

Telnet session.

including the ability to use certificate-based authentication like smart cards. SSH guards against eavesdropping on packets and IP redirection by encrypting the communications between the server and client. If available, SSH is preferred over Telnet for providing remote administration through the command line.

10.3.6 Designing for EMS

EMS is a collection of out-of-band management tools that enable the ability to manage a Windows Server 2003 computer when it is no longer responding to in-band management tools. You can access EMS through a terminal emulator, like **HyperTerminal**, that connects to a serial port on the server.

EMS is made up of standard Windows Server 2003 components that have been modified to redirect their output to the out-of-band communication port in addition to the video card. The following Windows components support out-of-band communication:

▲ Recovery Console
▲ Remote Installation Services (RIS)
▲ Text mode setup
▲ Setup loader

In addition to the standard Windows components, EMS includes two remote management consoles: **Special Administration Console (SAC)** and **!Special Administration Console (!SAC)**. Using the SAC is the most common way to access the EMS services on a Windows Server 2003 computer. SAC provides you with a command-line environment to manage the server when it is locked up, as shown in Figure 10-12.

Figure 10-12

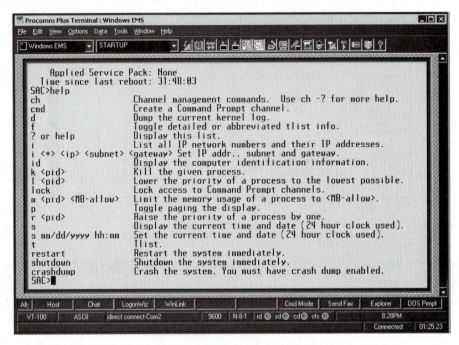

Special Administration Console.

The SAC will be available as long as the kernel of Windows Server 2003 is running. This means you can issue commands early in the boot process because as soon as the kernel is running, you can have access to the SAC, if it is enabled on your server. You can issue commands to the SAC to perform the following administration tasks:

▲ Restarting the server.

▲ Shutting down the server.

▲ Displaying the list of running processes.

▲ Killing a process.

▲ Configuring the IP address on the server.

▲ Starting a command prompt in the operating system, if possible.

▲ Generating a stop error so the server **dumps memory** (writes the contents of memory to a file).

The SAC provides **user mode access** (access to commands that run under the context of a user and can access memory available to user processes) through the cmd command, which launches a command prompt that you can use to start a command-line in-band management tool like Telnet to make managing the server easier. SAC also allows you to view the setup logs generated during the setup process to check on the progress of the setup or to diagnose problems with the setup. You can press "Esc+Tab" to switch to the SAC and view the setup logs during the GUI portion of the setup.

The !SAC is the fail-safe special management console that will load if the SAC fails to start for some reason. This is an automatic process. The !SAC does not provide all of the same functionality the SAC provides. In fact, it only provides two functions:

1. Restarting the server.
2. Redirecting stop error messages.

You can utilize the EMS services that are built into Windows Server 2003 to provide management of the server if the kernel is running or during loading. If you purchase additional hardware like a **service processor** (special processor that includes its own power supply and allows access to system management features using Telnet or a web-based interface), you can manage the server even if the kernel is not working.

You will need to decide how you will connect to the server to support EMS. Generally, you are going to connect to a serial connection on the server. You can purchase additional hardware to add network support for EMS. There are four basic designs for laying out your EMS infrastructure: direct serial connection, modem serial connection, terminal concentrator, and intelligent uninterruptible power supply (UPS). Let's take a look at each.

Using a Direct Serial Connection

A **direct serial connection** is the simplest of the out-of-band connections to a server. You can establish the connection by using a **null modem cable** (serial cable that allows two computers to connect to each other through serial ports by reversing the send and receive lines) between the management computer and the server running EMS (see Figure 10-13). The **management computer** is a computer that is running some kind of terminal emulation software. The easiest software to use is HyperTerminal because it comes with any Windows operating system, but almost any type of terminal emulation software will work.

You will need to make sure that the management computer and the server are physically secure to protect this design. The main benefit of direct serial connections is that they are easy to set up because they require no additional hardware.

The direct serial connection has a number of disadvantages:

▲ Computers need to be close to each other for physical security.
▲ It has the most limited functionality.
▲ It's difficult to manage more than a few computers using a direct serial connection.

Figure 10-13

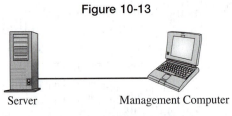

Server   Management Computer

Direct serial connection.

The direct serial connection is a great way to quickly connect a laptop computer to diagnose a server problem, like a hung server.

Using Modem Serial Connection

A **modem serial connection** is similar to a direct serial connection except that it involves putting a modem between the management computer and the servers. You would then dial into the modem and use a terminal emulation program. You have two connections to secure: the connection between the management computer and the modem and the connection between the modem and the server. Security on the connection between the management computer and the modem is based on security features found in the modem. For example, you could enable callback features in the modem to allow only connections from known numbers. Security on the serial connection between the modem and the server will need to be physically maintained. Figure 10-14 shows how a modem setup would look.

The benefits of using a modem for out-of-band communications are as follows:

▲ It's easy to set up and configure for use because there are no complicated devices to purchase and configure.

▲ The management computer can remotely connect to the server.

Figure 10-14

Serial Connection ┊ Phone Connection

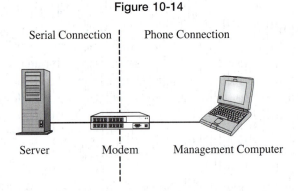

Server   Modem   Management Computer

Remote EMS through a modem.

There are some disadvantages, as follows:

▲ Security features in a modem are limited.
▲ It's difficult to manage more than a few computers using a modem.

Using a Terminal Concentrator

There are two problems with the direct serial or the modem serial connection to the server. The first problem is that the management computer is limited to two to four serial ports and therefore you can have only two to four EMS connections to your servers. The second problem is that the management computer needs to be physically secured to prevent access to the SAC. You can manage a larger number of servers and remove the necessity of physically securing the management computer by setting up a terminal concentrator to support a larger number of connections.

The **terminal concentrator** contains a larger number of serial ports than a server contains and can support a connection to a server for each port it contains. The terminal concentrator can then be connected to a network or a modem to provide terminal access to the servers it is connected to. This makes it easier to provide out-of-band communication to a larger amount of servers. A terminal concentrator also makes it easier to secure out-of-band communications.

You will need to physically secure the terminal concentrator's connection to the servers, just as you would any other serial connection. You should include the terminal concentrator in the locked server room with the servers that you will manage through it. The main difference is that the management computer and user can be authenticated by the terminal concentrator.

You usually connect to a terminal concentrator using a command-line terminal emulator like Telnet. Better yet, many concentrators support SSH, which can provide many options for authentication, including smart card and public key infrastructure (PKI). SSH also encrypts the traffic between the terminal concentrator and the management computer, further protecting the data from eavesdropping and manipulating. Figure 10-15 illustrates what a network with a terminal concentrator would look like.

The following are benefits of using a terminal concentrator:

▲ It supports logical authentication mechanisms.
▲ It can support encryption.
▲ It supports a larger number of servers for out-of-band management.
▲ It can support features in firmware like powering on and off the servers.

The main disadvantage is that you need to purchase additional hardware in the form of terminal concentrators.

Figure 10-15

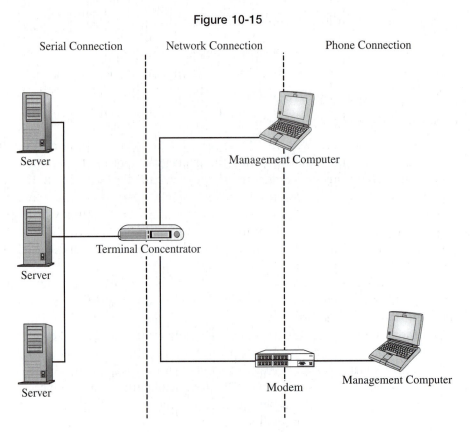

Using a terminal concentrator.

Using an Intelligent UPS

You might already have devices that can act as terminal concentrators in the form of an **intelligent uninterruptible power supply (intelligent UPS)**. The intelligent UPS can provide the same features a terminal concentrator provides. An intelligent UPS can form two connections to the server for use by EMS. It can connect using the standard serial connection and it can connect to the server through the AC power line. This means that not only can you manage the servers, but you can remotely control the power to the servers.

You need to manage and secure an intelligent UPS in the same way that you manage and secure a terminal concentrator. Physically secure the device in the server room with the servers and then use machine and user authentication to secure the network connection to the UPS. Having one device that performs two functions could save you the costs of purchasing separate terminal concentrators.

Figure 10-16 shows the configuration using an intelligent UPS.

Figure 10-16

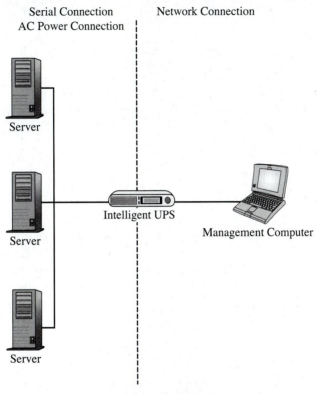

Serial Connection
AC Power Connection

Network Connection

Server

Server

Intelligent UPS

Management Computer

Server

Intelligent UPS setup.

FOR EXAMPLE

Ensuring 24x7 Uptime

Busicorp hosts web applications for a number of customers. Their highest level of service offers customers a dedicated server and offers a partial refund for service if the server is down more than 30 minutes. The Busicorp IT department currently has a rotating schedule for being on call. However, they have had to refund customer money due to the commute time for some IT staff members. IT wants to allow out-of-band remote management for these servers. There are currently ten customers who have purchased this level of service. The servers are running Windows Server 2003 and IIS.

You decide to purchase a terminal concentrator and allow out-of-bound remote management from a secure management computer on the internal network and from the IT administrators' laptop computers when they are connected through a modem. You require them to connect using SSH and authenticate with a smart card.

SELF-CHECK

1. Compare Remote Desktop and Remote Assistance.
2. Compare Telnet and SSH.
3. Identify the four ways to configure an out-of-band remote management solution using EMS.

SUMMARY

In this chapter, you learned how to ensure that your network remains operational and secure. The chapter began with a look at configuration control and creating a security update infrastructure to keep your software up-to-date. Next you learned about creating an audit trail to ensure you are notified of attempts to attack a computer. You also learned about some ways to configure secure remote management, including in-band management and out-of-band management.

KEY TERMS

!Special Administration Console (!SAC)

acct command

accton command

Audit

Auditing

Audit log

Audit trail

Automatic Updates

Change control

Clipping level

Configuration auditing

Configuration control

Configuration identification

Configuration item (CI)

Configuration management

Configuration status accounting

dcomcnfg

Direct serial connection

Distributed Component Object Model (DCOM)

Documentation control

Dumps memory

Emergency Management Services (EMS)

Event log

finger command

HyperTerminal

In-band remote management

Intelligent uninterruptible power supply (intelligent UPS)

Intrusion detection (ID)

last command

lastcomm command

lastlog command

Management computer

Modem serial connection

Monitoring

NetMeeting

Null modem cable

Out-of-band remote management

Packet Privacy

Patch

Penetration testing

Protocol analyzers

Remote Assistance

Remote Desktop for Administration

Remote Desktop Protocol (RDP)

Remote management plan

Remote procedure call (RPC)

Roaming disconnect support

Secondary network

Secure Shell (SSH)

Security access control list (SACL)

Security update

Security update infrastructure

Service processor

Software Update Services (SUS)

Special Administration Console (SAC)

Systems Management Server (SMS)

Telnet

Terminal concentrator

Terminal emulation

Terminal Services

User mode access

utmp command

War dialers

who command

Windows Server Update Services (WSUS)

Windows update

wtmp command

ASSESS YOUR UNDERSTANDING

Go to www.wiley.com/college/cole to assess your knowledge of ongoing security management.

Measure your learning by comparing pre-test and post-test results.

Summary Questions

1. Which of the following ensures that all system changes are approved before they are implemented?
   (a) configuration auditing
   (b) configuration control
   (c) configuration identification
   (d) configuration status accounting

2. Which free software update method can you use to automatically apply only approved updates to computers running Windows Server 2003 and SQL Server 2005?
   (a) SMS
   (b) SUS
   (c) Windows Update
   (d) WSUS

3. The only way to configure WSUS clients is through Group Policy. True or false?

4. Which command would you use to display the information in the wtmp file on a Linux computer?
   (a) finger
   (b) last
   (c) lastcomm
   (d) who

5. Which audit policy would you enable to log attempts to change trust relationships on a Windows computer?
   (a) audit directory service access
   (b) audit account management
   (c) audit policy change
   (d) audit process tracking

6. An out-of-band remote management tool is used when normal network communication cannot be established. True or false?

7. Which port would you need to open in a firewall to allow users to connect to a computer on the other side of the firewall using Remote Desktop?

(a) 22

(b) 23

(c) 135

(d) 3389

8. By default, the RDP protocol uses 128-bit encryption on a computer running Windows Server 2003. True or false?

9. Both Telnet and SSH can be used with smart card authentication. True or false?

10. You connect to a computer using the !SAC management console. What task can you perform?

(a) kill a process

(b) configure IP addressing

(c) restart the server

(d) display a list of running processes

11. You can use a terminal concentrator to connect multiple servers for out-of-band management. True or false?

Applying This Chapter

1. You have configured security for a Microsoft Exchange 2003 server and 40 client computers on a network. The client computers are running Windows XP Professional with Service Pack 2. They are also running Microsoft Office 2003. The computers are all members of an Active Directory® domain and are located at the same site. The business is a seasonal business. Most of the year the office supports about 40 users. However, in the summer, that number grows to 150. The additional users are supported using rented computers.

(a) What aspects of the network are most subject to change?

(b) Describe how you would handle security updates on the network. Explain why that is the most appropriate choice.

(c) The company is planning to upgrade to Exchange Server 2007. What should occur before the upgrade?

(d) You are concerned about unauthorized changes to Active Directory objects. How can you track attempted changes?

(e) If the Exchange server fails when you are not at work, you want to be able to restart it from home. What is the least expensive way to meet this requirement?

(f) When temporary employees are working at the site, they often have questions. You want to be able to help them with their problems without leaving your desk. What should you do?

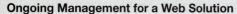

Ongoing Management for a Web Solution

You manage a website. The website includes a web server and a database server. The web server is located on the perimeter network. The database server is a headless server and is located on the internal network in a locked server room. SSL is used to encrypt communication between the clients and the web server and between the web server and the database server.

You need to be able to use the database management system user interface to manage the database server once a month.

The web application must have around-the-clock uptime. There are no IT administrators on-site between 8 p.m. and 7 a.m.

Both servers are running Windows Server 2003.

1. You are designing the configuration control plan for the servers. List some configuration items.

2. Identify the remote management requirements for this environment and describe how you would address them.

3. You want to ensure that only your laptop computer is used to log on to the database server remotely and that data is encrypted. What is the best way to achieve these requirements?

4. Discuss the drawbacks to enabling Automatic Updates on the web server.

5. How can you ensure that only you and the web server are accessing the database server?

11

DISASTER RECOVERY AND FAULT TOLERANCE

Starting Point

What You'll Learn in This Chapter

▲ Business continuity planning
▲ Disaster recovery planning
▲ Incident response planning
▲ Backup and restoration planning
▲ Redundant Array of Independent Disks (RAID)
▲ Storage area networks (SANs)
▲ Server clusters

After Studying This Chapter, You'll Be Able To

▲ Identify the purpose of a business continuity plan
▲ Identify the purpose of a disaster recovery plan
▲ Describe the methods of testing a disaster recovery plan
▲ Identify the purpose of an incident response plan
▲ List the steps you should take when responding to a security incident
▲ Create a backup strategy
▲ Compare and contrast various RAID implementations
▲ Identify a situation in which a SAN would be used
▲ Identify a situation in which you would implement a server cluster

INTRODUCTION

Regardless of all your mitigation efforts, attacks are going to happen. And unfortunately, they are not the only threat your network faces. Natural disasters, fires, and equipment failure also threaten the availability of your network. When planning your network security, you should always prepare for the worst. This chapter looks at the policies you should have in place to help you deal with worst case scenarios, minor attacks, or even natural disasters. The chapter then discusses some guidelines for creating a backup and restore plan. The chapter concludes by examining fault tolerance.

11.1 Planning for the Worst

A wide variety of events can impact the operations of a business and the information systems used by that business. These events can be either natural or man-made. Examples of disruptive events include the following:

▲ Sabotage
▲ Arson
▲ Security incidents
▲ Strikes
▲ Bombings
▲ Earthquakes
▲ Fire
▲ Floods
▲ Fluctuations in or loss of electrical power
▲ Storms
▲ Communication system failures
▲ Unavailability of key employees

This chapter examines three types of policies that can help a business continue to operate and recover from a security incident or other disruptive event: a business continuity plan, an incident response plan, and a disaster recovery plan.

11.1.1 Business Continuity Planning

The primary purpose of business continuity planning is to reduce the risk of financial loss and to enhance a company's capability to recover promptly from a disruptive event. The business continuity plan should also help minimize the cost and mitigate the risk associated with the disruptive event.

Business continuity plans should evaluate all critical information processing areas of the organization, such as workstations and laptops, networks, servers, application software, storage media, and personnel procedures.

A **business continuity planning committee** should be formed and given the responsibility to create, implement, and test the plan. The committee is made up of representatives from senior management, all functional business units, information systems, and security administration. The committee initially defines the scope of the plan, which should deal with how to recover promptly from a disruptive event and mitigate the financial and resource loss.

The business continuity planning process consists of four phases:

1. Scope and plan initiation: creation of the scope and the other elements needed to define the parameters of the plan.
2. Business impact assessment: a process to help business units understand the impact of a disruptive event.
3. Business continuity plan development: development of the business continuity plan. This process includes the areas of plan implementation, plan testing, and ongoing plan maintenance.
4. Plan approval and implementation: final senior management sign-off, enterprise-wide awareness of the plan, and implementation of a maintenance procedure for updating the plan as needed.

These elements are discussed in more detail in the following sections.

Scope and Plan Initiation

The **scope and plan initiation phase** is the first step to creating a business continuity plan. It entails creating the scope for the plan and the other elements needed to define the parameters of the plan. This phase includes an examination of the company's operations and support services. Scope activities could include creating a detailed account of the work required, listing the resources to be used, and defining the management practices to be employed.

Business Impact Assessment

A **business impact assessment** is a process used to help business units understand the impact of a disruptive event. This phase includes the execution of a **vulnerability assessment** (similar to a risk assessment).

The purpose of a business impact assessment is to create a document that will be used to help understand what impact a disruptive event would have on the business. The impact might be financial (quantitative) or operational (qualitative, such as the inability to respond to customer complaints).

A business impact assessment has three primary goals:

1. Prioritization of critical systems: Every critical business unit process must be identified and prioritized, and the impact of a disruptive event must be evaluated.

2. Estimation of downtime tolerance: The business impact assessment is used to help estimate the maximum tolerable downtime that the business can tolerate and still remain a viable company; that is, what is the longest period of time a critical process can remain interrupted before the company can never recover? It is often found during the business impact assessment process that this time period is much shorter than expected.

3. Identification of resource requirements: The resource requirements for the critical processes are identified at this time, with the most time-sensitive processes receiving the most resource allocation.

A business impact assessment is usually conducted in the following manner:

1. Gather the appropriate assessment materials. The business impact assessment process begins by identifying the critical business units and their interrelationships. You should also determine the factors that make the business successful.

2. Perform the vulnerability assessment. The vulnerability assessment usually includes quantitative (financial) and qualitative (operational) sections. The vulnerability assessment is smaller than a full risk assessment and is focused on providing information that is used solely for the business continuity plan and disaster recovery plan. **Quantitative loss criteria** include the following:

    (a) Incurring financial losses from loss of revenue, capital expenditure, or personal liability resolution.

    (b) The additional operational expenses incurred due to the disruptive event.

    (c) Incurring financial loss due to violation of contractual agreements.

    (d) Incurring financial loss due to violation of regulatory or compliance requirements.

    Typical **qualitative loss criteria** include the following:

    (a) The loss of competitive advantage or market share.

    (b) The loss of public confidence or credibility, or incurring public embarrassment.

    The vulnerability assessment should address critical support functions such as the physical infrastructure, accounting, payroll, and telecommunications systems.

3. Analyze the compiled information. Analyzing the information as part of the business impact assessment includes the following:

(a) Identifying interdependencies.

(b) Documenting required processes.

(c) Determining acceptable interruption periods.

4. Document the results and present recommendations. All processes, procedures, analyses, and results should be documented and presented to management, along with the associated recommendations. The report will contain the previously gathered material, list the identified critical support areas, summarize the quantitative and qualitative impact statements, and provide the recommended recovery priorities generated from the analysis.

Business Continuity Plan Development

The business continuity plan is developed by using the information collected in the business impact assessment to create the recovery strategy plan that will support the critical business functions. This process includes plan implementation, plan testing, and ongoing plan maintenance.

Plan Approval and Implementation

The object of this activity is to obtain the final senior management sign-off, create enterprise-wide awareness of the plan, and implement a maintenance procedure for updating the plan as needed.

▲ Senior management approval: Because senior management is ultimately responsible for all phases of the business continuity plan, they must have final approval. When a disaster strikes, senior management must be able to make informed decisions quickly during the recovery effort.

▲ Plan awareness: Enterprise-wide awareness of the plan is important and emphasizes the organization's commitment to its employees. Specific training might be required for certain personnel to carry out their tasks.

▲ Plan maintenance: Because of uncontrollable events, such as reorganization, employee turnover, relocation, or upgrading of critical resources, a business continuity plan might become outdated. Whatever the reason, plan maintenance techniques must be employed from the outset to ensure that the plan remains fresh and usable. Also, audit procedures should be put in place that can report regularly on the state of the plan.

Any costs for implementing the plan would also need to be approved at this point.

11.1.2 Disaster Recovery Planning

Disaster recovery planning is concerned with the protection of critical business processes from the effects of major information system and network failures, by quickly recovering from an emergency with a minimum impact to the organization.

A **disaster recovery plan** is a comprehensive statement of consistent actions to be taken before, during, and after a disruptive event that causes a significant loss of information systems resources.

Disaster recovery plans are the procedures for responding to an emergency, providing extended backup operations during the interruption, and managing recovery and salvage processes afterwards, should an organization experience a substantial loss of processing capability. Another objective of a properly executed disaster recovery plan is to allow the business to implement critical processes at an alternate site and to return to the primary site and normal processing within a time frame that minimizes the loss to the organization.

The disaster recovery planning process involves developing the disaster recovery plan, testing the plan, and executing it in the event of an emergency.

Developing the Disaster Recovery Plan

This first step involves developing the recovery plans and defining the necessary steps required to protect the business in the event of a disaster. Automated tools are available to assist in the development of the disaster recovery plan. These tools can improve productivity by providing formatted templates customized to the particular organization's needs.

Determining Recovery Time Objectives

Early in the disaster recovery planning process, all business functions and critical systems must be examined to determine their recovery time requirements. Recovery time objectives are assigned to each function or system in order to guide the selection of alternate processing procedures. Table 11-1 summarizes the rating classes and associated recovery time frame objectives.

When determining how to rate a particular function or system, you should consider the quantitative cost associated with downtime, any service level agreements you have in place with customers, and other costs that might be incurred

Table 11-1: Recovery Time Frames

Rating	Recovery Time Frame
AAA	Immediate
AA	Full functional recovery within 4 hours
A	Same business day
B	Up to 24 hours downtime permitted
C	24 to 72 hours downtime permitted
D	Greater than 72 hours downtime acceptable

by the system being down, such as loss of reputation or possible litigation. The more loss associated with a system being down, the higher that system should be rated.

Establishing Backup Sites

An important component of disaster recovery planning is maintaining a **backup site** that provides some degree of duplication of computing resources located away from the primary site. The types of backup sites are differentiated primarily by the extent to which the primary computing resources are replicated.

Hot sites, warm sites, and cold sites are the most common types of remote off-site backup processing facilities. They are differentiated by how much preparation is devoted to the site and, therefore, how quickly the site can be used as an alternate processing site. The characteristics of each of these sites are given as follows:

▲ **Cold site:** a designated computer operations room with heating, ventilation, and air conditioning (HVAC) that has no computing systems installed and, therefore, would require a substantial effort to install the hardware and software required to begin alternate processing. This type of site is rarely useful in an actual emergency.

▲ **Warm site:** an alternate processing facility with equipment installed, but without the current data set.

▲ **Hot site:** a site with all required computer hardware, software, and peripherals ready to begin alternate processing either immediately or within an acceptably short time frame. This site would be a duplicate of the original site and might only require synchronization of the most current data to duplicate operations.

Additional options for providing backup capabilities include the following:

▲ **Mutual aid agreements:** An arrangement with another company that might have similar computing needs. Both parties agree to support each other in the case of a disruptive event by providing alternative processing resources to the other party. Although appealing, this is not a good choice if the emergency affects both parties. Also, capacity at either facility might not be available when needed.

▲ **Rolling** or **mobile backup:** Contracting with a vendor to provide mobile power and HVAC facilities sufficient to stage the alternate processing.

▲ **Multiple centers:** In this scenario, the processing is spread over several operations centers, creating a distributed approach to redundancy and sharing of available resources. These multiple centers could be owned and managed by the same organization (in-house sites) or used in conjunction with a reciprocal agreement. If the centers are all owned by the same organization, the additional servers can also help manage the normal load.

▲ **Service bureaus:** An organization might contract with a service bureau to fully provide alternate processing services. The advantages of this type of arrangement are the quick response and availability of the service bureau, the possibility of testing without disrupting normal operations, and the possible availability of the service bureau for additional support functions. The disadvantages of this type of setup are the expense and the potential for resource contention during a large emergency.

Plan Testing

The disaster recovery plan must be tested and evaluated at regular intervals. Testing is required to verify the accuracy of the recovery procedures, verify the processing capability of the alternate backup site, train personnel, and identify deficiencies. The most common types of testing modes, by increasing level of thoroughness, are as follows:

▲ **Checklist review:** The disaster recovery plan is distributed and reviewed by business units for its thoroughness and effectiveness.

▲ **Tabletop exercise** or **structured walk-through test:** Members of the emergency management group meet in a conference room setting to discuss their responsibilities and how they would react to emergency scenarios by stepping through the plan.

▲ **Walk-through drill** or **simulation test:** The emergency management group and response teams actually perform their emergency response functions by walking through the test, without actually initiating recovery procedures.

▲ **Functional drill:** This approach tests specific functions, such as medical response, emergency notifications, warning and communications procedures, and equipment, although not necessarily all at once. It also includes **evacuation drills**, where personnel walk the evacuation route to a designated area where procedures for accounting for the personnel are tested.

▲ **Parallel test** or **full-scale exercise:** A real-life emergency situation is simulated as closely as possible. It involves all of the participants that would be responding to the real emergency, including community and external organizations. The test might involve ceasing some real production processing.

▲ **Full-interruption test:** Normal production is shut down and the disaster recovery processes are fully executed. This type of test is dangerous and, if not properly executed, can cause a disaster situation.

Implementing the Plan

If an actual disaster occurs, there are three options for recovery:

▲ Recover at the primary operating site.
▲ Recover to an alternate site for critical functions.
▲ Restore full system after a catastrophic loss.

Two teams should be organized to execute the recovery: the recovery and salvage teams. The functions of these teams are as follows:

▲ **Recovery team:** restore operations of the organization's critical business functions at the alternate backup processing site. The recovery team is concerned with rebuilding production processing. Getting a business's critical functions back online should be the highest priority task.
▲ **Salvage team:** repair, clean, salvage, and determine the viability of the primary processing infrastructure immediately after the disaster.

The disaster recovery plan should also address other concerns such as paying employees during a disaster, preventing fraud, media relations, and liaison with local emergency services.

11.1.3 Designing an Incident Response Procedure

The recovery plan is used in the event of a natural disaster or other catastrophic event. However, to respond to a security incident, you need a plan that specifically deals with the issues involved with recovering from a security incident. This is known as a **Computer Security Incident Response Plan (CSIRP)** and should provide you with the information you'll need at the moment that an attack is discovered or suspected. It should contain a list of the names and numbers of those to be notified.

The first step in putting together a CSIRP is to build a team referred to as a **Computer Security Incident Response Team (CSIRT)**. It is extremely important that each member of the team be given a finite scope of responsibility. It is always a good idea to include a broad range of skills on the team. A good team would include a network administrator who knows the topology of the network, a server administrator who knows the configuration of the servers, a desktop administrator who knows the configuration of the desktop workstations in the organization, an application specialist who is familiar with the applications that are running on the workstations and the servers, a security specialist whose main focus is on securing the organization, a team leader to facilitate the chain of communication, and a manager who has the authority to make a decision not covered by the plan.

Table 11-2: Severity Classifications

Severity	Example(s)
1	A small number of users receive an email with a virus attachment, which is caught by antivirus software on the computer.
2	A small number of scans detected on perimeter systems along with information concerning which computers will be targeted.
3	A large number of scans detected on perimeter systems; zero affect on production systems. A large number of computers infected with a known computer virus that is handled by antivirus software. Small number of isolated computers infected with unknown computer virus.
4	A breach of perimeter systems or successful denial-of-service attack with minimal impact on production.
5	A breach of perimeter systems or successful denial-of-service attack with major impact on production systems; poses a significant chance of financial or public relations damage.

Security Classifications

Once the entire team has been formed, the next step is to determine the severity level you'll assign to certain types of incidents. As you might imagine, some security incidents might not require the entire team being brought in. For example, an incident such as a small virus infecting a single computer would certainly not warrant the whole CSIRT to resolve the problem. There must be clear definitions of what severity an incident is and therefore who needs to work to resolve the issue. Table 11-2 shows an example of severity classification for ABC Corporation with some examples.

Based on Table 11-2, incidents with a severity of 3 or greater would result in the activation of the CSIRT, incidents with lower severity levels would be handled without the intervention of the incident response team. Instead, a network administrator or desktop support person would respond to resolve the problem.

Communication Procedure

The procedure should include a **determinate chain of notification** or **communication procedure** that describes how the information can flow to everyone who might be affected by the incident. One of the best ways to avoid mistakes when reacting to an incident is to have a procedure that spells out how the information should be disseminated to the various members of the team as well as to notify those individuals in need-to-know roles. Communication is key to the success of your security response team in properly defending and effectively reacting. For example, a scenario in which you suspect an employee is selling information to competitors typically spurs an internal investigation by the security team to audit the critical resources that are being leaked. Without a procedure specifying whom to notify, the workstation of the employee could be re-imaged by a desktop administrator, which would obviously erase most of the evidence on the machine. The desktop administrator should be made aware of the breach in security and trained well enough to know that re-imaging the workstation hard drive is not the appropriate response in this situation.

Methods of Responding to an Attack

There are typically two techniques for responding to an attack. One is to shut down or disconnect the system(s) that have been compromised (not the router that they came in through, unless it has been compromised). Shutting down or disconnecting the system(s) allows you to preserve the evidence before the attacker has the opportunity to hide his or her tracks. The other option is to isolate the system(s) so that you can monitor the activity of the attacker in order to gather more evidence and at the same time prevent other systems from being attacked. This option does, however, come with significant risk. The attacker might notice the changes, eliminate the evidence, and stop the attack. Allowing the attacker to continue, even in an isolated environment, should be an option only for a highly skilled security expert.

Incident Response Procedure Steps

The incident response procedure should include details for the following steps, with as much specific information as possible:

1. Declare the incident. The response procedure should include the conditions that must be met for an incident to be declared, as well as who is responsible for making the declaration. When an incident occurs that requires the team to respond, it should be declared. Typically, the team manager would be the individual making the declaration, and he or she would notify upper management that a security incident has occurred. The team manager would also be the person responsible for communicating the incident to the rest of the team.

2. Analyze the incident. The incident will need to be analyzed to determine the scope of the breach. It is at this stage that the details of the incident will be recorded.

3. Contain or resolve the incident. Depending on the type of incident that occurs, you might need to quarantine the systems that have been

compromised. Should a solution exist that can be applied and alleviate the situation, it should be carried out. Fixing the problem is better than containing it.

4. Resolve the problem. If the previous step led only to containment, the next step is to resolve the problem. This might begin with cleaning a system and then applying a patch or a service pack.

5. Prevent reoccurrence of problem. Take the appropriate steps to prevent the system(s) from being compromised again.

6. Document events. Log all of the events that have taken place, from the discovery of the breach to resolution. This documentation will be used in the post-incident evaluation.

7. Preserve evidence. Be sure to retain as much evidence as possible. As previously stated, this data can be used by the authorities to capture the attacker. The evidence can also be used to prevent future attacks that exploit similar vulnerabilities. It might be necessary to preserve the computer system as evidence, at least for a while, and to replace it with another computer.

8. Conduct a post-incident evaluation. Gather the team after the incident has been resolved to review all of the information that was collected. Identify areas in which the team could improve its response and paths of communication. Determine if a post-incident report should be provided to management and users.

FOR EXAMPLE

A Incident Response Procedure Will Prevent Mistakes

The first time that Steve fell victim to an external attack, he panicked and immediately shut down the router that the attacker entered through—he literally unplugged it. That was a knee-jerk reaction under the stress that obviously comes with being attacked. Turning off the router not only disconnected the attacker, it also stopped Internet email from entering the organization and prevented the company's users from sending external email and accessing the Internet entirely. Fortunately, the attackers (Steve found out later that it was significantly more than one) were only able to gain access to the company's public FTP servers and used them only to store and share files across the Internet.

Had there been a well-documented procedure dictating his response, Steve wouldn't have made such monumental mistakes. You will want to make sure that you have a procedure in place to prevent your response staff from making those mistakes.

11.2 Creating a Backup Strategy

If an incident, disaster, hard disk crash, or other catastrophic system failure occurs, you need to be able to recover data and services as quickly as possible. In many cases, this will mean reformatting and restoring from backup. Having a reliable backup strategy is essential to ensuring you can recover. This section discusses some guidelines for making sure your backup strategy can meet your business's recovery time frame requirements.

11.2.1 Analyzing Backup Requirements

When designing a backup strategy, the most important point is to ensure that your strategy is in line with the business's operational and data security requirements. As with other design tasks, the first step you must take is to analyze these requirements. You must identify the following:

▲ Recovery time frame requirements for each server on the network.
▲ The data stored on each server and on client workstations.
▲ How frequently each type of data changes.
▲ How the data is stored—is it in files or a database?
▲ Disk space required for the backup.
▲ The amount of data loss that can be tolerated if an incident occurs.
▲ Confidentiality requirements for the data.
▲ Is the data encrypted?
▲ How quickly the data needs to be brought back online.
▲ The cost of data loss, which includes the time necessary to reenter or recreate data.

You need to consider **transactional data**, such as that stored in a relational database; dynamic data, such as email on a **store and forward server** (a server that stores messages until they are picked up by the user or forwarded to the next email server on the route to its destination); documents stored on servers and on user workstations; server configuration data; and directory services and

Figure 11-1

	A	B	C	D	E	F
1	Data	Storage location	Estimated size	Data loss tolerance	Recovery time frame	Confidentiality
2	Accounts Receivable	AcctData1 database on SQL1	10 MB	4 hours	24 hours	Medium High
3	Orders	Sales database on SQL2	3 GB	None	4 hours	Medium
4	Inventory	Sales database on SQL3	1 GB	24 hours	1 hour	Medium Low
5	Marketing brochures	C:\MarketingShares on MKTG	20 GB	4 hours	72 hours	Low
6	User accounts	DC1, DC2, and DC3	4 GB	8 hours	1 hour	Very High

Data backup requirements spreadsheet.

user account data. If you have a public key infrastructure (PKI), you will also need a backup of all certificates. You will need to take special care to protect the backup of the root server certificate. If you use Encrypting File System (EFS) or another data encryption method, you will need to ensure that the certificates used to encrypt the data are also backed up.

When analyzing data backup requirements, you might want to use a spreadsheet like the one shown in Figure 11-1.

11.2.2 Backing Up System Configurations

You need to be able to ensure that you can recover each computer on the network to the state it was in before it was compromised or before a disaster occurred. This means having a reliable system configuration backup. On a Windows® computer, this backup is known as a **system state backup**. A system state backup on a domain control includes the directory services database.

You will also need to make sure you have a backup of any applications and application settings. The best way to do this is to periodically create a **full backup** (a backup of everything) of each server or to create an **image** using a utility like Symantec™'s **Ghost™** (a utility used to create a snapshot image of a computer's configuration that can be applied at a later time or to create an identical computer configuration). For client computers that have a standard configuration, creating an image using Ghost is a good way to ensure that you can quickly restore the client computer to a basic configuration. Remember that the image or full backup might not include the latest security updates, so make sure to apply them before connecting the computer to the network.

11.2.3 Choosing a Backup Tool

Another decision you will need to make is what tool to use to perform backups. Most operating systems include a backup utility. For example, Windows includes **Windows Backup**, shown in Figure 11-2.

Windows Backup allows you to select files and folders to back up, to back up system state, and to schedule recurring backups. It supports **volume shadow copy**,

Figure 11-2

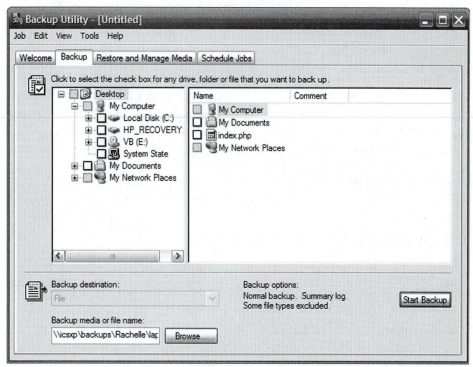

Windows Backup utility.

which allows you to back up files even if they are in use. There is also a command-line version of Windows Backup, called **ntbackup**.

There are also a number of third-party applications that can be used to perform backups. These applications differ in the features they support. For example, **Mondoarchive** supports backup of a Linux computer and is included with the Knoppix® distribution.

Some applications, such as database management systems, also include a backup feature. When they do, it is often best to create a backup using the application's software.

11.2.4 Choosing the Backup Media

Another important decision you need to make is the destination media for your backups. Your choice will depend on a number of factors, including the following:

▲ Media types supported by the backup tool.
▲ Cost.

▲ Storage capacity.

▲ Whether you need to run unattended backups.

▲ Security requirements.

▲ Off-site storage requirements.

Most backup solutions support backing up to a tape drive or network share. Some also support backing up to a CD. It is a good idea to keep a backup at a different location to ensure you can recover from a fire, flood, or other incident that affects the physical site. To do so, you will need to back up to removable media, such as a tape or CD, or burn the backups to a CD periodically. A backup kept at a different location is known as an **off-site backup**.

When backing up confidential data, you need to ensure that the backup media is physically secure. You should also protect backups by using a strong password.

11.2.5 Determining the Types of Backups

A full backup of data can be very time consuming and use a lot of disk space. Therefore, you will probably want to combine periodic full backups with supplemental backups. Two types of supplemental backups are common:

▲ **Differential backup:** A differential backup backs up all data that has changed since the last full backup.

▲ **Incremental backup:** An incremental backup backs up all data that has changed since the last full or incremental backup.

The time necessary to perform differential and incremental backups are compared in Figure 11-3.

Figure 11-3

Time required to back up

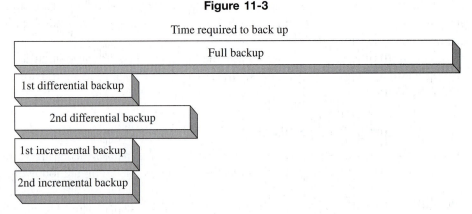

Relative time to perform backup.

Figure 11-4

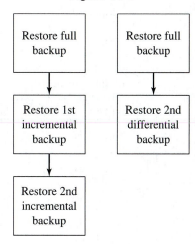

Restoration process.

The advantage to a differential backup is that you only need to restore two backups to restore the system: the full backup and the differential backup. The advantage to the incremental backup is that backups take less time and require less disk space. However, when restoring the computer, you need to apply the full backup and each incremental backup since the full backup. The restoration process is shown in Figure 11-4.

When backing up transactional data, such as that stored in a relational database, you can perform a **transaction log backup**, which creates a backup of the actions that have occurred on the data. A relational database management system writes changes to a file, known as a **transaction log**, before they are written to the database. A transaction log backup allows you to perform very frequent backups and to recover with minimal data loss. When recovering a database, you restore the database backup and then apply the transaction log backups in the order in which they are taken. If you were able to create a **tail-log backup** (a backup of the current transaction log) before backing up the database, you will apply that backup last and no data loss will occur. The procedure for restoring a transactional database is shown in Figure 11-5.

11.2.6 Determining Backup Frequency

Another key concern when designing a backup strategy is determining how frequently data needs to be backed up. This is one place your spreadsheet will come in handy because different data will have different backup frequency requirements, depending on the following:

Figure 11-5

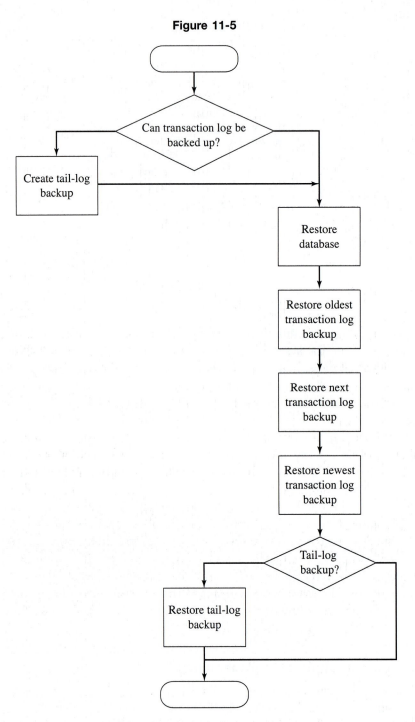

Database restoration process.

▲ How often the data changes.

▲ Business tolerance for data loss.

For example, you might need to back up the graphics files for the marketing department only once a week because they rarely change. However, the online order system and inventory database files change rapidly and there is little tolerance for data loss. Therefore, you might need to perform a daily full backup and hourly incremental backups of this data.

11.2.7 Assigning Responsibility for Backups

You will most likely want to automate backups so that they run on a scheduled basis. However, if you are backing up to removable media, such as a tape backup, someone needs to be responsible for changing the tape when it becomes full. Someone must also be responsible for auditing the backup process to make sure backups are run and for periodically testing the backups to ensure they can be restored if necessary.

Another consideration is that the backup operation must run under the security context of a user account. That user account must have permission to perform the backup. On a Windows system, that means the user must have either Read permission or the Back up files and directories user right (see Figure 11-6).

Permissions will vary for other backup programs. For example, the Mondoarchive program must run under the superuser account.

Backing Up Data on Client Computers

Implementing a reliable backup strategy that includes the data on client computers is difficult unless the data is stored on a central server. Most network operating

Figure 11-6

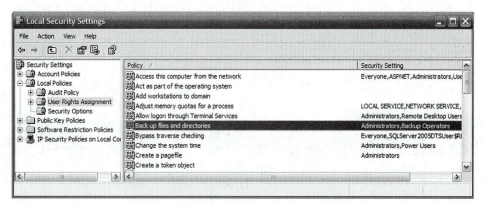

The Back up files and directories user right.

FOR EXAMPLE

Backups in a Distributed Environment

Many companies have resources dispersed across multiple geographic locations. Some of these locations might not even have an IT person on staff. When this is the case, how can you be sure that resources at those locations are being backed up?

Some vendors offer solutions for backing up servers that are geographically distributed. One example is Adaptec®'s Snap Server™. It provides a centralized backup location. If remote servers are running the Snap Enterprise Data Replicator (Snap EDR) agent, data can be automatically replicated to the Snap Server. A solution like this also off-loads the backup storage to a separate server.

systems allow you to store user data on a server. Some operating systems, such as Windows XP and Windows Vista™, have built-in support for synchronizing this centralized data with data stored on the client computer. This allows users to access their data when not connected to the network, while still allowing administrators to back up the data. If the data is stored on a computer running Windows Server 2003 or Windows Vista, users can also take advantage of **shadow copy**, which copies a file when it is changed and allows users to recover from user errors and file corruption. Shadow copy does not protect against hard disk failure.

11.2.8 Testing Recovery

A key element in your backup strategy should be guidelines for recovery of each system. You should periodically test recovery procedures using a test system. Doing so will help verify that your backup strategy is consistent and that employees understand the steps necessary for recovery. The more familiar those responsible are with recovery procedures, the less likely they are to make a mistake when under the pressure of a real security incident or disaster.

SELF-CHECK

1. Compare full backup, differential backup, and incremental backup.
2. Compare shadow copy and volume shadow copy.

11.3 Designing for Fault Tolerance

With Internet connectivity and global operations, many businesses today require **24×7 availability** (around-the-clock) for at least some of the resources on their network. In addition, some companies offer **Service Level Agreements (SLAs)** that put limits on how long a resource can be unavailable in the event of a security incident, system failure, or even a disaster.

If you manage a network that includes these types of resources, you need to design a **fault tolerant solution** to ensure you can meet the availability requirements. This section begins by discussing the concept of a single point of failure. It then moves on to discuss fault tolerant solutions for data storage. The section concludes with a look at server failover. The purpose of this section is not to make you an expert in designing fault tolerant solutions, but only to introduce you to the terms and concepts.

11.3.1 Eliminating Single Points of Failure

Consider the network in Figure 11-7. What happens if the database server fails? What happens if the domain name system (DNS) server is compromised? How long will it take for business operations to resume? The answer to these questions depends on how long it will take to obtain a computer, install an operating system, install applications, and restore data from backup. What if the database server stores patient medical records for a hospital? Chances are the time to restore the database server will be too long.

The problem with this network is that it has a number of single points of failure. A **single point of failure** is a server, hardware component, or network

Figure 11-7

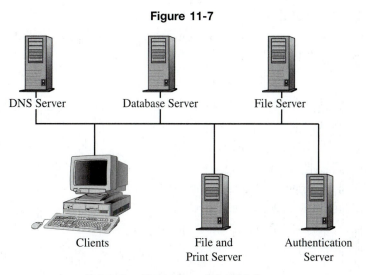

Network with single points of failure.

device that is not **redundant** (duplicated). If something happens to that component, the service it provides will not be available until the component is replaced. In the case of a file server, that might not be a problem. In the case of a domain controller or DNS server, it can prevent users from accessing the network at all.

The first step when designing a fault tolerant solution is to identify the single points of failure on your network. Then you can determine how to mitigate the risk of that system failing or being compromised.

11.3.2 Selecting Fault Tolerant Storage

One of the primary ways companies can improve availability is to invest in a **Redundant Array of Independent Disks (RAID)** solution for servers that require high availability or that contain data that cannot be lost due to drive failure. A RAID solution involves using multiple disks to improve reliability and performance. However, it should not be viewed as a replacement for regular backups. A RAID solution cannot be used to recover from a security incident.

When selecting a RAID solution, you need to choose the following:

▲ RAID level.
▲ Whether to use software or hardware RAID.

Your choices will depend on a number of factors, including availability requirements, performance requirements, capacity requirements, and budget.

We'll look first at the RAID levels and then look at the trade-offs between software and hardware RAID implementations. Finally, we'll look at how storage area networks can provide additional fault tolerance for data storage.

11.3.3 RAID Levels

There are multiple levels of RAID, each offering different levels of protection, performance, and disk capacity. These levels are

▲ RAID 0: disk striping
▲ RAID 1: disk mirroring
▲ RAID 1E: striped mirror
▲ RAID 5: striping with parity
▲ RAID 5EE: hot space
▲ RAID 6: striping with dual parity
▲ RAID 10: striped RAID 1 arrays
▲ RAID 50: striped RAID 5 arrays
▲ RAID 60: striped RAID 6 arrays

Let's take a brief look at how each of these works.

Figure 11-8

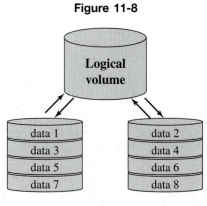

RAID 0.

RAID 0: Disk Striping

RAID 0 (disk striping) is not actually a fault tolerant solution. It is a disk array in which data is striped across multiple hard disks as shown in Figure 11-8. Its main benefit is that it offers better performance because data can be read from and written to multiple disks simultaneously. RAID 0 allows you to use 100% disk capacity for storage.

RAID 1: Disk Mirroring

RAID 1 (disk mirroring) provides fault tolerance by writing all data to two disks, as shown in Figure 11-9. RAID 1 requires exactly two disks. RAID 1 offers excellent read performance and good write performance when both disks are functioning. It can tolerate failure of a single hard disk. During failure and recovery, performance degrades to the level provided by a single disk. The primary disadvantage to RAID 1 is that it allows you to use only 50% of the total disk capacity.

Figure 11-9

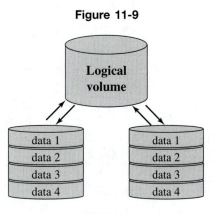

RAID 1.

Figure 11-10

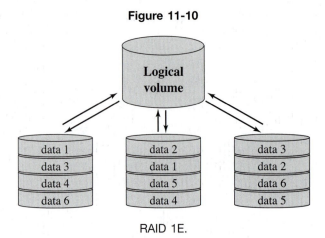

RAID 1E.

RAID 1E: Striped Mirror

RAID 1E (striped mirror) is a combination of RAID 0 and RAID 1. A stripe is written to 1 disk and mirrored to the next disk in the array, as shown in Figure 11-10. Like RAID 1, it can tolerate failure of a single disk and allows you to use only 50% of the total disk capacity. Its primary advantage is that you can include an odd number of disks in the array. You must have at least three disks to implement RAID 1E.

RAID 5: Striping with Parity

RAID 5 (striping with parity) works by striping data across the $n-1$ drives in the array and including a **parity stripe** on the drive that does not include data from that stripe, where n is the number of drives in the array. This is illustrated in Figure 11-11. A parity stripe is calculated from the data using an exclusive or (XOR) function.

Figure 11-11

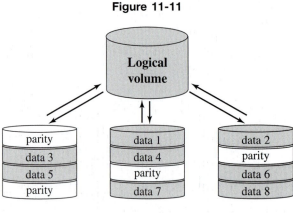

RAID 5.

Figure 11-12

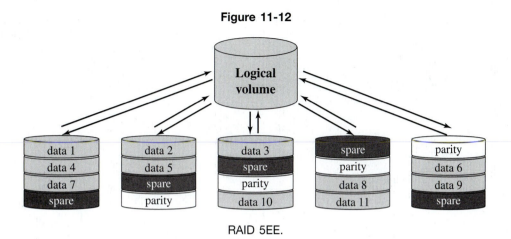

RAID 5EE.

RAID 5 protects against the failure of a single drive. It offers excellent read performance, but the write performance is somewhat degraded because of the calculation of the parity stripe. Performance during disk failure and recovery is also degraded. The primary benefit to a RAID 5 array is disk capacity. Between 67% and 94% of total capacity can be utilized, depending on the number of drives in the array. A RAID 5 array can support between 3 and 16 drives.

Some RAID 5 implementations include a **hot spare**, which is a drive that is automatically added to the array when a disk fails. Using a hot spare can decrease the amount of time the system operates with a failed drive and can decrease the likelihood that a second drive will fail before the stripe set is regenerated. If you have multiple RAID 5 arrays, they can share a single hot spare drive.

RAID 5EE: Hot Space

RAID 5EE (hot space) builds on the idea that many RAID 5 implementations use a hot spare and includes that hot spare as an active drive in the drive array. It does this by writing both a parity stripe and a spare stripe, as shown in Figure 11-12. This makes another disk available for read operations, and can improve read performance by approximately 25%. However, like RAID 5, RAID 5EE can only protect against the failure of a single drive. When using RAID 5EE, you must have between 4 and 16 drives. Available capacity will be between 50% and 88%, depending on the number of drives in the array.

RAID 6: Striping with Dual Parity

RAID 6 (striping with dual parity) is implemented by writing parity stripes to two disks instead of to just one, as shown in Figure 11-13. Its primary advantage is that two hard disk failures can occur without loss of data. Its disadvantage is

Figure 11-13

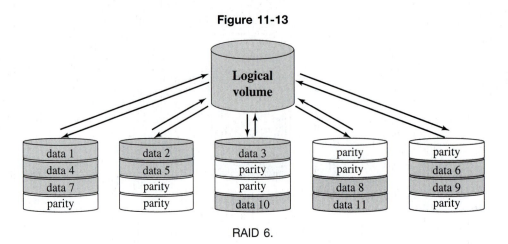

RAID 6.

that capacity is $n-2$ instead of the $n-1$ capacity provided by RAID 5. RAID 6 can be implemented with 4 to 16 disks, with available capacities between 50% and 88%, depending on the number of disks.

RAID 10: Striped RAID 1 Arrays

RAID 10 (striped RAID 1 arrays) works by creating a RAID 0 array from two or more RAID 1 mirror sets, as shown in Figure 11-14. This strategy provides

Figure 11-14

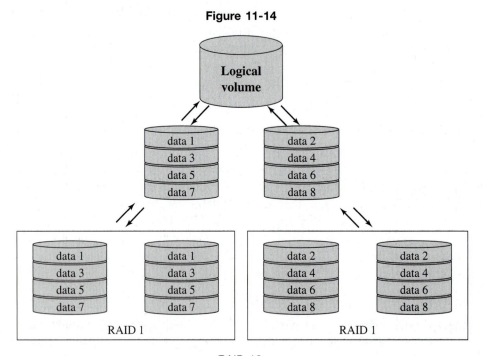

RAID 10.

two benefits: better fault tolerance because it can tolerate failure of one drive in each mirror set, and better performance when a drive fails because data can still be read from and written to multiple drives due to the RAID 0 striping. The primary disadvantage is that only 50% of drive capacity is available for data storage. RAID 10 is sometimes called **RAID 0+1.**

RAID 50: Striped RAID 5 Arrays

RAID 50 (striped RAID 5 arrays) works by creating a RAID 0 stripe set from multiple RAID 5 arrays, as shown in Figure 11-15. It protects against failure of up to one drive in a RAID 5 subarray. It requires at least 6 drives and allows you to use between 67% and 94% of capacity, depending on the number of drives in the subarrays.

RAID 60: Striped RAID 6 Arrays

RAID 60 (striped RAID 6 arrays) works by creating a RAID 0 stripe set from multiple RAID 6 arrays, as shown in Figure 11.16. It protects against failure of up to two disks in each subarray. It requires at least 8 drives and allows you to use between 50% and 88% of capacity, depending on the number of drives in the subarrays.

11.3.4 Choosing Between Hardware and Software RAID

Most current network operating systems, including Windows Server 2003, NetWare®, and Linux, offer at least some levels of software RAID. The primary

Figure 11-15

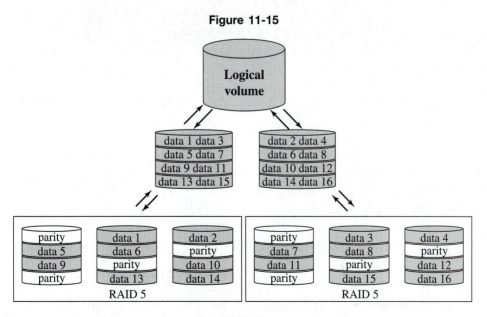

RAID 50.

Figure 11-16

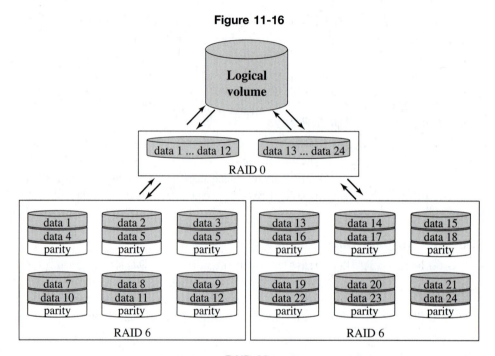

RAID 60.

benefit to using built-in software RAID is that it is included with the operating system so your only cost will be the cost of the disk drives. Operating system RAID can impact performance because the processor must perform RAID calculations. Another drawback is that RAID protection is not offered during the boot process, meaning that the only RAID type supported on an operating system boot volume is RAID 1.

There are four other options that offer better performance and better availability:

1. Hardware-assisted software RAID.
2. Hardware RAID on the motherboard.
3. Hardware RAID on a controller card.
4. A stand-alone disk subsystem.

Let's look at each of these.

Hardware-assisted Software RAID

With **hardware-assisted software RAID,** you install either a **host bus adapter (HBA)** that includes a RAID BIOS chip or a RAID BIOS chip on the motherboard and RAID software on the computer. This option is moderately inexpensive and offers RAID protection during the boot process.

Some of the RAID processing is performed by the RAID chip, but the computer's processor is still involved in the RAID processing. This means that performance is better than operating system RAID, but not as good as a pure hardware option. Another potential problem is that the RAID drivers can be affected by viruses.

Hardware RAID on the Motherboard

Some motherboards include a RAID processor and drive interfaces on board. This is known as **RAID-on-Chip technology**. This configuration is more expensive than hardware-assisted RAID, but offers better protection because it is not vulnerable to viruses and will not lose data during a power loss as write operations in progress are logged in non-volatile storage. It also offers better performance because the RAID processing is off-loaded to the RAID processor.

The primary drawback to hardware RAID on the motherboard is that it is on the motherboard and cannot be migrated to a different computer if the motherboard fails.

Hardware RAID on a Controller Card

The most effective (and most expensive) option is to buy a dedicated RAID controller card. This solution offers all the benefits of RAID-on-Chip, but also can be swapped to a different computer if necessary. Another benefit is that the RAID processing is completely isolated from the rest of the computer, so performance will be optimized.

Stand-alone Disk Subsystem

This solution is an external array of disks that includes a power supply and processing chips. Disk subsystems are available that can attach to a computer, to the network, or through a storage area network (SAN). The performance will be best if attached through a SAN. Let's take a closer look at SANs.

11.3.5 Storage Area Networks (SANs)

So far we have spoken of RAID in terms of **direct attached storage (DAS)**, meaning that the drives are attached directly to a single server. A solution that offers fault tolerance and better scalability than direct attached RAID is a **storage area network (SAN)**. A SAN device is a storage device that is directly attached to the network. Its storage space can be shared by multiple servers. This means that storage can be centralized for management, backup, and better utilization because all servers will have access to the same bank of storage. Figure 11-17 shows a SAN configuration.

Figure 11-17

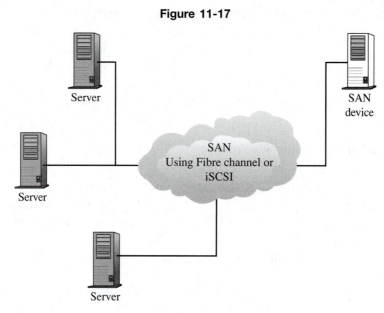

Storage area network (SAN).

A SAN device can connect to the servers using one of two interfaces:

1. **Fibre Channel:** A high-speed infrastructure of switches that can be used to connect the SANs and the servers.
2. **iSCSI:** A connection protocol that utilizes TCP/IP over Ethernet.

Let's look at the benefits and drawbacks of each.

Fibre Channel

A fibre channel is a standards-based high-speed protocol suite that can be implemented over copper wire or fiber optic cable. Storage devices and computers are connected to the network using fibre channel switches. A fibre channel network offers high speed data transfer (up to 4Gbps). Its primary drawback is the requirement for specialized equipment and expertise. Another drawback is that it can only support a range of 10 kilometers (km).

iSCSI

When you connect a SAN device using iSCSI, you are connecting it to your existing Ethernet network. iSCSI supports the SCSI (small computer system interface) protocol over a TCP/IP network. With Gigabit Ethernet, iSCSI can offer up to 1Gbps transmission rates. It is less expensive to implement than fibre channel because it does not require specialized switches or expertise. It transmission distance is limited only by the size of the network.

11.3.6 Designing a Failover Solution

Now that you have determined a strategy for redundant data storage, let's look at how to ensure redundancy for another resource on your network: the servers. Depending on a server's role, you can provide redundancy simply by including multiple servers that perform the same role on the network or you can implement **clustering** to configure **failover** between two or more servers that perform the same role. Clustering is a process by which multiple servers share the same role, host name, and IP address on a network.

An example of the first option is providing multiple domain controllers or DNS servers. Data is synchronized between them using replication or zone transfer. Another example is providing multiple Dynamic Host Configuration Protocol (DHCP) servers. In this case, data is not synchronized between them. Instead, you must configure non-overlapping scopes on each DHCP server. This method of providing redundancy is effective where it can be used because it allows for all servers to share the load between them when all are operational. It can also provide protection against some types of attacks. For example, if one DHCP server is the target of a denial-of-service attack, only that server needs to be taken offline. The other DHCP server can assume its role until the compromised server is replaced. The reason DHCP can automatically failover is that DHCP server discovery is achieved through broadcasts. Domain controllers can be located using SRV records on a DNS server. Clients can be configured with both a primary and a secondary DNS server address, adding automatic fault tolerance.

There are some server roles that cannot provide automatic failover simply by placing an additional server in that role on the network. One reason for this is that clients or applications are configured to access the server using its name or IP address. Consider the example of a database server. The database applications are configured to look for a specific server name on the network. If that server goes down, the application will not be able to automatically start using a different database server. In a server cluster (see Figure 11-18), multiple servers use the same public name and IP address. In actuality, these servers are attached to two networks: one in which they are seen as the same computer and a private network in which they can address each other as individuals.

A server cluster can consist of two types of nodes: active nodes and passive nodes. An **active node** is one that participates in handling service requests. A **passive node** is one that is inactive until a server configured as an active node fails. The number of nodes supported and the configuration supported depend on the operating system. For example, Windows Server 2003 supports up to eight nodes. A server cluster can use direct-attached storage or can connect to storage through a SAN.

Some companies are creating server clusters that span multiple geographic locations to provide failover in the event of a natural disaster or local catastrophe. One thing to keep in mind is that a server cluster will not protect against

Figure 11-18

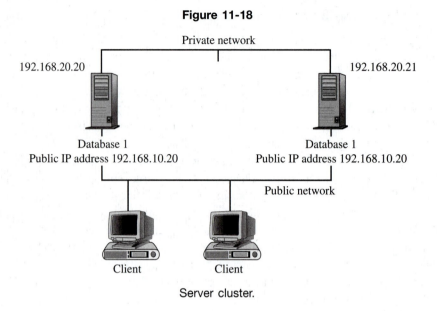

Private network

192.168.20.20   192.168.20.21

Database 1   Database 1
Public IP address 192.168.10.20   Public IP address 192.168.10.20

Public network

Client   Client

Server cluster.

FOR EXAMPLE

Eliminating Single Points of Failure—A Phased Approach

The web applications Busicorp hosts for customers use a database server. All data is currently stored on a single database server. The customer databases are stored on three internal hard disks. Busicorp currently performs a full backup of each database server nightly and transaction log backups hourly. One of the database server's hard disks fails. The customers with data stored on that database were unable to access their data for a four-hour period while the data was being restored. Several customers were very angry.

Busicorp decides it needs to change the configuration so that it can recover more quickly. Currently, there is no additional money in the budget, so it decides to reconfigure the hard disks to use software RAID 5. Fortunately, their system has enough capacity that they can implement RAID 5 without purchasing another hard disk.

As its customer base grows, Busicorp plans to purchase a SAN device that provides at least RAID 5 protection. Busicorp will implement the SAN using iSCSI so that it can utilize their current network infrastructure.

When the customer traffic warrants an additional database server, Busicorp plans to implement an active-active server cluster to allow failover if one of the database servers fails. The server cluster will utilize the SAN.

all types of attacks. In fact, depending on the nature of the attack, all nodes in the cluster might be compromised. Therefore, it is essential to have an offline server that you can quickly use to replace a compromised server if a security incident occurs.

SELF-CHECK

1. Describe the protection offered by each RAID level.
2. Compare fibre channel and iSCSI.
3. Compare an active node and a passive node.

SUMMARY

In this chapter, you learned how to develop plans that will help you recover network functionality in the event of a security incident, natural disaster, hardware failure, or other catastrophe. You examined guidelines for business continuity planning, recovery planning, and security incident response planning. You also learned about the factors you must consider when creating a backup strategy. The chapter concluded with a look at implementing fault tolerance, including disk fault tolerance using RAID, SANs, and server clustering.

KEY TERMS

24×7 availability

Active node

Backup site

Business continuity plan

Business continuity planning committee

Business impact assessment

Checklist review

Clustering

Cold site

Communication procedure

Computer Security Incident Response Plan (CSIRP)

Computer Security Incident Response Team (CSIRT)

Determinate chain of notification

Differential backup

Direct attached storage (DAS)

Disaster recovery plan

Disk mirroring

Disk striping

Evacuation drill

Failover

Fault tolerant solution

Fibre channel

Full backup

Full-interruption test

Full-scale exercise

Functional drill

Ghost

Hardware-assisted software RAID

Host bus adapter (HBA)

Hot site

Hot space

Hot spare

Image

Incremental backup

iSCSI

Mobile backup

Mondoarchive

Multiple centers

Mutual aid agreement

ntbackup

Off-site backup

Parallel test

Parity stripe

Passive node

Qualitative loss criteria

Quantitative loss criteria

RAID 50

RAID 5

RAID 5EE

RAID-on-Chip technology

RAID 1

RAID 1E

RAID 6

RAID 60

RAID 10

RAID 0

RAID 0+1

Recovery team

Redundant

Redundant Array of Independent Disks (RAID)

Rolling backup

Salvage team

Scope and plan initiation phase

Service bureau

Service Level Agreement (SLA)

Shadow copy

Simulation test

Single point of failure

Storage area network (SAN)

Store and forward server

Striped mirror

Striped RAID 5 arrays

Striped RAID 1 arrays

Striped RAID 6 arrays

Striping with dual parity

Striping with parity

Structured walk-through test

System state backup

Tabletop exercise

Tail-log backup

Transactional data

Transaction log

Transaction log backup

Volume shadow copy

Vulnerability assessment

Walk-through drill

Warm site

Windows Backup

ASSESS YOUR UNDERSTANDING

Go to www.wiley.com/college/cole to assess your knowledge of disaster recovery and fault tolerance.

Measure your learning by comparing pre-test and post-test results.

Summary Questions

1. A business impact assessment should be part of a disaster recovery plan. True or False?

2. A business continuity planning committee should include representatives from which of the following?
   (a) senior management and information systems only
   (b) senior management, all functional units, information systems, and security administration
   (c) information systems and security administration only
   (d) senior management and security administration only

3. Which type of backup site can allow you to get critical systems online the fastest if a disaster occurs?
   (a) cold site
   (b) hot site
   (c) warm site

4. Which type of disaster recovery test could result in an actual disaster if not performed correctly?
   (a) full-interruption test
   (b) functional drill
   (c) parallel test
   (d) full-scale exercise

5. A CSIRP is used only in the event of a security incident. True or Fase?

6. Which step should be performed AFTER you isolate the compromised system?
   (a) analyze the incident
   (b) declare the incident
   (c) reformat the compromised system
   (d) prevent reoccurrence of the problem

7. What backup strategy will require you to restore at most two backups during recovery?
   (a) full backup with incremental backups
   (b) full backup with transaction log backups
   (c) full backup with differential backups

8. On a computer running Windows Vista, shadow copy is the only backup necessary. True or False?

9. Which RAID level allows you to recover from the failure of any two disks?

   (a) RAID 10

   (b) RAID 6

   (c) RAID 50

   (d) RAID 5EE

10. An iSCSI SAN can be created using the existing TCP/IP network infrastructure. True or False?

11. A server cluster can only be implemented by servers at the same geographic location. True or false?

Applying This Chapter

1. You have been hired by a company to evaluate their network and procedures and to help them prepare for a security incident or natural disaster. The servers on the company's network are shown in Figure 11-19.

   (a) What information will you need to gather to create a business continuity plan?

   (b) Why is a business impact assessment important?

   (c) When will the disaster recovery plan be used?

Figure 11-19

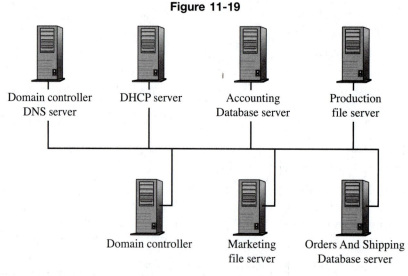

Domain controller   DHCP server   Accounting   Production
DNS server   Database server   file server

Domain controller   Marketing   Orders And Shipping
                     file server   Database server

Servers on the network.

(d) Which type of test would you perform to allow response teams to perform their functions without actually initiating recovery procedures?

(e) How would a person know who to contact if a security incident is suspected?

(f) Why would you isolate a compromised server and replace it with a different server?

(g) What information do you need to gather before you can create a backup policy?

(h) On which servers could you perform a transaction log backup?

(i) Which services represent a single point of failure for network operations?

(j) During the business impact analysis, it is determined that the resource that must be restored the soonest is the OrdersAndShipping database. What is the advantage of implementing a RAID 1 solution?

(k) What is the disadvantage to implementing a RAID 1 solution?

(l) Why are backups still important even if you implement a RAID 1 solution?

(m) You find that disk space on the OrdersAndShipping database server is at 80% utilization, while disk space on the Accounting database server is at 30% utilization. How could a SAN help provide better storage utilization?

(n) What protection would be offered by implementing server clustering on the OrdersAndShipping database server?

(o) How could you eliminate the DNS server as a single point of failure?

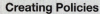
Creating Policies

You learned about several different policies you should create to prepare for the worst. Consider the company where you work and answer these questions:

1. Does your company have a business continuity plan in place?
2. Does your company have a disaster recovery plan in place?
3. Have you ever been involved in a disaster recovery plan test? If so, describe your experience.
4. Does your company have a CSIRP in place?
5. What divisions should be included on your company's CSIRT team?
6. Why is it important to conduct a post-incident evaluation?

Creating a Backup Strategy

FS1 contains files that are critical to business operations. The files change by 20% on a daily basis. Most of these changes affect the same files. The company can afford to lose only 8 hours worth of changes to the files. A full backup takes 2 hours to complete and the same amount of time to restore. The company operates around-the-clock.

The company's current backup plan calls for a full backup every Friday at 8 p.m. and incremental backups every other night at 8 p.m.

1. If the hard disk fails at 7 p.m. on Thursday night, how much data will be lost?
2. How long will the server take to restore?
3. Why would differential backups be a better solution?
4. How could you change the backup plan to meet the company's requirements.
5. What is the best way to allow for fast recovery if the server's processor fails?
6. What type of incident would your solution to step 5 not protect against?

Evaluating RAID Solutions

Consider the following RAID configurations and identify the storage capacity available and the protection offered.

1. Three 20GB hard disks configured in a RAID 5 array.
2. Five 40GB hard disks configured in a RAID 5EE array.
3. Five 20GB hard disks configured in a RAID 6 array.
4. Eight 40GB hard disks configured in a RAID 60 configuration.

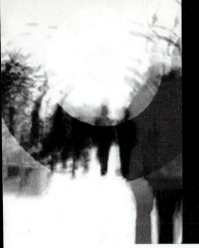

12

INTRUSION DETECTION AND FORENSICS

Starting Point

Go to www.wiley.com/college/cole to assess your knowledge of intrusion detection and forensics.
Determine where you need to concentrate your effort.

What You'll Learn in This Chapter

▲ Intrusion detection systems
▲ Intrusion protection systems
▲ Honeypots
▲ Collection and preservation of evidence

After Studying This Chapter, You'll Be Able To

▲ Describe the role of an intrusion detection system
▲ Describe the role of an intrusion protection system
▲ Describe the role of a honeypot
▲ Explain the importance of proper handling of evidence
▲ List the steps you should take to prepare a drive for a forensics investigation
▲ Identify the types of information you must gather before shutting down the computer
▲ Describe techniques for locating evidence on a hard drive

INTRODUCTION

Even with prevention mechanisms in place, at some point an attack will occur. The more time that elapses between the start of an attack and the time you realize that an intrusion has occurred, the more damage the hacker will do. Therefore, it is essential that you have systems in place to alert you to a possible attack.

In addition, if an attack does occur, you need to be able to analyze how the attack occurred and document evidence of the attack. Only by understanding the nature of the attack can you build defenses against it occurring in the future. Also, if you decide to prosecute the attacker, you will need to preserve a chain of evidence that will be admissible in court.

This chapter looks at mechanisms for detecting an intrusion. Then it examines the purpose of a honeypot. Finally, the chapter looks at some forensics procedures.

12.1 Intrusion Detection

Intrusion detection encompasses a variety of categories and techniques. The primary approaches involve determining if a system has been infected by viruses or other malicious code and applying methods for spotting an intrusion in the network by an attacker. This chapter focuses on detecting an intrusion on the network. To this end, the next sections discuss different types of intrusion detection systems and intrusion protection systems.

12.1.1 Intrusion Detection and Response

Intrusion detection (ID) is the task of monitoring systems for evidence of intrusions or inappropriate usage. The response to a detected intrusion is defined in a Computer Security Incident Response Policy (CSIRP) and includes notifying the appropriate parties, determining the extent of the severity of an incident, and recovering from the incident's effects.

12.1.2 Intrusion Detection Systems

An **intrusion detection system (IDS)** is a system that monitors network traffic or audit logs to determine whether any violations of an organization's security policy have taken place. An IDS can detect intrusions that have circumvented or passed through a firewall or that are occurring within the local area network (LAN) behind the firewall.

Various types of IDSs exist. The most common approaches to ID are statistical anomaly (also known as behavior-based) detection and signature-based (also known as knowledge-based or pattern-matching) detection. Intrusion detection systems that operate on a specific host and detect malicious activity on that host only are called **host-based IDS (HID)**. ID systems that operate on network segments and analyze that segment's traffic are called **network-based IDS (NIDS)**. Because there are pros and cons of each, an effective ID strategy should use a combination of both network- and host-based IDSs. A truly effective IDS will detect common attacks, including distributed attacks, as they occur.

Let's look first at the two approaches to ID. Next we'll examine the difference between host-based and network-based IDSs.

Signature-based IDSs

In a **signature-based IDS** or **knowledge-based IDS**, signatures or attributes that characterize an attack are stored for reference. Then, when data about events is acquired from audit logs or from network packet monitoring, this data is compared with the **attack signature database**. If there is a match, a response is initiated. This is a similar approach to that used by antivirus applications.

This method is more common than using behavior-based IDSs. Signature-based IDSs are characterized by low false alarm rates (or **false positives**) and, generally, are standardized and understandable by security personnel.

A weakness of the signature-based IDS approach is the failure to characterize slow attacks that extend over a long period of time. To identify these types of attacks, large amounts of information must be held for extended time periods. Another issue with signature-based IDSs is that it can only detect an intrusion if its attack signature is stored in the database. Additional disadvantages of signature-based IDSs include the following:

▲ The IDS is resource-intensive. The knowledge database continually needs maintenance and updating with new vulnerabilities and environments to remain accurate.

▲ Because knowledge about attacks is very focused (dependent on the operating system, version, platform, and application), new, unique, or original attacks often go unnoticed.

Statistical Anomaly-based IDSs

Statistical anomaly IDSs or **behavior-based IDSs** dynamically compare usage patterns with learned patterns of "normal" user behavior and trigger an alarm when a deviation occurs.

With this method, an IDS acquires data and defines a "normal" usage profile for the network or host that is being monitored. This characterization is accomplished by taking statistical samples of the system over a period of normal use. Typical characterization information used to establish a normal profile includes memory usage, CPU utilization, and network packet types. With this approach, new attacks can be detected because they produce abnormal system statistics. The advantages of a behavior-based IDS include the following:

▲ The system can dynamically adapt to new, unique, or original vulnerabilities.
▲ A behavior-based IDS is not as dependent upon specific operating systems as a knowledge-based IDS.
▲ The system can help detect abuse-of-privileges types of attacks that do not actually involve exploiting any security vulnerability.

Some disadvantages of a statistical anomaly IDS are that it will not detect an attack that does not significantly change the system-operating characteristics, and it might falsely detect a nonattack event that caused a momentary anomaly in the system. Also, behavior-based IDSs are characterized by the following:

▲ High false alarm rates. High false positives are the most common failure of behavior-based ID systems and can create data noise that can make the system unusable or difficult to use.
▲ Activity and behavior of the users of a networked system might not be consistent enough to effectively implement a behavior-based ID system.
▲ The network might experience an attack at the same time the intrusion detection system is learning the behavior.

Network-based IDSs

Network-based IDSs (NIDSs) reside on a discrete network segment and monitor the traffic on that segment. They are usually implemented as a network appliance with a network interface card (NIC) that is operating in **promiscuous mode** (a mode in which it can see all other packets on the network) and is intercepting and analyzing the network packets in real time.

A network-based IDS involves looking at the packets on the network as they pass by a sensor. The sensor can only see the packets that happen to be carried on that particular network segment. Network traffic on other segments and traffic on other communication media (such as phone lines) can't be monitored properly by a network-based IDS.

Packets are identified to be of interest if they match a signature. Three primary types of signatures are as follows:

1. **String signatures**: String signatures look for a text string that indicates a possible attack.
2. **Port signatures**: Port signatures watch for connection attempts to well-known, frequently attacked ports.
3. **Header condition signatures**: Header condition signatures watch for dangerous or illogical combinations in packet headers.

An NIDS usually provides reliable, real-time information without consuming network or host resources. An NIDS is passive when acquiring data and reviewing packets and headers. It can also detect denial-of-service (DoS) attacks. One problem with an NIDS system is that it will not detect attacks against a host made by an intruder who is logged in at the host's terminal.

Implementing an NIDS in a switched environment poses challenges. This issue arises from the basic differences between standard hubs and switches. Hubs exclude only the port the packet came in on and echo every packet to every port on the hub. Therefore, in networks employing only hubs, NIDS sensors can be placed almost anywhere in the infrastructure. However, when a packet comes into a switch, a temporary connection in the switch is first made to the destination port, and then the packets are forwarded. This means more care must be exerted when placing IDS sensors in a switched environment to ensure the sensor is able to see all of the network traffic.

Some switches permit spanning port configuration, which configures the switch to behave like a hub only for a specific port. The switch can be configured to span the data from a specific port to the IDS port. Unfortunately, some switches cannot be guaranteed to pass all the traffic to the spanned port, and most switches only allow one port to be spanned at a time.

Another option is to use an inline NIDS. An inline NIDS acts like a bridge between a router and a switch or between two switches, as shown in Figure 12-1. The network adapter used to perform monitoring is generally not assigned an IP address so that it cannot be the direct recipient of traffic. Most NIDSs will include a separate network adapter as a management interface.

Host-based IDSs

Host-based IDSs (HIDS) use small programs (**intelligent agents**) that reside on a host computer. They monitor the operating system detecting inappropriate activity, writing to log files, and triggering alarms. Host-based systems look for activity only on the host computer; they do not monitor the entire network segment.

Figure 12-1

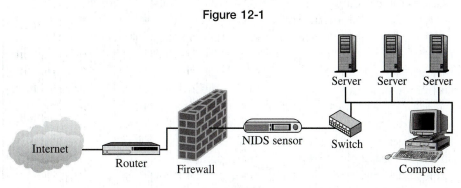

Inline NIDS.

An HIDS can review the system and event logs to detect an attack on the host and to determine whether the attack was successful. Detection capabilities of an HIDS are limited by the incompleteness of most audit log capabilities. In particular, HIDSs have the following characteristics:

▲ They monitor access and changes to critical system files and changes in user privileges.
▲ They detect trusted insider attacks better than an NIDS.
▲ They are relatively effective at detecting attacks from the outside.
▲ They can be configured to look at all network packets, connection attempts, or login attempts to the monitored machine, including dial-in attempts or other non–network-related communication ports.

12.1.3 IDS Issues

Many issues limit the effective use of an IDS. These include the following:

▲ The use of more complex, subtle, and new attack scenarios.
▲ The use of encrypted messages to transport malicious information.
▲ The need to interoperate and correlate data across infrastructures with diverse technologies and policies.
▲ Ever-increasing network traffic.
▲ Attacks on the IDSs themselves.

FOR EXAMPLE

The IDS that Cried Wolf

An IDS is only useful if someone monitors the logs. However, if the logs include a large number of false positives, the job can be tedious and actual attempts at an attack can be missed. Many signature-based sensors are configured with all signatures enabled. Although this might be appropriate in some environments, consider the case where you are running an application that generates traffic similar to one of the signatures. A large number of entries are added to the log file. The administrator responsible for reviewing the log file soon tires of looking at false positives and stops reviewing the log. An attack occurs and the IDS logs the traffic as suspicious. Unfortunately, because of all the false positives, no one reviews the log and the attack goes unnoticed until customers complain that they can't access the application server.

▲ Unacceptably high levels of false positives and false negatives, making it difficult to determine true positives.

▲ The lack of objective IDS evaluation and test information.

▲ The fact that most computing infrastructures are not designed to operate securely.

An issue with the implementation of intrusion detection systems is the performance of the IDS when the network bandwidth begins to reach saturation levels. Obviously, there is a limit to the number of packets that a network intrusion detection sensor can accurately analyze in any given time period. The higher the network traffic level and the more complex the analysis, the more the IDS might experience high error rates, such as prematurely discarding copied network packets.

12.1.4 Intrusion Prevention Systems (IPS)

An **intrusion prevention system (IPS)** is similar to an IDS, except that it not only detects and logs suspected intrusion attempts, it also attempts to prevent them. An IPS can be host-based or network-based. It can use attack signatures or anomalies as the basis for blocking traffic. One potential drawback to an IPS is that false positives will prevent legitimate network traffic.

SELF-CHECK

1. Compare a signature-based IDS with an anomaly-based IDS.
2. Compare an NID and an HID.

12.2 Honeypots

A different approach to intrusion detection and response is the use of a honeypot. A **honeypot** is a monitored decoy mechanism that is used to entice a hacker away from valuable network resources and provide an early indication of an attack. It also provides for detailed examination of an attacker's methods during and following a honeypot exploitation.

Honeypots can be employed for either research or production purposes. In the research mode, a honeypot collects information on new and emerging threats, attack trends, and motivations, and, essentially, characterizes the attacker community. When applied on a production network, honeypots are used for preventing attacks, detecting attacks, and responding to attacks.

12.2.1 Preventing, Detecting, and Responding to Attacks

Honeypots are effective in preventing attacks by doing the following:

▲ Slowing or impeding port scanning by detecting scanning activity.

▲ Consuming an attacker's energy through interaction with a honeypot, while the attack is detected, analyzed, and handled.

▲ Deterring an attack by a cracker who suspects that a network employs honeypots and is concerned about getting caught.

Honeypots provide a way to detect an attack that is taking place or has occurred. Honeypots have the following advantages in detecting attacks:

▲ The ability to capture new and unknown attacks.

▲ Reduction in the amount of data that has to be analyzed by capturing only attack information.

Responding to an attack on a production network is challenging and not always effective. There are constraints that hamper the response process, such as not being able to take a critical application offline to analyze the attack and having to sort through myriads of IDS data.

Honeypots offer solutions to these problems because a honeypot does not perform a business-related function and can be taken offline to analyze data and prepare a response. Secondly, because they do not handle legitimate user traffic, honeypots generate small amounts of data that are the direct result of an attack, so the data can be reviewed more efficiently and a response can be implemented in a shorter time period.

One way to use a honeypot is to position it on your internal network, as shown in Figure 12-2. When a honeypot is located on the internal network, it

Figure 12-2

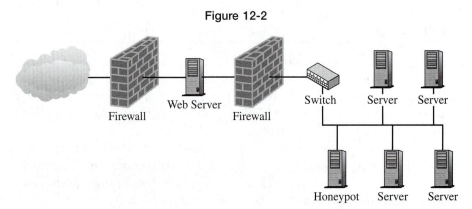

Honeypot on the internal network.

can log traffic that warns of malicious software running on the network, such as a worm. Attack traffic logged on a honeypot located on the internal network might also indicate that your perimeter defenses are insufficient.

Another configuration is to place the honeypot on the perimeter network, as shown in Figure 12-3. This strategy allows you to examine the types of attacks that can breach the firewall between the Internet and your perimeter network and can give you forewarning about attacks that might target your resources on your internal network as well. The less protected the honeypot is, the more information you will gather. However, consider that some of the information will not be useful if you already have defenses set up to protect against those types of attacks. Therefore, in a production environment, you would not be likely to put a honeypot directly on the Internet.

12.2.2 Honeypot Categories

In general, there are two types of honeypots: low-interaction honeypots and high-interaction honeypots. In this context, **interaction** refers to the level of activity provided by the honeypot to the attacker.

Low-interaction Honeypots

A **low-interaction honeypot** supports a limited emulation of an operating system and system services. Thus, an attacker's actions are limited by the low level of emulation that the honeypot provides. An obvious advantage of this type of honeypot is its lack of complexity and ease of deployment.

Because the honeypot has minimal capabilities, it also reduces the risk of an attacker compromising the honeypot to launch an attack on other network

Figure 12-3

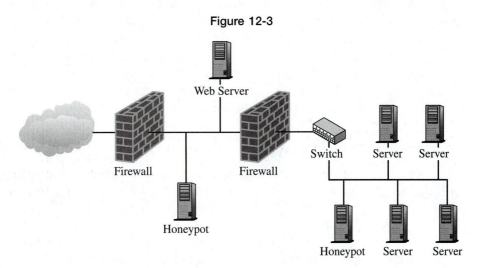

Honeypot on the perimeter network.

resources. However, the simplicity of a low-interaction honeypot is its primary weakness, in that its limited interaction makes it easier for an attacker to determine that he or she is engaged with a honeypot.

An example of a low-interaction honeypot is **Honeyd**. Honeyd is an open-source honeypot developed by Niels Provos. Honeyd 0.8 was released under the **GNU General Public License (GNU GPL)** in January of 2004. Honeyd updates are available regularly, with version 1.5 released in August of 2006. Honeyd is a daemon that can run on Unix®, Linux, and Windows® operating systems. You can configure it to simulate a specific operating system and to emulate common services, including Hypertext Transfer Protocol (HTTP) and File Transfer Protocol (FTP). Honeyd operates in the following fashion:

1. It monitors connection attempts to **unused IP space** (unassigned addresses in the subnet).
2. It checks connections to TCP and UDP ports.
3. It intercepts connections and pretends to be a system service or operating system.
4. It logs attacker's interaction with the service or operating system emulated by the honeypot.
5. It captures information such as passwords, command instructions, and attack targets.

High-interaction Honeypots

High-interaction honeypots are more complex than low-interaction honeypots in that they provide for more complex interactions with attackers by incorporating actual operating systems and services. This type of honeypot can capture a large amount of information about an attacker and his or her behavior. But, because it runs actual operating systems and services, a high-interaction honeypot is susceptible to compromise and being used as a base to launch an attack against other network components. Also, a high-interaction honeypot requires additional resources for deployment and maintenance. An example of this type of honeypot is the Symantec™ Decoy Server.

12.2.3 When to Use a Honeypot

As discussed earlier in this chapter, a honeypot is used in either a research or production mode. The research type of honeypot has high levels of interaction with an attacker and performs the following functions:

▲ Through a honeynet, it captures information on the behaviors, intentions, characteristics, and identities of attackers. A **honeynet** is a controlled network of high-interaction honeypots that are intended to be targets of attacks.

▲ It provides information on the activities of specific organizations and associated threats.

▲ It gathers data on attacks occurring globally (distributed research honeypots).

A production honeypot is designed to emulate an actual operating system and services on a computer system for the express purposes of identifying vulnerabilities and acquiring information that can be used to detect and apprehend attackers. Specifically, a production honeypot can do the following:

▲ Determine how an attacker gained access to the network.

▲ Monitor the attack in real time.

▲ Indicate that an attack is occurring.

▲ Isolate the attacker from the remainder of the network.

▲ Acquire information about the attacker.

12.2.4 Legal Considerations

Deploying a honeypot requires careful consideration of the legal issues involved with monitoring, gathering information on, and prosecuting an individual based on the use of a honeypot. Some of the legal concerns are as follows:

▲ The liability of your organization if your honeypot is used to attack another organization's network.

▲ Privacy rights of individuals being monitored on your network.

▲ The possibility that an attacker apprehended through the use of a honeypot will claim entrapment.

▲ Relevant laws of different jurisdictions outside of the United States.

FOR EXAMPLE

Honeynet Project

The **Honeynet Project** was established in 1999 as a network security research activity using honeynets and honeypots to explore and discover an attacker's behaviors, motives, tools, and approaches, and to apply the lessons acquired from this effort. During the first two years, the Honeynet research group was limited to 30 members. In 2002, the Honeynet Research Alliance was formed to include a larger number of contributors, including researchers from India, Mexico, Greece, Brazil, and Ireland. The team members volunteer their time and contribute hardware and software to the project. More information about the Honeynet Project is available at www.honeynet.org.

Deployment and use of honeypots without an understanding of the national, state, and local laws can lead to civil and criminal penalties for violating an individual's privacy rights through illegal monitoring of his or her activities. For example, evidence obtained by an agent of the U.S. government or a private individual acting at the behest of an agent of the U.S. government can be in violation of the Fourth Amendment of the U.S. Constitution. A private individual who is not acting as an agent of the U.S. government is not bound by the Fourth Amendment and can deploy a honeypot. However, that individual is still bound by state and federal privacy laws that might be applicable to monitoring a person's communications.

Another legal consideration is the 1968 Federal Wiretap Act, which is sometimes referred to as Title III. This Act was expanded in 1986 and establishes procedures for court authorization of real-time surveillance of electronic communications. The types of activities for which wiretaps can be authorized were increased by the United States Patriot Act.

SELF-CHECK

1. Describe the role of a honeypot.
2. What are the legal issues involved with using a honeypot?

12.3 Forensics

When an intrusion occurs, your first thought will probably be how to keep the critical business processes running. However, when dealing with an attack that might require criminal prosecution, you need to take a step back and think about the evidence you will need to prosecute and how you can obtain it so that it is admissible in court. To do this, you need to know about forensics.

Forensics is the science of gathering and preserving evidence. This section will not make you an expert in forensics. A detailed discussion of forensic practices would require a book of its own. Instead, this section introduces some key concepts that will help you secure the evidence you need—or at least not damage it before the forensic expert your company hires arrives.

12.3.1 Understanding Evidence

Evidence is information presented in court that attempts to prove a crime was committed. When your network or a computer on your network is attacked, evidence can take several forms. For example, evidence might include the following:

▲ A hardware device, such as a computer, router, or hard drive. This type of evidence is known as **physical evidence** or **real evidence**.

▲ Log files.

▲ Files on a hard disk.

▲ Captures of a computer's state.

▲ Database files.

Data retrieved from a computer that provide documentation of what occurred is known as **documentary evidence**. Guidelines for the types of evidence you should collect are available in **RFC 3227**.

One of the challenges you will face is that computer data is easy to modify. Therefore, you need to be sure you can prove that the evidence was not planted on the computer. You need to take the necessary precautions when handling compromised computers to avoid making the data inadmissible in court. These precautions include the following:

▲ Preventing bits on the hard disk from being changed.

▲ Avoiding environmental or power-related damage to the physical device.

Evidence should be stored in a secure location to protect it from tampering. Another critical step you must take is to create a **chain of custody** for each item that might be considered evidence. A chain of custody provides detailed documentation of every action performed on a piece of evidence, including the date and time the item was removed from storage, the person performing the action, a detailed description of the action, and the date and time the item was returned to storage.

12.3.2 Gathering Evidence on a Live System

Depending on the nature of the attack, you might need to document the current state of the system. Some information about what is happening on a computer is lost when you shut down (or unplug) the computer. This information is known as **volatile data**. Information you might need to gather from a live system include the following:

▲ Listening ports

▲ Network connections

▲ Running applications

When gathering this information, you will want to be extremely careful not to modify the system or write the data to the hard disk. One way to gather data is to write it to a USB drive. Special forensics tools are available for gathering data. A discussion of specific tools is beyond the scope of this chapter. However, certain operating system utilities can be used to gather important information— we'll look at those.

Viewing Information about Listening Ports and Network Connections

You can view information about listening ports and established network connections by using the Netstat –a command-line utility. It displays the protocol; the local address, including the port; the foreign address, including the port; and whether the connection is listening or established. An example of running Netstat –a is shown in Figure 12-4.

To save the output to a file instead of displaying it on the screen, you would execute the following:

```
Netstat -a > path
```

For example, to save the output to a file named “netstat.txt” on the USB drive referenced by E:, you would run

```
Netstat -a >e:\netstat.txt
```

Figure 12-4

```
Command Prompt - netstat -a
Microsoft Windows [Version 5.2.3790]
(C) Copyright 1985-2003 Microsoft Corp.

J:\Documents and Settings\Administrator>netstat -a

Active Connections

  Proto  Local Address          Foreign Address        State
  TCP    server1:ftp            server1.busicorp.com:0  LISTENING
  TCP    server1:domain         server1.busicorp.com:0  LISTENING
  TCP    server1:http           server1.busicorp.com:0  LISTENING
  TCP    server1:kerberos       server1.busicorp.com:0  LISTENING
  TCP    server1:epmap          server1.busicorp.com:0  LISTENING
  TCP    server1:ldap           server1.busicorp.com:0  LISTENING
  TCP    server1:microsoft-ds   server1.busicorp.com:0  LISTENING
  TCP    server1:kpasswd        server1.busicorp.com:0  LISTENING
  TCP    server1:593            server1.busicorp.com:0  LISTENING
  TCP    server1:ldaps          server1.busicorp.com:0  LISTENING
  TCP    server1:1024           server1.busicorp.com:0  LISTENING
  TCP    server1:1025           server1.busicorp.com:0  LISTENING
  TCP    server1:1027           server1.busicorp.com:0  LISTENING
  TCP    server1:1038           server1.busicorp.com:0  LISTENING
  TCP    server1:1041           server1.busicorp.com:0  LISTENING
  TCP    server1:1050           server1.busicorp.com:0  LISTENING
  TCP    server1:pptp           server1.busicorp.com:0  LISTENING
  TCP    server1:3268           server1.busicorp.com:0  LISTENING
  TCP    server1:3269           server1.busicorp.com:0  LISTENING
  TCP    server1:5900           server1.busicorp.com:0  LISTENING
  TCP    server1:ldap           server1.busicorp.com:1032  ESTABLISHED
  TCP    server1:ldap           server1.busicorp.com:1033  ESTABLISHED
  TCP    server1:ldap           server1.busicorp.com:1034  ESTABLISHED
  TCP    server1:ldap           server1.busicorp.com:1046  ESTABLISHED
  TCP    server1:1032           server1.busicorp.com:ldap  ESTABLISHED
  TCP    server1:1033           server1.busicorp.com:ldap  ESTABLISHED
  TCP    server1:1034           server1.busicorp.com:ldap  ESTABLISHED
  TCP    server1:1046           server1.busicorp.com:ldap  ESTABLISHED
  TCP    server1:epmap          server1.busicorp.com:2395  ESTABLISHED
  TCP    server1:epmap          server1.busicorp.com:2400  ESTABLISHED
  TCP    server1:netbios-ssn    server1.busicorp.com:0  LISTENING
  TCP    server1:ldap           server1.busicorp.com:1043  ESTABLISHED
  TCP    server1:ldap           server1.busicorp.com:2397  TIME_WAIT
  TCP    server1:ldap           server1.busicorp.com:2398  TIME_WAIT
  TCP    server1:ldap           server1.busicorp.com:2399  TIME_WAIT
  TCP    server1:ldap           192.168.10.10:1064     ESTABLISHED
  TCP    server1:ldap           192.168.10.10:1070     ESTABLISHED
  TCP    server1:ldap           192.168.10.10:1085     ESTABLISHED
  TCP    server1:ldap           192.168.10.10:1089     ESTABLISHED
```

Netstat -a.

Viewing Information about Running Applications

You should also save information about the applications running on the computer. On a Windows computer, **Task Manager** allows you to view the processes running on the computer, as shown in Figure 12-5. However, it does not allow you to save the data to a file. Another drawback is that Task Manager lists several instances of **svchost.exe**. That is because a number of services run under the context of the svchost.exe application. These services could include malware.

The **tasklist** command-line utility allows you to output a list of processes running on the computer. Use the /svc option to identify each service running within a process, as shown in Figure 12-6.

As with Netstat, you can use the > operator to cause the output to be stored to disk. For example, to save the output to a file named "tasklist.txt" on drive E, you would execute

```
Tasklist /svc >e:\tasklist.txt
```

Figure 12-5

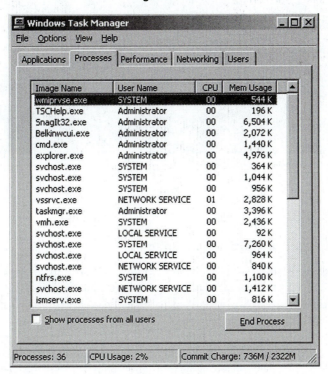

Task Manager.

Figure 12-6

```
cx  Command Prompt                                                       _|□|x|

J:\Documents and Settings\Administrator>tasklist /svc

Image Name                    PID Services
============================= ======== =========================================
System Idle Process              0 N/A
System                           4 N/A
smss.exe                       588 N/A
csrss.exe                      716 N/A
winlogon.exe                   768 N/A
services.exe                   820 Eventlog, PlugPlay
lsass.exe                      832 HTTPFilter, kdc, Netlogon, PolicyAgent,
                                   ProtectedStorage, SamSs
svchost.exe                    996 DcomLaunch
svchost.exe                   1208 RpcSs
svchost.exe                   1292 Dhcp, Dnscache
svchost.exe                   1328 LmHosts, W32Time
svchost.exe                   1340 AeLookupSvc, AudioSrv, Browser, CryptSvc,
                                   dmserver, EventSystem, helpsvc,
                                   lanmanserver, lanmanworkstation, Netman,
                                   Nla, RasMan, RemoteAccess, Schedule,
                                   seclogon, SENS, ShellHWDetection, winmgmt,
                                   wuauserv, WZCSVC
spoolsv.exe                    480 Spooler
msdtc.exe                      512 MSDTC
acs.exe                        620 ACS
dfssvc.exe                     668 Dfs
dns.exe                        704 DNS
svchost.exe                    952 ERSvc
inetinfo.exe                  1144 IISADMIN, MSFtpsvc
ismserv.exe                   1160 IsmServ
ntfrs.exe                     1252 NtFrs
svchost.exe                   1616 RemoteRegistry
vmh.exe                       1652 vmh
vssrvc.exe                    1808 Virtual Server
svchost.exe                   1852 W3SVC
svchost.exe                   2208 TermService
svchost.exe                   2224 TapiSrv
wmiprvse.exe                  3620 N/A
explorer.exe                  2864 N/A
Belkinwcui.exe                2972 N/A
SnagIt32.exe                  2996 N/A
TSCHelp.exe                   3080 N/A
wuauclt.exe                    212 N/A
iexplore.exe                   456 N/A
cmd.exe                       2956 N/A
tasklist.exe                  2676 N/A
wmiprvse.exe                   360 N/A

J:\Documents and Settings\Administrator>
```

Tasklist /svc.

12.3.3 Preparing a Hard Drive Image

If you are going to present any portion of the contents of a hard disk as evidence in a trial, you will need to be able to prove that the data on the hard disk was not modified. To do so, you need to take the following steps before examining a hard drive's contents:

1. Create a checksum or Message-Digest algorithm 5 (MD5) hash of the drive. You will use this hash to compare against a disk image you create to ensure that the data has not been changed.

2. Create a bitstream image of the drive. A **bitstream image** copies each bit on the drive exactly, meaning that the checksum or MD5 hash of the image will be identical to that of the drive. You need special tools to create a bitstream image.

3. Create a checksum or MD5 hash of the image. You will periodically create a new hash of the image to verify that nothing has changed. If at any point the checksums do not match, you will need to repeat steps 2 and 3 before proceeding.

One way to ensure that you don't change the image inadvertently is to use a **write blocker**. You can purchase software write blockers or hardware write blockers. In either case, they work by preventing write operations from occurring.

Another point to keep in mind is that the destination disk for the image must be **sanitized**. Sanitizing a disk is more than just deleting the data from it or formatting it. You must ensure that there are no remnants left of the data it previously contained. The United States Department of Defense guidelines for sanitizing a disk are to write a specific value to each byte on the first pass and write its **complement value** on the second pass. For example, "00001111" would be written on the first pass and "11110000" would be written on the second pass.

A number of different tools are available that allow you to prepare a hard drive image. When you select a tool, you need to verify that it has been validated for use in forensics. If it hasn't been, the defense might be able to use that fact to invalidate your evidence. The National Institute of Standards and Technology (NIST) tests forensic tools and publishes the results of those tests on its website. You should investigate the forensic tools you plan to use to make sure they are accepted by the governing bodies in the locales where you are planning to present the evidence in court. If a tool has been used in other cases and you have documentation to that effect, it is more likely to be accepted as credible by the judge and jury.

FOR EXAMPLE

Choosing the Right Tool for the Right Job

Although Symantec's Ghost™ is a popular tool among network administrators, it is not the right tool for creating a disk image to be used for a forensic investigation. Ghost does not perform a bitstream copy of the disk. Therefore, when you try to compare hash values, they are likely to be different. Make sure the tool you use to create the image is forensically sound. One popular tool is the **dd utility** included with many Linux and Unix distributions. A Windows version is also available. Some tools, such as **WinHex** by X-Ways Forensics, can be used to sanitize the destination disk, create the hash, and make the bitstream copy.

12.3.4 Searching for Data on a Hard Drive

After you have created a bitstream image of the drive, you can mount the image using a write blocker and begin to search for data. You should use a write blocker to ensure that you do not modify the data on the image, which would require you to create a new image because the checksum would have changed. In this section, we'll look at some of the standard places you can find data using operating system features. These include the following:

▲ Log files

▲ Hidden files

▲ Temporary Internet files

▲ Temporary application files

▲ Deleted files

▲ Email

The specific examples we give will be mostly Windows examples. However, the same basic concepts apply regardless of the operating system the compromised computer is running.

Log Files

Operating systems store information about events in log files, as do some applications and services. A good place to start looking for information about the potential attack is to examine the log files on the computer. The Windows Security log, shown in Figure 12-7, shows security events that have occurred, provided the

Figure 12-7

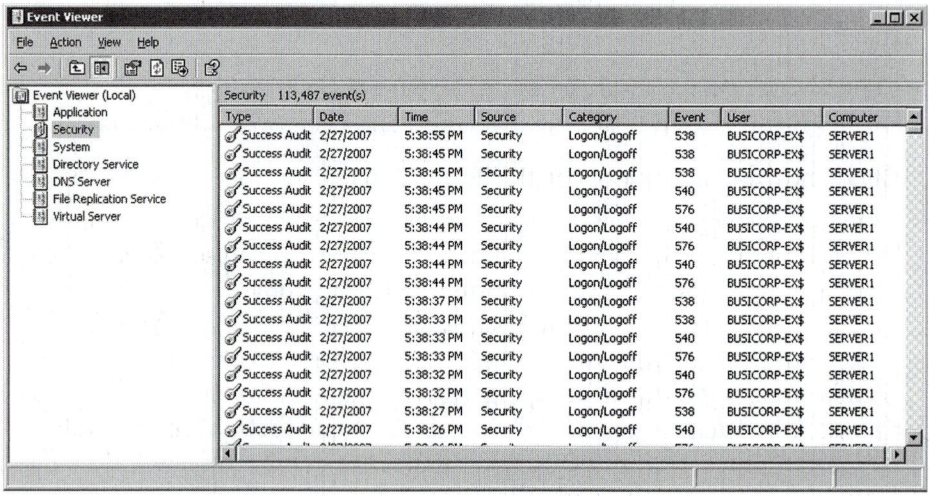

Security log.

system is configured to log those events. Other log files can be viewed through Event Viewer. The Application log is a log file used by a number of applications. Also, some applications create their own log files; one example is DNS Server.

Other applications create log files that cannot be read by Event Viewer. Consult the application's documentation for information about where to locate these log files. You might also check the directory where the application is installed.

Hidden Files

Users might try to hide their tracks by hiding malicious files. They might do so by changing the name or file extension of a file so that it looks like something benign. Or they might set the **Hidden attribute** on a Windows file or folder, as shown in Figure 12-8.

A more advanced tactic might be to also set the System attribute on a file. By default, Windows does not display files with the System attribute set to

Figure 12-8

Hidden attribute.

Figure 12-9

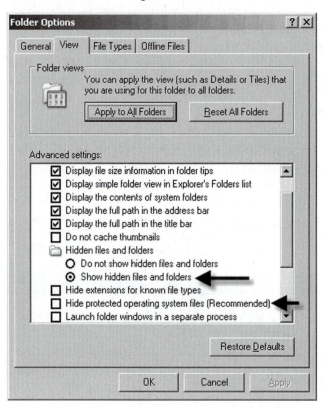

Showing hidden and system files.

"True." You can change this behavior and cause Windows to display hidden files through Folder Options, as shown in Figure 12-9:

On a computer running Linux or Unix, you can create a hidden directory by using three periods (...) as the first three characters of the filename. You can create a hidden file by starting the filename with a period. To view hidden files on a Unix or Linux computer, execute

```
ls -a
```

Temporary Internet Files

Another possible place to look, especially when examining a computer from which you suspect an attack was launched, or if you suspect an employee is downloading harmful content, is the **Temporary Internet Files** cache. A number of websites download temporary files to a user's hard disk to allow a web page to load more quickly on subsequent requests or to maintain data between requests using cookies. Figure 12-10 shows some temporary files stored by Internet Explorer®.

Figure 12-10

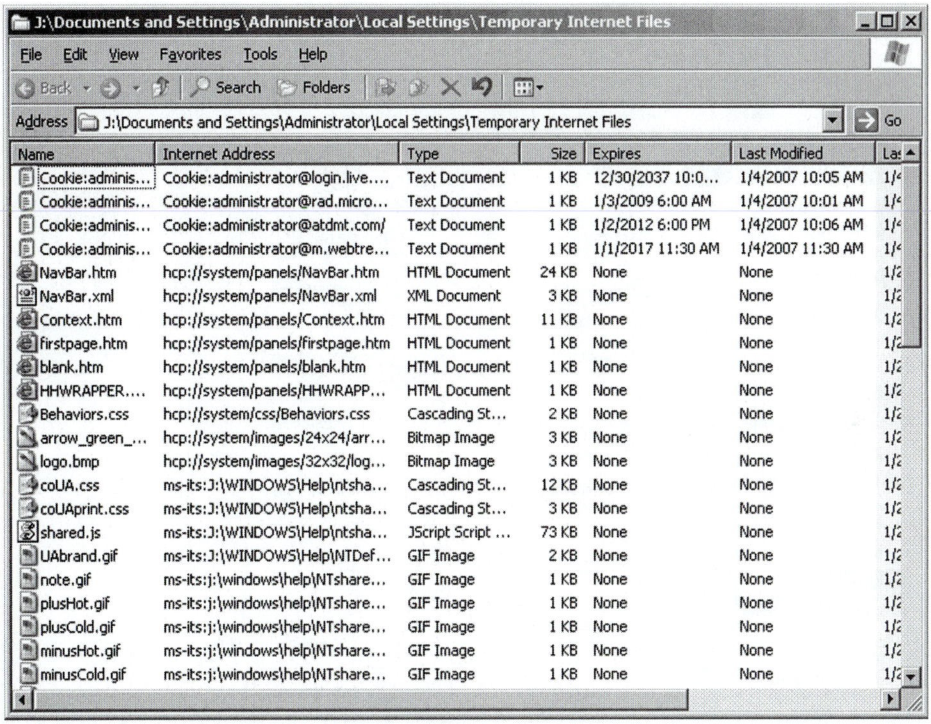

Temporary Internet Files.

The path to the temporary files will be different depending on the browser. For example, Internet Explorer stores temporary files at My Documents\Local Settings\Temporary Internet Files.

Temporary Files

Another type of **temporary file** is that created by some applications, such as Word processing applications. Although applications sometimes delete the temporary files they create, some do not. These files might contain valuable information. On a Windows computer, the first character in a temporary file name is a tilde (~). Figure 12-11 shows some temporary files left behind by Microsoft® Word while writing this book.

Deleted Files

When a user deletes a file, is it gone? The answer is no. On a Windows computer, a deleted file will be moved to the **Recycle Bin**, as shown in Figure 12-12.

Figure 12-11

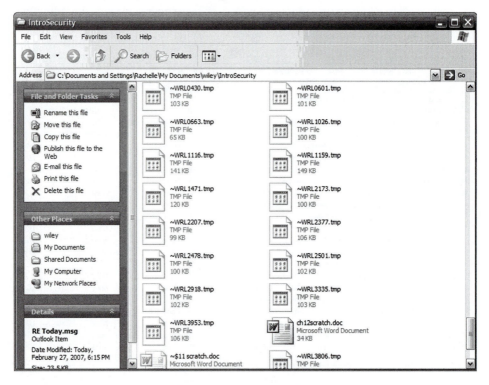

Temporary application files.

Figure 12-12

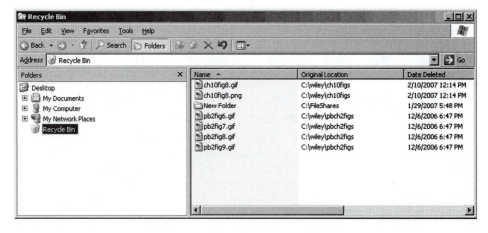

Recycle Bin.

Figure 12-13

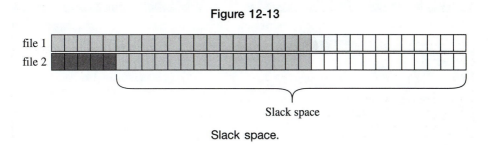

Slack space.

However, even when the Recycle Bin is emptied, deleted files (or remnants of them) still remain on the hard disk. This is because a file is written to the hard disk in clusters. When a file is deleted, the first character of the filename is changed to "0xE5" (hexadecimal E5), and the area of the hard disk where that file was stored becomes available. Until those bits of the hard disk are over-written with other data, some (or all) of the file contents will be available. Some-times a file will not take an entire cluster. If this is the case, the remnants left behind by the previous file will still be on the disk. For example, suppose you have a file that is 20 KB and a cluster is 32 KB. When the 20 KB file is deleted, its contents are left behind on the disk. Now suppose the next file created at that location is only 5 KB. The leftover area in the cluster will still contain 15 KB of the data from the previous file (see Figure 12-13). The data left over in the cluster is known as **slack space** and can be analyzed by some forensics and data recovery applications, such as the forensics version of WinHex by X-Ways Software Technology.

Email

If the attack was based on malware distributed through email, a spam attack, or a phishing attack, you might want to gather information through email. You might also be able to use email as evidence if the attacker is an employee. One thing to keep in mind is that an email has a header that allows you to view its path from its source to its destination. Figure 12-14 shows the **email header** displayed using Microsoft Outlook® 2003.

Hidden Shares

Another thing to look for as evidence of an attack is a **hidden share** planted by the attacker. You can use the net share command, as shown in Figure 12-15 to view all shares, including hidden shares on a Windows System. A hidden share is one with a "$" appended to the share name. A hidden share does not show up when browsing shares in My Network Places.

Figure 12-14

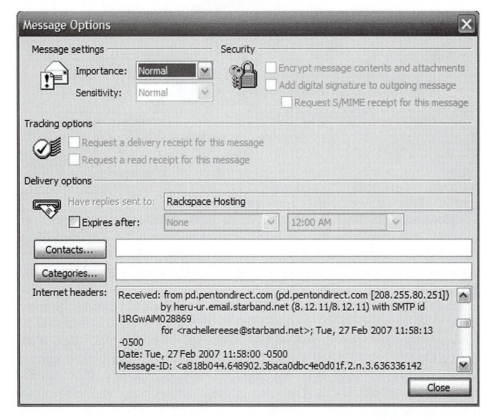

Email header.

Figure 12-15

Hidden shares.

FOR EXAMPLE

Forensically Speaking

Although some information can be gathered using operating system tools, if you want to be sure your evidence is forensically sound, you'll need to obtain forensics tools and use them to protect the hard disk, create the image, and gather data. Some tools, such as **The Sleuth Kit** are freely downloadable. The Sleuth Kit is a command-line utility available for Unix, Linux, Mac® OS X, and Windows. On a Unix, Linux, or Mac OS X system, it utilizes the **Autopsy Forensic Browser**, which is a free graphical user interface.

Some companies have some free tools and some that are available for purchase. For example X-Ways Software Technology offers WinHex as a free download and **X-Ways Forensics** for purchase. Although you can download a free trial of X-Ways Forensics, its features are limited.

Part of your security planning should be researching the forensics tools available and creating your own forensics tool kit. That way, you'll be ready if you need it.

SELF-CHECK

1. Describe a chain of custody.
2. Identify the steps you should take to ensure a disk examination is forensically sound.
3. Why must you gather some evidence before shutting down the computer?
4. Describe slack space.

SUMMARY

In this chapter you learned about ways to handle an attack when it occurs. We began with a discussion of intrusion detection systems, including a description of how they work and the difference between an NIDS and an HIDS. You also learned that an intrusion prevention system is an IDS that can automatically take steps to prevent an attack. From there we moved on to discuss honeypots. You learned that a honeypot is another way to detect a potential attack and that it allows you to better analyze the nature of the attack. Finally, we discussed forensics. You learned the importance of taking precautions when gathering evidence and the steps to take to prepare a hard disk for a forensic investigation. You also learned some of the things to look for during an investigation.

KEY TERMS

Attack signature database

Autopsy Forensic Browser

Behavior-based IDS

Bitstream image

Chain of custody

Complement value

dd utility

Documentary evidence

Email header

Evidence

False positive

Forensics

GNU General Public License (GNU GPL)

Header condition signature

Hidden attribute

Hidden share

High-interaction honeypot

Honeyd

Honeynet

Honeynet Project

Honeypot

Host-based IDS (HIDS)

Intelligent agent

Interaction

Intrusion detection (ID)

Intrusion detection system (IDS)

Intrusion prevention system (IPS)

Knowledge-based IDS

Low-interaction honeypot

Network-based IDS (NIDS)

Physical evidence

Port signature

Promiscuous mode

Real evidence

Recycle Bin

RFC 3227

Sanitized

Signature-based IDS

Slack space

Statistical anomaly IDS

String signature

svchost.exe

Task Manager

Tasklist

Temporary file

Temporary Internet files

The Sleuth Kit

Unused IP space

Volatile data

WinHex

Write blocker

X-Ways Forensics

ASSESS YOUR UNDERSTANDING

Go to www.wiley.com/college/cole to assess your knowledge of intrusion detection and forensics.

Measure your learning by comparing pre-test and post-test results.

Summary Questions

1. A knowledge-based IDS must have its attack database kept up-to-date. True or False?

2. What type of IDS acts like a bridge?
   (a) HIDS
   (b) NIDS
   (c) inline NIDS

3. What type of device can be used as a decoy to distract attackers from accessing legitimate resources?
   (a) HIDS
   (b) honeypot
   (c) NIDS
   (d) IPS

4. Evidence collected from files on a computer is known as real evidence. True or False?

5. What type of data must be collected before shutting down a compromised computer?
   (a) a list of the processes running on the computer
   (b) a list of files in the Recycle Bin
   (c) the files in the Temporary Internet Files cache
   (d) any temporary application files

6. Which of the following steps should you take after creating an image of a disk, but before beginning your investigation of the disk's contents?
   (a) Create an MD5 hash of the disk.
   (b) Create an MD5 hash of the image.
   (c) View a list of processes running on the computer.
   (d) Install a forensics tool kit on the disk.

7. What tool can you use to view information about open network connections?
   (a) dd utility
   (b) Ghost
   (c) Netstat
   (d) Tasklist

8. A Windows file is permanently deleted when you empty the Recycle Bin. True or False?

9. Which of the following Linux directories would be hidden?

   (a) &hideme

   (b) nothere

   (c) $gone

   (d) ...hidn

10. Which of the following Windows files is a temporary application file?

   (a) ~goingaway

   (b) ^gonebutnotforgotten

   (c) ...solong

   (d) $byenow

Applying This Chapter

1. Busicorp has asked you to recommend a strategy for detecting possible attacks on the network. Busicorp has hired a two-person security team. Part of their jobs will be to watch for signs that indicate an attack. Busicorp's development team builds web applications for customers and deploys them on a perimeter network. Each application will have a different network access pattern. One of Busicorp's concerns is that a detection system will trigger false alarms when a new customer application is deployed.

   (a) What type of intrusion detection will you recommend? Explain why.

   (b) What would be the maintenance concern for this type of IDS?

   (c) Would you recommend the use of a honeypot? If so, where would you position it?

2. You are a security consultant who has been called in to investigate an attack against a company's client database. The company is most likely going to try to prosecute the attacker if his or her identity can be discovered.

   (a) Describe the importance of maintaining a chain of custody for all evidence.

   (b) What precautions will you take before attempting to find evidence on the hard disk?

   (c) When you arrive at the site, you find the customer has already shut down the system. What evidence have you lost?

   (d) List some areas you might check to determine whether there is a rootkit or other malicious software hidden on the computer.

   (e) One of the compromised computers is a Linux web server. How would you check for hidden files?

YOU TRY IT

Detecting and Analyzing Intrusions

An intrusion detection strategy is only valuable if someone looks at the logs of suspicious activity. A honeypot's value is also dependent on someone reviewing the information it provides. Think about the systems described in this chapter and consider how you could make reviewing the data easier. Describe some "best practices" for each of the following systems:

▲ Signature-based IDS
▲ Statistical anomaly IDS
▲ Honeypot

Always Be Prepared

Probably the most important guideline in recovering from an attack is to be prepared to do so. Consider the forensics procedures we have discussed so far.

1. Describe how being prepared can help you prevent damaging the admissibility of evidence or the evidence itself?
2. Discuss why a bitstream image of each hard disk you examine is essential.
3. Describe what is meant by volatile data.
4. Why is it important to investigate data recovery and disk imaging tools before you use them in an investigation?

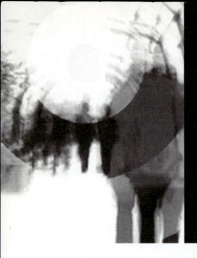

GLOSSARY

%systemroot%   An environmental variable that stores the path to the folder where Windows® is installed (usually C:\Windows).

.NET Passport authentication   See Windows Live™ authentication

/etc/group file   A file on a Unix® or Linux computer that stores a list of groups.

/etc/passwd file   A file on a Unix or Linux computer in which user accounts are stored.

/etc/profile file   A file on a Unix or Linux computer that stores information about the actions to take when a user logs in.

24x7 availability   The requirement for a resource to be available seven days a week, twenty four hours a day.

3DES   A symmetric encryption algorithm that applies the DES algorithm three times for a key length of 168 bits. Stands for Triple DES.

802.11a   A wireless networking standard that operates at 54Mbps, but only has a short range.

802.11b   A wireless networking standard that supports speeds of up to 11Mbps and uses the same part of the radio spectrum as 802.11g.

802.11g   A wireless networking standard that supports speeds of up to 54Mbps and uses the same part of the radio spectrum as 802.11b.

802.11i   A wireless security protocol that incorporates TKIP, 802.1x, and Advanced Encryption Standard (AES).

802.1Q   A specification that defines the standard tagging protocol most widely used on VLANs.

802.1x   A wireless security standard that requires TKIP for data integrity and EAP-TLS or PEAP for authentication. 802.1x requires a RADIUS server.

A record   See Host record.

Acceptability   A criterion for evaluating a biometric system that considers privacy, invasiveness, and psychological and physical comfort when using the system.

Access client   The TACACS term for a person or device that dials in to an ISP.

Access token   An object that contains information about a user who is logged on, including the user SID and any group membership SIDs.

Account Operators   An Active Directory built-in Domain Local group whose members can manage user and group accounts on a domain controller.

Accountability   Audit information must be selectively kept and protected so that actions affecting security can be traced to the responsible party.

acct command   A command that records all executed commands on a Linux or Unix® system.

accton command   A Linux or Unix command that can be used to enable accounting.

ACE   A part of a DACL or SACL that identifies a user or group, a type of access, and whether access is granted or denied. Stands for access control entry.

ACK message   A packet used to acknowledge the receipt of a packet with a specific sequence number. Stands for acknowledgement message.

ACL (DAC)   A table that lists the access level each subject should have to an object. Stands for access control list.

ACL (Windows)   A list of security protections that apply to an object or to one or more object properties. Stands for access control list.

Active Directory®   The directory system used by Windows 2000 and Windows Server 2003.

Active Directory Application Mode (ADAM)   A technology that allows encrypted directory data to be transmitted to a server on the perimeter network, such as the Edge Transport server role in Microsoft® Exchange 2007.

Active Directory client extensions   Software that can be installed on legacy Windows operating systems to allow them to use NTLMv2 as the authentication protocol.

Active Directory database   The storage location for domain security principals and other domain objects in a Windows 2000 or Windows Server 2003 domain.

Active Directory forest   One or more domains that trust each other and share the same forest root domain.

Active Directory–Integrated (ADI) zone   A zone that is stored in the Active Directory® database and can be replicated between domain controllers.

Active node   A cluster node that handles service requests.

Active Server Pages (ASP)   Microsoft®'s server-side programming technology that allows you to write scripts that are interpreted by the server.

ActiveX   A technology developed by Microsoft for creating reusable content that can be distributed over the Internet or through an application installation.

ActiveX control   A user-interface element that is created using ActiveX® and embedded in a web page. An ActiveX control must be downloaded to the client.

Ad hoc mode   A peer-to-peer communication mode for a wireless network. Ad hoc mode does not utilize a wireless access point.

Add-on   See Plug-in.

Address Resolution Protocol (ARP) spoofing tool   A tool that intercepts and modifies email packets at some point in their transmission path in order to launch a man-in-the-middle attack.

Administrative shares   See Hidden shares.

Administrators   An Active Directory built-in Domain Local group whose members have full control over any computer in the domain.

Adware   A type of malware that displays targeted or random ads, either in pop-up windows or on web pages.

AES   A symmetric encryption algorithm that has three key sizes: 128, 192, and 256 bits. AES has been approved by the National Security Agency for protecting confidential U.S. government data. Stands for Advanced Encryption Standard.

AH   A component of IPsec that provides integrity and authentication, but does not provide confidentiality. Stands for Authentication Header.

AirSnort   A product that can be used to break WEP encryption.

Algorithm   A series of steps that define how to perform a task.

Analysis paralysis   A phenomenon that occurs when you keep breaking attack tree subgoals into smaller and smaller units, basically overanalyzing the problem.

Anonymous access   A method of access that does not require authentication. Instead, a specific user account is always used as the security context, regardless of the user's identity.

Anonymous FTP   A site running File Transfer Protocol (FTP) that does not require authentication. Users log on using *anonymous* as the username and their email address as the password.

Anti-malware   A program that combines the features of an anti-spyware and antivirus program to scan for and remove any type of malware it is configured to detect.

Anti-spyware   A program that scans for and removes spyware from a computer.

Antivirus   A program that scans for and removes viruses, worms, and Trojan horses.

Application layer (OSI model)   The layer of the OSI model that provides services such as email, file transfers, and file servers.

Application layer (TCP/IP model)   Equivalent to the Application, Presentation, and Session layers of the OSI model.

Application proxy firewall   A Layer 7 firewall that uses a proxy to substitute for a service. The proxy forwards user requests to the service and responses to the user. A proxy isolates the user from the actual service.

Appropriate use policy   A set of security rules employees will be expected to follow.

ARP   A protocol that maps IP network addresses to the hardware MAC addresses used by a data link protocol. The ARP protocol functions as a portion of the interface between the OSI network and data link layers. Stands for Address Resolution Protocol.

ARP spoof attack   An type of man-in-the-middle attack in which an attacker gets between two hosts in the email transmission path.

AS   A Kerberos service that is responsible for authenticating a user or computer and responding with a session key. Stands for authentication service.

ASCII   An encoding standard used by Unix, DOS, and Windows operating systems. Stands for American Standard Code for Information Interchange.

ASP   A Session layer protocol used to set up a session between an ASP server application and an ASP workstation application or process. Stands for AppleTalk® Session Protocol.

ASP.NET   Microsoft's latest server-side programming technology that allows you to create compiled server-side applications based on the .NET Framework.

Asymmetric encryption   An encryption method that requires two keys: a private key and a public key.

Attack script   A script that automates a specific type of attack, making it easy for a script kiddie to launch an attack without knowledge of the vulnerability.

Attack signature database   The repository of attack signatures in a signature-based IDS.

Attack tree   A hierarchical diagram that illustrates how an attack might occur.

Audit   A onetime or periodic event to evaluate security.

Audit log   See Audit trail.

Audit trail   A log of events that provides a history of occurrences in an IT system. Also referred to as an audit log or an event log.

Auditing   An ongoing process that examines the system or user activities and writes events to an audit log. Also referred to as monitoring.

Authentication   The property that the proposed source of the data can be verified to be true; the process of verifying an identity (for example, a user).

Authentication data   A variable number of 32-bit words containing an integrity check value (ICV) computed over the ESP packet, but not including the Authentication data field.

Authentication protocol   A set of rules that define how the credentials are stored on the authentication server and passed between the client and the server.

Authenticator   A Kerberos object that is presented to a server to prove that the security principal requesting access is the one that was granted the ticket. An authentication includes a timestamp to prevent replay attacks.

Authorization   The process of determining the resources the user can access once authenticated.

Authorizing entity   A person who grants or denies permission to access an object when operating under discretionary access control.

Automatic Updates   The Windows® operating system component that allows the Windows Update website or another update server to be checked for updates on a schedule.

Autopsy Forensic Browser   A graphical user interface that works with The Sleuth Kit. Only available for Linux, Unix®, and Mac® OS X.

Autorun macro   A script that runs when a Microsoft Office document is opened.

Availability   Prevention of unauthorized withholding of information or resources.

Back-to-back configuration   A perimeter network configuration in which a screened subnet is placed between two firewalls. One firewall filters traffic between the Internet and the screened subnet. The other firewall filters traffic between the screened subnet and the internal network.

Backdoor   An application installed on a computer to allow an attacker to circumvent security measures on the system.

Backup Operators   An Active Directory built-in Domain Local group whose members can run backup and restore operations.

Backup site   A location where you can restore critical services to maintain business operations during a disaster.

Baseline template   A security template that contains settings relevant to all member servers and that is linked high in the OU hierarchy.

Basic authentication   An IIS authentication method that sends credentials as clear text, but works with most browsers.

Bastion host   A host that allows other computers on the network to access the Internet. A bastion host has two network adapters: one on the Internet and one on the internal network.

Behavior-based IDS   See Statistical anomaly IDS.

BIND   A popular DNS implementation. Stands for Berkeley Internet Name Domain.

BIND name server   A type of DNS server that runs on Unix® or Linux.

Biometrics   An automated means of identifying or authenticating the identity of a living person based on physiological or behavioral characteristics.

Bitstream image   A bit-by-bit copy of a disk so that the hash of the source drive and the hash of the image are identical.

Blacklist   A database of known domain names or IP addresses used by spammers.

Block cipher   A symmetric encryption algorithm in which a message is broken into blocks before being encrypted.

Blum-Blum-Shub pseudorandom generator   A pseudorandom number generator that is considered secure because cracking it requires factoring large numbers.

Boot sector virus   A virus that infects the boot sector of a floppy and that is transmitted to a hard drive boot sector when the user starts the computer using the floppy.

BootP   A protocol that provides a diskless workstation with its IP address based on its MAC address.

Border security   The process of adding perimeter defenses, such as firewalls, between network segments.

Break the stack   A condition in which data entered into a string variable exceeds the size of the string buffer and puts malicious commands on the stack to be executed.

Broadcast domain   The grouping of computers that receive all packets sent to a specific segment. A router or a switch can be used to segment a network into multiple broadcast domains.

Broadcast packet   A packet that is sent to all computers on a segment.

Browser parasite   A program that changes browser settings or adds features, such as toolbar buttons to a browser, in order to perform a malicious act.

Brute force attack   An attack in which software tries different combinations of letters, numbers, and symbols until a match to the password is found.

Brute force methods   The process of enumerating through all possible keys until the proper key is found.

Buffer overflow attack   An attack which exploits a program by entering data that exceeds the amount of memory allocated to a variable to cause malicious commands to be put on the execution stack.

Business continuity plan   A plan that allows a company to recover from a catastrophic or disruptive event.

Business continuity planning committee   A group made up of members of senior management, functional business units, information systems, and security administration. Responsible for creating the business continuity plan.

Business impact assessment   The second step in creating a business continuity plan. It is the process in which you evaluate the impact of a disruptive event in terms of financial and operational costs.

CA   The entity responsible for issuing, validating, and managing certificates. Stands for certificate authority.

Callback   A dial-up server security measure that requires the remote access server to call the client back. When used with a predefined number, it provides security at the expense of flexibility.

CAPolicy.inf file   A file that is used to publish the CPS to subordinate CAs.

CBC   A block encryption mode in which the cipher text of the previous block is XORed with the next block of plain text before being encrypted. A modification to the plain text will propagate to all subsequent blocks. A change in the cipher text will corrupt the block in which the change was made and invert the bit in the next block. Stands for cipher-block chaining.

CER   A biometric system characteristic that reports the percent in which the FRR equals the FAR. Stands for crossover error rate

Certificate   See X.509 certificate and CA.

Certificate path   See Chain of trust.

Certificate policy   The policy that defines how certificates are issued and managed.

Certificate request   The document that contains the public key of the requestor, along with identifying information. A certificate request is sent to a CA for validation.

Certificate template   A template used by Microsoft® Certificate Services on Windows Server 2003 for generating certificates for specific applications.

CFB   A block encryption mode in which the previous cipher-text-block result is XORed with the results of encrypting the current block. If a bit in the cipher text is changed, the block in which the change occurs will have that bit inverted, and the subsequent block will be corrupted. Stands for cipher feedback.

Chain of custody   A detailed tracking of each action performed on a piece of evidence, including the date and time it was taken out of storage, the person who checked it out, a detailed description of what was done with it while it was checked out, and the date and time it was returned to storage.

Chain of trust   The validation path for a CA hierarchy. In a chain of trust, if the client computer trusts the root CA, it implicitly trusts the CAs validated by the root CA or any of its subordinates.

Challenge Handshake Authentication Protocol (CHAP)   An industry standard remote access authentication protocol that transmits passwords using one-way hash, but requires passwords to be stored using reversible encryption.

Challenge-and-response   A method of requesting credentials from a user in which the server sends a challenge and the client appends the password to the challenge and hashes it before sending it to the server.

Change control   See Configuration management.

ChangeCipherSpec message   A message in an SSL session that indicates that subsequent records should be protected with the new cipher suite and keys.

CHAP   An authentication protocol used to validate remote access users. It requires passwords to be stored as reversibly encrypted. Stands for Challenge-Handshake Authentication Protocol.

Chargen   A service that returns a random string of characters. It operates on port 19.

Checklist review   A disaster recovery plan test in which business units review the plan.

chgrp command   A Unix command used to change the group associated with a file.

chmod command   A Unix command used to change the permissions of a file.

chown command   A Unix command used to change the owner of a file.

CIA   The acronym used to refer to the three main goals of cryptography: confidentiality, integrity, and authentication.

Cipher spec   The cryptographic parameters agreed upon for an SSL session.

Cipher text   Data in its encrypted, unreadable form.

Clearance   A level of authorization used in MAC to determine access.

Client certificate   A digital certificate requested by and issued to a computer that acts as a client in a session.

ClientHello message   A message sent by a client to begin negotiation for an SSL conversation.

Clipping level   A baseline value for an activity, set on a firewall or intrusion detection system to identify a normal level for that type of activity.

Clustering   A technology that allows automatic failover between two or more servers.

Code Red 2   A variant of the Code Red worm.

Code Red worm   A worm that attacks Internet Information Services (IIS) using a buffer overflow error in Index Server.

Cold site   A backup site that is a computer operations room without computers or a network infrastructure installed.

Common Gateway Interface (CGI)   The original solution for creating a server-side web component.

Communication procedure   See Determinate chain of notification.

Compiled   Converted from human-readable source code to binary machine language.

Complement value   The reverse of a binary value. In a complement each 1 becomes a 0 and each 0 becomes a 1. For example, the complement of "01" is "10."

Computationally secure   The amount of time needed to compute all possible combinations is so large that it cannot be done in any reasonable amount of time.

Computer security   Implementing measures to secure a single computer.

Computer Security Incident Response Plan (CSIRP)   A procedure that should be followed if a security incident occurs.

Computer Security Incident Response Team (CSIRT)   The team responsible for creating the CSIRP.

Confidentiality   Prevention of unauthorized disclosure of information; the property that only the parties that should be able to obtain information are able to obtain it.

Configuration auditing   The quality assurance aspect of configuration management that verifies that all configuration management policies are enforced and that the accounting information is consistent and complete.

Configuration control   A means of ensuring that all system changes are approved before they are implemented and that implementation is complete and accurate.

Configuration identification   The process of decomposing a system into discrete configuration items.

Configuration item (CI)   An identifiable, understandable, manageable, and trackable unit for which configuration must be managed.

Configuration management   The process of tracking and approving changes to a system. Also referred to as change control.

Configuration status accounting   The documentation of configuration control activities.

Connection-oriented protocol   A type of transmission protocol that guarantees the delivery of packets and that the packets will be delivered in the same order as they were sent.

Connectionless protocol   A type of transmission protocol that transmits packets on a best effort basis—delivery is not guaranteed.

Cookie   An ASCII file that is downloaded from a website to a browser. It is usually used to maintain state information or to store a user's logon credentials.

Countermeasures   Actions to mitigate the risks of attacks against networks.

CPS   A document that describes how CAs are managed in the organization. Stands for Certificate Practice Statement.

Crackers   Programs used by attackers to launch dictionary attacks on passwords and other sensitive authentication information present on internal networks.

Credentials   Proof that the user is who he or she claims to be.

CRHF   A hash function that is resistant to hash collisions. Stands for Collision Resistant Hash Function.

CRL   A list of certificates that are not valid because they have been revoked. Stands for certificate revocation list.

Cross-certification   A process that allows certificates issued by a CA from one organization to be trusted by another organization.

Cryptanalysis   The process of analyzing a cryptographic algorithm to discover how it can be cracked.

Cryptanalyst   A person who analyzes and cracks cryptographic algorithms.

Cryptographic primitives   The four key areas of cryptography: random number generation, symmetric encryption, asymmetric encryption, and hash functions.

Cryptography   The science of developing algorithms for encrypting data.

Custom role   A SQL Server role created and managed by a user.

Custom template   A security template that you define. A custom template can be based on a predefined template or created from scratch.

Cyclic redundancy check (CRC)   A file verification technique that involves calculating the file size and dividing by a predetermined number to obtain the remainder. The remainder is then compared to the remainder of a future calculation.

DAC   An access control model in which an authorizing entity grants or denies permission to access an object. Access control is at the discretion of the object's owner. Stands for discretionary access control.

DACL   The part of the security descriptor that grants or denies specific users and groups access to the object. Stands for discretionary access control list.

Data encapsulation   The process of attaching a header at each layer to the data being sent across the network.

Data integrity   The state that exists when computerized data is the same as that in the source documents and when it has not been exposed to accidental or malicious alteration or destruction.

Data Link layer   The layer of the OSI model that provides error checking and transfer or message frames.

dbcreator role   A SQL Server fixed server role that grants members permission to create databases.

db_backupoperator role   A SQL Server fixed database role that grants its members permission to back up a database.

db_securityadmin role   A SQL Server fixed database role that grants its members permission to create custom database roles, manage their permissions, and manage their memberships.

dcomcnfg   A Windows tool for configuring DCOM.

dd utility   An open source utility that can be used to make a bitstream copy of a disk. Included with most Linux and Unix distributions. A Windows® version is also available.

Defense-in-depth   The security strategy in which multiple controls are implemented to offer multiple layers of protection instead of relying on a single control.

Denial-of-service attack   An attack that prevents a server from performing its normal job.

Depth   The point at which a pseudorandom number generator will cycle.

DES   A symmetric key encryption algorithm that uses a key length of 56 bits. Stands for Data Encryption Standard.

Determinate chain of notification   A description of how information should flow to people who might be affected by a security incident. Also referred to as communication procedure.

DHCP scope   A range of IP addresses to assign to DHCP clients.

DHCPINFORM message   A DHCP message sent by Windows® 2000 and Windows Server 2003 DHCP servers to verify that it is authorized with the domain controller.

Dictionary attack   An attack in which all the words in the dictionary are tried until a match with the password is found.

Differential backup   A backup that backs up all data that has changed since the last full backup. Only the full backup and most recent differential backup need to be restored.

Diffie-Hellman key exchange   A key agreement protocol in which both parties agree on a prime number and a base, then select secret numbers independently.

Digest   The fixed-size message generated by a hash function.

Digest authentication   An IIS authentication method that authenticates users using Active Directory. Although credentials are sent across the network as a hash, they must be stored as using reversible encryption on the domain controller. Digest authentication does not require Internet Explorer®.

Digital certificate   See X.509 certificate.

Digital signature   A method of providing authentication by encrypting a message or its digest with a private key.

Direct attached storage (DAS)   One or more hard disks attached directly to a computer.

Disaster recovery plan   The set of actions that should be taken to prepare for and recover from a natural disaster or other catastrophic event.

Discrete logarithm problem   The mathematic problem of calculating the discrete logarithm. In order for the Diffie-Hellman key exchange algorithm to be broken, there must be an efficient algorithm to solve the discrete logarithm problem.

Disk mirroring   See RAID 1.

Disk striping   See RAID 0.

Distributed Component Object Model (DCOM)   A Windows programming interface for accessing an application running on a different computer using RPCs.

Distributed denial-of-service (DDoS) attack   An attack in which Trojan horse code on zombie computers launches an attack against a target, overwhelming the target and making it difficult to track down the source of the attack.

Distributed File System (DFS)   Service that manages the Windows Server feature and that allows multiple file shares to be represented as a single logical volume.

DMZ   A noncritical, somewhat secure region located between a private internal network and a public network, such as the Internet. Stands for demilitarized zone.

DNS   A distributed database system that matches host names to IP addresses and vice versa. Stands for domain name system.

DNS cache   A location on a DNS server that contains information retrieved from queries to other DNS servers.

DNS namespace   The name of the domain, represented as a fully-qualified domain name. For example, busicorp.com or corp.busicorp.com.

DNSUpdateProxy group   A Windows group to which DHCP servers are assigned to prevent them from owning the records they register in DNS.

Documentary evidence   Evidence that provides documentation of what occurred. It can include files and other data collected from a computer.

Documentation control   The process of ensuring that all configuration documentation is complete and up-to-date.

Domain   A security boundary in a Windows NT® 4.0 client/server network or an Active Directory network.

Domain Admins   An Active Directory Global group that is a member of the Administrators group.

Domain Computers   An Active Directory Global group in which all computers that have been joined to the domain are members.

Domain controller   A server in a domain that stores credentials and authenticates security principals based on their domain account.

Domain Controller Baseline Policy (DCBP)   A GPO that contains the baseline security settings for the domain controllers in an organization and that is linked to the Domain Controllers OU.

Domain Controllers   An Active Directory Global group in which all domain controllers for the domain are members.

Domain Guests   An Active Directory Global group that is a member of the Guests group.

Domain Local group   An Active Directory group that can be used in native mode or mixed mode. Permissions are generally assigned to Domain Local groups.

Domain Name System (DNS) server   A server responsible for resolving host names to IP addresses.

Domain Users   An Active Directory group in which all users in the domain are members. It is a member of the Users group.

DoS attack   See Denial-of-service attack.

DREAD methodology   A qualitative risk analysis scheme that helps you assign ratings for assets, vulnerabilities, and threats.

Drop-off Directory   A writable area of an anonymous FTP server.

DSA   A standard that defines an algorithm for generating digital signatures. Stands for Digital Signature Algorithm.

Dumps memory   Writes the contents of memory to a file.

Dynamic DNS updates   See Dynamic updates.

Dynamic Host Configuration Protocol (DHCP) server   A server responsible for automatically assigning TCP/IP configuration settings.

Dynamic updates   A feature of some DNS servers that allows clients to automatically create and update their DNS records.

EBCDIC   A legacy character encoding standard originally developed for IBM servers. Stands for Extended Binary Coded Decimal Interchange Code.

ECB   A block encryption method in which each block is encrypted independently. It does not provide integrity because a change to the cipher text in one block only invalidates that block. Stands for electronic code book.

Echo   A TCP/IP utility that echoes a string back to the display. It operates on port 7.

Edge Transport   A Microsoft Exchange server role that acts as a mail proxy by residing in the perimeter network and checking incoming mail for viruses, attachments, and spam.

Effective NTFS permissions   The permission that determines whether a user's access attempt will be granted. Effective permissions consider group membership, inherited permissions, and explicit permissions.

EFS   The feature of the NTFS file system on a Windows 2000, Windows XP, or Windows Server 2003 system that provides file encryption. Stands for Encrypting File System.

Elevation of privilege   An attack in which a user gains more privileges on a computer system than he or she is entitled to.

Email header   A part of an email message that includes the source address of the sender and all hops along the path to the recipient.

Email replay attack   An attack in which the packet or packets associated with an email are intercepted and played back to the destination mail server.

Emergency Management Services (EMS)   Windows Server 2003 out-of-band management tools.

Encapsulating   Wrapping a datagram inside headers and trailers to allow it to be transmitted over a network medium that does not normally accept that type of packet.

Enigma   A cryptography machine invented by the Germans in World War II. It used the speed of rotors to generate the keys.

Enrollment strategy   The process of requesting and installing certificates for users, computers, and services.

Enrollment time   The time that it takes to initially register with a system by providing samples of the biometric characteristic to be evaluated.

Enterprise CA   A CA that is integrated with Active Directory.

ESP   An IPsec component that provides confidentiality, authentication, integrity, some replay protection, and limited traffic flow confidentiality. Stands for Encapsulating Security Payload.

Ettercap   An ARP spoofing tool.

Evacuation drill   A test of the evacuation procedures portion of the disaster recovery plan.

Event log   See Audit trail.

Everyone group   A special identity on Windows computers that includes all users.

Evidence   Information presented in court that attempts to prove a crime was committed.

Extensible Authentication Protocol (EAP)   A standard that allows support for multiple remote access authentication protocols.

External consistency   See Data integrity.

Failover   The process by which one server takes over the operations of another.

Failover system   An identical copy of a server and its data that can be used in the event of an attack, natural disaster, or server failure.

False positive   An access pattern flagged as suspicious that is actually benign.

FAR   A biometric characteristic that reports the percentage of invalid subjects that are falsely accepted. Stands for false acceptance rate.

Fault tolerance   A method of providing a backup server that can assume the role of a server that has failed.

Fault tolerant solution   A solution that can automatically recover from failure of a device or component.

Fault-tolerant computing   A computer configuration that can tolerate the failure of a component.

Fibre channel   A suite of protocols that creates a high-speed infrastructure for transferring data between storage devices and servers.

File Replication Services (FRS)   Service responsible for transferring files and the directory database between domain controllers.

Filter   A set of rules that determine which packets should be allowed through a firewall, which should be rejected, or which should be dropped.

Finger   A utility that allows you to determine information about a user and logon sessions based on an email address. It operates on port 79.

finger command   Unix or Linux command that allows you to obtain information about a user.

Fixed database role   A SQL Server role automatically created at the database scope for which permissions cannot be changed, but membership can.

Fixed server role   A SQL Server role automatically created at the server scope for which permissions cannot be changed, but membership can.

Footprint   To use a port scanner or other technique to gain information about the operating systems and services running on a network.

Forensics   The science of gathering and preserving evidence.

Forward lookup   The type of DNS query used to find out the IP address of a computer when you know its host name.

Frequency analysis   A cryptanalysis technique that uses the fact that some letters in a specific language appear more frequently than others.

FRR   A biometric characteristic that reports the percentage of valid subjects that are falsely rejected. Stands for false rejection rate.

FTP   An Application layer protocol that provides for authenticated transfer of files between two computers and access to directories. Stands for File Transfer Protocol.

Full backup   A backup of all selected files and folders.

Full-interruption test   A test of the disaster recovery plan in which normal production is shut down and all recovery processes are executed.

Full-scale exercise   See Parallel test.

Functional drill   A test of the disaster recovery plan that tests one or more specific functions of the plan.

Gateway-to-gateway security   The act of securing data between two gateways, but not between the gateway and the client. Used to support non-IPsec-aware clients.

Generic Routing Encapsulation (GRE)   A PPTP subprotocol that adds a header to a PPP packet.

Ghost™   A software utility created by Symantec™ that can be used to create an image of a computer's configuration.

GID   A 16-bit number that identifies a group on a Unix computer. Stands for group identity.

Global catalog   A database that contains a subset of Active Directory objects and object attributes for every domain in the forest.

Global catalog server   A domain controller that hosts the global catalog for the forest.

Global group   An Active Directory group that can be used in native mode or mixed mode. It is normally added as a member of a Domain Local group, Local group, or Universal group.

GNU General Public License (GNU GPL)   A licensing structure for open source and freely distributed software.

GPO   An Active Directory object that is used to centrally manage user and computer configuration settings, including security settings. Stands for Group Policy Object.

Group Policy   Active Directory's centralized management technology for user and computer configuration settings.

Group transient key (GTK)   In 802.11i, a temporal key that protects multicast and broadcast data.

Groups   Collections of one or more users.

Guests   An Active Directory built-in Domain Local group whose members are more limited than members of the Users group.

Half-open connections   Connections that have not completed the handshake process and are in the SYN_RECV state.

Hardware-assisted software RAID   Involves installing either a host bus adapter that includes a RAID BIOS chip or a RAID BIOS chip on the motherboard and RAID software on the computer.

Hash   See Digest.

Hash collisions   The probability that the same hash will be generated from different data.

Hash function   A function that computes a smaller, fixed-size digest from a message of any size.

Header condition signature   A combination of data in packet headers that indicates an attack.

Headless server   A server that does not have a monitor attached.

Heterogeneous environment   A network environment that runs multiple operating systems.

Hexadecimal commands   A computer command represented in base 16.

Hidden attribute   A Windows file attribute that causes a file to not be displayed unless the Show hidden files and folders option is enabled.

Hidden share   A share that cannot be seen when browsing the network. On a Windows computer, a hidden share is created by appending a "$" to the end of the share name.

High-interaction honeypot   A honeypot that allows an attacker to perform complex interactions because it uses actual operating systems and services.

Home directory   A directory on a Unix computer associated with a specific user.

Honeyd   An open source low-interaction honeypot created by Niels Provos.

Honeynet   A controlled network of high-interaction honeypots.

Honeynet Project   A multinational organization that researches attacker methods using honeypots and honeynets.

Honeypot   A monitored decoy system that can be used to research attack methods and help prevent an attack by distracting the attacker from an actual target.

Host   A file in which a virus resides.

Host bus adapter (HBA)   An adapter for connecting hard drives to a motherboard. It can include a RAID BIOS chip or a RAID processor.

Host name   The name of a computer on a TCP/IP network.

Host record   A DNS server record that identifies a computer on the network and is used for forward lookup.

Host-based IDS (HIDS)   An IDS that runs on a specific host and can detect only malicious activity targeted at that host.

Host-to-Host layer   Layer in the TCP/IP model that is similar to the OSI Transport layer.

Hot site   A backup site that has all required hardware, software, and peripherals installed and that can be up and running by synchronizing the data.

Hot space   See RAID 5EE.

Hot spare   A drive in a RAID 5 array that does not participate in the array until another drive fails, but that is added to the array automatically when a failure occurs. A hot spare can also be used without RAID.

HTTP   A protocol used for sending web pages and information to other locations on the Internet. Stands for Hypertext Transfer Protocol.

HTTPS   A protocol that encrypts data sent over HTTP. It uses a digital certificate on a web server to provide the encryption key. Stands for Hypertext Transfer Protocol over SSL.

Hyperlink   A clickable area on a web page that loads a different URL.

HyperTerminal   A terminal emulation program included with Windows operating systems.

HyperText Markup Language (HTML)   The language used to create most web pages. A browser uses the HTML to determine how to render content.

IAS proxy   An IAS server that is configured to forward RADIUS traffic to another server.

ICMP   A troubleshooting protocol and member of the TCP/IP protocol suite used to identify problems with the successful delivery of diagnostic packets within an IP network. For example, Ping uses ICMP. Stands for Internet Control Message Protocol.

ICV   A hash of the ESP packet, not including the Authentication data field. Used to verify that the message has not been tampered with. Stands for integrity check value.

Identification   The process of supplying the credentials the authenticating server will user to prove a user's or computer's identity.

Identity theft   Using somebody else's identity to gain access to a resource or service.

Identity-based access control   An access control model in which a user's identity is managed by a different person or organization than the one that manages permissions and privileges.

IKE protocol   A protocol for authentication, shared key generation, and managing the negotiation of cryptographic algorithms, authentication methods, and key generation and exchange in an IPsec session. Stands for Internet Key Exchange protocol.

IKEv2   The latest version of Internet Key Exchange protocol, defined in RFC 4306.

ILOVEYOU virus   A virus that propagates through email by sending an infected message to everyone in a user's address book (contacts folder).

Image   A snapshot of a computer's configuration that can be applied to the same computer or a different computer.

Impersonate   The act of using another user's credentials to gain access to a server.

Impersonation token   An access token that is created when a client application accesses a server on behalf of the user.

In-band remote management   The process of accessing and managing a computer that is operational and can be accessed using standard network communication.

Incremental backup   A backup that backs up all files that have changed since the last full or incremental backup. To recover using incremental backups, you must restore the full backup and then each incremental backup in the order in which they were taken.

Incremental template   A security template that contains settings relevant to a specific server role.

Index Server service   A Windows service that indexes files on a hard disk for faster search access.

Infrastructure mode   A wireless networking mode in which clients connect to a wireless access point.

Inherited permission   A permission that is configured at an object higher in the hierarchy and that flows down to the objects lower in the hierarchy. Active Directory objects inherit permissions from the organizational unit hierarchy. File system objects inherit permissions from the folder hierarchy.

Initialization vector (IV)   A varying value that is used along with the shared secret when performing WEP encryption.

Inode   A structure in a Unix file that includes the UID of the owner, the GID of the group that owns the file, and the permissions granted to owner, group, and other.

Integrated Windows authentication   An IIS authentication method that authenticates users using either Active Directory or the local account database and sends credentials as a hash, but requires Internet Explorer on the client.

Integrity   Prevention of unauthorized modification of information; the property that data has not been modified or changed in any way.

Intelligent agent   A small program that resides on a host computer and monitors the computer for suspicious activity.

Intelligent uninterruptible power supply (intelligent UPS)   A device that provides power conditioning and fault tolerance in case of power failure, and can be used to connect servers to serial ports or through the AC power line.

Interaction   The level of activity provided by the honeypot to the attacker.

Intermediate CA   A CA that issues certificates on behalf of the root CA.

Internet Authentication Service (IAS)   Microsoft®'s implementation of a RADIUS server.

Internet Connection Sharing (ICS)   A simplified NAT service that issues dynamic IP addresses in the 192.168.0.x range and can operate on Windows 2000 Professional or Windows XP.

Internet layer   Layer of the TCP/IP model that performs a similar function to the Network layer of the OSI model.

Internet Server Application Programming Interface (ISAPI)   An application programming interface (API) that allows you to create compiled web components that can run on Internet Information Services (IIS).

Internet zone   The Internet Explorer® and Outlook® security zone that contains all addresses not on the local network that have not been added to either the trusted sites zone or the restricted sites zone.

Intersite Messaging service (IsmServ)   Allows communication between domain controllers at different Active Directory sites.

Intrusion detection (ID)   The act of detecting and analyzing activities to determine whether an attempt was made to gain unauthorized access to a system.

Intrusion detection system (IDS)   A system or appliance that monitors network traffic or audit logs to determine whether an attack might be underway.

Intrusion prevention system (IPS)   A system that not only detects and logs suspicious activity, but also takes action to prevent the attack.

IP   The Network layer protocol in the TCP/IP suite. It provides a best effort, or unreliable service, for connecting computers to form a computer network. It does not guarantee packet delivery. Stands for Internet Protocol.

IP address   A four-byte address that is assigned to every host on the Internet or on a network running TCP/IP.

IP address filtering   The process of limiting the client IP addresses that can connect to a server.

IP packet filtering   The process of limiting the protocols or ports on which a computer will accept a request.

IP within IP   See Tunnel mode.

IPsec   A security protocol that operates at the Internet layer of the protocol stack. It can provide traffic filtering, confidentiality, integrity, authentication, and some protection against replay attacks. Stands for IP (Internet Protocol) security.

IPsec policy   A collection of rules defining how IPsec should permit, block, or protect specific types of traffic.

IPX   A protocol maintained by Novell® that transmits and receives packets. It works with SPX. Stands for Internetwork Packet Exchange.

iSCSI   A connection protocol for communicating between storage devices and servers that uses the existing Ethernet and TCP/IP infrastructure.

ISO 17799   A standard that provides best practices for defining security policies.

Issuing CA   A CA at the lowest level of the hierarchy. It is responsible for enrolling, deploying, and renewing user and computer certificates.

IUSR_*computername* account   A special Windows account that is created when IIS is installed. It provides the security context for anonymous access to web sites.

IV sequencing discipline   A feature of TKIP in which the receiver discards packets that are out of sequence. This feature helps to prevent replay attacks.

Java applets   A program written in Java that runs on a user's workstation and is subject to specific limitations to help increase security.

JavaScript®   A scripting language based on the Java programming language.

Java™   A programming language in which applications can be compiled once and then executed on multiple different operating systems, provided a Java Virtual Machine (JVM) is installed.

JPEG   Standard for graphics defined by the Joint Photographic Experts Group. Stands for Joint Photographic Experts Group.

KDC   A Kerberos service that is responsible for storing credentials in a database and managing the exchange of keys between clients and servers on the network. Stands for key distribution center.

Kerberos   A trusted authentication protocol based on symmetric key cryptography that authenticates clients to other entities on the network. Kerberos implementations are available for many operating systems, including Windows, Unix, NetWare®, and Macintosh.

Kerberos key distribution center (KDC)   A domain controller service required on all domain controllers to perform authentication.

Key   A piece of data used for encryption and decryption. A strong key is a random piece of data that cannot be easily discovered.

Key agreement protocol   A method of generating shared keys on the fly.

Key block   A set of keys used to protect data transmission in an SSL session.

Key confirmation key (KCK)   In 802.11i, a member of the PTK that binds the PMK to the client station and access point.

Key encryption key (KEK)   In 802.11i, a member of the PTK that is used to distribute the group transient key.

Keystroke logging program   Utilities that can log a user's keystrokes and that can be used to store and forward passwords to an attacker.

Knowledge-based IDS   See Signature-based IDS.

L0phtcrack   A program used to crack passwords.

LAN Manager protocol   An authentication protocol used by older Microsoft operating systems, such as MS-DOS® and Windows 95. It has a maximum password length of 14 characters and stores passwords in a format that is easy to crack.

last command   A Unix or Linux command used to display login information. When used without parameters, it shows all logins in the wtmp file.

Last-in-first out (LIFO)   An execution order in which the last command placed on the stack executes first.

lastcomm command   A Unix or Linux command that shows the commands that have been executed.

lastlog command   A Unix or Linux command that records the last time a user logged in.

Layer 2 Tunneling Protocol (L2TP)   An industry-standard VPN protocol that uses IPsec for encryption. Through IPsec, it offers computer authentication using either certificates or pre-shared keys.

Layered architecture   The decomposition of network functions into layers. Layered models include the OSI model and the TCP/IP model.

LC4   See L0phtcrack.

Letter salad   A technique used to try to circumvent spam filters by misspelling words that are commonly used in spam.

Limiting the attack surface   The process of removing or disabling unnecessary services, closing unnecessary ports, and removing unnecessary input and output devices.

Link Control Protocol (LCP)   A subprotocol of PPP that detects loopback links, accommodates limits on packet sizes, sets up encapsulation options, and negotiates peer-to-peer authentication.

Link establishment phase   The phase of a PPP conversation in which the two devices establish specific network parameters, such as frame size, compression, and the authentication protocol.

LMHosts file   A file that contains NetBIOS name resolution information and that can be used as an alternative to WINS.

Local intranet zone   The Internet Explorer and Outlook security zone that contains all addresses on the internal network.

Local Service account   A built-in Windows account that has very limited permissions on the computer and that cannot access other computers across the network.

Local System account   A built-in Windows account that has extensive permissions on the computer and that can access other resources across the network.

Logic bomb   A type of Trojan horse that remains dormant until a triggering condition occurs.

Logical Link layer   The sublayer of the OSI model's Data Link layer that is responsible for setting up the communication link and formatting the data into frames.

Low-interaction honeypot   A limited emulation of an operating system and system services.

ls command   A Unix command that is used to list the files and directories and information about them.

MAC   An access control model in which a subject is given clearance and an object is given a sensitivity classification. Access is determined by matching the subject's clearance to the object's sensitivity. For example, a subject with a secret clearance can access secret objects, but not top secret objects. Stands for mandatory access control.

MAC address   The unique address assigned to each network adapter. It comprises a 6-byte number. The first three bytes of a MAC address identify the manufacturer. The remaining three bytes represent the serial number of the device.

MAC address filtering   A security method in which a wireless access point is configured with a list of MAC addresses that should be allowed to connect.

Macro Virus Protection   A Microsoft Office feature that can be used to prevent macros from running unless the user explicitly allows them.

Mail proxy   See Mail relay.

Mail relay   A server that resides in the perimeter network and checks incoming email for scripts, viruses, questionable attachments, and spam. Also known as a mail proxy.

Malcode   See Malware.

Malware   Code that performs a malicious act. Viruses, worms, Trojan horses, spyware, and adware are all examples of malware. Also known as malcode.

Man-in-the-middle attack   An attack in which the attacker intercepts a message and alters it before sending it on to the recipient. A man-in-the-middle attack can be used to compromise a key agreement unless authentication is also used.

Manage Documents permission   A permission granted on a Windows printer to allow a user to manage the print queue.

Manage Printer permission   A permission granted on a Windows printer to allow a user to configure the printer and install drivers.

Managed computer   A computer that is configured through a centralized policy. One example of a managed computer is an Active Directory® client that is configured through Group Policy.

Management computer   A computer running terminal emulation software used to manage a computer using EMS.

MasterSecret   A 48-byte value derived from the PreMasterSecret, "master secret," and the random number selected by the client and the server in an SSL session. The MasterSecret provides the input to construct a key block.

MD5   A hash function. Stands for Message-Digest algorithm 5.

MD5–Challenge   A test package for EAP that should be used to troubleshoot connections. It requires configuring the server and client with a shared secret.

Media Access layer   The sublayer of the OSI model's Data Link layer that is responsible for supporting a computer's access to packet data and for regulating a computer's permission to transmit packet data.

Melissa   A virus that attaches itself to Microsoft Word files and infects Normal.dot when the file is opened. Once it resides in Normal.dot, it infects other Word files opened on the computer.

Message Integrity Code (MIC)   A unique, unambiguous representation of the transmitted message that will change if the message bits change.

Michael   The 64-bit MIC used by TKIP.

Michelangelo   An early logic bomb that used Michelangelo's birthday as the trigger. It was designed to overwrite the hard drive.

Microsoft Challenge Handshake Authentication Protocol (MS-CHAP)   A Microsoft version of CHAP that transmits both a LAN Manager hash and an NTLM hash. It does not require the server to store passwords using reversible encryption.

Microsoft Challenge Handshake Authentication Protocol Version 2 (MS-CHAPv2)   An improved version of MS-CHAP that offers mutual authentication and does not transmit a LAN Manager hash.

Microsoft Passport authentication   See Windows Live authentication.

Microsoft Point-to-Point Encryption (MPPE)   The encryption method used by PPTP. The session keys are generated from the MS-CHAP or EAP passwords.

MIME   Enables the use of non–US-ASCII textual messages, nontextual messages, multipart message bodies, and non–US-ASCII information in message headers in Internet mail. Stands for Multipurpose Internet Mail Extensions.

Mitigate   Reduce the likelihood or impact of a risk.

Mixed mode domain   A Windows Active Directory domain that includes Windows NT 4.0 domain controllers or that has not yet been converted to native mode.

Mobile backup   A vendor that supplies mobile power and HVAC facilities to allow a company to perform processing during an emergency. Also referred to as a mobile backup.

Modem serial connection   Similar to a direct serial connection except that it involves putting a modem between the management computer and the server(s).

Mondoarchive   A backup utility for Linux systems.

Monitoring   See Auditing.

MPEG   Standard for the compression and coding of motion video. Stands for Moving Picture Experts Group.

Multicast packet   A packet that is sent to all computers on a network that are listening on a specific multicast address.

Multicasting   Sending a message to multiple computers listening on the same IP address. Multicasting is often used for distributing presentations to multiple hosts.

Multihomed computer   A computer with multiple network interfaces.

Multiple centers   An emergency strategy that spreads processing across multiple geographic locations.

Mutual aid agreement   An arrangement with another company to provide processing resources to each other in the event of a disaster.

Mutual authentication   A type of authentication in which the client must prove its identity to the server and the server must prove its identity to the client.

MX record   A DNS record that identifies a mail server.

Naive Bayes classifier   A method of classification used to determine whether an email is spam based on whether the email contains words that are frequently used in spam.

NAT   A service that translates private addresses that are normally internal to a particular organization into routable addresses on public networks such as the Internet. Stands for Network Address Translation.

Native mode domain   A Windows Active Directory domain in which all domain controllers are running Windows 2000 Server or Windows Server 2003 and that has been converted to native mode.

NAT–Traversal   An Internet Engineering Task Force (IETF) draft standard that uses User Datagram Protocol (UDP) encapsulation to wrap the IPsec packet inside a UDP/IP header.

Need to know   The access control condition that a subject must have a need to access a specific classified document in order to perform assigned duties.

Need-to-access environment   An access control environment in which users are given permission to access only the data they need to perform their jobs.

Need-to-know environment   An access control environment in which users are given permission to read only the data they need to perform their jobs.

Nest   To make an object of one specific type a member of an object of the same type. In Active Directory native mode, Global groups can be nested.

NetBIOS application   An application that uses the NetBIOS application layer protocol to communicate on the network.

NetBIOS name   The name of a computer that is compatible with NetBIOS applications and legacy Windows operating systems.

NetMeeting®   An online conferencing application.

Netstat   A Windows troubleshooting tool that allows you to see which ports a computer is listening on, as well as other information about the network.

Network Access layer   Layer of the TCP/IP model that performs a similar function to the Data Link and Physical layers of the OSI model.

Network access server (NAS)   A server in a TACACS configuration that processes requests for connections and transmits authentication credentials to the TACACS server.

Network Address Translation (NAT) server   A server responsible for acting as a gateway between the Internet and computers on the internal network.

Network Configuration Operators   An Active Directory built-in Domain Local group whose members have some rights to manage the network configuration parameters for computers in the domain.

Network Control Protocol (NCP)   A subprotocol of PPP that is used for configuring, managing, and testing data links.

Network layer   The layer of the OSI model that performs packet routing across networks.

Network security   Protecting all the resources on a network from threats.

Network Service account   A built-in Windows account has the same local permissions as Local Service, but can also access computers across the network.

Network stack   A stack of protocol layers.

Network-based IDS (NIDS)   An IDS that listens to traffic on a network segment and can detect an attack targeted at any host on that segment.

newgrp command   A Unix command that allows a user to associate their user account with a different group.

Next Header   A field in an ESP pack that shows the next protocol field on the normal IP packet.

NFS   A Session layer protocol that supports the sharing of files among different types of file systems. Stands for Network File System.

Nimda worm   A variant of the Code Red worm.

NIST   A United States government agency that performs research, develops technical standards, and promotes technological advances. Stands for National Institute of Standards and Technology.

Nonpersistent cookie   A cookie that is stored in memory, not on the hard drive, and is deleted when a session ends or the computer is rebooted.

Nonrepudiation   The inability to deny that a specific action occurred.

Nonrepudiation of delivery   The act of collecting and providing evidence that a message was delivered to a specific recipient.

Nonrepudiation of origin   The act of collecting and providing evidence about the sender of a document.

NSA   A United States government agency responsible for collecting and analyzing foreign communications and protecting the confidentiality of U.S. government data. Stands for National Security Agency.

ntbackup   The command-line version of Windows® Backup.

NTFS permissions   Permissions that are configured for a file or folder on a Windows system. Stands for NT File System permissions.

NTLM protocol   An authentication protocol that is used for Windows NT 4.0 domains and local SAM account authentication in Windows 2000 and Windows XP.

NTLMv2 protocol   An authentication protocol that provides more secure password transmission than NTLM and that also provides mutual authentication.

Null modem cable   A special serial cable that allows two computers to connect to each other through serial ports by reversing the send and receive lines.

Nyxem worm   A logic bomb that is activated on the third of every month. It disables file sharing security, antivirus protection, and deletes Microsoft Office files, .zip files, and .rar files.

Object   A passive entity to which permission is granted or denied.

OFB   A block encryption mode in which the output of the encryption algorithm is XORed with the plain text continuously throughout the blocks. If any bits are lost, the message cannot be recovered. Stands for output feedback.

Off-site backup   A backup stored at a different location, usually in a secure vault or safety deposit box.

One-time pad   A cryptographic algorithm in which the cryptographer uses a pad of random numbers to provide the shift value for each letter of the message.

One-time password   An automatically generated password that can only be used for a short amount of time or for a single logon.

One-way hash   A hash created with a shared secret. The hash is created on both ends of the conversation and compared. However, you cannot decode the hash to retrieve the actual data.

Originating domain   The domain from which a cookie is downloaded.

OSI model   A network architecture model that consists of seven functional layers. The OSI model was developed around 1981 by the International Organization for Standardization (ISO). Stands for Open Systems Interconnection model.

OSPF   A routing protocol that selects the least-cost path from a source computer to a destination computer. Stands for Open Shortest Path First.

OU   A container in an Active Directory domain. An OU can be used to group objects for delegation of administration or for applying Group Policy. Stands for organizational unit.

Out-of-band remote management   The process of connecting to and managing a server that does not respond to standard network communication.

Outlook postmark   A puzzle of varying complexity that is added to legitimate email to help distinguish it from spam.

OWA   An Internet-facing server that allows access to Microsoft Exchange through HTTP. Stands for Outlook® Web Access.

Packet checksum   The result of a mathematical calculation on a packet that is added to the packet to verify its integrity.

Packet filtering   A technique used by firewalls. Each packet is compared against a filter and the packet is either allowed to pass, is rejected, or is dropped.

Packet Privacy   The method of encryption used by DCOM.

Packet sniffer   Software or hardware that captures traffic on the network and allows a user to view the packet headers and data.

Packet tampering   An attack in which data packets are modified.

Pad length   A field in an ESP packet that provides the length of the padding field.

Padding   A technique in which extra characters are added to plain text before generating the cipher text. Padding is used with block ciphers to produce blocks of a specific length and with stream ciphers to provide randomness for a common message.

Pairwise master key (PMK)   In 802.11i, a symmetric key possessed by an access point and a client station which is used to authorize access to the 802.11 medium.

Pairwise transient key (PTK)   In 802.11i, a collection of operational keys, including key encryption key, key confirmation key, and temporal key.

PAM   Software that runs on a Unix computer to provide a standard interface that allows you to use a variety of authentication protocols. Stands for pluggable authentication module.

Parallel test   A simulation of an emergency situation that involves all participants and that might include some interruption in production processing. Also referred to as a full-scale exercise.

Parity stripe   An XOR calculated from data stripes and written to a disk in the array for fault tolerance.

Passive node   A cluster node that sits idle until it needs to take over for an active node.

Passphrase   A password that can contain many characters, including spaces.

Password Authentication Protocol (PAP)   A legacy remote access authentication protocol in which the username and password are passed in clear text.

Patch   See Security update.

Payload data   A variable-length field containing the Transport layer network message.

PCBC   A block encryption mode that is similar to CBC, except that changes to the cipher text are propagated through the remainder of the message. Stands for propagating cipher-block chaining.

PDU   A network message at a specific layer in the network stack. Stands for protocol data unit.

Peer-to-peer network   A network that does not implement centralized security. Users on a peer-to-peer network share resources with other users and manage the security of those resources.

Penetration testing   The process of probing a network's defenses to try to find vulnerabilities.

Per-packet mixing function   A TKIP feature that involves generating a temporal key that is used along with the packet sequence counter to build the packet key. It causes different clients to create different per-packet encryption keys, mitigating the risk of IV discovery.

Perimeter network   See DMZ.

Permission attributes   The individual security protections for an object, including users who are allowed and denied access.

Persistent cookie   A cookie that is stored on a user's hard drive and can be accessed by spyware.

Personal firewall   Firewall software that runs on a server to limit the traffic that server accepts.

Personal firewall   Firewall software that runs on a user's computer to protect it against unwanted and potentially harmful traffic.

Phishing attack   A type of social engineering attack in which a user is tricked into supplying confidential information by an email that spoofs a legitimate site, such as an online banking site, PayPal®, or eBay®.

Phishing filter   A feature of Internet Explorer 7 that attempts to determine whether a website is legitimate or a spoofed website used in a phishing attack.

Physical entry point   An interface on a computer that allows input or output.

Physical evidence   A physical item that can be presented as evidence. For example, a piece of equipment.

Physical layer   The layer of the OSI model that defines standards for transmission media.

PID   An identifier associated with a process (subject) on a Unix computer. Stands for process ID.

Ping   A command that can be used to check whether computers on a network can communicate.

Ping of death   A denial of service attack that uses a Ping request that is larger than the maximum size of 65,536 bytes.

PKI   The technology, software, and services that allow an organization to securely exchange information and validate the identity of users, computers, and services. Stands for public key infrastructure.

Plain text   Data in its unencrypted, readable form.

Plug-in   An extension to a browser that allows a user to display a specific type of content in the browser.

Point-to-Point Protocol (PPP)   A remote access protocol that can encapsulate IP, IPX, and other network protocols.

Point-to-Point Tunneling Protocol (PPTP)   A VPN protocol that uses the PPP infrastructure and authentication mechanisms. Developed by Microsoft, it is primarily used for VPN access to a Windows® network.

Poisoning the cache   Changing data in the DNS cache on a downstream DNS server so that one or more records point to a bogus or malicious address.

Policy CA   See Intermediate CA.

Polyalphabetic substitution   The method used by the Vigenere cipher in which multiple alphabetic shifts are used as the key instead of the single shift used by the substitution cipher.

POP3   The latest version of POP.

POP   An Application layer protocol used to retrieve email from a mail server. Stands for Post Office Protocol.

Port   A logical entity associated with a number on which the TCP/IP protocol listens for messages associated with a specific protocol.

Port scanner   A utility that scans a computer or network for open TCP/IP ports.

Port signature   A set of connection attempts to frequently attacked ports.

Portable Document Format (PDF)   A standard document format that can be read by Adobe® Acrobat® or Acrobat Reader®. Many websites use PDF to allow users to view content.

Post Office Protocol 3 (POP3)   A protocol used to receive email.

PPP   A protocol used for transmitting data over point-to-point links. It does this by encapsulating the datagrams of other protocols. PPP was designed as a replacement for SLIP in sending information using synchronous modems. Stands for Point-to-Point Protocol.

Pre-shared key (PSK) mode   An 802.11i mode in which there is no authentication exchange and a single private key can be assigned to the entire network or to an access point/client pair.

Pre-shared secret   A key that is shared between two parties before communication begins.

PreMasterSecret   A 48-byte random value used in a function to calculate the Master Secret for an SSL session.

Presentation layer   The layer of the OSI model that provides encryption, code conversion, and data formatting.

Primary token   An access token that is associated with the user who is logged on to the computer where the process is running.

Principal   See Subject.

Principle of least permission   The best practice of granting only the permissions a user needs to perform a job.

Principle of least privilege   See Principle of least permission.

Print job   A document that has been sent to a printer.

Print Operators   An Active Directory built-in Domain Local group whose members can manage printers in the domain.

Print permission   A permission granted to a Windows printer to allow the user to send documents to be printed.

Print queue   A list of documents (print jobs) that have been sent to the printer.

Print Spooler service   A Windows service that manages print queues and print jobs.

Privacy   Protection of personal data.

Private key   A key that is only known to its owner. Used in asymmetric encryption.

Private network   An organization's network that is for internal access. It often must handle confidential and proprietary data.

Promiscuous mode   A network adapter operating mode that allows the adapter to see packets on the network that are destined for other computers.

Propagated   Spread from computer to computer.

Protected Extensible Authentication Protocol (PEAP)   A protocol that allows a user to authenticate using a password on a wireless network protected by 802.1x.

Protocol   A formal set of rules that describe how computers transmit data and communicate across a network.

Protocol analyzer   See Packet sniffer.

Protocol analyzers   Software or hardware that captures packets on the network.

Proxy agents   Application- and protocol-specific implementations that act on behalf of their intended application protocols.

Pseudorandom numbers   Numbers that appear to be random. The key attribute of pseudorandom numbers is that they cannot be predicted.

PTR record   A record used to perform a reverse lookup for a host.

Public key   A key that is only known to the world. Used in asymmetric encryption.

Public network   A network that can be accessed by anyone.

Purple   A cryptographic machine invented by the Japanese in World War II. It used telephone stepping switches to generate the keys.

Qualitative loss criteria   A category of potential loss that includes losses that cannot be accurately estimated as a dollar amount, including loss of competitive advantage, market share, or public opinion.

Qualitative risk analysis   A method of risk analysis in which values are taken from domains without an underlying mathematical structure, such as the advice of security experts.

Quantitative loss criteria   A category of potential loss that can be estimated as a dollar amount, including loss of revenue, expenditure, or liability resolution.

Quantitative risk analysis   A method of risk analysis in which values are taken from a mathematical domain, such as monetary value or probability of occurrence.

Quarantining attachments   Removing attachments from an email before the email is delivered to the recipient.

Query   A command written in SQL and sent to a database.

RADIUS client   A dial-in server, VPN server, or wireless access point that uses a RADIUS server to perform authentication, authorization, and/or auditing.

RADIUS server   A server that provides authentication, authorization, and/or auditing for RADIUS clients.

RAID 0   A technology in which data is striped across multiple disks. It offers better performance, but does not provide redundancy. Also referred to as disk striping.

RAID 0+1   See RAID 10.

RAID 1   A technology in which data is mirrored to a second disk. It protects against failure of a single hard disk. Also referred to as disk mirroring.

RAID 1E   A technology in which data is mirrored in stripes across three or more disks. It protects against failure of a single hard disk. Also referred to as a striped mirror.

RAID 5   A technology in which data is striped across disks and a parity stripe is written to allow recoverability if a single disk fails. Also referred to as striping with parity.

RAID 5EE   A technology in which data is striped across disks and a spare stripe is also created to prevent performance degradation when a disk fails. Protects against a single disk failure. Also referred to as hot space.

RAID 6   A technology in which data is striped across disks and a parity stripe is written to two disks. Protects against two drive failures. Also referred to as striping with dual parity.

RAID 10   A technology in which data is mirrored and then striped to provide better performance and protection against a single drive failure. Also referred to as RAID 0+1 or striped RAID 1 arrays.

RAID 50   A technology in which multiple RAID 5 arrays are striped to provide better performance and protection against a drive failure in each array. Also referred to as striped RAID 5 arrays.

RAID 60   A technology in which multiple RAID 6 arrays are striped to provide better performance and protection against two drive failures in each array. Also referred to as striped RAID 6 arrays.

RAID-on-Chip technology   A type of hardware RAID in which the RAID processor and drive interfaces are built onto the motherboard.

RARP   A protocol that enables a computer in a LAN to determine its IP address based on its MAC address. Stands for Reverse Address Resolution Protocol.

RBAC   An access control model in which permissions are granted to one or more roles and users are assigned to one or more roles. Therefore, the role serves as an intermediate layer. Stands for role-based access control.

Real evidence   See Physical evidence.

Recovery team   A team with the responsibility of restoring business operations during a disaster.

Recycle Bin   A temporary repository for deleted files on a Windows computer.

Redundant   Duplicated.

Redundant Array of Independent Disks (RAID)   A technology that uses multiple disks to eliminate the disk as a single point of failure and to protect data against the failure of one (or sometimes more) disks.

Registry   A database on a Windows computer that stores hardware and software configuration settings.

Remote access server   A server that provides network access through a dial-up connection.

Remote access server (RAS)   A server responsible for providing network access to dial-up or virtual private network (VPN) clients.

Remote Assistance   A remote management technology that allows one user (the novice) to invite another user (the helper) to access the novice's computer remotely.

Remote Authentication Dial-in User Service (RADIUS)   A standard for implementing centralized authentication, authorization, and auditing for remote and wireless access.

Remote Desktop for Administration   A management tool that allows you to connect to a Windows desktop as if you were logged in interactively.

Remote Desktop Protocol (RDP)   The protocol used to access a computer using Remote Desktop for Administration.

Remote login   A command in UNIX that begins a terminal session between an authorized user and a remote host on a network. The user can perform all functions as if he or she were actually at the remote host.

Remote management plan   A plan that identifies computers that must be managed remotely, the tools that will be used, and any security requirements for remote management.

Remote procedure call (RPC)   The protocol used when one application accesses another application on the network using DCOM.

Remote Procedure Call Locator (RpcLocator)   Service that allows computers to find a server running the remote procedure call (RPC) service.

Replay attack   An attack in which an attacker captures and then replays a packet sent between a browser and a web server or an email. The attacker might optionally modify the packet before replaying it.

Replays   Attacks in which data are captured and replayed with or without modification.

Replicate   To reproduce by creating a copy of itself.

Repudiated   Denied.

Restricted sites zone   The Internet Explorer and Outlook security zone that contains addresses that should be treated with more stringent security restrictions than address in the Internet zone.

Reverse lookup   A DNS query sent to retrieve the host name of a host when the IP address is known.

Reversible encryption   An encryption method that can be decrypted. A one-way hash is not reversibly encrypted. Symmetric or asymmetric encryption is reversible.

RFC 1994   The Request for Comment that describes the CHAP protocol for PPP.

RFC 2401   The Request for Comment that defines the security architecture for IPsec.

RFC 2402   The Request for Comment that defines the Authentication Header component of IPsec.

RFC 2406   The Request for Comment that defines the Encapsulating Security Payload (ESP) component of IPsec.

RFC 2409   The Request for Comment that defines the Internet Key Exchange (IKE) protocol.

RFC 2488   The Request for Comment that describes MS-CHAP.

RFC 2898   The Request for Comment that describes 802.11i pre-shared key mode.

RFC 3227   A Request For Comment that details the guidelines for collecting documentary evidence.

RFC 4306   The Request for Comment that defines IKEv2.

Rijndael   A symmetric encryption algorithm that is a variant of AES. It supports both key and block sizes of any multiple of 32 bits between 128 bits and 256 bits.

RIP   A routing protocol that sends routing update messages to other network routers at regular intervals and when the network topology changes. Stands for Routing Information Protocol.

Risk   The possibility that some incident or attack can cause damage to your enterprise.

Risk analysis   The process of identifying a risk and assessing its likelihood and impact.

Risk analysis tool   Software that systematically analyzes a system or network to identify vulnerabilities.

Rlogin   See Remote login.

Roaming   The process of moving between wireless access points.

Roaming disconnect support   A feature of Remote Desktop that allows the programs you start to run even if you are disconnected.

Rogue DHCP server   An unauthorized DHCP server that assigns addresses from the wrong scope or from an overlapping scope.

Role   Job or task used to determine the necessary access.

Rolling backup   See Mobile backup.

root   The username of the superuser account on a Unix computer.

Root CA   The first CA you install. It has a self-signed certificate and is responsible for validating the CAs beneath it in the hierarchy.

Rooted   A condition in which a backdoor has been installed.

Routing and Remote Access Server (RRAS)   The component of Windows Server 2003 that allows you to support dial-up and VPN access.

RPC   A Session layer protocol that supports procedure calls where the called procedure and the calling procedure might be on different systems communicating through a network. RPC is useful in setting up distributed, client-server-based applications. Stands for remote procedure call.

RSA   An asymmetric encryption algorithm developed by Ron Rivest, Adi Shamir, and Len Adleman.

RSA pseudorandom generator   A pseudorandom number generator that is considered secure because cracking it requires factoring large numbers.

rsh   A Unix utiltiy that allows you to execute shell commands remotely. Stands for remote shell.

Rule base   See Filter.

Rule-based access control   A type of mandatory access control (MAC) in which rules determine access privileges.

Ruleset   See Filter.

S/MIME   A technology used to encrypt and digitally sign email messages. Stands for Secure/Multipurpose Internet Mail Extensions.

SA   Information about the algorithms and key to use during an ESP transmission. Each side of the conversation requires a SA. Stands for security association.

SACL   The part of the security descriptor that dictates which events are to be audited for specific users or groups. Stands for system access control list.

Safe for execution   A security level for an ActiveX control. The developer certifies that the control will not do anything harmful if it is embedded in a web page.

Safe for scripting   A security level for an ActiveX control. The developer certifies that there are no properties that can be set in script in such a way that they do harm to the client computer.

Salting   The addition of random data to a message before it is hashed.

Salvage team   A team that is responsible for repairing, cleaning, salvaging, and determining the viability of the primary processing infrastructure.

SAM database   A database that stores user credentials on a computer running Windows NT 4.0, Windows 2000, Windows XP, or Windows Server 2003. Stands for Security Accounts Manager database.

Sanitized   The status required for a destination disk when creating a forensic disk image. Sanitizing a disk is a process of removing all previous contents from the disk.

Scope and plan initiation phase   The first step in the business continuity planning process. It defines the scope of the plan and examines the company's operations and support services.

Screened subnet   A protected area on the network that is used to run services that are shared outside the organization. See DMZ.

Script kiddies   An attacker who has little insight into the vulnerabilities or features of a system, but uses a script to launch an attack.

Scripts   Code that is executed by a scripting host or macro and does not need to be compiled as an executable.

SCTP   A protocol similar to TCP, except that it transmits multiple streams of messages instead of a single stream of bytes (TCP can only send a single stream of bytes). Stands for Stream Control Transmission Protocol.

Secondary logon   The feature in Windows 2000, Windows XP, and Windows Server 2003 that allows you to change your security context when running a specific application by launching the application using the Run As command.

Secondary network   A network dedicated to accessing a computer for remote management.

Secrecy   Protection of data belonging to an organization.

Securable   See Object.

Secure baseline   A plan for applying the pieces of a trusted computing base to computers.

Secure by default   A characteristic of an operating system or application that ensures that when a user installs it using a default installation, known security vulnerabilities are closed and features that might cause security holes are turned off.

Secure Shell (SSH)   A terminal emulation program that allows you to use strong authentication and encryption.

Secure updates   A type of dynamic update in which only computers that are members of the domain can create or modify its host record. Secure updates can only be used on Active Directory–integrated zones.

Security access control list (SACL)   A part of an Active Directory® object, file system object, or printer that lists the users groups for whom access should be audited and the events that should be audited.

Security Configuration and Analysis snap-in   A Microsoft Management Console (MMC) snap-in that is used to analyze a computer's configuration against a security template.

Security Configuration Wizard (SCW)   Microsoft Windows Server 2003 wizard that simplifies the configuration of a server that hosts one or more roles. Includes an XML database of recommended security settings for various roles.

Security descriptor   A part of an object that contains the security information for that object. A security descriptor includes a DACL, a SACL, and the object owner.

Security group   An Active Directory group that has an SID, and therefore can be assigned access permissions.

Security manager   A part of the Java Virtual Machine that monitors what an applet does and prevents it from performing tasks that might be harmful.

Security policy   A document that defines the objects that should be protected and how that protection should be performed.

Security principal   An authenticated user or computer. A user, computer, or group that can be assigned access to a resource.

Security template   A file that contains a definition of security settings that should be configured for a computer.

Security Templates snap-in   A Microsoft Management Console (MMC) snap-in that is used to create, view, and modify security templates.

Security update   A software update that fixes a security vulnerability. Also referred to as a patch.

Security update infrastructure   A system or set of systems that automates the deployment of security updates and service packs.

Self-propagation   A method by which malware reproduces without requiring a user's assistance.

Self-signing   The process in which a CA validates its own certificate.

Semi-private network   A network that might carry confidential information and that has some regulations about who can access it.

Separation of services   The security strategy in which each major service runs on its own host.

Sequence number   A field in an ESP packet that allows the sender to determine whether the packet is part of a legitimate conversation or used in a replay attack.

Serial Line Internet Protocol (SLIP)   An early dial-up networking protocol that allows remote access using TCP/IP.

Server Operators   An Active Directory built-in Domain Local group whose members can manage domain member computers.

Server role   The job a server performs on a network.

Server-side program   A web component that executes on the web server and sends HTML to the browser.

serveradmin role   A SQL Server fixed server role that allows members to modify server configuration settings, start the server, and stop the server.

ServerHello   A server's response to an SSL ClientHello message. The ServerHello message selects the cipher to use and sends the client a certificate chain for authentication.

Service bureau   An organization that provides alternate processing services during an emergency.

Service Level Agreement (SLA)   An agreement in which a company promises that a resources will be available within a certain amount of time after an incident, system failure, or disaster.

Service processor   A special processor that includes its own power supply and allows access to system management features if the kernel is not running. Can be located on a motherboard or expansion card.

Service set identifier (SSID) An identification number that clients use to connect to a wireless network. Both the client and the WAP must use the same SSID. However, by default, WAPs broadcast the SSID.

Session cookie See Nonpersistent cookie.

Session hijacking A type of man-in-the-middle attack in which an attacker captures traffic that includes either authentication credentials or an authentication cookie and then uses that data to impersonate the client.

Session layer The layer of the OSI model that negotiates and establishes a connection with another computer.

Sessionless A communication in which each request is sent independently from all other requests between the client and server.

SFTP A protocol that is replacing FTP. It provides increased security because it includes strong encryption and authentication. SFTP is a client that is similar to FTP and uses SSH or SSH-2 to provide secure file transfer. Stands for Secure File Transfer Protocol.

SGID program A program configured to run under a specific group account, regardless of who is executing it. Stands for set groupID program.

SHA-1 A standard algorithm for hashing data.

Shadow copy A Windows Server 2003 and Windows Vista™ technology that saves multiple copies of a file so that a user can revert to a previous copy if a user error or file corruption occurs.

Share permissions Permissions that protect a network share. Share permissions are only used to determine access when a user connects using Windows file sharing.

Shared folder A folder on a Windows computer that has been shared to the network.

Shift The offset in a substitution cipher. The shift is used to build the table that serves as the key.

Shiva Password Authentication Protocol (SPAP) A legacy remote access authentication protocol in which passwords are transmitted using a reversible encryption format.

Shoulder surfing A social engineering attack in which a person looks over a person's shoulder as the person types his or her password.

SID A machine-readable unique identifier for a security principal, such as a user, computer, or group. Stands for security identifier.

Signature-based IDS An IDS that uses attack signatures to characterize an attack. Activity is compared against the attack signature database to determine whether suspicious activity is occurring.

Simple file sharing A type of file sharing in which the Guest account is used to access files and the user is not actually authenticated.

Simple Mail Transfer Protocol (SMTP) A protocol used to send email.

Simulation test A test of the disaster recovery plan in which the response teams perform their response functions, but do not initiate recovery procedures. Also referred to as a walk-through drill.

Single point of failure   A weakness in a network that can cause a resource to be unavailable because the component's function is not redundant.

Single sign-on   The ability for a user to gain access to multiple servers by authenticating a single time.

Single-key encryption   See Symmetric encryption.

Site   A grouping of computers that usually represents a geographic location.

Slack space   Space in a cluster that is left over when a file does not require the entire cluster.

Slag code   See Logic bomb.

SLIP   A legacy protocol that defines a sequence of characters that frame IP packets on a serial line. It is used for point-to-point serial connections running TCP/IP, such as dial-up or dedicated serial lines. Stands for Serial Line Internet Protocol.

Slogin   The secure version of Rlogin, used by SSH.

Smart card   A special card contaning a chip that can store digital certificates and private keys. A user must have the card and know the PIN number in order to be authenticated; this type of authentication is known as two-factor authentication.

SMB   A protocol used for file sharing on a Windows network. Stands for Server Message Block.

SMB signing   The process of adding a keyed hash to each SMB packet to provide authentication and integrity, but not confidentiality. Stands for Server Message Block signing.

SMTP   An Application layer protocol that supports the transmission and reception of email. Stands for Simple Mail Transfer Protocol.

Smurf attack   A type of denial-of-service attack in which the attacker sends an ICMP echo request with a spoofed sender address to a broadcast address of a network. The responses flood the spoofed sender's address and make it too busy to respond to legitimate requests.

SNMP   An Application layer protocol that supports the exchange of management information among network devices through a management entity that polls these devices. It is a tool used by network administrators to manage the network and detect problem areas. Stands for Simple Network Management Protocol.

Social engineering   An attack that involves people, not computers. A social engineering attack is one in which the attacker convinces a victim to provide information, such as a password, that can be used to launch an attack.

Sockets   Programs used to access the TCP/IP protocol services.

Software Update Services (SUS)   A freely downloadable server application that can be used to download updates from the Windows Update website for approval and distribution.

Spam   Unwanted email. Spam can include email containing malware or advertisements.

Spam DoS attack   A denial-of-service attack launched by sending so much spam using a forged address that it overloads the mailbox of the forged address and prevents the legitimate use of the address or causes the forged address to be blacklisted.

Spam filter   Software that attempts to identify spam based on the content of the message and other information it can gather about the message or its sender.

Spammer   A person or organization that sends spam.

!Special Administration Console (!SAC)   An EMS remote management console that runs when SAC cannot, but provides only limited capabilities.

Special Administration Console (SAC)   An EMS remote management console that can be used as long as the kernel is running and that allows you to issue user mode commands.

SPI   A 32-bit field in an ESP packet, uniquely identifying the security association for the datagram, the destination IP address, and the security protocol (ESP). Stands for Security Parameters Index.

Spoof   The act of pretending to be someone or some computer that you are not.

Spooled   A condition in which a print job is temporarily stored on the hard disk while waiting to be sent to the printer.

SPX   A protocol maintained by Novell that provides a reliable, connection-oriented transport service. Stands for Sequenced Packet Exchange.

SpyBlast   A browser parasite that claims to locate and eradicate spyware, but that in actuality displays pop-up advertisements.

Spyware   An application that gathers information about a workstation or user. The information gathered is most commonly used to launch advertising campaigns, but could sometimes be used for identity theft.

SQL injection attack   A type of attack against a database server in which the attacker enters data in a field that causes a dynamically constructed query to execute malicious commands.

SRV record   A record that identifies a computer that provides a specific service.

SSH   A secure remote administration technology for Unix that provides authentication and encrypted transmission (over TCP/IP), so is more secure than its predecessor, Telnet. Stands for Secure Shell.

SSH-2   The latest version of SSH.

SSL   A protocol that resides between the Transport layer and Application layer of the protocol stack to provide authentication, integrity, and confidentiality. Stands for Secure Sockets Layer.

SSL Handshake Protocol   The component of SSL that agrees on the cryptographic parameters for the session.

SSL Plaintext records   The data in an SSL transmission that has been broken into fragments but not yet encrypted.

SSL Record Layer   The component of SSL that fragments and encrypts data.

Stack   An internal structure where the operating system places the commands that should execute in a last-in-first-out (LIFO) order.

Stand-alone CA   A CA that is not integrated with Active Directory.

State   Information about the current session between a web browser and a website. One way to manage state is by using cookies.

State table   The table that stores connection information in a stateful inspection firewall.

Stateful inspection   See Stateful packet filtering.

Stateful packet filtering   A firewall technique that uses a table to keep track of connection pairs and that compares each packet against that table.

Statistical anomaly IDS   An IDS that profiles normal usage patterns and compares them with the current usage pattern to detect suspicious activity.

Stealth mode   A wireless access point mode in which the SSID is not broadcast, so the client must be manually configured with the SSID in order to connect.

Sticky bit   A Unix permission bit used to prevent a file from being deleted. To set the sticky bit, set the Execute bit to t instead of x.

Storage area network (SAN)   A network that includes storage devices that can be shared among servers. A storage area network uses either fibre channel or iSCSI for communication.

Store and forward server   An email server that stores messages until they are picked up or routed to the next stop in the route to their destination.

Stream cipher   A symmetric encryption algorithm in which each byte in the plain text is processed with the bytes preceding it.

STRIDE threat model   A list of threat categories created by Microsoft.

String buffer   A memory location set aside to store a specific number of characters.

String signature   A text string that indicates a possible attack.

Striped mirror   See RAID 1E.

Striped RAID 1 arrays   See RAID 10.

Striped RAID 5 arrays   See RAID 50.

Striped RAID 6 arrays   See RAID 60.

Striping with dual parity   See RAID 6.

Striping with parity   See RAID 5.

Strong password   A password that is difficult to guess or crack using a dictionary or brute force attack.

Structured Query Language (SQL)   The ANSI standard relational database query language.

Structured walk-through test   See Tabletop exercise.

Subject   An entity that is granted or denied permission to use an object. Usually an individual or a process.

Subordinate CA   A CA that has a certificate signed by another CA in the hierarchy.

Substitution cipher   A cryptographic algorithm in which each letter in the plain text is replaced by a different letter to create the cipher text.

SUID program   A program configured to run under a specific account, regardless of the user who is running it. Stands for set userID program.

superuser   The all-powerful user on a Unix system (root user).

Support_388945a0   A built-in Windows user account used by the Help and Support feature. It is normally disabled.

svchost.exe   A Windows application that allows multiple services to run within its context.

Switch   A network device that limits the traffic to the destination associated with a specific port. A switch can be used to create smaller broadcast domains.

Symmetric encryption   A method of encryption is which the same key is used to encrypt and decrypt the data.

Symmetric master key   A key that is known by the authentication server and client station for the positive access decision.

SYN message   A packet used to request a conversation or to synchronize sequence numbers.

Systat   A Unix troubleshooting tool that reports information about the processes running on a system.

System state backup   On a Windows computer, the backup of the operating system configuration.

Systems Management Server (SMS)   A comprehensive change management and configuration solution that can deploy applications and manage security updates and other assets.

Tabletop exercise   A test of the disaster recovery plan in which members of the emergency management group discuss their responsibilities and step through the plan verbally. Also referred to as a structured walk-through test.

TACACS+   An enhancement to TACACS that provides dynamic passwords, two-factor authentication, and improved auditing.

Tag   An identifier used to group computers onto a VLAN.

Tail-log backup   A backup of a relational database transaction log that is taken immediately before performing recovery.

Task Manager   The Windows utility that allows you to view a list of running processes.

Tasklist   A Windows command-line utility that allows you to view a list of running processes, including the services running under each process that hosts multiple services.

TCP   A highly reliable, connection-oriented protocol used in communications between hosts in packet-switched computer networks or interconnected networks. Stands for Transmission Control Protocol.

TCP session hijacking   An attack in which an attacker opens a legitimate connection to a server to obtain a sequence number, then impersonates a client by changing the source IP address in a packet and changing the sequence number to a best guess based on the attacker's legitimate request.

TCP SYN flooding attack   A denial of service attack in which a large number of SYN packets is set to a server without completing the conversation initiation handshake.

TCP/IP model   A layered model that defines the layers at which the members of the TCP/IP protocol operate.

Telnet   A remote administrator protocol that operates in clear text. Telnet presents a security risk. *Also* A terminal emulation program that sends data in clear text.

Temporal key   A key that protects transmitted data and varies with time.

Temporal Key Integrity Protocol (TKIP)   A strategy for managing wireless network encryption keys that is based on the WEP algorithm but eliminates some of its vulnerabilities.

Temporary file   A file created by an application. Usually deleted when the application is closed, sometimes they remain on disk.

Temporary Internet files   Files downloaded from a website by a browser. They can include graphics, cookies, and other files.

Terminal Access Controller Access Control System (TACACS)   An authentication protocol that provides centralized remote access authentication and related services, such as event logging. Similar to RADIUS.

Terminal concentrator   A hardware device that contains a number of serial ports and that can be used to connect multiple servers for EMS management.

Terminal emulation   A program that allows a user to execute commands on a remote system.

Terminal Services   An earlier version of Remote Desktop for Administration used in Windows 2000. Terminal Services is also supported in Windows Server 2003 for running applications remotely.

TFTP   Reduced version of FTP; it does not provide authentication or accessing of directories. Stands for Trivial File Transfer Protocol.

TGS   A Kerberos service that is responsible for supplying the client with a ticket-granting ticket (TGT). Stands for ticket-granting service.

TGT   An object that is presented to the ticket-granting service to request a ticket for another server. Stands for ticket-granting ticket.

The Sleuth Kit   A freely downloadable set of command-line forensics tools available for Unix, Linux, Mac OS X, and Windows.

The wild   A term used to refer to a public network, such as the Internet.

Third-party cookie   A cookie that is downloaded from one domain and that sends data back to another domain.

Threat   An action by an adversary that tries to exploit a vulnerability to damage assets.

Three-pronged configuration   A perimeter configuration in which a device has three network adapters: one on the Internet, one on the screened subnet, and one on the internal network.

Throughput rate   The rate at which the system processes and identifies or authenticates individuals.

TIFF   A public domain raster file graphics format. It does not handle vector graphics. TIFF is platform-independent and was designed for use with printers and scanners. Stands for Tagged Image File Format.

Time bomb   A logic bomb that uses a date or time as the triggering event.

TLS   The latest version of SSL. Stands for Transport Layer Security.

Total cost of ownership (TCO)   The total cost of purchasing, implementing, supporting, and maintaining a computer.

Transaction log   A file that stores changes to data in a relational database before they are written to the database.

Transaction log backup   A backup of a relational database transaction log.

Transaction Signatures (TSIG)   A cryptographic signature that verifies the identity of a DNS server receiving a zone transfer.

Transactional data   Data stored and managed by a relational database management system.

Translation table   In NAT, a table that maps public IP addresses to internal private IP addresses.

Transport layer (OSI model)   The layer of the OSI model that supports reliable end-to-end delivery of data.

Transport layer (TCP/IP model)   See Host-to-Host layer.

Transport mode   An ESP mode in which the upper-layer protocol frame, but not the IP header, is encapsulated. Provides end-to-end encryption.

Trapdoor   See Backdoor.

Trojan horse   A program that masquerades as a legitimate program, while performing a covert function that is usually malicious.

Trojan horse applications   Software that pretends to be legitimate applications, but actually performs malicious tasks.

Trust relationship   An association that allows computers and users in Domain A to trust computers and users in Domain B based on its authentication by an authentication server in Domain B.

Trusted computing base   The total combination of protection mechanisms in a computer system.

Trusted host   A Unix host that is trusted because the user name is the same on both the local and remote computers.

Trusted sites zone   The Internet Explorer and Outlook security zone that contains addresses that should be treated with fewer security restrictions than the Internet zone.

Trusted zones   DNS domains that for which Internet Explorer® enforces fewer restrictions.

Tunnel   To send data through an unsecure network by encapsulating the data inside protocol headers and trailers.

Tunnel mode   An ESP mode in which the entire IP datagram is encapsulated within an outer IP datagram. This mode allows gateway-to-gateway security for hosts that are not IPsec-aware.

Two-factor authentication   A type of authentication in which you must present two different authentication factors—for example, something you have and something you know.

Type 1 authentication   A type of authentication in which the credential provided is something you know. The most common example of type 1 authentication is using a password.

Type 2 authentication   A type of authentication in which the credential you provide is something you possess.

Type 3 authentication   A type of authentication in which the credential you provide is something you are. Biometrics is an example of type 3 authentication.

Type I error   See False rejection rate.

Type II error   See False acceptance rate.

UDP   An "unreliable" protocol in that it transmits packets on a best-effort basis; it does not provide for error correction or for the correct transmission and reception sequencing of packets. Stands for User Datagram Protocol.

UID   A 16-bit number that identifies a user on a Unix computer. Stands for user identity.

Unicast packet   A packet that is sent to a single computer.

Uniform Resource Locator (URL)   The path to a web site. It takes the form *protocol:\\hostname_or_IPaddress\\path\filename?querystring*. The path, filename, and query string are optional.

Universal group   An Active Directory group that is available in native mode domains only. Its members can be accounts, Global groups from any domain, and other Universal groups.

Unused IP space   Unassigned addresses in an IP subnet.

UOWHF   A hash function that is resistant to hash collisions. Stands for Universal One Way Hash Function.

UrlScan   An ISAPI filter that screens and analyzes URLs and other web server requests before Internet Information Services (IIS) processes them.

User mode access   Access to commands that run under the context of a user and that can access memory available to user processes.

User-based access control   A method in which a user is authenticated and the user's SID is used to determine resource access permissions.

User-directed discretionary access control   A type of discretionary access control in which a user can alter access privileges.

Users   An Active Directory built-in Domain Local group whose members have limited access in the domain.

utmp command   Unix or Linux command that records accounting information used by the who command.

Verb   A type of HTTP command that tells the web server to perform a specific action.

Vigenere cipher   A cryptographic algorithm in which a repeating keyword is used as the key for generating the cipher text.

Virtual machine   Runs an operating system and one or more applications. To network clients, it is accessed as if it is a physical server.

Virtual private network (VPN)   A secure tunnel through a non-secure network such as the Internet.

Virtualization   The process of installing multiple virtual machines on a single physical host.

Virus   Code that attaches itself to legitimate software, such as an application or data file. A virus requires a host to transport it from computer to computer.

Virus signature   A pattern of bits inside a virus that the antivirus program uses to identify it.

Visual Basic script (VBScript)   A script written in the Visual Basic® scripting language. Visual Basic is a programming language that evolved from BASIC.

VLAN 1   The default VLAN to which a host belongs if no tag is specified.

VLAN   A logical network segment that is defined by grouping computers based on organizational requirements instead of on physical location. Stands for virtual local area network.

VLAN hopping   An attack in which the attacker modifies the VLAN ID (tag) on a packet to bypass Layer 3 devices, such as routers and firewalls.

VLAN ID   See Tag.

Volatile data   Information that is destroyed when a computer is shut down.

Volume shadow copy   The Windows technology that allows a file to be backed up even if it is in use.

Vulnerability   A weakness of a system that could be accidentally or intentionally exploited to damage assets.

Vulnerability assessment   Performed during the business impact assessment. Similar to a risk assessment.

Vulnerability scanner   See Risk analysis tool.

Walk-through drill   See Simulation test.

War chalking   The process of leaving a mark on a building or sidewalk to let others know the location of an unsecured wireless access point.

War dialers   Devices that automatically dial phone numbers looking for a remote access server.

War driving   The process of searching for unsecured wireless access points by driving around with a wireless network card and software that can detect unsecured access points.

Warez list   A list of anonymous FTP and vulnerable writable directories. Often used by attackers to transfer pirated software.

Warm site   A backup site that has most peripheral equipment installed, but the principal computers are not installed.

Web beacon   A link to a graphic or other resource on a web server that logs the email addresses that open the link. This tells the attacker that the email is being opened.

Well-known ports   Ports numbered between 0 and 1024 that are identified with a specific TCP/IP Application layer protocol.

Well-known SID   An SID used on every computer or in every domain. For example, the Everyone SID is always S-1-1-0.

WEP open authentication   A WEP authentication method in which the client is authenticated solely on the basis of its knowledge of the SSID.

WEP shared key authentication   A type of challenge-response authentication used with WEP. It is inherently weak because the challenge string is transmitted as clear text, the IV is transmitted in clear text, and the IV must be reused frequently.

who command   A Unix or Linux command that displays the users who are logged in to the computer and when the connection began. It might also display the name of the computer where the user is logged in interactively.

Wi-Fi®   See Wireless fidelity.

WiFi Protected Access (WPA)   An authentication and encryptions strategy for wireless networks that prevents some WEP vulnerabilities but provides backward compatibility with existing hardware. WPA uses TKIP.

Windows Backup   The backup utility included in Windows operating systems.

Windows Internet Name Service (WINS) server   A server responsible for resolving NetBIOS names to IP addresses.

Windows Live authentication   A public central authentication server that issues credentials to users on the Internet. Applications on the Internet can interface with Windows Live to authenticate users.

Windows Server Update Services (WSUS)   The latest enhancement to SUS. It can deploy not only updates for operating system, but also those for supported Windows applications.

Windows update   A website hosted by Microsoft that contains the latest service packs and patches for Windows operating systems and some Microsoft applications.

WinHex   A forensics utility for Windows that can be used to sanitize a disk, create a hash, and make a bitstream copy.

WINS replication   The process of copying WINS records from one WINS server to another.

Wired Equivalent Privacy (WEP)   An encryption method for wireless networks that authenticates users based on their knowledge of a shared secret and uses that shared secret along with an initialization vector to encrypt message packets.

Wireless access point (WAP)   A networking device for a wireless network. A WAP can allow clients to connect in infrastructure mode and can act as a bridge to a wired network.

Wireless fidelity (Wi-Fi)   A general term used to describe a wireless network that connects two or more computers.

Wireless LAN (WLAN)   A LAN that uses a wireless connection medium based on an 802.11 standard.

Word salad   A technique to try to circumvent spam filters by inserting random or nonsense words into the body of a message.

Worm   Malicious code that is self-propagating and exploits a vulnerability in a program.

Write blocker   Hardware or software that prevents a hard disk's contents from being modified.

Written security policy   Set of written laws, rules, and practices that regulate how an organization manages, protects, and distributes resources to achieve specified security policy objectives.

wtmp command   The Unix or Linux command that stores information about each time a user logs in or logs out.

X-Ways Forensics   A forensics tool kit for Windows.

X.509 certificate   An electronic document that contains information about its owner, the public key of its owner, and the signature of a validator.

XOR function   A binary operation performed on two strings of bits. If the bits are the same, the result is a 0. If the bits are different, the result is a 1.

Zombie   A host on which a Trojan horse is installed in order to launch a distributed denial-of-service attack.

Zone   A container on a DNS server that corresponds to a DNS namespace. A zone contains DNS records.

Zone transfer   A method of sharing DNS records with one or more other DNS servers.

INDEX

$ character, 455
%systemroot%, 170
|| symbol, 203–04
~ character, 453
> operator, 446, 447

A

A record, 280
Acceptability, 131
Access client, 238
Access control. *See also* Authorization and access
        control
    Active Directory object permissions, 163–64
    discretionary access control, 150–51
    examples, 153, 161, 173, 180
    files and folders, 165–71
    mandatory access control, 151–52
    overview, 150
    principle of least permission, 154
    role-based access control, 152–53
    standards, 22
    Unix objects, 176–81
    Unix overview, 174
    Unix principals, 174–75
    user rights assignment, 172–73
    Windows model, 161–63
    Windows overview, 154
    Windows principals, 154–61
Access control entries (ACE), 161, 162, 173
Access control list (ACL), 150, 151, 161, 173, 299
Access control settings, 13
Access tokens, 161, 162–63
Account Lockout policy, 139–40
Account Logon, 140
Account operators, 158
Accountability, 6, 9–10
acct command, 369
ACE (access control entries), 161, 162, 173
Acknowledgement (ACK) message, 189–90
ACL (access control list), 150, 151, 161, 173, 299
Acrobat Reader, 337
Active Directory
    authentication, 124
    client extensions, 133
    database, 120
    802.1x configuration, 248–50
    forest, 158
    Group Policy, 288
    integrated zones, 277
    introduced, 110
    object permissions, 163–64
    reversible encryption, enabling, 227–28
    routing and remote access service, 224, 225
Active Directory Application Mode (ADAM), 349
Active Directory-integrated (ADI) zones, 277
Active node, 425
Active Server Pages (ASP), 299
ActiveX, 324–25
ActiveX controls, 324–25
Ad hoc mode, 240
ADAM (Active Directory Application Mode), 349
Add-ons, 324
Address Resolution Protocol (ARP), 37
Address Resolution Protocol (ARP) spoofing tool,
        338, 340
ADI (Active Directory-integrated) zones, 277
Administrative (hidden) shares, 169–71
Administrators, 158
Advanced Encryption Standard (AES), 87–88
Adware, 322
AH (authentication header), 206
AirSnort, 234
Algorithms, cryptographic, 75
"All People Seem to Need Data Processing"
        pneumonic, 32
American National Standards Institute (ANSI), 301
American Standard Code for Information
        Interchange (ASCII), 34, 319
Analysis paralysis, 15
Anonymous access, 123
Anonymous FTP, 295–96, 297
Anti-malware, 317
Anti-spyware, 317–18
Antivirus software, 317
AppleTalk Session Protocol (ASP), 35
Applets (Java), 325–26
Application authentication, 123–25
Application layer
    OSI model, 33–34
    TCP/IP model, 41–42
Application proxy firewalls, 64
Application servers, securing
    database servers, 301–03
    overview, 298, 304
    web servers, 298–300
Appropriate use policy, 21
ARP (Address Resolution Protocol), 37
ARP (Address Resolution Protocol) spoofing tool,
        338, 340

AS (authentication service), 136
ASCII (American Standard Code for Information
        Interchange), 34, 319
ASP (Active Server Pages), 299
ASP (AppleTalk Session Protocol), 35
ASP.NET, 299
Assets, 12, 16, 18, 20, 22
Asymmetric encryption, 80, 90–92, 99
Attack signature database, 435
Attackers
    evidence left behind, 370, 406, 442–43
    firewalls and, 64–65
    profile, 4
Attacks. *See also* Malware protection; Server security
    automated, 4
    brute force, 14
    buffer overflow, 303
    definition, 11
    denial-of-service. *See* Denial-of-service (DoS)
        attacks
    dictionary, 14
    flooding, 9
    hijacking, 327–28
    honeypots. *See* Honeypots
    man-in-the-middle, 8, 89, 337–39, 340
    phishing, 341–42, 343
    replay, 136, 328–29, 339–41, 342
    response to, 405–06
    scripts, 15
    smurf, 9
    social engineering, 4–5
    spam, 342–45
    SQL injection, 301–03
    TCP session hijacking, 189–91
    against third parties, 3
    tree, 14–15
Audit, 366
Audit logs/audit trails, 367–68, 370
Auditing
    baseline templates, 265
    configuration, 359
    definition, 366
    files and folders, 292–93, 294, 295
    monitoring, 368
    security audits, 366
    security templates, 269
    standards and guidelines, 367–68
    Unix, 368–69
    Windows, 285, 369–71
Authentication
    application, 123–25
    biometrics, 129–31
    in CIA, 98
    computer, 120–21
    credentials, 125–31

    definition, 119
    examples, 123, 127, 128, 130, 135, 142–43
    interactive logon, 119–20
    mutual, 121–22
    overview, 119, 143
    password and account best practices, 136–41
    protocols, 131–36
    strategy, 226–27
    wired equivalent privacy. *See* Wired equivalent
        privacy (WEP)
Authentication data, 207
Authentication header (AH), 206
Authentication service (AS), 136
Authenticator, 136
Authorization, 119
Authorization and access control
    Active Directory object permissions, 163–64
    examples, 153, 161, 173, 180
    mandatory access control, 151–52
    models, 150
    overview, 150, 182
    principle of least permission, 154
    role-based access control, 152–53
    Unix objects, 176–81
    Unix overview, 174
    Unix principals, 174–75
    Windows model, 161–63
    Windows overview, 154
    Windows principals, 154–61
Authorizing entity, 150
Automatic Updates (Windows), 361, 367
Automating updates, 360
Autopsy Forensic Browser, 457
Autorun macros, 312
Availability, 6, 8–9

B

Backdoors, 314–15
Back-to-back configurations, 196, 197
Backup Operators, 159
Backup sites, 401–02
Backup strategy
    assigning responsibility, 413–14
    frequency, 411–13
    media selection for, 409–10
    overview, 407
    requirements, analysis, 407–08
    system configurations, 408
    testing recovery, 414
    tools, 408–09
    types of backups, 410–11
Backups, 55–56
Baseline template, 265
Baselines

example, 272
implementing, 265
Linux servers, 272–73
secure, 264
Security Configuration Wizard, 270–71
security templates, 265–69
trusted computing base, 263–64
virtualization, 273–74
Basic authentication, 124
Bastion host, 195–96
Behavior-based IDS, 435–36
Berkeley Internet Name Domain (BIND), 33
Best practices
authentication, 136–41
compliance with standard, 23
network security, 45–49
risk analysis, example, 18
security policy, example, 24
BIND (Berkeley Internet Name Domain), 33
BIND name server, 277–78
Biometrics, 129–31
Bitstream image, 449
Blacklist, 344
Block ciphers, 85–88
Blocking ports, 52–53
Blum-Blum-Shub pseudorandom generator, 81
Boot sector viruses, 311
BootP, 34
Border security
application proxy firewalls, 64
example, 66
firewalls, general, 58–60, 64–65
network address translation, 65–67
overview, 57
packet-filtering firewalls, 60–62
perimeter defense, 58
segmenting a network, 57–58
stateful packet-filtering, 62–63
"Break the stack," 303
Broadcast domain, 198
Broadcast packets, 61
Browser parasites, 313
Browsers. See Web browser security
Brute force attack, 14
Brute force methods, 77
Buffer overflow attack, 303
Business continuity planning, 22, 396–99
Business impact assessment, 397–99

C

CA. See Certificate authority (CA)
Cache poisoning, 281–83
Calculating risk. See Risk analysis
Callback option, 228

CAPolicy.inf file, 108
Castle security metaphor, 47–48
CBC (cipher-block chaining), 86
CD-ROM drives, 54–55
CER (crossover error rate), 131
Certificate authority (CA)
definition, 99–100
designing hierarchy, 103–07
from other organizations, 108–09
PKI role, 101
public vs. private, 104–05
renewals, 110–11
revocation, 111–12
smart cards, 128–29
Certificate path, 107
Certificate policy, 108
Certificate requests, 101–02
Certificate revocation list (CRL), 111–12
Certificate templates, 100
Certificates
digital, 99–100, 105
secure socket layers, 330–31
Certification Practice Statement (CPS), 108
CFB (cipher feedback), 87
CGI (Common Gateway Interface), 299
Chain of custody, 445
Chain of trust, 107
Challenge Handshake Authentication Protocol
(CHAP), 139, 223–24, 227
Challenge-and-response, 223–24
Change control, 358
ChangeCiperSpec message, 205
Characters, cryptography, 82
Chargen, 51
Checklist review, 402
chgrp command, 180
chmod command, 179
chown command, 180
CIA (confidentiality, integrity, authentication),
80, 97–99
Cipher feedback (CFB), 87
Cipher spec, 202
Cipher text, 76
Cipher-block chaining (CBC), 86
Ciphers
block, 85–88
historical, 79
one-time pad, 78–79
stream, 84–85
substitution, 75–77
Vigenere, 77–78
CIs (configuration items), 359
Clearance, 151
Client certificate, 122
ClientHello message, 202, 203

Clipping levels, 368
Clustering, 425, 426
Code Red 2, 303
Code Red Worm, 303
Cold site, 401
Collision Resistant Hash Function (CRHF), 94
Common Gateway Interface (CGI), 299
Communication procedure disaster recovery, 404–05
Compiled, 311
Complement value, 449
Compliance, 23
Computationally secure, 84
Computer authentication, 120–21
Computer Management MMC, 171, 377–78
Computer Security Incident Response Plan (CSIRP),
    403, 434
Computer Security Incident Response Team
    (CSIRT), 403
Confidentiality, 2, 6–7, 11. *See also* Cryptography
Confidentiality, integrity, authentication (CIA), 80,
    97–99
Configuration, server, 49–59
Configuration auditing, 359
Configuration control, 359
Configuration identification, 359
Configuration items (CIs), 359
Configuration management, 357–60
Configuration status accounting, 359
Connectionless protocol, 36
Connection-oriented protocol, 36
Consistency, external, 8
Continuity planning, 396–99
Cookies, 327, 328, 331–34
Costs
    account risk analysis, 140–41
    firewall installation, 64–65
    infrastructure design, 192
    risk analysis, 16
    security design, 46–47
Countermeasures
    description, 16–19
    TCP SYN flooding attacks, 192
CPS (Certification Practice Statement), 108
Crackers, 60
CRC values, 312
Credentials
    authentication, 125–31
    definition, 119–20
CRHF (Collision Resistant Hash Function), 94
CRL (certificate revocation list), 111–12
Cross-certification, 108–09
Crossover error rate (CER), 131
Cryptanalysis, 75
Cryptanalysts, 76
Cryptographic mechanisms, 10

Cryptographic primitives, 75
Cryptography
    asymmetric encryption, 80, 90–92
    characters (fictional examples), 82
    CIA, achieving, 97–99
    definition, 75
    examples, 83, 90, 92, 94, 96, 99, 109, 112
    history, 75–79
    MMC, 377
    overview, 75, 113
    primitives, 79–81
    public key infrastructure, 99–112
    symmetric encryption, 80, 83–90
    XOR function, 81–82
CSIRP (Computer Security Incident Response Plan),
    403, 434
CSIRT (Computer Security Incident Response
    Team), 403
Custom roles, 153
Custom templates, 268–69
Cyclic redundancy check (CRC), 312

D
DAC (discretionary access control), 150–51
DACL (discretionary access control list), 161–62
DAS (direct attached storage), 423
Data
    alteration, 190
    backing up. *See* Backup strategy
    definition, 12
    encapsulation, 31
    integrity, 8
    searching for on hard drive, 450–57
    transmission, 193–94
Data Encryption Standard (DES), 84
Data Link layer, 33, 37–38
Data transmission protection protocols, 201–05
Database servers
    restoring, 412
    securing, 301–03
Db_backupoperator roles, 153
Db_securityadmin roles, 153
Dbcreator roles, 153
DCBP (Domain Controller Baseline Policy), 289
DCOM (Distributed Component Object
    Model), 378
dcomcnfg, 378
dd Utility, 449
DDoS (Distributed Denial-of-service) attacks, 313
Decryption. *See* Cryptography
Default permissions, 167
Defense-in-depth principle, 47–49
Deleted files, 453–55
Demilitarized zone (DMZ), 58, 195

Denial-of-service (DoS) attacks
   availability, 8–9
   definition, 3–4, 189
   description, 190
   example, 17–18
   incorrect zone data, 276
   likelihood, 19
   Network-based IDS (NIDS), 436–37
   spam, 343–44
   as threat, 13
   WINS servers, 287
Depth, 81
DES (Data Encryption Standard), 84
Design
   client authentication, 135
   Emergency Management Services, 383–89
   failover solution, 425–27
   incident response procedure, 403–06
   securing network transmission, 192–93
   security systems, 46–47
Determinate chain of notification, 404–05
DFS (Distributed File System), 291
DHCP scopes, 284
DHCP servers, 274, 284–87, 288, 425
DHCPINFORM message, 284
Dial-up networking
   authentication protocols, 223–28
   examples, 228, 235
   limiting access, 228–29
   preventing access, 229–30
   protocols, 222–23
Dictionary attack, 14
Differential backup, 410
Diffie-Hellman key exchange, 89, 90
Digest, 93
Digest authentication, 124
Digital certificates, 99–100, 105
Digital Signature Algorithm (DSA), 214
Digital signatures, 10, 92, 94, 341
Direct attached storage (DAS), 423
Direct serial connection, 385–86
Disaster recovery. *See also* Fault tolerance
   backup frequency, 411–13
   backup requirements, 407–10
   backup responsibilities, 413–14
   backup types, 410–11
   business continuity planning, 396–99
   examples, 406, 414
   incident response procedures, designing, 403–06
   overview, 396, 427
   planning for, 396, 399–403
   testing recovery, 414
Disaster recovery plan, 400
Discrete logarithm problem, 89
Discretionary access control (DAC), 150–51

Discretionary access control list (DACL), 161–62
Disk mirroring (RAID 1), 417
Disk stripping (RAID 0), 417
Distributed Component Object Model (DCOM), 378
Distributed Denial-of-service (DDoS) attacks, 313
Distributed File System (DFS), 291
DMZ (demilitarized zone), 58, 195
DNS (domain name system), 33, 51, 291
DNS cache, 281, 282
DNS namespace, 275
DNSUpdateProxy group, 286
Documentary evidence, 445
Documentation control, 360
Domain, 120
Domain Admins, 159
Domain Computers, 159
Domain Controller Baseline Policy (DCBP), 289
Domain controllers, 120, 159, 289–92
Domain Guests, 159
Domain Local groups, 158–61
Domain name system (DNS), 33, 51, 291
Domain name system (DNS) servers, 274, 275–83
Domain principals, 156, 157
Domain Users, 159
DoS attacks. *See* Denial-of-service (DoS) attacks
DREAD methodology, 16
Drop-off directories, 296
DSA (digital signature algorithm), 214
Dumps memory, 384
DVD drives, 54–55
Dynamic DNS updates, 285–87
Dynamic Host Configuration Protocol (DHCP)
        servers, 274, 284–87, 288, 425
Dynamic outbound packets, 67
Dynamic updates, 280–81

E
EAP (Extensible Authentication Protocol), 226
EBCDIC (Extended Binary Coded Decimal
        Interchange Code), 34
ECB (electronic code book), 86
Echo, 51
Edge Transport, 349
Effective permissions, 167
EFS (Encrypting File System), 90
802.1Q, 198
802.1x standard
   Active Directory configuration, 248–50
   description, 247–48
   Protected Extensible Authentication Protocol,
      250–51, 252
   RADIUS, 251
   re-keying, 247–48
   wireless network vulnerabilities, 254

802.11a, 239
802.11b, 239
802.11g, 239–40
802.11i standard, 252–53
Electronic code book (ECB), 86
Elevation of privilege, 13
Email header, 455, 456
Email replay attack, 339–41, 342
Email security
    architectural considerations, 347–49
    email header, 455, 456
    example, 349
    malcode propagated by, 345–46
    man-in-the-middle attacks, 337–39, 340
    overview, 336
    phishing attacks, 341–42, 343
    replay attacks, 339–41, 342
    spam, 342–45
Emergency Management Services (EMS), 374, 383–89
Encapsulating, 222
Encapsulating security payload (ESP), 206–08
Encrypting File System (EFS), 90
Encryption. See Cryptography
Enforce password history, 137
Enigma (encryption machine), 79
Enrollment strategy, 110
Enrollment time, 131
Enterprise CA, 110
ESP (encapsulating security payload), 206–08
/etc/group, 175
/etc/passwd, 174
/etc/profile, 175
Ettercap, 338
Evacuation drills, 402
Event logs, 367–68, 370
Everyone group, 168
Evidence, 444–45
Extended Binary Coded Decimal Interchange Code
    (EBCDIC), 34
Extensible Authentication Protocol (EAP), 226
External consistency, 8. See also Integrity

F

Failover, 425
Failover solution, 425–27
Failover system, 55–56
False acceptance rate (FAR), 130
False positives, 435, 436, 438
False rejection rate (FRR), 130
Fault tolerance. See also Disaster recovery
    definition, 263
    example, 426
    failover solution, designing, 425–27
    overview, 415, 427

RAID hardware and software, 421–23
RAID levels, 416–21
single points of failure, 415–16, 426
storage, 416
Storage area networks, 423–24
Fault tolerant solution, 415
Fault-tolerant computing, 8
Fibre Channel, 424
File Replication Services (FRS), 291
File servers, securing, 292–93
File Transfer Protocol (FTP), 33, 51
Files and folders
    backing up, 413
    deleted, 453–55
    designing access control, 165–71
    hidden, 451–52
    securing file servers, 292–93
    simple sharing, 120
    temporary Internet, 452–53
    Unix security attributes, 179–81
Filters, 60. See also Firewalls
Finger, 51
finger command, 368
Firefox, 332, 334, 336, 338
Firewalls
    back-to-back configuration, 196, 197
    bastion host, 195, 196
    as border security, 58–65
    disadvantages, 64–65
    lack of, 19
    personal, 56, 318
    secure socket layers, 201–02
    TCP session hijacking, 191
    three-pronged configuration, 196, 197
    weak, 13
Fixed database roles, 153
Fixed server roles, 153
Flooding attacks, 9
Floppy drives, 55
Folders and files. See Files and folders
Footprint, 198
Forensics. See also Intrusion detection (ID)
    data searching on hard drive, 450–57
    definition, 444
    examples, 449, 457
    gathering evidence on a live system, 445–48
    hard drive image, 448–49
    overview, 444, 458
    understanding evidence, 444–45
Forward lookup, 280
Frequency analysis, 76–77
FRR (false rejection rate), 130
FRS (File Replication Services), 291
FTP (File Transfer Protocol), 33, 51
FTP servers, securing, 295–97

Full backup, 408
Full-interruption test, 402
Full-scale exercise, 402
Functional drill, 402

G

Gateway-to-gateway security, 208
Generic Routing Encapsulation (GRE), 231
Ghost, 408, 449
GIDs (group identities), 174
Global catalog, 160
Global catalog servers, 160
Global groups, 158, 159
GNU General Public License (GNU GPL), 442
GPOs. *See* Group Policy Objects (GPOs)
GRE (Generic Routing Encapsulation), 231
Group identities (GIDs), 174
Group Policy, 110, 288
Group Policy Objects (GPOs)
    computer authentication, 121
    security templates, 265–66
    SUS client configuration, 363–64
    user rights assignment, 172
Group transient key (GTK), 252
Groups, 152, 158–61, 175
Guests, 159

H

Half-open connections, 192
Hard drive image, 448–49
Hardware
    as asset, 12
    remote management security, 373–74
    securing, 193
Hardware-assisted software RAID, 422–23
Hash collisions, 94
Hash functions, 80, 93
Hashes
    CIA, achieving, 99
    digital signatures, 92, 94
    disabling LAN Manager, 132
    encryption, 93–96
    examples, 94, 96
HBA (host bus adapter), 422–23
Header condition signatures, 436
Headless servers, 55
Heterogeneous environment, 119
Hexadecimal commands, 303
Hidden (administrative) shares, 169–71
Hidden attribute, 451
Hidden files, 451–52
Hidden shares, 455, 456
High-interaction honeypots, 442

Hijacking attacks, 327–28
Home directory, 176–77
Honeyd, 442
Honeynet Project, 442–43
Honeypots
    appropriate use of, 442–43
    attack prevention and detection, 440–41
    definition, 439
    high-interaction, 442
    legal considerations, 443–44
    low-interaction, 441–42
Host, 311
Host bus adapter (HBA), 422–23
Host name, 274
Host record, 280
Host-based IDS (HID), 435, 437–38
Host-to-Host layer, 41
Hot site, 401
Hot space (RAID 5EE), 419
Hot spare, 419
Hyperlink, 299
HyperTerminal, 383
Hypertext Markup Language (HTML), 299
Hypertext Transfer Protocol (HTTP), 3, 35
Hypertext Transfer Protocol over SSL (HTTPS), 3

I

IAS (Internet Authentication Service), 236
IAS proxy configuration, 236–37
ICMP (Internet Control Message Protocol), 9, 37
ICS (Internet Connection Sharing), 284
ICV (integrity check value), 207
ID. see Intrusion detection (ID)
Identification, 125
Identity theft, 3
Identity-based access control, 151
IEEE. see Institute of Electrical and Electronics
        Engineers (IEEE)
IKE (internet key exchange) protocol, 209
IKEv2, 209
ILOVEYOU virus, 312
Image, 408, 448–49
Impersonate, 123
Impersonation token, 162
In-band remote management, 373
Inbound remote management, 376–82
Incorrect zone data, 275–76
Incremental templates, 266
Index Server service, 303
Information disclosure, 13
Information leakage, 276
Information Systems Audit and Control Association
        (ISACA), 367
Infrastructure design, for security, 192–93

Infrastructure mode, 240
Inherited permissions, 164
Initialization vector (IV), 242
Inode, 176
Input and output devices, 53–55
Insider fraud, 4
Institute of Electrical and Electronics Engineers
     (IEEE), 38, 239–40
Integrated Windows authentication, 124
Integrity, 6, 7–8, 11, 97. *See also* Hashes
Integrity check value (ICV), 207
Intelligent agents, 437
Intelligent UPS (uninterruptible power supply),
     388–89
Interaction, 441
Interactive logon, 119–20
Intermediate CA role, 106
Internet Authentication Service (IAS), 236
Internet Connection Sharing (ICS), 284
Internet Control Messaging Protocol (ICMP),
     9, 37
Internet Engineering Task Force, 212
Internet Explorer
     cookie policies, 333
     phishing filter, 342
     zones, 334–36
Internet Information Services (IIS), 379
Internet Key Exchange (IKE) protocol, 209
Internet layer, 41, 42
Internet Protocol (IP)
     address network classes, 40–41
     definition, 36
     TCP/IP model, 39–43
Internet Protocol security. *see* IP security (IPsec)
Internet Server Application Programming Interface
     (ISAPI), 299
Internet zone, 334–35
Internetwork Packet Exchange (IPX), 36
Intersite Messaging service (ismServ), 291
Intrusion detection (ID). *See also* Forensics
     definition, 434
     examples, 438, 443
     honeypots, 439–44
     issues affecting, 438–39
     overview, 434, 457
     prevention systems (IPS), 439
     systems (IDS), 434–38
Intrusion detection system (IDS), 253, 368,
     434–38
Intrusion prevention systems (IPS), 439
Investigative searching, 298
IP. *see* Internet Protocol (IP)
IP address
     description, 39
     filtering, 199–200

network address translation, 65
     static configuration, 67
IP packet filtering, 61, 200
IP security (IPsec)
     authentication header, 206
     configuration, 210–11
     creating rules, 212
     definition, 37
     encapsulating security payloads, 206–08
     IKE protocol, 209
     overview, 205–06
     security associations, 208–09
     subnet securing, 214
     WINS server security, 287–88
IP within IP, 208
IPsec VPN clients, 234
IPX (Internetwork Packet Exchange), 36
ISACA (Information Systems Audit and Control
     Association), 367
ISAPI (Internet Server Application Programming
     Interface), 299
iSCSI, 424
ISO 17799 security standard, 20–23
ISO OSI model. *see* Open systems interconnection
     (OSI) model
Issuing CA role, 106
IUSR_computername account, 123
IV (Initialization vector), 242
IV sequencing discipline, 245

J

Java applets, 325–26
JavaScript, 326
Joint Photographic Experts Group (JPEG), 35

K

Kerberos, 87, 134–36
Kerberos key distribution center (KDC), 292
Kerberos realm, 134
Key agreement protocol, 89
Key block, 204
Key confirmation key (KCK), 252
Key distribution center (KDC), 136
Key encryption key (KEK), 252
Key hierarchy, 248
Key reuse, 247–48
Keyed hash functions, 96
Keys
     definition, 76
     DES and stream cipher, 84
     802.11i standard, 252–53
     sharing, 88–90
     Vigenere cipher, 78

Keystroke logging programs, 127, 314
Knoppix permissions, 181
Knowledge-based IDS, 435

L

L0phtrack (LC5), 127
L2TP (Layer 2 Tunneling Protocol), 233–34, 235
LAN Manager protocol, 132
LAN Manager-based protocols, 131–34
last command, 369
lastcomm command, 369
Last-in-first-out (LIFO), 303
lastlog command, 368
Layer 2 Tunneling Protocol (L2TP),
        233–34, 235
Layered architecture, 31
Layers, ISO OSI model
    Data Link, 37–38
    Logical Link, 37
    Media Access, 37
    Network, 36–37
    Physical, 38
    Presentation, 34–35
    Session, 35
    Transport, 35
Layers, TCP/IP model
    Application, 41
    encapsulation, 42–43
    Host-to-Host, 41
    Internet, 42
    Network Access, 42
    Transport, 41
LC5 (L0phtrack), 127
LCP (Link Control Protocol), 223
Legal issues and honeypot deployment,
        443–44
Letter salad, 344
Level of criticality, 13
LIFO (Last-in-first-out), 303
Limiting the attack surface, 50
Link Control Protocol (LCP), 223
Link establishment phase, 223
Linux
    BIND name server, 277–78
    malware programs, 316
    secure baseline configuration, 272–73
LMHosts file, 287
Local intranet zones, 335–36
Local Service account, 52
Local System account, 52
Log files, 450–51
Logging programs. see Keystroke logging programs
Logic bombs, 313
Logical Link layer, 37

Low-interaction honeypots, 441–42
ls command, 176

M

MAC (mandatory access control), 151–52
MAC (Media Access Control) address, 34, 241
Macro Virus Protection, 312
Mail proxy, 347
Mail relay, 347
Malcode. see Malware protection
Malware protection
    email security, 336–49
    examples, 315, 322, 349
    overview, 311, 350
    spyware, 314
    Trojan horses, 312–13
    viruses, 311–12
    web browser security. see Web browser security
    workstation, 315–22
    worms, 312
Manage Documents permission, 293–94
Manage Printer permission, 294
Managed computer, 318
Management. see Security management (ongoing);
        Updates, managing
Management computer, 385
Mandatory access control (MAC), 151–52
Man-in-the-middle attack, 8, 89, 337–39, 340
MasterSecret, 203, 205
MD5 (Message-Digest algorithm 5), 93, 448
MD5-Challenge, 226
Media Access Control (MAC) address, 34
Media Access layer, 37
Media for backups, 409–10
Melissa (virus), 311–12
Message Integrity Code (MIC), 245–46, 247
Message-Digest algorithm 5 (MD5), 93, 448
Michael, XXX
Michaelango (virus), 313
Microsoft Challenge Handshake Authentication
        Protocol (MS-CHAP), 225
Microsoft Challenge Handshake Authentication
        Protocol Version 2 (MS-CHAPv2), 225–26
Microsoft Exchange, 349
Microsoft NetMeeting, 381
Microsoft Outlook, 346, 348
Microsoft Passport, 123–24
Microsoft Point-to-Point Encryption (MPPE), 231–32
MIME (Multipurpose Internet Mail Extensions), 34
Mitigation of risk, 16–19
Mixed mode domain, 158
MMC (Microsoft Management Console), 171, 377–78
Mobile (rolling) backup, 401
Modem serial connection, 386–87

Modems, 54

Mondoarchive, 409

Monitoring, 368. *See also* Auditing

Monitors, 55

Moving Picture Experts Group (MPEG), 34

MPPE (Microsoft Point-to-Point Encryption), 231–32

MS-CHAP (Microsoft Challenge Handshake Authentication Protocol), 225

MS-CHAPv2 (Microsoft Challenge Handshake Authentication Protocol Version 2), 225–26

Multicast packets, 61

Multihomed computer, 275

Multipurpose Internet Mail Extensions (MIME), 34

Mutual aid agreements, 401

Mutual authentication, 121–22

MX records, 276

N

n and n-1, 418

Naive Bayes classifier, 344

NAS (network access server), 238

NAT (Network Address Translation) servers, 65–67, 275, 289

National Institute of Standards and Technology (NIST), 87

National Security Agency (NSA), 88

Native mode domain, 158

NAT-Traversal, 234

NCP (Network Control Protocol), 223

Need-to-access, 49

Need-to-know, 49, 151

Nest, 159

.NET Passport, 123–24

Net share command, 171

NetBIOS applications, 287

NetBIOS name, 275

NetMeeting, 381

Netstat, 44, 51, 446

Network Access layer, 41, 42

Network access server (NAS), 238

Network adapters, 54

Network Address Translation (NAT) servers, 65–67, 275, 289

Network Configuration Operators, 159

Network Control Protocol (NCP), 223

Network File System (NFS), 35

Network infrastructure servers, 274–89

Network layer, 33

Network security

examples, 5, 10, 20

integrity, 8

overview, 2, 24

traffic requirements, 189–94

Network Service account, 52

Network stack, 31

Network traffic, security requirements, 189–94

Network transmission, securing. *see* Securing network transmission

Network-based IDS (NIDS), 435, 436–37

newgrp command, 175

Next Header, 207

NFS (Network File System), 35

Nimda worm, 303

NIST (National Institute of Standards and Technology), 87

Nonpersistent cookie, 327, 332

Nonrepudiation, 6, 10

Nonrepudiation of delivery, 10

Nonrepudiation of origin, 10

NSA (National Security Agency), 88

ntbackup, 409

NTFS permissions, 165–67

NTLM protocol, 133

NTLMv2 protocol, 133, 135

Null modem cable, 385

Nyxem Worm, 313

O

Objects

definition, 150

Unix, 176–81

OFB (output feedback), 87

Off-site backup, 410

One-time pad, 78–79

One-time passwords, 128

One-way-hash, 224

Open access point, 253, 254

Open Shortlist Path First (OSPF), 37

Open systems interconnection (OSI) model, 32–38

Organizational security infrastructure, 21

Organizational security policy, 21

Organizational unit (OU), 163, 265–66

Originating domain, 332

Outlook postmark, 349

Outlook Web Access (OWA), 127

Out-of-band remote management, 373–74. *See also* Emergency Management Services (EMS)

Output and input devices, 53–55

Output feedback (OFB), 87

P

Packet checksums, 253

Packet Privacy, 378

Packet sniffer, 45, 189

Packet tampering, 190

Packet-filtering firewalls, 60–62

Pad length, 207

Padding, 84, 207
Pairwise master key (PMK), 252
Pairwise transient key (PTK), 252
PAMs (pluggable authentication modules), 120
Parallel test, 402
Parity stripe, 418
Passive node, 425
Passphrase, 126
Password Authentication Protocol (PAP), 223
Passwords
    account lockout, 139–40
    age and length, 137–38
    attack tree, 14
    authentication, 125–28
    forgetting, 96
    policies, 137–39
    preventing storage of LAN Manager, 291
    weak, 19
Patch, 360
Payload data, 207
PCBC (propagating cipher-block chaining), 87
PDF (Portable Document Format), 324, 337
PDU (protocol data unit), 207
PEAP (Protected Extensible Authentication Protocol),
    250–51, 252
Peer-to-peer network, 119, 120
Penetration testing, 368
Perimeter network, 58
Perimeter security, 58, 195–200
Permission attributes, 161
Permissions. see specific types of permissions
Per-packet mixing function, 244–45
Persistent cookie, 327, 333
Personal firewall, 56, 318
PGP (pretty good privacy), 99
Phishing, 341–42, 343
Phishing filter, 342
Physical entry point, 53–54
Physical evidence, 444–45
Physical layer, 33, 38
Physical server security, 50
PID (process ID), 175
ping command, 37
Ping of death, 65
PKI. see Public key infrastructure (PKI)
Plain text, 76
Planning
    business continuity, 396–99
    disaster recovery, 396, 399–403
Pluggable authentication modules (PAMs), 120
Plug-ins, 324, 337
PMK (Pairwise master key), 252
Point-to-Point Protocol (PPP), 38, 222, 224
Point-to-Point Tunneling Protocol (PPTP), 231–33
Poisoning the cache, 281–83

Policies, 20–21, 264
Policy CA, 106
Polyalphabetic substitution, 77
Poor authentication, 59
Port scanners, 53
Port signatures, 436
Portable Document Format (PDF), 324, 337
Ports
    blocking, 52–53
    personal firewalls, 56
    TCP/IP, 43–45
    USB, 55
Post Office Protocol (POP3), 337
Power supply, uninterruptible, 388–89
PPP (Point-to-Point Protocol), 38, 222, 224
PPTP (Point-to-Point Tunneling Protocol), 231–33
Predefined security templates (Windows Server
    2003), 266–69
PreMasterSecret, 203, 204, 205
Presentation layer, 33, 34–35
Pre-shared key (PSK) mode, 253
Pre-shared secret, 88
Pretty good privacy (PGP), 99
Primary tokens, 162
Primitives, cryptographic, 79–81
Principals
    definition, 150
    Unix, 174–75
    Windows, 154–60
Principle of least permission, 154
Principle of least privilege, 154
Print jobs, 294
Print Operators, 159
Print permission, 293
Print queue, 294
Print servers, securing, 293–95
Print Spooler service, 293
Privacy. see Confidentiality
Private certificate authorities, 104–05
Private key, 90
Private networks, 58
Process ID (PID), 175
Promiscuous mode, 45, 436
Propagated, 311
Propagating cipher-block chaining (PCBC), 87
Protected Extensible Authentication Protocol (PEAP),
    250–51, 252
Protocol analyzers, 45, 368
Protocol data unit (PDU), 207
Protocols
    Address Resolution, 37
    AppleTalk Session, 35
    authentication, 131–36
    connectionless, 36
    connection-oriented, 36

Protocols *(Continued)*
    definition, 31
    Hypertext Transfer, 3, 35
    Hypertext Transfer over SSL, 3
    Internet, 36
    Internet Control Messaging, 9, 37
    Point-to-Point, 38
    port numbers, 43
    proxy agents for, 64
    Reverse Address Resolution, 37
    review, 31–32
    Routing Information, 37
    Serial Line Internet, 38
    Stream Control Transmission, 36
    Transmission Control, 35
Proxy agents, 64
Pseudorandom generator, 81
Pseudorandom numbers, 80–81, 95–96
PSK (pre-shared key) mode, 253
PTK (Pairwise transient key), 252
PTR record, 280
Public certificate authorities, 104–05
Public key, 90
Public key infrastructure (PKI)
    CA hierarchy, designing, 103–07
    certificate renewal, 110–11
    certificate revocation, 111–12
    certificates from other organizations,
        108–09
    configuring trust, 102–03
    definition, 100–101
    digital certificates, 99–100
    enrollment and distribution strategy, 110
    examples, 109, 112
    Extensible Authentication Protocol, 226
    overview, 99
    security policy, 107–08
Public networks, 57
Purple (encryption machine), 79

Q

Qualitative loss criteria, 398
Qualitative risk analysis, 15–16
Quantitative loss criteria, 398
Quantitative risk analysis, 15
Quarantining attachments, 349
Query, 301

R

RADIUS (Remote Authentication Dial-in User
        Service), 235–37, 251
RADIUS client, 236
RADIUS server, 236

RAID (Redundant Array of Independent Disks),
        416–23
RAID 0 (disk stripping), 417
RAID 1 (disk mirroring), 417
RAID 10 (striped RAID 1 arrays), 420–21
RAID 1E (striped mirror), 418
RAID 5 (striping with parity), 418–19
RAID 50 (striped RAID 5 arrays), 421
RAID 5EE (hot space), 419
RAID 6 (striping with dual parity), 419–20
RAID 60 (striped RAID 6 arrays), 421, 422
RAID-on-Chip technology, 423
Random number generation, 80–81
RARP (Reverse Address Resolution Protocol), 37
RBAC (role-based access control), 152–53
RDP (Remote Desktop Protocol), 379, 381
Real evidence, 444–45
Recovery team, 403
Recovery time frames, 400
Recovery time objectives, 400–401
Recycle Bin, 453, 454
Redundant, 416
Redundant Array of Independent Disks (RAID),
        416–21
Registry, 267
Re-keying, 247–48
Remote access. *See also* Wireless security
    authentication strategy, 226–27
    dial-up networking, 222–30
    examples, 228, 235, 238
    overview, 222, 255
    RADIUS and TACACS, 235–38
    virtual private networks, 230–35
Remote access servers (RAS)
    challenge and response, 224
    definition, 275
    dial-up networking, 54, 222
    RADIUS and TACACS, 235–38
    securing, 288
Remote administration
    backup recovery, 414
    deployment planning, 375–76
    Emergency Management Services, designing for,
        383–89
    examples, 378, 390
    management plan, 372–74
    overview, 371–72
    security considerations, 374–75
    TCP/IP remote management, 382–83
    Windows inbound management tools,
        376–82
Remote Assistance, 381–82
Remote Authentication Dial-in User Service
        (RADIUS), 235–37, 251
Remote Desktop for Administration, 378–81

Remote Desktop Protocol (RDP), 379, 381
Remote login (Rlogin), 34
Remote management plan, 372
Remote procedure call Locator (RpcLocator), 292
Remote procedure call (RPC)
    definition, 35
    Distributed Component Object Model, 378
    securing domain controllers, 292
    separation of services, 51
Remote shell (rsh), 191
Replay attack, 136, 328–29
Replays, 190
Repudiated delivery, 10
Repudiation, 13
Reputation, 12
Responsibility
    for backups, 413–14
    for security, 6
Restricted site zones, 336
Reverse Address Resolution Protocol (RARP), 37
Reverse lookup, 280
Reversible encryption
    enabling, 227–28
    password storing, 138–39
    password transmission, 223
RFC 1994, 223
RFC 2401, 206
RFC 2402, 206
RFC 2406, 206
RFC 2409, 209
RFC 2488, 225
RFC 2898, 253
RFC 3227, 445
RFC 4306, 209
Rijndael, 88
RIP (Routing Information Protocol), 37
Risk
    calculating, 15–16
    e-commerce websites, 3
    mitigation, 16–19
Risk analysis
    costs, 16, 140–41
    definition, 11
    examples, 17–18, 48
    qualitative, 15–16
    quantitative, 15
    tools, 13
Rivest, Shamir, Adleman (RSA), 81, 91, 128
Rlogin, 34
Roaming, 253
Roaming disconnect support, 379
Rogue DHCP servers, 284, 288
Role, 152
Role-based access control (RBAC), 152–53
Rolling (mobile) backup, 401

Root CA role, 105–06
Rooted, 314–15
Routing and Remote Access Service (RRAS),
    224, 225
Routing Information Protocol (RIP), 37
RPC. see Remote procedure call (RPC)
RSA (Rivest, Shamir, Adleman), 81, 91, 128
Rule base (ruleset), 60
Rule-based access control, 151

S

SA (security associations), 208–09
SACL (system access control list), 162, 369
Safe for execution, 324
Safe for scripting, 324
Salting, 95
Salvage team, 403
SAM (Security Accounts Manager) database, 120
Sanitized, 449
SANs (Storage area networks), 423–24
Scanners, vulnerability, 13
Scope and plan initiation phase, 397
Screened subnets, 58, 195
Script kiddies, 4
Scripts, 311
SCTP (Stream Control Transmission Protocol), 36
SCW (Security Configuration Wizard),
    270–71
Secondary logon, 120
Secondary network, 375
Secrecy. see Confidentiality
Securable, 150
Secure baseline, 263
Secure by default, 17
Secure File Transfer Protocol (SFTP), 34, 297
Secure shell (SSH), 34, 212–14, 382–83
Secure socket layer (SSL), 201–05
Secure sockets layer (SSL), 2, 299, 330–31
Secure updates, 281
Secure/Multipurpose Internet Mail Extensions
    (S/MIME), 105
Securing network transmission
    data, 193–94
    design considerations, 192–93
    examples, 194, 198, 199, 200, 204, 214
    IP address and packet filtering, 199–200
    IP security (IPsec), 205–11
    overview, 189, 214–15
    secure shell, 212–14
    server message block signing, 211–12
    SSL and TLS, 201–05
    subnets, 195–96
    switches and VLANS, 196–99
    traffic security requirements, 189–94

Security
  awareness and training, 23, 24
  basics, 6–11
  definition, 5–6
  importance, 2–6
  ISO 17799 standard, 20
  overview, 2, 24
  personnel, 22
  physical and environmental, 22
  policies and standards, 20–23
  responsibilities, 23
  wireless. *see* Wireless security
Security access control list (SACL), 162, 369
Security Accounts Manager (SAM) database, 120
Security associations (SA), 208–09
Security Configuration and Analysis snap-in,
  269–70
Security Configuration Wizard (SCW), 270–71
Security descriptors, 161–62
Security groups, 158–61
Security identifiers (SID), 120, 154, 156–58
Security management (ongoing). *See also* Intrusion
  detection (ID)
  auditing and logging, 366–71
  Emergency Management Services, 383–89
  examples, 366, 370, 378, 390
  overview, 357, 389–90
  remote management deployment, 375–76
  remote management plan, 372–74
  remote security considerations, 374–75
  TCP/IP remote management, 382–83
  updates, 357–66
  Windows inbound management tools, 376–82
Security manager, 325–26
Security parameters index (SPI), 207
Security policy, 107–08
Security principal, 119
Security template, 263, 265–69
Security Templates snap-in, 268–69, 290
Security update infrastructure, 360
Self-propagation, 311
Self-signing, 106
Semi-private networks, 57–58
Separation of services, 50–51
Sequence number, 207
Sequenced Packet Exchange (SPX), 36
Serial Line Internet Protocol (SLIP), 38, 222
Server message block (SMB) signing, 211–12, 213
Server Operators, 159
Server roles
  baselines, 263–74
  definition, 263
  examples, 272
  overview, 263
  virtualization, 273–74

Server security
  application servers, 298–303
  best practices for, 45–49
  border security, 57–67
  DHCP servers, 284–87, 288
  domain controllers, 289–92
  examples, 45, 48, 56, 66, 281, 296, 303
  file and print servers, 292–97
  NAT servers, 289
  network infrastructure servers, 274–89
  network protocol review, 31–32
  open systems interconnection (OSI) model, 32–38
  overview, 31, 67
  RAS, 288
  replay attacks, 328–29
  securing, procedure for, 49–56
  TCP/IP model, 39–43
  TCP/IP ports, 43–45
  WINS servers, 287–88
Serveradmin roles, 153
Server-side program, 299
Service bureaus, 402
Service Level Agreements (SLAs), 415
Service processor, 385
Service redirection, 275–76
Service Set Identifier (SSID), 241
Session cookie, 327
Session hijacking, 327–28
Session layer, 33, 35
Sessionless, 324
Set, 369
Set groupID (SGID), 178–79
Set userID (SUID), 178–79
SFTP (Secure File Transfer Protocol), 34, 297
SGID (set groupID), 178–79
SHA-1, 93
Shadow copy, 414
Share permissions, 168–69
Shared folders, 168
Sharing keys, 88–90
Shift, 76, 77
Shiva Password Authentication Protocol (SPAP), 223
Shoulder surfing, 14
SID (security identifiers), 120, 154, 156–58
Signature-based IDSs, 435
Signatures
  digital, 10, 92, 94, 214, 341
  header condition, 436
  port, 436
  string, 436
  transactions, 278–79
  virus, 317
Simple file sharing, 120
Simple Mail Transfer Protocol (SMTP), 33, 50, 337
Simulation testing, 402

Single points of failure, 415–16, 426
Single sign-on, 120
Single-key encryption. *see* Symmetric encryption
Site, 291
SLA (Service Level Agreements), 415
Slack space, 455
Slag code, 313
Sleuth Kit, 457
SLIP (Serial Line Internet Protocol), 38, 222
slogin, 34
Smart cards, 105, 128–29
SMB (server message block), 211–12, 213
S/MIME (Secure/Multipurpose Internet Mail
        Extensions), 105
SMS (Systems Management Server), 361
SMTP (Simple Mail Transfer Protocol), 33, 50, 337
Smurf attack, 9
SNMP (Simple Network Management Protocol), 34
Social engineering attack, 4–5
Sockets, 39
Software, 12
Software Update Services (SUS), 361, 362–65
Spam, 342–45
Spam DoS attacks, 343–44
Spam filters, 344
Spammers, 342–43
SPAP (Shiva Password Authentication Protocol), 223
Special Administration Console (SAC), 383–85
!Special Administration Console (!SAC), 383–85
SPI (security parameters index), 207
Spoofing
    definition, 9, 13
    description, 190
    firewalls and, 60
Spooled, 294
SPX (Sequenced Packet Exchange), 36
SpyBlast, 322
Spyware, 314
SQL injection attack, 301–03
SRV records, 276, 277
SSH (secure shell), 34, 212–14, 382–83
SSID (Service Set Identifier), 241
SSL (secure socket layer), 2, 201–05, 330–31
SSL handshake protocol, 202–03
SSL plaintext records, 202
SSL record layer, 202
SSL VPN clients, 234–35
Stack, 303
Stand-alone CA, 110
Standards, 20–23
State, 328
State tables, 63
Stateful inspection (stateful packet-filtering), 62–63
Static IP address configuration, 67
Statistical anomaly IDS, 435–36

Stealth mode, 241
Sticky bit, 177
Storage area networks (SANs), 423–24
Store and forward server, 407
Stream ciphers, 84–85
Stream Control Transmission Protocol (SCTP), 36
STRIDE threat model, 13, 16
String buffer, 303
String signatures, 436
Striped mirror (RAID 1E), 418
Striped RAID 1 arrays (RAID 10), 420–21
Striped RAID 5 arrays (RAID 50), 421
Striped RAID 6 arrays (RAID 60), 421, 422
Striping with dual parity (RAID 6), 419–20
Striping with parity (RAID 5), 418–19
Strong passwords, 137
Structured Query Language (SQL), 301
Structured walk-through test, 402
Subjects, 150, 175
Subordinate CA, 106
Substitution ciphers, 75–77
SUID (set userID), 178–79
Superuser (root), 174, 175
Support_388945a0, 290
SUS (Software Update Services), 361, 362–65
svchost.exe, 447
Switch, 193
Symmetric encryption, 80, 83–90, 99, 242. *See also*
        Kerberos
Symmetric master key, 252
SYN message, 189
Systat, 51
System access control list (SACL), 162
System backups, 55–56
System development and maintenance, 22
System failure attacks, 3–4
System state backup, 408
Systems Management Server (SMS), 361

T

Tabletop exercise, 402
TACACS (Terminal Access Controller Access Control
        System), 235, 237–38
TACACS+ (Terminal Access Controller Access
        Control System Plus), 238
Tag, 198
Tagged Information File Format (TIFF), 35
Tail-log backup, 411
Tampering (data), 13
Task Manager, 447
Tasklist, 447, 448
TCO (total cost of ownership), 264
TCP (Transmission Control Protocol), 35–36
TCP session hijacking, 189–91

TCP SYN flooding attacks, 191–92
TCP/IP model, 39–43
TCP/IP ports, 43–45
TCP/IP session
    hijacking attack, 189–91
    initiation, 190
    remote management, 382–83
Telnet, 34, 50, 382–83
Temporal Key Integrity Protocol (TKIP), 244,
        246, 247
Temporal key (TK), 252
Temporary files (applications), 453, 454
Temporary Internet Files, 452–53
Terminal Access Controller Access Control System
        Plus (TACACS+), 238
Terminal Access Controller Access Control System
        (TACACS), 235, 237–38
Terminal concentrator, 387–88
Terminal emulation, 382
Terminal Services, 379
Testing
    backup recovery, 414
    disaster recovery plan, 402
TFTP (Trivial File Transfer Protocol), 33, 51
Third parties attack, 3
Third-party cookies, 332
Threat assessment, 15
Threats, 11–16
Three-pronged configurations, 196, 197
Throughput rate, 131
Ticket-granting service (TGS), 136
Ticket-granting ticket (TGT), 136
TIFF (Tagged Information File Format), 35
Time bomb, 313
TKIP (Temporal Key Integrity Protocol), 244,
        246, 247
TLS (Transport Layer Security), 3, 201–05
Total cost of ownership (TCO), 264
Traffic, 189–94
Traffic analysis, 7
Transaction log, 411
Transaction log backup, 411
Transactional data, 407
Transactions Signatures (TSIGs), 278–79
Translation table (NAT system), 65
Transmission Control Protocol (TCP), 35–36.
        See also TCP/IP model
Transmissions, securing. see Securing network
        transmission
Transport layer (OSI model), 33, 35–36
Transport Layer Security (TLS), 3, 201–05
Transport layer (TCP/IP model), 41
Transport mode, 207–08
Trapdoors, 314–15
Triple DES (3DES), 87

Trivial File Transfer Protocol (TFTP), 33, 51
Trojan horse applications, 127, 312–13
Trust relationship, 134
Trusted computing base, 263
Trusted host, 191
Trusted zones, 281, 336
TSIGs (Transactions Signatures), 278–79
Tunnel, 222
Tunnel mode, 208
24 x 7 availability, 415
Two-factor authentication, 125
Type 1 authentication, 125
Type 1 errors, 130
Type 2 authentication, 125
Type 2 errors, 130
Type 3 authentication, 125

U

UDP (User Datagram Protocol), 36
UIDs (user identities), 174–75
Unicast packets, 61
Uniform Resource Locator (URL), 298
Uninterruptible power supply (UPS), 50
Universal groups, 158, 159–60, 161
Universal naming convention (UNC),
        169–70
Universal One Way Hash Function (UOWHF), 94
Universal Serial Bus (USB) ports, 55
Unix
    access control, implementing, 174
    auditing, 368–69
    BIND name server, 277–78
    example, 180
    Kerberos support, 134
    objects, 176–81
    principals, 174–75
Unused IP space, 442
UOWHF (Universal One Way Hash Function), 94
Updates, managing
    automating, 360
    configuration management, 357–60
    creating infrastructure, 360–62
    example, 366
    overview, 357
    Software Update Services, 362–65
    Windows network, 361
    Windows Server Update Services, 362, 363
UPS (uninterruptible power supply), 50
URL (Uniform Resource Locator), 298
UrlScan, 300
USB (Universal Serial Bus), 55
User Datagram Protocol (UDP), 36
User identities (UIDs), 174–75
User mode access, 384–85

User rights assignments
    access control, implementing, 172–73
    DCBP, 289–90
    malware protection, 318–19
    secure baseline, 264
User training, 320–22
User-based access control, 120
User-directed discretionary access control, 151
Users, 159
/usr/adm/lastlog, 368
utmp command, 369

V

Values. *see* Assets
/var/adm/acct, 369
/var/adm/utmp, 369
/var/adm/wtmp, 369
Verbs, 300
Vigenere cipher, 77–78
Virtual local area network (VLAN), 196–99
Virtual machines, 274
Virtual private network (VPN), 230–35
Virtualization, 273–74
Virus signature, 317
Viruses, 311–12
Visual Basic script (VBScript), 312
VLAN (virtual local area network), 196–99
VLAN hopping, 198
VLAN ID, 198
VMWare, 274
Volatile data, 445
Volume shadow copy, 408–09
VPN (Virtual private network), 230–35
Vulnerabilities
    definition, 12–13
    passwords, 94–95, 126
    wireless design, 253–55
Vulnerability assessment, 397
Vulnerability scanners, 13

W

Walk-through drill, 402
WAP (Wireless access point), 240
War chalking, 241
War dialers, 368
War driving, 240–41
Warez lists, 296
Warm site, 401
Web beacon, 320
Web browser security
    configuration, 329–33
    examples, 337
    Firefox, 332, 334, 336, 338

Internet Explorer security zones,
    334–36
    overview, 323
    risks, 323–24
    session threats, 327–29
    technologies, 324–27
Web servers, securing, 298–300
Well-known ports, 43
Well-known security identifier (SID), 156
WEP (Wired equivalent privacy), 241–44, 246
WEP open authentication, 234
WEP shared key authentication, 234–35
who command, 369
Wi-Fi (wireless fidelity), 239
Wi-Fi Protected Access (WPA), 244–46
"the Wild," 195
Windows
    access control, implementing, 154
    access control model, 161–63
    access control, principals, 154–61
    Active Directory object permissions,
        163–64
    auditing, 285, 369–71
    Automatic Updates, 361, 367
    Backup, 408–09
    credentials, 120
    inbound management tools, securing,
        376–82
    Kerberos support, 134
    LAN Manager-based protocols, 131–34
    managing services, 51–52
    Security Configuration Wizard, 270–71
    Server 2003 (predefined security templates),
        266–69
    sharing tab, 168
    smart cards, 128–29
    updating network, 360–62
    user rights assignment, 172–73
Windows Internet Name Service (WINS) servers,
    274–75, 287–88
Windows Live authentication, 123–24
Windows Security log, 450–51
Windows Server Update Services (WSUS), 361,
    362, 363
Windtalkers, 83
WinHex, 449, 455
WINS replication, 287
Wired equivalent privacy (WEP), 241–44, 246
Wireless access point (WAP), 240
Wireless LAN (WLAN), 239
Wireless security
    802.1x standard, 246–52
    802.11i standard, 252–53
    example, 255
    networking standards, 239–40

Wireless security (Continued)
  open access point design, 253, 254
  overview, 239, 255
  preventing intruders from connecting,
      240–41
  vulnerabilities, 253–55
  Wi-Fi Protected Access, 244–46
  wired equivalent privacy, 241–44
  wireless modes, 240
Word salad, 344
Workstation protection, 315–22
Worms, 312
WPA (Wi-Fi Protected Access), 244–46
Write blocker, 449
Written security policy, 24

WSUS (Windows Server Update Services), 361,
      362, 363
wtmp command, 369

X
X.509 certificates, 99–100
XOR function, 81–82
X-Ways Forensics, 457

Z
Zombie, 313
Zone transfer, 276
Zone transfer vulnerability, 276–79
Zones, 275